Niv

The authorised biography of

DAVID NIVEN

Also by Graham Lord

Novels

Marshmallow Pie
A Roof Under Your Feet
The Spider and the Fly
God and All His Angels
The Nostradamus Horoscope
Time Out of Mind
A Party to Die For
Sorry, We're Going to Have to Let You Go

Autobiography

Ghosts of King Solomon's Mines

Biography

Just the One: The Wives and Times of Jeffrey Bernard
James Herriot: The Life of a Country Vet
Dick Francis: A Racing Life
Arthur Lowe

Niv

The authorised biography of DAVID NIVEN

GRAHAM LORD

First published in Great Britain in 2003
by Orion Books Ltd
The Orion Publishing Group Ltd
Orion House
5 Upper Saint Martin's Lane
London WC2H 9EA

A CIP catalogue record for this book is available from the British Library.

ISBN 0 75285 306 6

Typeset by Selwood Systems,
Midsomer Norton

Printed in Great Britain by Butler & Tanner Ltd,
Frome & London

For all of Niv's family and friends
who loved him so much and miss him still

Contents

Every effort has been made to trace the copyright holders of the photographs included in this book but, if any have been inadvertently overlooked, the author and publishers will be pleased to make the necessary changes at the first opportunity

1, 2, 3 & 4 – Grizel Niven; 5 – private collection; 6 – Bodelian/Conservative Central Office; 7, 8 & 9 – Stowe School; 10 – RMA Sandhurst; 11 – private collection; 12 – Fiona Niven; 13 – BBC Hulton Picture Library; 14, 15 & 16 – private collection; 17 – private collection; 18, 19, 20, 21 & 22 – private collection; 23 – the Estate of Michael Trubshawe; 24 – RMA Sandhurst; 25 – Fiona Niven; 26 – Photo Source; 27, 28 & 29 – private collection; 30 – private collection; 31 – *Illustrated London News*; 32, 33, 34 & 35 – private collection; 36 & 37 – private collection; 38 – *Vanity Fair*; 39, 40 & 41 – private collection; 42, 43, 44 & 45 – private collection; 46 – Fiona Niven; 47 – the Hon. William Feilding; 48 & 49 – Graham Lord; 50 – private collection; 51 – Fiona Thyssen; 52 – Camera Press/Robert Penn; 53 – private collection; 54 – Roderick Mann; 55 – Rex Features; 56 – Hedi Donizetti; 57 – Graham Lord; 58 – Fiona Niven; 59 – Peter Watson; 60 – Rex Features; 61 – Leslie Bricusse

Illustrations

Plate section 3

Plate section 4

Preface

David Niven, whose friends called him Niv, was an hilarious, utterly charming, delightfully engaging fantasist and fibber. His gloriously funny autobiography, *The Moon's a Balloon*, is stuffed with errors of fact, anecdotes that are hugely exaggerated and superb stories that are completely untrue.

Does this matter? Of course not. He was a great raconteur, and raconteurs polish their anecdotes and make things up. His stories hurt no one, were never malicious, and he told them to brighten our lives and make us chuckle. Almost everyone who knew him has told me that he was a lovely man: kind, considerate, understanding, extremely funny and determined to cheer other people up even though his own life was stained at times by deep unhappiness. So who cares if he told a few fibs? Novelists and politicians do it all the time.

Unfortunately as Niv's biographer it is my job to try to sort out the truth from the fibs. When he claimed that he fought for a rebel army in Cuba in 1934, when he certainly did not, I have a duty to say so. But my adjustments to Niv's version of his life are not meant to show him up or put him down. He was an actor and writer who tailored his life to make millions laugh, and one excellent joke is worth a hundred facts. And he told his stories so often for so many years that by the time he came to write *The Moon's a Balloon*, when he was sixty, he had probably come to believe that all his fibs and exaggerations were actually true. We all readjust our memories, few of us with such splendid effect as he did.

So if at times you are irritated by my corrections to his stories, please remember this: Niv was the twinkling star, the meteor who lit up every room he entered; I am just the dreary drudge whose job it is to try to tell the truth.

I loved every minute researching and writing this book. Here was a man whose courage, kindness and *joie de vivre* were an inspiration for us all. I wish so much that I had met him.

Graham Lord
June 2003

One

'The Most Poisonous Little Bastard'
1910–1923

When twenty-four-year-old David Niven signed his first Hollywood film contract in 1935 the studio's publicity director decided that his background was not nearly exotic enough, so he tarted it up. Instead of being the son of a humble second lieutenant in the British army he was said to be the son of 'General William G. Niven, famed Scottish war hero'. Instead of being born in London he was said to come from Kirriemuir in Scotland and the fibs were so successful that when he died in 1983 even *The Times* said in its obituary that he was born in Kirriemuir. 'Even I get confused about my father,' his elder son, David, told me in 2002. 'Was he born in Scotland or not?'

Not – though when you consider Niv's reputation as an irresistible ladies' man, Kirriemuir would have been a perfect birthplace, judging by the raucous, bawdy Scottish rugby drinking song 'The Ball of Kirriemuir':

Four and twenty virgins came doon from Inverness,
And when the Ball was over there were four and twenty less!
Singin' balls to your partner, arse agin' the wall!
If ye cannae get laid on a Saturday nicht ye cannae get laid at all!

Niv was in fact born in a bustling London street in a mansion block of houses and shops just beside the busy clang and clatter of Victoria railway station. His father was a rich, thirty-two-year-old country landowner, a gentleman of leisure and a part-time second lieutenant in the Berkshire Imperial Yeomanry. Niv liked to pretend that the family was deeply

Scottish but his father had also been born in London, his Niven grandfather had been an English Justice of the Peace and director of the London *Evening News* and *Hampshire Telegraph*, and Niv's half-French mother had been born in Wales. If there was any Scotch in his veins it was not blood.

James David Graham Niven, the future film star, was born in Belgrave Mansions, Grosvenor Gardens, London SW1, on 1 March 1910, St David's Day, just ten days before the American film director D. W. Griffith released the first movie ever to be made in the little village of Hollywood near Los Angeles – a seventeen-minute love story, *In Old California*, starring Mack Sennett. Belgrave Mansions was a classy address, close to Buckingham Palace, where the neighbours included the Rt Hon. Baron Killanin, Sir Alexander Bannerman and Sir Alfred Dent. Niv's father, William Niven, was not just the rich, spoiled, layabout son of a newspaper executive. In 1904, when he was twenty-seven and on safari in Kenya, he shot four lions in one morning and four more over the next few days. 'I got all these alone, and was really very lucky not to get into any trouble,' he wrote in a letter home. 'Eight lion skins with their heads on are really very fine trophies, especially for a two months' trip, and I am told that four lions in a morning make a record for East Africa.'

Courage and a sense of adventure flowed strong in the blood of the Nivens. One of the baby David's great-great-uncles had been a British general. Another had been a major in the 21st Fusiliers, and a great-great-great-uncle had been killed at the Battle of Waterloo. The baby's maternal forebears were equally militaristic. Niv's thirty-two-year-old mother, Henriette Degacher, was descended from an eighteenth-century Sieur of the Château de Caumont de Marivault and the family motto stressed the virtue of courage: *Coeur vaillant se fait royaume* (a brave heart creates its own nobility). Her father had been a captain in the British 24th Foot Regiment and had fought in the Kaffir and Zulu Wars in South Africa from 1877 to January 1879, when he was killed during the Battle of Isandhlwana, at which 1700 British soldiers were slaughtered by more than 20,000 Zulu. Her maternal grandfather and great-uncle had both been British generals, and when her mother remarried in 1888 she chose a lieutenant-general who had served in Afghanistan, Bengal and India, had been wounded at the Siege of Lucknow and decorated four times. Niv was proud of his family legacy and when he died in 1983 his papers included a bundle of his maternal grandparents' letters to each other, a family tree, and two locks of his grandfather's hair – one a fine tuft of baby hair dated 16 July 1841, when his grandfather had been fifteen months old.

When Niv's father registered his birth in 1910 he gave as his address the family's 300-year-old Jacobean country seat, Carswell Manor at Buckland near Faringdon which was then in Berkshire but is now in Oxfordshire. It was a three-storey, seven-bedroom, pale stone house that had been in the Niven family for more than fifty years, with a dovecote, walled garden, hundreds of acres of farmland, and the family's helmet-and-visor crest set in stone above the front porch along with the family motto, *Vivis Sperandum* (Place Your Hope in the Living). But before the year was out William Niven sold the house 'rather ingloriously' to pay his 'racing and other debts', said Niv forty years later. Today Carswell Manor is a co-ed prep school, St Hugh's, where a drawing of the house by William Niven still hangs in a corridor, and across the main road to Oxford the local golf club has named its restaurant Niven's. 'I don't think David would be terribly pleased,' chuckled the headmaster, Derek Cannon, in 2002. 'They serve hamburgers and chips, so he wouldn't be rushing to eat there!'

One reason for William Niven's debts may have been the size of his family, for the new baby was his fourth child. He and Henriette already had a ten-year-old daughter, Joyce; a seven-year-old son, Henry, who was always known as Max; and a three-year-old daughter with an odd Scots name, Grizel, pronounced Grizzle. They had a butler, footmen, governesses, gardeners, gamekeepers, grooms and horses, and led an extravagant life in London as well as the country. 'I remember my father only very slightly,' Grizel told me in 2002. 'He seldom came home and we weren't all that close as a family.' As Niv wrote sixty years later in his autobiography, *The Moon's a Balloon*, he saw little of his father 'except when I was brought down to be shown off before arriving dinner guests or departing fox-hunting companions. I could always tell which were which because the former smelt of soap and perfume and the latter of sweat and spirits . . . sweaty, hearty, red-faced, country squires.' His father also had to meet the cost of a rented house in Scotland – Craig Lodge at Dalmally in Argyllshire – and Niv's son Jamie told me in 2002 that although William was rich he had 'a sizeable investment in Argentine railroad bonds and got literally wiped out' when the bonds crashed.

After the sale of Carswell Manor the Nivens moved to Golden Farm at Cirencester and then to Fairford Park in Gloucestershire, which is where they were living when the First World War began in August 1914 and Niv's father went off to join the Berkshire Yeomanry in battle along with his valet, two grooms and a gardener. They were sent to Turkey and the Dardanelles, and there, on 21 August 1915, in the Gallipoli Peninsula, William Niven was killed as he and his comrades stormed the Turkish trenches at Suvla Bay – just one of more than half a million men who died during the doomed Dardanelles campaign. His body was never found and it was three months before the British Red Cross wrote to Henriette to say that a Trooper W. Deacon had reported that he and Lieutenant Niven had actually reached the Turkish trenches in the dark when Niven was shot in the head. The letter added optimistically that this 'does not of course exclude the possibility of your husband having been taken prisoner by the Turks'. It was not until seventeen months later that Henriette received official confirmation of his death, though she was granted probate in his estate in August 1916. Short of money, she moved the family to a couple of small, rented seaside houses in Folkestone, and it was not until February 1919 that she managed to track down another Berkshire Yeoman, Private A. W. Calder, who had witnessed William's death and could tell her that he had been shot in the head and killed instantly. 'He was a most popular Officer & loved by all,' wrote Calder.

William left everything to Henriette, but once his debts were paid his estate totalled just £5760 11s 8d, the equivalent in 2003 of about £200,000 – not much with which to buy a house and raise four children aged sixteen, thirteen, nine and six. She rented a house in London, at 38 Onslow Square, South Kensington, where according to *The Moon's a Balloon* she entertained 'pale, gay young men who recited poetry and sang to my mother . . . She was very beautiful, very musical, very sad and lived on cloud nine.' In fact Henriette may not have been quite as sad as Niv believed. 'I don't think my mother was deeply unhappy when my father died,' Grizel told me. 'I don't remember her crying. She was tall, very good-looking and had a good figure, and she could be quite flirtatious with men. I wouldn't be at all surprised if she had one or two boyfriends while she was married to my father. David and I thought it was very odd that he and I had fair, curly hair and bright blue eyes but Joyce and Max had brown eyes and straight, dark hair.' Sixty years later, according to Niv's elder daughter, Kristina, 'Daddy used to say that Joyce and Max didn't really look like him and Grizel, and that maybe his mother had had an affair with someone else.' The film critic Tom Hutchinson told me that Niv had confided that he had not liked his mother much because she had rejected him as a child and was a flirtatious socialite with a reputation for having loose sexual morals. 'David gave me the impression that his mother treated him not just casually but almost with contempt,' said Hutchinson. 'He told me that once when he was a boy he had had to spend an entire Christmas Day on his own because she was out at some social occasion. There weren't any presents. He told me: "I wished myself a merry Christmas, and cried." When Niv saw the film *Psycho* he said, "it's an indictment of all mothers, damn them all!" ' He told the *Telegraph Sunday Magazine* in 1977 that he came from a family 'that didn't give much of a damn', and Grizel said that they never saw much of their mother: 'We always had a nurse or governess, but I don't know what [mother] did all day. She didn't do any work or painting, cooking or gardening.'

If Henriette did have lovers one was almost certainly Thomas Walter Comyn Platt, a forty-eight-year-old bachelor diplomat who liked to hyphenate his last two names to Comyn-Platt. He had served the Foreign Office in London, Turkey, Greece, Uganda and South Africa, had been a Gold Staff Officer at the coronations of Edward VII and George V and had stood unsuccessfully as a Conservative candidate for Louth in Lincolnshire in the parliamentary election of 1906. During the First World War, according to *Who's Who*, Platt had served as a railway officer and interpreter in France but had been invalided out and had become a member of the Game Committee at the Ministry of Food. 'I think it's quite likely that he was in love with my mother while she was still married to my father,' Grizel told me, and Henriette solved her financial problems by marrying him.

Several years later, in 1925, Comyn-Platt published a book, *By Mail and Messenger*, which makes it plain that for many years he had had a close relationship with Henriette, whom he called Etta. It was a collection of letters that he had written from abroad to a woman in England, describing his adventures during his many travels through Asia Minor, central Asia and Africa from 1904 onwards, and he sent them from Constantinople, Samarkand and Baghdad, from Tripoli, Cairo, Aden, Mombasa, Entebbe. It was a vivid compendium of travellers' tales, anecdotes and legends, and the letters were almost certainly written to Etta because in the book's preface he says that they 'induced One to start on Life's journey with me; a journey which, I pray, may be as long as it has been happy'. Etta was his only wife, and they had been wed for eight years when he published them, and he would surely not have published the book had they been sent to someone else. They must have been written to her even though she was married to William Niven, and they are so astonishingly loving, romantic and filled with longing that Platt and Etta must have been lovers. 'You are continually in my thoughts,' he wrote in one of them, 'and to be with you again is to look forward to another Land of Beulah, where there are flowers and grapes and songs of birds, and the sun shines night and day.'

They met in London in 1904, when he was thirty-five and she was twenty-six, at a magnificent ball at Carlton House Terrace in the presence of Edward VII, Queen Alexandra and 'all the beauty and fashion of London' – among them Lady Londonderry, Lady Warwick, Lady Herbert and several knights of the Garter. He wrote his first letter the next day, as his train roared through the fields of Kent and bore him towards Calais, the Continent and his first diplomatic posting in the embassy at Constantinople, and he made it plain that he was already obsessed by her. On the train, he told her, he had spotted a woman who was wearing a veil, and had thought it was her. 'For the last hour,' he wrote on the ferry to Calais, 'I have searched every portion of the ship in the hope of finding you on board . . . Carried away by Hope, I convinced myself that the veiled lady was you.'

Niv always hated Comyn-Platt and sneered at him in *The Moon's a Balloon* as 'a second line politician who did not fight in the war . . . a tall, ramrod straight creature with immensely high, white collars, a bluish nose and a very noisy cuff-link combination which he rattled at me when I made an eating error at mealtime'. To underline his unhappiness over the wedding Niv claimed that it took place cruelly on his sixth birthday, 1 March 1916, but it was in fact more than a year later, on 22 May 1917, and not at All Saints church in Sloane Street, as he claimed, but at St Margaret's, Westminster – the House of Commons' parish church in the grounds of Westminster Abbey. It was an appropriately political venue because Comyn-Platt was an active member of the Conservative Party, the Carlton Club and the 1900 Club, an influential Tory dining club. On the marriage certificate he described his profession as 'Gentleman'. Among the guests was Margot Asquith, the influential wife of Herbert Asquith, who had recently been replaced as Prime Minister by David Lloyd George, and during the service seven-year-old David Niven, who was now calling Platt 'Uncle Tommy' and was dressed embarrassingly as a pageboy in a primrose suit with mother-of-pearl buttons and a white lace collar, announced in a shrill voice that the hook-nosed Mrs Asquith was a witch, an opinion with which many politicians were inclined to agree. So too did the sexy Hollywood actress Jean Harlow, who once made the mistake of calling her Mar-*gott*. 'No, dear,' said Mrs Asquith sharply. 'The t is silent, as in Harlow.'

Since Comyn-Platt had been writing such loving letters to Etta ever since 1904, it seems quite possible that he may have been Grizel's and

David's real father. They both suspected that their father was not their father and it was common in Edwardian times for wealthy upper-class women to have lovers and illicit children, and judging by the only photograph of Comyn-Platt that has survived, which shows that he was not ugly at all, he and Niv shared a startling resemblance. The photo is a head-and-shoulders shot that appeared on Comyn-Platt's election leaflet when he stood for Parliament for Southport in the general election of December 1923, when he was fifty-four, and at the same age Niv looked remarkably like him. They had the same slightly bulbous chin, sensitive mouth, long straight nose and sloping forehead, and both began to go bald early. They also shared a remarkable facility for reinventing the truth. In *Who's Who* Comyn-Platt claimed that he was born in 1875 whereas he was in fact born in 1869, and he lopped ten years off his age when listing each of his diplomatic posts. He even claimed that during the war he was invalided out in 1916 whereas it happened in January 1915, just five months after the war started, which raises a doubt as to whether he ever really was a railway officer and interpreter in France. Carelessly he told *Who's Who* not only that he had been born in 1875 but also that he had stood for Parliament in 1891, when he would have been just sixteen and too young to vote, but nobody noticed, and when he died in 1961 *The Times* and the *Daily Telegraph* both said he was eighty-five when in fact he was ninety-two.

Like Niv, Platt was an excellent raconteur and his book is extremely vivid and well written:

> Through the window one could just see the rising moon clearing the top of a distant hill, where the trees stood out like the teeth of a fret saw; and, below in the valley, a dark sheet of water with a silver patch, the reflection of some huge star. Weird sounds now and then broke the night silence: the croaking of a frog, the bark of a fox, the cry of some frightened bird. But, more persistent than all, the plaintive hoot of the widdah owl. Do you know the bird I mean? Its note is the saddest in the animal world. The peasants will tell you that it loses its way in the forest and arrives home only to find its young dead.

In another letter he wrote:

> The moon is a circle of gold set in an ebony sky. Towards the west, near by that huge rock on the desert edge, is the Mosque of Omar. See how the white marble glistens in the moonlight; and that clump of

palm trees – are they not exactly like feathered aigrettes on silver poles? It really is wonderful, you must admit. And those rafts, drifting idle downstream; do you hear the three notes of the fisherman's pipe? Can you see his lantern at the stern? Both are to attract the fish.

Like Niv, Comyn-Platt wrote about the famous people he had met – Lord Kitchener, Winston Churchill's mother, the opera singer Dame Nellie Melba – but he was not always as kind about his acquaintances as Niv was. Cecil Rhodes, for instance, was 'the essence of dullness'. Like Niv, too, some of Platt's stories seem wildly larger than life. When he trekked from Mombasa on the Indian Ocean into the heart of Uganda in 1898 to serve at the British high commission in Entebbe he said that he walked for a nightmarish three months almost all the way to Lake Victoria, at an average of fifteen miles a day, menaced all the way by lions, jiggers and malaria with a hundred porters carrying his goods, chattels and food on their heads, and a mule that he dressed in a canvas coat and trousers to protect it from 'the deadly bite of some vile fly'. And when he arrived he then spent months in a mud hut with a grass roof and two holes for windows. One evening, he said, he looked through one of the holes and saw a crocodile seize a young girl on the edge of the lake, and although she screamed and he ran 300 yards to her rescue he was too late and the girl disappeared shrieking beneath the water.

If Comyn-Platt was indeed Niv's and Grizel's real father it is a tragic story, for their relationship was dreadful. He seems to have had little time for children and Grizel told me with passion: 'Oh, we all *hated* him. I can't imagine why my mother liked him. He was tall and ugly and didn't like us and he tried to be bossy. He denigrated us all the time. The first time I was given a knife to use instead of a spoon he said "how stupid the girl looks". We couldn't stand him.'

Yet Comyn-Platt had some admirable qualities. He was surprisingly independent and unconventional for a diplomat, and wrote in one of his letters: 'I really believe that if the Chancelleries of Europe were to close down for six months in the year half the World's troubles would be avoided.' He was amusing: 'Have you ever thought what punishment is likely to be meted out to snobs in the next world? I have. I am quite convinced that they will be compelled to sit for all eternity in a back row, wearing red hot coronets.' He was intelligent, well read, and imaginative: in the middle of a forest he once saw a magical, beautiful, 'luminous' bird and thought it was his beloved Etta in disguise, and he was convinced that he saw her face in the wisps of smoke drifting from an old man's pipe. And in one letter he wrote:

> It is related in the *Mesnevi*, a book of Persian verse, that the Soul knocked at the door of the Divine Spirit craving admission to the Kingdom of Happiness. 'Who is there?' asked the voice from within. 'It is I,' was the reply. 'This house will not hold me and thee,' came the answer, and the Soul departed in sorrow. But true Love is ever persistent, and so, after a year's wandering, the Soul returned once more to the eternal threshold and in answer to the question, 'Who is there?' replies 'It is thou': 'Let myself enter,' says the voice, and the Soul, in unison with the Divine Spirit – and not till then – enters the Kingdom of Happiness. Does my story appeal to you?

Platt was brave and adventurous: riding on horseback through the desert with two Arabs, he had to separate them when they started to fight. He foresaw the end of European power in the Middle East decades before it dwindled. He could be kind and generous: in Constantinople he met a poor girl who was trying to collect a thousand piastres so as to free her beloved fiancé from prison, where he was serving a sentence for smuggling, and 'she was so brave and resigned about it all', wrote Platt, 'that my feelings got the better of me, and I gave her the rest of the money he needed. How grateful she was, and how she blessed me! I can see her now, her eyes full of tears, as she looked at the gold coins.'

There also seems no doubt that Platt loved Etta deeply. The last few letters in his book were written after they had married, when he went back to Constantinople, and he called her 'dear Heart' and 'dearest' and wrote: 'have you realized that tomorrow week is the anniversary of our wedding day? I pray we may never spend another apart. Bless you.' Later he wrote: 'I shall always hate leaving you. And to think that we should not be together on the anniversary of our wedding day . . . the happiest day of our lives.' Describing his journey through the Balkans, he added, 'I would have given anything for you to have been with me . . . I think of you always, and shall be only really happy when I am with you again.'

Perhaps he was not at all the ogre that Niv said he was. Maybe the boy David hated him so much precisely *because* he made his mother so happy and resented him Oedipally for hijacking her love. Many years later Niv told his daughter Kristina that Comyn-Platt 'beat him a lot' when he was a boy, and in 1974 Niv told Bart Mills of the *Guardian* that he was always telling amusing stories and trying to make people laugh because 'I want to be loved. It comes from being hit by my stepfather', but Grizel told me that this was not true. On the other hand, Grizel and David were not alone in disliking Platt, who was to be knighted in 1922 in the New Year Honours list for his work as secretary to the British Commission in Uganda in 1898. The archaeologist and traveller Gertrude Bell met him in Baghdad in 1926 and advised her mother to avoid him in London because 'he is such a bore', and it is disconcerting that in *Who's Who* he recorded under 'Recreations': 'none'. Yet he was still sufficiently adventurous at the age of sixty-six, in 1936, to be described in *The Times* as 'the noted traveller' when he went off around the world – to Ceylon, Malaya, the West Indies and British Honduras – to estimate for the Society for the Preservation of the Fauna of the Empire the danger of any rare species becoming extinct in those countries. In 1935 he published two more books, *The Turk in the Balkans* and *The Abyssinian Storm*, and in the 1940s and 1950s he wrote intelligent letters regularly to the *Daily Telegraph* – about income tax, politics, architecture, food rationing, nutrition, elocution, history – that were sometimes witty and always notable for their common sense.

In later life, certainly, Comyn-Platt became curmudgeonly and misanthropic, but many very old men do. In 1953 he joined the Turf Club, where a fellow member was Niv's thirty-four-year-old brother-in-law, Andrew Rollo. 'He was a bit forbidding,' Rollo told me, 'tall and thin with a grumpy face, like a Dickensian villain, and long grey hair and a large pair of spectacles. You'd cross the street to avoid him.' But to be fair to Sir Thomas he was now eighty-four, a lonely widower and in pain. The Turf Club's sixty-five-year-old head barman, Jimmy Holland, told me: 'I got to know him well and when he was on form he was fun and he'd make jokes, and he had an account with a bookmaker and sometimes he'd put a fiver on a horse. But when he was on bad form that would last for six months. He could be miserable, a real Scrooge figure, about six foot two, with a bony face and moustache, but he was lonely and would come in every day at lunchtime and stay until about ten o'clock at night, even at weekends.' He did, however, develop one unattractive habit. 'He never went to the toilet,' Holland told me. 'The gents' toilet was a long way downstairs in the basement, and we had open fires, and he used to pee in the fire, right in front of people. It would splash everywhere. He'd call the porter and say, "The fire's gone out again," and the porter would say, "You've pissed in the fire again, Sir Thomas." '

When Comyn-Platt died in 1961 his friend Henry Maxwell, in an affectionate tribute in *The Times*, admitted that he was gaunt, angular, old-fashioned and out of sympathy with the modern world, but what old man of ninety-two is not? 'Below the austere and aloof exterior,' wrote Maxwell, 'was a warm humanity and a quickness of wit and humour which many a younger man might have envied. He pulled people's legs, using his deafness on occasion [*and*] of his qualities the one which I think was outstanding was his courage. Old age, infirmity when it came, enforced isolation, and physical suffering, he fought them step by step to the end.'

By the time Etta married Platt in 1917 Grizel and David, now nine and seven, had become very close. Their elder brother Max was fun, Grizel told me, but by now he was a naval cadet at Dartmouth and not often at home. Their elder sister Joyce was seventeen and living at home but 'she was too bossy', Grizel said, and 'we didn't like her and she didn't like us'. But Grizel and David were always together, looked alike and shared a rebellious nature. Because she was so clumsy and always losing things Niv nicknamed her 'Gump' – the slang word then for a lunatic – and they went swimming, played cricket and fought together, and she admitted that sometimes he was unruly and uncontrollable. 'We were such good friends,' Grizel said. 'David was great fun as a boy, always very naughty,' which may explain why his mother and Comyn-Platt decided it was time to send him to a private boarding prep school in Worthing to learn a little discipline. Niv was appalled. 'For years I was bitter about this miscarriage of justice and found it hard to forgive my stepfather and my mother for what they had done,' he wrote in a ghosted series in the *Sunday Express* in 1958. He deeply resented being sent away from home, even though Grizel was at a boarding school in Norfolk. 'It was a *foul* school,' he told the British television chat-show host Michael Parkinson in 1981. 'There was a dreadful amount of bullying of the smaller boys by the older boys and the masters. I remember being hung out of a window from the third floor, and the window was shut on the middle of my back, and two terrified children were holding my feet, and being beaten with a cane. Another charming fellow would beat your hand with a ruler. I've never been so frightened in my life as I was of those masters. And there was a mad matron. I went to her with a boil because the food was so bad and she said, "Oh, that's nothing," and lopped off the top of it with rusty scissors so I got a terrible infection and was sent to hospital. Then my mother caught on.'

In *The Moon's a Balloon* Niv described the teachers as 'sadistic perverts who had been dredged up from the bottom of the educational barrel' and claimed that he had been dangled by a teacher called Croome out of a fourth-floor window. Ten years later, when he was a strapping rugby-forward cadet at the Royal Military Academy at Sandhurst, he went back to the school, determined to revenge himself on Croome, and discovered to his embarrassment that the school was deserted and the window was in fact close to the ground. And when *The Moon's a Balloon* was published in 1971 the headmaster's daughter protested publicly that her father had run an excellent school, and that he and his teachers had had a dreadful struggle to knock at least some sense and knowledge into young Niven's thick and bolshie skull.

Whether David was justified in all his complaints or not, 'I have very few pleasant memories,' he wrote in the *Sunday Express*.

> Even the few happy moments brought undeserved penalties. I was allowed to visit the London Zoo once, and a very special treat it was. But shortly afterwards I was sent to the hospital with tuberculosis of the jugular vein – they traced it to some tainted milk I had drunk at the Zoo – and my mother was told I would never be back. The doctors took a desperate chance, removed three and a half inches of the jugular vein and replaced it temporarily with a silver tube. Eight operations later I had developed a substitute network of veins and was released as a rare medical freak who should have died and didn't.

After the infected boil David was sent to Heatherdown, an expensive prep school at Ascot that he came to love. Etta can hardly have been as poor as Niv always claimed if she could afford to send Max to Dartmouth, Grizel and David to boarding schools, and to put David's name on the waiting list for Eton. In *The Moon's a Balloon* he claimed that 'only a token subscription to the family coffers was being made by Uncle Tommy and she still had her thumb in the dyke of my father's debts', but that same year, 1919, she bought a house at Bembridge in the Isle of Wight, Rose Cottage, and to pay for all that she must have had a great deal of financial help from Comyn-Platt. It was a rose-covered Regency house, in the middle of the village, of which David was thoroughly ashamed because it was so much smaller than his posh school friends' houses. 'That place was awful,' he told Lionel Crane of the *Sunday Pictorial* in 1957. 'When the east wind blew the back door wouldn't open, and when the west wind blew the front door wouldn't shut.' Nevertheless, the family spent the summer there and David came to love Bembridge because he could go sailing and, best of all, because Uncle Tommy rarely joined them during the holidays but stayed in London, where in 1920 he bought

47 Cadogan Place, an elegant, five-storey terraced town house in a quiet Chelsea street that was cossetted by several acres of quiet, leafy private gardens and had as its neighbours Sir Felix Schuster in number 48, the Honourable Edwin Portman in number 46, as well as a baroness and six other titled knights and ladies. Despite her comparatively meagre inheritance, Etta and her children never had to slum it; Comyn-Platt must have been much more generous than David claimed.

David, now nine, reckoned that Heatherdown was 'schoolboy heaven': the masters were kind, the matrons motherly, the food delicious and there were big green playing fields, a lake and a swimming pool. The forty-one-year-old headmaster, Sammy Day, had captained Cambridge University at cricket and played for Kent, and the boys were from a much better class than those at Worthing: they were the sons of dukes and marquesses, he said, 'very carriage-trade ... very snobbish. Everybody went from there to Eton.' He realised that after years of feeling unloved he could make himself popular by playing the clown. 'It was total insecurity,' he confessed to the *Telegraph Sunday Magazine* in 1977. 'The other boys were frightful, but I developed a dreadful urge to please them. They had all the unimaginable snobbery that went with money and large houses in the England of those days.' He told Michael Parkinson: 'I ate chocolate all the time and got very fat and obnoxious ... Everybody who becomes an actor probably becomes an actor because he wants to be liked.' So he clowned in chapel when he was singing a solo and his voice broke, and was caned by the Head. He was made responsible for the bellows that controlled the air for the organ and succeeded in making it emit a loud fart during a sermon by the Bishop of Ripon, which led to another painful visit to the Head's study. On a school walk through Ascot he deliberately split the seat of his trousers and displayed his buttocks to the public gaze. He was caught trying to slip into Ascot racecourse. He posted to his Bembridge friend Brian Franks, who was sick in the sanatorium at another school, a parcel that contained a ripe dog dropping, a gift that did not amuse the matron who opened the parcel. Finally, in a vain attempt to win a prize in the school's annual Speech Day flower show, David stole a giant marrow from the girls' school next door, Heathfield, and lied that he had grown it himself. That was it. After eighteen months Heatherdown had had enough of him. He was caned again, expelled, and Eton removed him from its waiting list. Etta and Uncle Tommy were at their wits' end to know what to do with the boy: he was only ten but already he seemed to be quite impossible.

It did not help that Etta was so vague and incapable of exercising any discipline. She did promise to give him £50 if he refrained from smoking until he was eighteen and he never did smoke, but otherwise during that summer of 1920 he was 'up to every prank you could think of', his Bembridge friends John Cockburn and Alec Mellor told Sheridan Morley for his biography *The Other Side of the Moon*. 'There wasn't much discipline and every night he'd be off to the local Garland Club, which was the centre of adult activity.' He stole apples and was clipped round the ear by the local bobby, PC Summers, and when he climbed over an iron fence he impaled his thigh on a spiked railing and had to be helped home, soaked in blood. His mother was out that night yet again – at a fancy dress party, dressed as a nun.

David's keenest interest was the sea. His mother had become a member of Bembridge Sailing Club and he started to learn to sail, and loved messing about in boats and dinghies. A friend's father taught him to fish with hand line, net or spinner, to pick up crab pots at dawn, to catch lobsters by hand among the rocks, to spear giant conger eels. He was even allowed to lend a hand with the ropes when the lifeboat crew returned at night from a mission of mercy. Because of this his mother and Uncle Tommy decided that he should follow Max into the navy, and they sent him to a school in Southsea that specialised in handling difficult boys and was run on strict lines by an ex-Royal Navy officer, Lieutenant Commander Bollard, and his wife. According to *The Moon's a Balloon* the establishment was a small, grimy terraced house with a dozen pupils with criminal tendencies, little better than a reformatory, and Bollard was a vicious, drunken brute, 'a gigantic man . . . with a magenta coloured face and tufts of hair sprouting on his cheek bones' who thrashed the boys regularly 'for nothing' and punished David by locking him in a dark cellar full of rats. As for Mrs Bollard, she was apparently a 'thin-lipped, blue-veined' alcoholic who starved the boys. 'Every day was torture for me,' wrote Niv. Feeling neglected and rejected yet again, he joined a gang of boys who went shoplifting on Saturday afternoons and sold their booty to a fence in Southampton. If this all sounds just a little too Dickensian to be true, Niv did admit in a letter to his publisher Jamie Hamilton in 1966 that he was 'undoubtedly the most poisonous little bastard that God ever put breath into'. And the experience lasted only a month, after which he went back home to Bembridge – with a stick of rock given to him by Commander Bollard, which suggests that the man was not always a monster.

To pass the entrance exams for Dartmouth naval college Niv was sent to yet another expensive establishment, this time a crammer in a vicarage at Penn Street in Buckinghamshire that was run by the Reverend Arthur Browning, a grandson of the poet Robert Browning. According to Niv, Browning was another 'evil-tempered, vain old tyrant' and the dozen or so boys 'without exception loathed him', but Mrs Browning's food was good, a couple of the masters were unexpectedly nice, and his two years there turned out to be so enjoyable that he tried at last to do some serious work and was not especially upset when a large Old Etonian plied him with ice-cream cornets, lured him into some woods and interfered with him.

Despite every effort David failed to get into Dartmouth. His English, French, history and geography were adequate but in 1923 he failed the vital maths exam. Once again he had been rejected and once again his self-esteem had been battered. At the age of thirteen he seemed to be on the scrapheap already. But then just in time a new public school, Stowe, was founded and Uncle Tommy managed to get him a place. It was to give him the polished personality, manners and wit that were to make him a classic 1920s English gentleman, a film star, and deeply loved all over the world.

Two

The Making of an English Gentleman
1923–1928

Stowe School opened in May 1923 at Stowe House, a few miles southwest of Buckingham, a vast, magnificent, classically eighteenth-century mansion that had for more than 200 years been the country seat of the Dukes of Buckingham and Chandos and their heirs. It was a breathtaking setting for a public school with its massive grandeur, elegant colonnades, the north portico built by Vanbrugh, the sweeping Corinthian south loggia designed by Robert Adam. It had sumptuous state rooms, a domed oval marble saloon with pink marble pillars, a huge dining room, a chapel, and scores of stupendous paintings, and it was set in 280 acres of wooded grounds, lawns and landscaped parkland where Capability Brown had begun his career as an under-gardener. There were streams, lakes, waterfalls, avenues, numerous little follies, statues, *temples d'amour*, a triumphal arch and everywhere glorious views. Stowe even had its own zoo where the boys were allowed to keep pets. For an Old Boy of Commander Bollard's Southsea reformatory to be sent to Stowe was akin to being wafted suddenly to Paradise. This was just what thirteen-year-old David needed: style, elegance, space to grow and compensation at last for all that he and his family had lost when his father was killed. Yet never in his memoirs did he mutter even a grudging word of gratitude for Sir Thomas Comyn-Platt, who must have been paying his fees since Etta never worked. 'I was brought up under an umbrella of miserable crushing debt,' he complained to the *Daily Express* in 1960. Not at Stowe, he wasn't. There he lived like a prince.

Best of all, the first headmaster, J. F. Roxburgh, was a man of such liberal elegance and good breeding that he was to provide young David at last with the male role model that he needed so desperately. Roxburgh was a father figure whom David was to idolise and emulate for the rest of his days. Without J. F. Roxburgh and Stowe there would have been no witty, elegant film star called David Niven.

John Fergusson Roxburgh, who was always known as J. F., was thirty-five when Stowe opened with its ten assistant masters and ninety-nine boys aged thirteen to fifteen, one of them a future British Cabinet minister, John Boyd-Carpenter, who was to describe Roxburgh in his memoirs as 'the greatest schoolmaster of his generation ... he had the rarest of all qualities in his profession, the power to arouse interest and curiosity, and to inspire by example. It was impossible not to admire him, and not to do one's best not to disappoint him.' Previously an assistant master at Lancing in Sussex, he was tall, thin, beautifully dressed and renowned for his stylish suits, coloured silk handkerchiefs, tumbling ties, and his habit of calling even the youngest boy 'my dear fellow'. His vision was to start a happy public school very different from the old-fashioned, regimented ones that existed already. He treated the boys as adults, respected each for his individual abilities, no matter how unusual, and gave them much more freedom and leisure than was normal in public schools so that they might have time to develop their own interests. 'There was an exhilarating sense of freedom,' wrote Boyd-Carpenter. 'There were no bounds; bicycles were encouraged; and there were few rules ... But a high standard of good manners was insisted on.' Roxburgh knew the dates of each boy's birthday and each came to believe that J. F. actually cared about him individually. Above all, he tried to instil in them an elitist delight in art, architecture and literature. As he said in his first speech as headmaster, 'Every boy who goes out from Stowe will know beauty when he sees it all the rest of his life.'

Noel (later Lord) Annan, who joined Stowe as a pupil in 1930, wrote in the *Daily Telegraph* in 1988 that J. F. 'accepted the public school system – houses, prefects, fagging and the rest. But he wanted to make the schools more humane, less regimented, less dominated by the worship of games, and, above all, less philistine. Roxburgh civilised their outlook and enlarged their substance.' Annan added – and this would be particularly important for David Niven – that Roxburgh 'tried to make the lot of the ill-adjusted, the lonely and the scruffy, happier. Boys who pottered, boys who preferred country pursuits to team games, boys who had not found themselves were to be encouraged.' And he had a nice, dry sense of humour. To one small boy who was sitting in class with untidy hair, J. F. asked genially, 'My dear fellow, what is the French for a hairbrush?' As for punishment, he did occasionally use the cane as a last resort for offences such as drinking, smoking or cheating, but generally, said Annan, 'he tried to make boys feel it was childish or inelegant to behave badly [*and*] he made boys more generous-minded and more honourable. He taught them to hope – and put their trust in life.' One of David's contemporaries, Peter Sherwood, told Sheridan Morley that although Niv 'was always getting into scrapes . . . he found in Roxburgh a wonderful and clever mentor who knew exactly how to handle him. He would only have to say, "My dear David, I don't think that is very helpful," and David would say, "I suppose not, sir, I'm awfully sorry." '

Some felt that Stowe was not sufficiently intellectual and Roxburgh was said to be snobbish, racist and much better with the boys than he was with his staff, but David was to blossom under his otherwise liberal, tolerant, graceful regime. In five years he grew up and was transformed from a lively but insecure, rebellious problem child into the charming, well-spoken, life-enhancing English gentleman – bubbling with *joie de vivre*, beautifully dressed and gleaming with good manners – that he was to be for the rest of his life. Niv always knew how much he owed to Roxburgh. 'I worshipped the man,' he said.

He joined the school at the start of its second term, in September 1923, along with 207 other new boys, and was put into Chandos House where he found a second important role model in his housemaster, Major Richard Haworth, a regular soldier who had won the Distinguished Service Order and had been a senior instructor at Sandhurst. 'Haworth was a gentleman of the old school and the reverse of a martinet,' wrote Annan in his biography of Roxburgh, and an added attraction for David was that Haworth was to found the school's sailing club. 'The thing about Stowe was the amount of friendship on equal terms,' wrote one of its first teachers, twenty-seven-year-old Hugh Heckstall-Smith, in his autobiography. 'Every day almost everyone was seeing a number of people it was a joy to see . . . The feeling of the place was like the feeling at the beginning of some of the earlier Dialogues of Plato, of friends meeting casually at some rather delightful spot.'

Dudley Steynor, a sprightly ninety-three-year-old contemporary of Niven's who was in the same class, Remove B, told me in 2002: 'I cannot convey the admiration we had for Roxburgh. One winter he put up on the board a rule that when the Octagon Lake was frozen over no one should skate on it until he had tested it. The next day someone had carved his initials – JFR – with skates right across the ice. At breakfast he said he wanted to see the boys who had done it. Four of them had no hesitation in owning up straight away and he gave them each four strokes of the cane.'

With David safely out of the way at boarding school for three months, Sir Thomas Comyn-Platt stood again for Parliament in the snap general election that the Prime Minister, Stanley Baldwin, called in November 1923, this time for the northern seaside constituency of Southport in Lancashire – 'Vote for COMYN-PLATT, AND KEEP HOME FIRES BURNING' exhorted his leaflet – but even though he was defending a Conservative seat he was beaten by his Liberal opponent by 928 votes. He was not alone: Tories were losing their seats all over the country, Baldwin lost his majority, his government fell, and Ramsay MacDonald became Britain's first Labour Prime Minister.

At Stowe David was no doubt jubilant at Uncle Tommy's defeat, but otherwise he kept a low profile that first year. He was still addicted to milk chocolate and became so fat that his schoolfellows called him Podger or Binge. 'I had this great round face and I couldn't run very fast,' he told the *Sunday Express* columnist Roderick Mann, who was to become one of his closest friends, in 1966. 'I and another fat boy hated having to shower after football because we both turned pink under the hot water. We were both so gross that eventually we sent off for some tubes of stuff we'd seen advertised as fat dissolvents. Fearful smelling stuff and every night we'd rub it on our stomachs. As we kept hacking away at the chocolate whirls during the day it was hardly likely to have any effect. I just stayed fat. But I do remember I entered for the half-mile, and as I thundered round 150 yards behind the field everyone roared with laughter and I started clowning and I realized then and there that I didn't mind being last as long as people laughed at me.' He was never going to be an intellectual – Roxburgh himself said that David was 'not clever, but useful to have around' – and although he was not stupid he was lazy, but he soon became fitter and lost weight and by March 1924 he was playing rugby for the Chandos House 2nd XV. Like many rugby players he developed a taste for alcohol and told the *People* in 1969 that 'soon after my fourteenth birthday I was found face down in a rhododendron bush after finishing off half a bottle of brandy. But thereafter I learned to drink and to hold my drink like a gentleman.'

In 1924 the Comyn-Platts moved into another large Chelsea house nearby where they were to settle for nine years. It was at 110 Sloane Street, again a five-storey terrace. It had to house not only Sir Thomas and Etta but also Joyce (who was twenty-four), Grizel (sixteen), David (fourteen) and at least one maid, if not two. Max, who was now a zany, restless twenty-two, had left the navy, joined the army, served in India, and resigned his commission by sending his commanding officer a telegram that read: 'DEAR COLONEL REQUEST PERMISSION RESIGN COMMISSION LOVE NIVEN.' David was so amused by this that he pinched the story and claimed in *The Moon's a Balloon* that it was he who sent that telegram himself when he came to resign from the army in 1933. After leaving the army Max had then become the Starter at Bombay racecourse and was now working as a jackaroo on a cattle ranch in Australia. Even so the house was simply not big enough for the whole family, and David was sent away each night during the Easter holidays to sleep a mile and a half away, in St James's Place, off Piccadilly, in what he called 'a minute cubicle in a boarding-house [*with an*] iron bed, wooden floor [*and*] stained jug'.

'Every night after dinner,' he told Michael Parkinson on television in 1972, 'this creepy stepfather I had used to give me tuppence for the bus and I'd get off at the Ritz Hotel and go down to this ghastly burrow with a pot under the bed, and eventually I got more adventurous and walked down to Piccadilly.' There he would cruise the bright, exciting, vibrant night streets around Piccadilly Circus and ogle the pretty young prostitutes in their cloche hats and short skirts who wiggled and winked under the benign supervision of the winged statue of Eros, the Greek god of love. For the rest of his life Niv delighted in telling the story of how he was mesmerised by a gorgeous, seventeen-year-old blonde tart with blue eyes, fabulous legs and a deliciously lively manner who used to solicit in Bond Street. Her name was Nessie and he became besotted instantly. From them on he searched for her in the wicked streets and followed her around. On the fourth night she stopped suddenly and asked him if he was looking for a good time. Niv's story in *The Moon's a Balloon* of how she initiated him into the joys of sex for free in her little flat in Cork Street, with a record of 'Yes, We Have No Bananas' playing on the wind-up gramophone, is wonderfully vivid, funny and touching, and he said that after that they would meet regularly in the afternoons for tea, or to go to the cinema or music hall together, before returning to Cork Street for more sex. 'By the time the Easter holidays ended,' Niv wrote, 'Nessie had become the most important thing in my life . . . she gave me something that so far had been in rather short supply – call it love, understanding, warmth, female companionship or just "ingredient X" – whatever it was, it was all over me like a tent . . . there grew up between us a brother-sister relationship that was to last for many years.' He claimed that she even visited him regularly at Stowe that summer, when he ravished her on a tartan rug in the school grounds, and that he introduced her to Roxburgh as they sat watching cricket one Saturday afternoon and she said to J. F. boldly, 'Don't look a bit like a schoolmaster dew yew, dear?' Fifty years later he told Don Short of the *People*, in 1974, that when he left Stowe in 1928 and she broke off the relationship 'I was heartbroken . . . I was really in love with her.'

Some of Niv's closest friends are cynical about this classic old story of the Golden-hearted Whore. It is certainly likely that the teenage David consorted with young prostitutes in the West End of London and launched his enthusiastic lifelong pursuit of female flesh maybe as young as fourteen, but many of his friends reckon that Nessie never existed and was either a romantic invention or an idealised composite of several young tarts whom David enjoyed in those years. One of his contemporaries at Stowe, Frith Banbury, told me: 'We all knew about this prostitute and he had this very exciting reputation, but I never saw her.' Dudley Steynor remembered that Niv did once bring 'an extraordinarily pretty girl with a huge, wide straw hat' to a cricket match at Stowe and introduced her to Roxburgh, but Reg Gadney, the son of David's Stowe friend Bernard Gadney, who went on to captain England at rugby during the 1930s, told me that his father did not believe that Nessie existed. Nor did Roderick Mann, who told me: 'It didn't ring true.' Tom Hutchinson agreed and said that Niv once confided that in fact he had lost his virginity to a school matron at Stowe, 'a woman all the boys fancied'. The American writer William F. Buckley, who became a very close friend of Niv's in the 1960s, told me that Niv had told him he had been seduced at the age of fifteen 'by this woman who looked after him', and Dudley Steynor said, 'There *was* a young matron at Stowe – oh, *yes*! – in her late twenties or early thirties and there was a story that one of the prefects was sleeping with her.' Niv himself told the *People* in 1969: 'I certainly sowed bigger wild oats than most youngsters. Sex? I was at it as soon as I knew what it was all about. I'd certainly lost my virginity by the time I was sixteen. And seduction was a wonderful sport in those days, with half a dozen petticoats to fight your way through!' And the girls loved him. Reg Gadney's mother, whose brother was at Stowe, told her son that whenever she visited the school 'David would wear an extravagant buttonhole, invite her to sample its scent, and then steal a kiss.'

But there was also a private, reserved side to David's nature even then. 'Dad gave me the impression,' said Gadney, 'that David, formidably good-looking, charming and mature for his years, was a self-contained, even solitary, figure whom it was hard to know.' Peter Sherwood agreed: 'There was always something faintly reserved behind all that charm,' he told Morley. 'You felt that if you could really strip it off ... a quite different David might emerge.' Back at Stowe for the summer term of 1924, David 'didn't have a special friend but he was an extremely pleasant fellow', Steynor told me, 'an extrovert and very charming even then, a little mischievous and up to minor pranks but not nasty or vicious.' Sherwood did recall one Niven prank that was less than kind: 'I remember him once when we were teenagers rushing out of Waterloo Station into the back of a cab and saying to the driver, "King's Cross, and drive like hell!" and then slipping out again through the other door so that the cab would arrive totally empty at the other station.' Still, maybe taxi drivers are considered fair game by comic actors and comedians. At the end of a taxi ride in London the great Tommy Cooper liked to tuck a little something into the cabby's top pocket and rumble 'have a drink on me', at which the cabby would remark 'ta very much, guv', poke his fingers into his top pocket and retrieve a teabag.

Niv's jokes and pranks 'were always much the same', Sherwood told Morley. 'They were repetitive but somehow he always made them work and got the laughs, and I suppose that was where it all started. He also used to do a lot of impersonations, men who'd eaten mothballs thinking they were peppermint lumps, gracious ladies having to be polite about ghastly Christmas gifts, that kind of thing. His face would become contorted with grotesque smiles and he'd keep the routine going for five or ten minutes.'

Before long David was polishing these vignettes and turning them into short sketches that he would perform on stage during the Chandos House shows that he helped to organise at the end of each term. 'I started doing concerts at school to be liked,' he told Michael Parkinson in 1981. Already he was a keen actor with a natural gift for comedy, and he was to base many of his sketches on the Aldwych farces that were popular in London at the time. In the autumn of 1924 Major Haworth founded an Officer Training Corps, Niven and Sherwood both joined, and soon the regular camp concerts gave them yet another outlet for their thespian talents. In the summer of 1925 they spent ten days at an Officer Training Corps camp on Salisbury Plain along with several hundred boys from other schools and David performed a sketch in front of them all in the camp concert that was held in a huge circus tent. He based his act on a monologue about a dim politician canvassing in an election that the comedian Milton Hayes had recorded. In David's adaptation the figure of fun was a slow-witted inspecting officer, Major General Sir Useless Eunuch, and to play the part he wore a uniform, a shaggy grey moustache and a monocle. 'I experienced, for the first time, that delicious terror that has never left me,' he wrote in *The Moon's a Balloon*, '– stage fright ... with rubbery knees, dry lips and sweating palms.' He need not have worried. He was a huge success right from the start, when he shambled onto the stage, peered at the red-jacketed officers sitting in the front three rows and barked, 'Sergeant-Major, why is it that these members of the band have no instruments?' For ten minutes he bumbled on – 'what we must do with this camp, Sergeant-Major, is find out where we stand, then get behind ourselves and push ourselves forward' – and was given a standing ovation at the end of it. 'Milton Hayes and I were a riotous success that night,' he said, 'and the harpoon of craving success as a performer was planted deep inside me.'

'David's impressions became an annual event at the camps,' said Sherwood, 'and were so popular that the audience used to chant "We want Niven!" whenever any other poor schoolboy got up to do a turn.' Another of his favourite acts was to pretend to be drunk. 'None of us really thought he would go on the stage but he had a wonderful, boisterous sense of humour,' said Steynor. Frith Banbury, who would become a stage actor and director, felt then that David might develop into a comic song-and-dance man rather than a straight actor. 'Acting in plays seemed to inhibit him,' he told me, 'whereas doing turns was always what suited him best. He was always arsing about, being the funniest boy in the class.'

By Christmas 1924 Stowe had 342 boys, a figure that increased to 420 by the end of 1925. A huge playing field was built, a science block with physics and chemistry laboratories, more dormitories and classrooms, a sanatorium, gymnasium, squash and tennis courts, a golf course, and on 17 July 1924 Queen Victoria's grandson, Prince Arthur of Connaught, unveiled a tablet to mark the gift to the school of the beautiful Grand Avenue of elms and beeches that ran for nearly two miles from the lodge gates to the Corinthian Arch and had been bought by Old Etonians as a generous gesture of welcome from an ancient school to a new one. Even Sir Thomas Comyn-Platt was moved to buy tennis racquets for the team that won the house tennis tournament.

In January 1925 David went off to Savognin in Switzerland on a skiing trip with a group of Stoics. Once across the Channel he and a boy called Griffin managed to get lost in Boulogne, but they rejoined the rest of the party in Basle the following day 'cheerful but exhausted', according to a report in the March 1925 issue of the school magazine, *The Stoic*. Perhaps it is best not to ask why two teenage boys on the loose in a French town should have become so exhausted. In Switzerland they enjoyed glorious weather, and although David did not shine at skiing he came into his own at evening sing-songs during which, according to *The Stoic*, 'Woods, as an irate sergeant, and Niven, as a slightly muddled recruit, were a source of great amusement'.

Back in the Isle of Wight, Etta splashed out yet again and bought a twenty-five-year-old, 14ft sailing dinghy, *Merlin*, for David and Grizel to mess about in, and he and his friend Brian Franks founded the Bembridge Sailing Dinghy Club for children with Brian as captain, David as secretary and Ralph Gore, who was later to become Sir Ralph and a famous helmsman, as treasurer. They started with twenty-three members, held races, printed their own stationery and programmes, bought their own burgees and made a profit of £6 14s 0d in the first year.

At Stowe the next term David helped to start a Chandos House magazine, *The Chandosian*, and played the drum, cymbals and trombone in the eight-strong school jazz band, a picture of which was published in *The Stoic* in 1925 and shows David toying with a drumstick and dressed like the other boys in the same dapper suit-and-tie style that the Beatles would wear in the Sixties. David joined a drama group, the Bruce Players, that Sherwood had started in March and they began to put on occasional one-act plays and sketches that David had written. He also developed a mischievous talent for drawing and during lessons would make witty little thumbnail sketches or cartoons which would then be passed surreptitiously around the room to the amusement of the rest of the class. For weeks David thought that none of the teachers had noticed his little hobby but at the end of term, when one master was discussing with the class what exams they ought to take, he said, 'Niven, I think you should take drawing.' The class roared with laughter and for once the laugh was on him.

Another prank that might well have been David's concerned a statue of Lord Cobham which stood in the school grounds at the top of a tall column with a spiral staircase that was protected by barbed wire because it was strictly out of bounds. One morning Roxburgh told the school assembly that several signatures had been found on the statue and he promised serious trouble for the next person to write his signature up there. The next day he announced that there was now indeed another signature at the top: it read 'J. F. Roxburgh'. According to another Stowe contemporary, Terence Prittie, on one occasion when David really did go too far and Roxburgh decided that he had to beat him he was unable to go ahead because as he prepared to address Niv's buttocks with his cane he saw his face grinning at him upside-down between his legs.

Despite David's taste for mischief he started to work quite seriously, for Major Haworth had persuaded him to aim for Sandhurst and the army, for which he would have to pass several specified subjects in the School Certificate exams in 1926, when he was sixteen. He was still hopelessly weak at maths and had to have special coaching, but his best subject was English and 'our English master, Mr Arnold, was always praising David's essays and stories', Steynor said. Niv certainly had a keen and lively eye and a light touch with words, judging by an amusing little story that he wrote when he was fifteen for *The Stoic* describing a shambolic school expedition during a second trip to Switzerland at the start of 1926. Entitled 'A Tailing Party at the Swiss Camp', it read in full:

> The procession prepared to start in the following order: first, a couple of sinister-looking horses; second, Antoine, or 'The Last Bandit', or 'Why-cause-a-lot-of-trouble-by-pushing-your-rich-uncle-over-the-cliff-when-you-can-have-him-quietly-stabbed-for-one-franc-fifty'; third, a sleigh full of lunch; and fourth, the cream of the Hotel Valbella on luges, reading from left to right – an Etonian, a Rugbeian, Hartland-Swann, a Reptonian, me, a Cantab, and Reptonian II.
>
> While Antoine put the finishing knots to the luges, we all stood round admiring the Etonian's apricot ski-ing suit. 'Take your seats, please!' from the Rugbeian. We sat down. The Rugbeian took Hartland-Swann's feet on his lap; Reptonian I took mine; Cantab took Reptonian II's; the Etonian, alone in front, nursed a guide book.
>
> 'En avant!' cried the Etonian, in his best taught-in-twelve-lessons accent. Antoine muttered an oath to his animals. They pulled bravely. The rope snapped – and they trotted gaily down the hill with Antoine.
>
> We hurried after them with the luges . . .
>
> 'It's a good joke,' said the Cantab, when this happened the third time, 'but personally I'm fed up with it.' Antoine, who seemed full of rope, produced a fourth piece and tied a knot that would have made even Major Haworth envious. We settled down again.
>
> Once more Antoine cursed his horses, and once more they pulled bravely . . . And this time we went with them. 'The idea all along,' I explained to Hartland-Swann.
>
> We fell to discussing why we should enjoy the journey more in our

present position than we had done coming up from the station a few days before in a comfortable sleigh, feeling bitterly cold and extremely bored.

'It's the possibility of an accident,' explained the Rugbeian. 'At any moment somebody may fall off.'

'My dear chap,' said the Etonian, turning round to take part in the conversation, 'why anybody should fall off –' We went suddenly round a corner, and quietly the Etonian left his luge and rolled on to the track.

As soon as we had recovered our powers of speech, we called upon Antoine to stop. He indicated with the back of his neck that it was dangerous to stop just then; and it was not until we were at the bottom of the hill, almost a mile from the place where the Etonian had left us, that the procession halted and gave itself up to laughter.

Ten minutes later a brilliant sunset was observed approaching from the North. A little later it was seen to be a large dish of apricots and cream – or shall we say the Etonian? When he had arrived and told us all about our lineage and future, he lapsed into a gloomy silence.

'Let's get on, then,' said the Rugbeian. We resumed our seats once more. The Etonian clung tight to his seat with both hands.

'Right!' said the Cantab. Antoine swore at the horses. They pulled bravely. The rope snapped, and they trotted gaily up the hill with Antoine.

We hurried after them with the luges . . .

Even now that he was swotting for his School Certificate exams, David was as mischievous as ever. Another contemporary, James Reeves, later a poet, told Morley that as they went into hall for lunch one day they passed a line of trolleys loaded with huge pink blancmanges and David smacked each one flat with his hand. It was 'an episode which may seem tepid enough today', said Reeves, but at the time it was 'irresistibly funny, a touch of creative comic genius'. Hugh Heckstall-Smith, who was trying to teach David physics as well as maths, reported that if he turned his back in class he always suspected that David was up to something nefarious in the back row. When he was working out an equation on the blackboard he felt much more comfortable if he kept David in sight and he would call him up to the front of the class and ask him to point at the equations he was working on. At fifteen David was very big for his age, and if he was asked in the physics laboratory to fetch a test tube, David and his much smaller friend Stewart-Wallace would turn the whole thing into a major farcical performance in which David marched smartly to the end of the lab and back with the diminutive Stewart-Wallace marching in step right on his heels. David was equally mischievous in his chemistry lessons and another contemporary, John Doubleday, told Peter Haining, the author of *The Last Gentleman: A Tribute to David Niven*, that during one chemistry lesson 'Niven had surreptitiously emptied a glass of sulphuric acid and refilled it with a similarly-coloured solution. Then, at a suitable moment, he had stood up, unstoppered the bottle, and before the science master's horrified gaze had poured the contents into his mouth, clutched his throat and gasped, "This is the end!" '

Even so, by the time David was sixteen he was so mature, charming and well spoken that Roxburgh chose him to show prospective parents around the school, even if it meant missing lessons for a whole morning. In July 1926 Roxburgh also decided to make him one of the four prefects – or monitors as they were known – in a new house, Grafton, that was to open the next term with Bernard Gadney as the head house prefect. 'It will do him a world of good to have something to "run" and the feeling that something really depends upon him,' Roxburgh wrote to Etta, and Niv recalled in *The Moon's a Balloon*: 'My prospects in the new house were very exciting, my fat had disappeared, I had many friends at school and at Bembridge, I had Nessie in the background and I was at last beginning to get to know and to love my mother.' But three days later he was caught cheating during his School Certificate Latin exam. He was perfectly competent at Latin but wanted to get the exam over quickly so that he could leave early, and persuaded his clever friend Archie Montgomery-Campbell, who was at the next desk, to translate the verse section and drop a crumpled copy onto the floor between their desks so that David could retrieve it and copy it. 'I am thankful for the sake of the School that I found out what had happened before the papers were sent to the Examiners,' wrote Roxburgh to Etta. 'I wish David would think a little more before he does these impulsive things, which are so entirely below his proper level, and which cannot help lowering him in the estimation of us all.'

Roxburgh nearly expelled him, which would have destroyed any chance of him going to Sandhurst, but Niv was one of his favourites and instead he gave him twelve strokes of the cane and this time there was no grinning upside down between the legs. Even worse than the pain – for a boy of sixteen who was already as big as a man and about to be made a prefect – must have been the indignity and the fact that the entire school, even the smallest thirteen-year-old, knew about it, and the knowledge that he had let Roxburgh down. Yet J. F. still made him a prefect when he returned to Stowe the next term, a brilliant psychological move that was finally to be the making of Niv because now he felt he owed Roxburgh everything and was determined to thank him by being the best monitor ever. 'Although I say it myself I was the best in the school,' he told Lionel Crane.

He was certainly the most popular prefect. Terence Prittie, who was a small thirteen-year-old in Grafton House, remembered that he and his fellows jostled to sit near David at meals because he was so friendly even to juniors and his conversation was always a delight. During the holidays at Bembridge he continued to take chances, most notably when he, Cockburn and Mellor regularly borrowed a car at night, even though none of them had a driving licence or insurance, and drove six miles to the holiday-resort town of Shanklin in pursuit of girls, and Etta was such an easygoing mother that she built an extension to Rose Cottage so that Niv and his girlfriends could misbehave in private and give her a little peace. She called it The Sin Wing.

At Stowe he was as carefree as ever. 'He was given his own study in Grafton,' Reg Gadney said, 'and enlisted a fashionable London decorator to furnish it in what was considered the modern style. He invited Roxburgh and Dad to tea – hot buttered crumpets and Gentleman's Relish – and Roxburgh's reaction was only to observe: "My dear Niven, I am bound to say that this room absolutely stinks of curtains."

"Yes, headmaster," said David, "but they're terribly contemporary." '

That term the impresario Sir Oswald Stoll gave the school an expensive movie projector because he believed that it was the public schools that would provide educated producers to run the British film industry. Little did he dream that sitting in the audience at Stowe was a boy who would become one of the biggest British film stars of all, though one wonders whether David was able to sit through all the films that were to be shown over the next new terms, among them *The Morris Motors Works Film* and *The Reconstruction of the City and South London Tube*.

At the end of December there was another two-week Stowe skiing expedition to Savognin in Switzerland, and at the start of the new year David was elected a member of the Debating Society, where the star was the future politician John Boyd-Carpenter. David soon became a regular speaker, beginning in March with a maiden speech supporting the motion that 'This house approves the policy of His Majesty's Government towards China' – a bold task since a Chinese Nationalist army was about to capture Shanghai and endanger British interests there, the Chinese Communists were about to launch a general strike, and the British consulate in Nanking was to be attacked and British properties looted.

In March too David wrote another article for *The Stoic* in which he described a sporty weekend that he and fifteen other boys had spent playing football, tennis, billiards, ping-pong and darts at the Hoxton Manor Club in London and he was nearly arrested for having travelled in a first-class railway carriage with a third-class ticket. He had never shone particularly at sport but in February 1927 he played in his first rugby house match for Grafton against Cobham and started to make a mark in the tennis and squash house matches. He swam for Grafton, won a hundred-yard race and was awarded a medallion after taking a life-saving exam in July, and was described by the examiner as 'the best all-round competitor'. In May he was promoted to lance-corporal in the Officer Training Corps and that summer he started to play regularly for the school's 2nd XI cricket team, and at the end of June he was awarded his 2nd XI colours. In *The Moon's a Balloon* he claimed that he was 'a frequent performer . . . in the 1st XI cricket, the 1st XV Rugby Football and in the fencing and boxing teams', but in fact he never fenced or boxed for the school and played only once for the rugby 1st XV.

He played his first of many matches for the cricket 1st XI on 18 June against Trinity College, Oxford, and although he did not bat – he never went in higher than number 9 – his skill was as a fast opening bowler. He took two wickets for thirty-two before making his first Debating Society paper speech that evening, speaking second against the motion 'That this House deplores the modern tendency to encourage education'.

According to Heckstall-Smith

> Niven got picked for the Second Eleven at away matches at cricket more for his effect on the team's morale than for what he could do with bat or ball . . . On the bus he could usually be relied on to give his famous impersonation of The Man who got a Mothball instead of a Peppermint when he was Having Dinner with the Queen. He said no word and made no movement except of the expression of his face, but the whole story was clear: the natural nervousness, the polite smile of acceptance, the first doubt, the suppression of the first doubt, the renewal of the doubt, the dawning certainty, the final certainty, the resolve to swallow (come what may), the first attempt, its abandonment, the working up of determination to make another attempt, the second attempt and its abandonment, the third and successful

attempt, the immediate relief, the short carefree period, the first doubt of the second series, the realisation that there was really little more that could be done about it . . .

At the end of July 1927 David took the School Certificate exams again and failed, and Roxburgh, Etta and Uncle Tommy began seriously to worry that he might never get into Sandhurst. The School Certificate was usually taken by boys of fifteen or sixteen, and David was now nearly seventeen and a half. With signs of desperation he was entered to sit the exams yet again at the end of the year.

During the winter he played rugby, as a hefty forward, just once for the 1st XV but regularly for the 2nd XV and was awarded his 2nd XV colours. His junior military career was progressing well, too, and in November he was promoted to corporal in the Officer Training Corps and awarded an 'A' Certificate. His School Certificate, however, was a very different matter. He sat the exams for a third time and failed yet again.

Roxburgh was worried. 'I too am grieved about David, who failed with extraordinary completeness,' he wrote to Etta. 'He did not get a "Credit", in any single subject! I have had a talk with him and we have together come to the conclusion that he and we must make a terrific effort to pass him through in July . . . David has all the brains required to get a Certificate, but he has always found real application difficult. However, he did begin to work properly last term, and the feeling that he is now really "up against it" should provide the necessary spur. With reasonable luck he will pass in July, I feel pretty sure.'

He was right. Niv was almost eighteen and far too old to be struggling still with School Certificate exams, and to fail yet again would have been pathetic when boys two or three years younger were passing with ease. In February he played rugby again for the 2nd XV, which thrashed Eton 53–0, and in March he made a major speech in the Debating Society as the main speaker deploring a ban by the official censor of a controversial new war film, *Dawn*, in which Sybil Thorndike played the British nurse Edith Cavell, who had been shot by the Germans during the First World War, because the censor felt it was unfairly anti-German and against the spirit of the League of Nations. But otherwise David worked solidly that term.

At the start of his final term, in May, he was promoted to sergeant in the OTC and in June took part in a military field day during which squads of uniformed boy soldiers from Stowe, Rugby and Radley schools played a war game across the broad grounds of Stowe for an audience of

1000 spectators. At one stage of the battle, according to the subsequent report in *The Stoic*, 'the platoon commander . . . took advantage of natural features . . . and drove a herd of cows into the enemy'.

David also played cricket regularly that summer for the 1st and 2nd XIs, though he never won his 1st XI colours, despite taking 5 wickets for 87 against the Crusaders. *The Stoic* singled him out as the 2nd XI's star bowler thanks to some excellent performances when he took 5 for 36 against Eton, 5 for 42 against the Welsh Guards, and 6 for 69 against Bradfield. A week later, on a perfect summer's day, he crowned his sporting career at Stowe by winning the senior backstroke event during the swimming sports and came second in the senior breaststroke. But the achievements that must have given him the greatest pleasure – and relief – came when he passed the army entrance exam for Sandhurst in June and then in July passed all the necessary School Certificate exams at last. On David's army interview form Roxburgh wrote in his rough draft: 'An excellent type of boy. Improved enormously since he came here. Not clever but . . . He will be popular wherever he goes and unless he gets in to bad company – which might be dangerous for him as he likes to get on with everybody – he would be a useful officer who would count for something . . . and do well with the men. I recommend him.'

The day before David left Stowe in July 1928 Roxburgh gave as always a talk to all the leavers. 'He began with a mnemonic: the four Ls, Language, Letters, Love, L.s.d.,' said Noel Annan in his biography of Roxburgh. 'The wisdom of the mnemonic consisted in remembering the following rules for life: restrain your language; answer letters the same day; keep your financial resources in such good order that a wedding present can be despatched to whatever friend was about to commit the classic act of folly; and above all if you fell in love yourself before twenty-five, take a single ticket to the North Pole and *be very careful what you write to women*.' Roxburgh was adamant. 'Gentlemen,' he begged them, 'whatever else you may have to do with women – however great the temptation, whatever the provocation – never, gentlemen, I implore you, I entreat you, never write to them. Women always keep letters, never destroy them, always know when to produce them.' Once when his Latin class was translating a passage about grasping Roman mistresses Roxburgh warned the boys, 'Gentlemen, they're not worth it: they're like coffee – they smell better than they taste.' Wrote Annan: 'He had little experience of women and none of sex,' and he was perhaps homosexual though there is no evidence that he ever indulged himself physically. His advice about women was probably the only topic on which David would disagree profoundly since two of the greatest joys of Niv's life were to be sex and the friendship of women. But on another question he agreed completely with Roxburgh: 'When we left Stowe,' said Steynor, 'Roxburgh said, "people will tell you that your schooldays are the happiest in your life, but that's all utter nonsense because the best time of your life is always ahead of you. Never forget that." ' It was a wonderfully optimistic, life-enhancing philosophy that David was to follow energetically all his life.

Niv's final school report was affectionate but critical: 'No society could say goodbye to David without a very real sense of loss but it is time he passed on. His eternal good humour, courtesy, and kindliness to all alike will win him friends everywhere he goes. Impulses will have to be curbed and more self-discipline learned. There is still that dangerous necessity of impressing his heroes and being the leading light in any company.'

In the Isle of Wight that summer, now that he was eighteen, he joined the adult Bembridge Sailing Club, enjoyed the sailing during Cowes Week and for another week kicked his heels as he waited nervously for his official acceptance by Sandhurst. Given his acting talent and popularity on stage it seems strange that he decided to go into the army rather than the theatre. He was not the only one in the family with a talent for acting: Grizel had it too and after being presented at court as a debutante (not something that a poor family could afford) she had gone to RADA – the Royal Academy of Dramatic Art – and would soon be touring in repertory theatre with another young student, Robert Morley, and appearing on the West End stage as Edith Evans's maid. But soldiering was in the family blood and Niv told Lionel Crane in 1957: 'It wasn't that I was in love with the army. It was the best thing we could think of to get a job that paid nice and quick.' In 1960 he complained to the *Daily Express* that 'as soon as I was old enough I was pushed into the regular army', but Tom Hutchinson did not think that he needed much pushing: 'I think he had an instinctive urge to join up because he had never had a proper family and the army would have been a huge family for him. It would give him comradeship and a sort of manly love.'

On 9 August he went for a second interview before a panel of seven generals and a clergyman, and was at last offered a place at Sandhurst. Delightedly he wrote to Roxburgh that weekend: 'I want to thank you very very much for all you did in connection with getting me in.' Then he added nervously, 'I had had something that I have been wanting to say to you for a long time and I decided to say it to you at the end of term, but when the time came, I am afraid my heart failed me! You may think it a colossal piece of cheek, and indeed it is, but please forgive me as it certainly is sincere. I want to congratulate you personally, Sir, on your wonderful achievement in bringing Stowe to what it is. I think it is marvellous and so, I know, does everyone. And I always wish I could have done something to help. Once again very many thanks, Sir, for your help in getting me into Sandhurst. I do hope you are not offended by what I have written, but I could not leave Stowe without expressing my appreciation and admiration.'

It is easy to imagine a ripple of ghostly applause from David's distinguished military ancestors: *The boy's come good at last, thank God. He's going to be all right.*

Three

Sandhurst and the Hairy-Legged Irish
1928–1933

David was one of five young men from Stowe who joined more than 400 other Gentlemen Cadets at the Royal Military College at Sandhurst on 31 August 1928 to be trained for fifteen months to become officers in the British army. The college's buildings were not nearly as stylish as those of Stowe but they were old and elegant, and the grounds extremely spacious, with acres of woodland, a lake and a river. The course cost £300, the equivalent of about £9000 in 2003, but Sir Thomas Comyn-Platt may have had to pay only £45 (£1400 today), the fee for the son of a dead officer. David was assigned to the junior platoon of No. 1 Company, where the senior cadet in charge was called Wright – 'a shifty-looking customer', he wrote in *The Moon's a Balloon*, 'a singularly unattractive piece of work' – who later changed his name to Baillie-Stewart and was imprisoned for selling military secrets to the Germans.

On his second Sunday at the college David and the other newcomers, all smartly dressed in traditional Sandhurst tweed caps, were inspected by the seventy-eight-year-old Field Marshal Duke of Connaught, the third son of Queen Victoria, and for ten weeks they were drilled ferociously by the Company Sergeant Major, 'Robbo' Robinson of the Grenadier Guards. They were paraded, shouted at, marched, yelled at, made to run, bawled at, exercised, sworn at, inspected, bellowed at, drilled again and shouted at again. They were taught to salute, climb ropes, use a bayonet and ride horses, and they polished everything in sight, over and over again: rifles, bayonets, boots, buttons. If they failed to be perfect at any of their tasks they were arrested and locked in the guardroom or made to drill yet again in full battle order at the end of the day when everyone else had collapsed, exhausted. A cadet who was caught pilfering was tarred and feathered by his fellows, horsewhipped across a vast field and thrown into the freezing lake. An unpopular chap might have his room smashed up, his moustache shaved off, or be thrown into the lake after dinner – a regular retribution. David was popular right from the start, but those first ten weeks were 'sheer, undiluted hell', he wrote. 'Life at Sandhurst was tough but it was exhilarating and the cadets were a dedicated *corps d'élite*.'

John Masters, who joined Sandhurst as a cadet three years later and went on to become a lieutenant-colonel in the Indian army and the author of bestselling novels such as *Nightrunners of Bengal* and *Bhowani Junction* in the 1950s, reckoned that the college was 'undoubtedly brutal'. Of his first weeks there he wrote in his autobiography *Bugles and a Tiger*: 'The drill step increased from 120 to 150, 160, 170 paces a minute – anything, just as fast as our legs would carry us. Faster. The sergeants twinkled along beside us like demented sheepdogs, their pace sticks twirling, their mouths baying and yapping an endless series of commands, threats and objurgations' – bull-necked sergeants who were technically inferior in rank to the Gentlemen Cadets and would call David 'Mr Niven, sir' before bawling at him, though according to an old Sandhurst maxim a Gentleman Cadet was almost an officer and not quite a gentleman. When King George V's third son, Henry Duke of Gloucester, had been a Sandhurst cadet just after the First World War an infuriated sergeant had bellowed at him: 'Mr Prince 'Enry, if I was your father, I'd – I'd – I'd *habdicate* – sir!'

For those first ten weeks the new cadets were not allowed to leave the college, but the exhausting routine did not diminish Niv's sparky sense of fun. 'In the life-saving exercises in the pool he would grab people round the shoulders when it was his turn to be saved and shout "Save me! Save me! Save me!" ' his contemporary General Sir Charles Harington told me, 'and once when we were doing mock court-martials and Niven wasn't paying any attention as usual and the commanding officer said, "What do you think the sentence should be in this case, Niven?" he said, "Death, sir!" The CO said, "But he's only been late coming back to barracks!" and Niven said, "All right: confined to barracks for two weeks".' General Harington also recalled that 'Niven lived a Walter Mitty life at Sandhurst and would make things up, as he did all his life.'

At the end of ten nightmarish weeks the new cadets suddenly realised that they were as fit as they would ever be, and although the drilling was now a part of their lives they were able at last to think sometimes and to study military law, tactics, administration and man management. They even had time for leisure. They could buy tea, buns and cigarettes in the Fancy Goods Store, which was known for some reason as Jesus, or beer and port with their meals, and they could raise extra money by leaving their bicycles, watches or suits with the local pawnbroker, Mrs Hart, otherwise known as the Duchess of Camberley. The nearest pub in bounds to cadets was at Frimley Green, Aldershot had a cinema and Camberley two prostitutes. Two other favourite amusements were bicycle polo and throwing bicycles off the roof on Sunday evenings. They were allowed out of bounds on Saturday nights and Sundays, a bus was provided to take them to London if they wished, and those in their senior year were allowed to have cars and raced them to London at night, though the privilege was removed, according to Masters, after 'too many civilians had been killed'. Generally the cadets' favourite method of relaxation was to drink too much. One Gentleman Cadet contemporary of David's told Alan Shepperd for his history of Sandhurst that 'some GCs found signing in after a weekend leave rather an ordeal. The orderly officer sat at a table at the entrance of the Old Building. Many would not have passed a breathalyser test, but as long as some sort of a signature was attempted and the GC remained upright most orderly officers were satisfied; if not, a charge of drunkenness was treated very seriously by the Commandant!' Also forbidden were the mid-week late-night expeditions when a cadet might meet a girl even though he could be expelled if he was caught. He would climb out of a window after lights-out, dodging the college policemen, the 'Bluebottles', and run across an open sports field before being picked up in a hired car.

Young Niven made an immediate impact at Sandhurst. He was soon selected to play in the scrum for the rugby 1st XV, and after just five weeks he appeared on stage at the college theatre in a variety show in which he performed a duologue entitled 'Searching for the Supernatural' with the college's reigning star actor and comic, R. E. Osborne-Smith. 'A valuable recruit, who deservedly made the hit of the evening, was David Niven,' said the college's *R. M. C. Magazine and Record*. 'He is a great find, with the most exquisite meandering manner.'

At the end of David's first ten weeks of purgatory he was made a lance-corporal, one of six promoted in No. 1 Company, and a week later he had a large part in his first Sandhurst play, *The Creaking Chair*, a three-act murder mystery in which he played a Fleet Street crime reporter and was praised by the college magazine as 'an irresistible hero'. At the end of

November he was awarded a rugby Blue and wrote a proud six-page letter to Roxburgh to list his string of successes but also to report ruefully: 'I met the R.M.C. champion heavyweight in the Boxing Competition. Altogether eight blows were struck. I struck the first two, he struck the next six – I went down six times!!' There were now nine Old Stoics at Sandhurst, and his pride in Stowe and loyalty to Roxburgh shone through his letter. 'When the King and Queen come down to Stowe for the opening of the chapel,' he suggested, 'if there are enough of us, do you think the Sandhurst contingent could form an extra guard of honour behind the O.T.C. one?' and he concluded, 'Everybody here has a very high opinion of Stowe, as of course they should, and we will see that that is kept up.' On 8 March he was deeply touched to receive a letter from Roxburgh wishing him a happy birthday.

He learned to play the bagpipes and was chosen to be one of the commandant's two orderlies that term, a post that provided a huge breakfast with the commandant every Sunday and allowed Niv to be excused the drill parade every Saturday morning so that he could go up to London early for the whole day. On Sunday mornings he and his fellow orderly would escort the CO to parade, chapel and a full inspection of the whole college, slow-marching and carrying silver sticks and beautiful embossed silver Victorian message boxes attached to their belts. As a joke Niv kept in his box a roll of lavatory paper and a dozen condoms, and to his horror one morning the commandant, Major-General Eric Girdwood, decided that he ought to inspect his orderlies and their message boxes. He opened Niven's box and gazed at its contents. There was a long silence. 'Niven,' he said eventually. 'Thank you very much. You are very considerate.'

David's dream after Sandhurst was to join the glamorous Argyll and Sutherland Highlanders, and in March he wrote to Roxburgh: 'I have just heard definitely that I am certain to get either the Argylls or the Blackwatch, I only pray that it is true.' His mother – 'whom I had finally grown to love and to appreciate,' he wrote in *The Moon's a Balloon* – had been pulling every possible string with influential Scottish friends to get him into the regiment, though her and David's motives were not quite as basic as those of the drunk middle-aged major of a Highland regiment who once remarked to John Masters as he propped himself up in a public lavatory, 'Join a Highland regiment, me boy. The kilt is an unrivalled garment for fornication and diarrhoea.' Lady Comyn-Platt had even managed to wangle an introduction to the colonel of the Argylls, the McClean of Loch Buie, who had taken a shine to David and introduced him to the regiment's honorary colonel, the sixty-two-year-old Princess Royal, Princess Louise, George V's sister, who became fond of him too. David spent a day with the officers of the regiment, who were about to sail off to the West Indies, and got on so well with them that they told him he was certain to be offered a commission in the Argylls and would soon be joining them in the Caribbean. He took this so much for granted that when he had to fill in a War Office form listing in order of preference the three regiments for which he would like to be considered, he wrote '1. The Argyll and Sutherland Highlanders; 2. The Black Watch' and then added cheekily, '3. Anything but the Highland Light Infantry.' It was to prove one joke too many.

During that term his stage career blossomed. At the end of February 1929 he appeared in another Sandhurst variety show in an item he had written himself entitled 'Why Every Married G. C. Should Have a Wife', of which the local paper reported, 'Mr J. D. G. Niven's witty talk . . . was, perhaps, the most popular item of the evening.' The *R. M. C. Magazine and Record* was equally impressed and said, 'Niven biffled away so delightfully that one wondered whether any institution provides a richer store for humour than the R. M. C.' A month later he performed what the local paper said was 'a very amusing sketch' of 'sparkling wit' as well as delivering a duologue with another cadet, both of whom were 'excellent' according to the college magazine. Three weeks later he was back again on stage in his first starring part – for two nights at the RMC theatre and then for a third at the Drill Hall in Camberley – in a three-act farce, *It Pays to Advertise*, in which he was the only cadet in the cast and played the lead opposite Mrs Barkas, the wife of one of the officers. His role was that of a charming, layabout, twenty-four-year-old son of a millionaire businessman – precisely the sort of light, charming, comic part that was to make him famous in Hollywood – and the local paper reported that 'Gentleman Cadet David Niven kept the audience continually in laughter' although 'his acting at times was a trifle exuberant'. The college magazine was enthusiastic too. This was 'quite the best show we have enjoyed for a long while', it reported, and 'the part of Rodney Martin exactly suited David Niven with his very attractive, easy manner. One feels so completely "at home" with him, so sympathetic when his troubles overwhelm him; proud of him when he keeps his flag flying; delighted when he wins through. He can make you "emote" . . . one minute and laugh with him the next. That is acting . . . He and Capt. Teversham together are a joy.'

That week Niv took part in an inter-company sports contest in No. 1

Company's shot-put team and five weeks later he was promoted to the rank of corporal. In June he had yet another cause for celebration. Comyn-Platt – who now had living with him and Etta at 110 Sloane Street both twenty-nine-year-old Joyce and twenty-two-year-old Grizel – stood for Parliament for the third time in a general election and was beaten by his biggest margin yet even though his seat at Portsmouth Central had previously had a 3503 Tory majority. Once again the Conservatives were losing all over the country to Labour, whose leader Ramsay MacDonald was again about to replace Stanley Baldwin as Prime Minister.

In June David invited a girl – he said she was Nessie – to the annual Sandhurst Ball and they danced in the big, beautifully decorated gymnasium to the strains of the college's military band. The ball 'was probably the most colourful function in prewar England', said John Masters, 'and was annually attended by about two thousand people ... The cadets and the women acted as a backdrop for the brilliance of nearly every mess kit of the British Empire – scarlet and gold, chocolate and French grey, royal blue and silver, dark green and light blue, white and crimson; kilts and trews; sporrans and aiguillettes and shoulder chains – and then the naval officers in their boat cloaks! The sight of the officers gathering was intoxicating but awe-inspiring.'

David had also found himself a new girlfriend: the beautiful, blonde, twenty-year-old English actress Ann Todd, who was soon to make the first of her thirty-seven films, to become one of Britain's most popular stars of the 1930s and 1940s, and to marry the director David Lean. Niv first saw her in a play in Portsmouth, bought a programme, drew two hearts on it with an arrow piercing both, and had it delivered to her. She decided immediately to have nothing to do with such an impertinent young man, but he started turning up at the theatre every night and sending her more programmes with hearts drawn beside her name. 'I got very uptight about that because it seemed so childish,' she told Sheridan Morley, but on the last night David wangled his way into her dressing room by persuading the playwright, Ian Hay, to introduce him. 'He was very cocky,' she said years later. '*Very* cocky. Very full of himself but now, thinking it over, I suspect very insecure inside.' Every Saturday night he would cadge a lift to London to see her, and although she said they never became lovers 'he was just a lovely person. People adored him even when he was very young,' and they developed a lifelong brother-and-sister relationship, the first of many platonic friendships that Niv was to have with beautiful women.

That summer he spent his last holiday in Bembridge sailing and chasing girls – 'I had a heart like a hotel with every room booked,' he wrote in *The Moon's a Balloon* – and enjoyed it all the more because his restless, ebullient twenty-six-year-old brother Max was briefly home on leave after his five-year stint as a cowboy in Australia before setting off for the South Pacific to manage a banana plantation on Norfolk Island. One shadow over that Bembridge summer was that Etta had begun to suffer dreadful pains that she tried to shrug off but that were in fact the first symptoms of the cancer of the colon that was to kill her three years later. In her last years, when she was often bedridden, David became closer to her and she told him and Ann that she dearly wished they would get married. Although David and his mother had never been especially close, Ann Todd told Morley, 'he was the baby of the family and she really loved him.'

At the start of David's final term at Sandhurst he was promoted yet again, this time to the giddy rank of junior under-officer – a rare achievement since No. 1 Company had only one senior under-officer and four juniors. One cadet under David's command that term was the future Major-General David Belchem, who wrote in his memoirs: 'He kept us, and everyone else, in good humour. He was, inevitably, constantly in trouble himself through committing minor military transgressions (such as leaving his bicycle in the wrong place, a heinous offence). But his personality and charm enabled him to get away with it.'

In October David took part in another variety show, this time appearing in three sketches with H. A. L. Montgomery-Campbell, a Stowe contemporary who had joined Sandhurst with him. One was about a seance, one about a Beau Geste firing squad, and 'Niven and Montgomery-Campbell were as good as ever we have seen them,' reported the *R. M. C. Magazine and Record*. 'Each is a splendid foil to the other. And when Miss Watson-Smyth comes to help them we get a finale raising the quality of a truly high-class entertainment.' During that final term he also played the juvenile lead in the Sherlock Holmes mystery *The Speckled Band*, turned out often for the 1st XV, and won his rugby Blue again. He certainly looked a formidable rugby opponent: the 1929 1st XV portrait shows a tough, frowning, intimidating nineteen-year-old bruiser with no resemblance at all to any theatrical luvvie.

When he took his final exams at Sandhurst he found them ominously easy and was convinced that his entry into the Argylls would be a simple formality, but when the results were published he came very low in the final order of merit: 122nd out of 148 cadets, despite being given bonus marks for having been an under-officer. As one Sandhurst examiner once wrote about another cadet, 'This candidate sets himself remarkably low standards, which unfortunately he fails to live up to.' To be certain of a commission in his first-choice regiment David should have done much better and was devastated to learn that he would not be going to the Argylls after all but to the very regiment that he had sneered at, the Highland Light Infantry, the HLI, or Hairy-Legged Irish as they were jocularly known by the other Scots regiments – the only Highland regiment to wear not the kilt but tartan trews with weird vertical and horizontal stripes.

He left Sandhurst on 18 December 1929, deeply depressed not to be going to the Caribbean, without winning any distinctions or prizes, and after a six-week Christmas break he was gazetted as a second lieutenant in the Highland Light Infantry (City of Glasgow Regiment) on 31 January 1930. His mother was shocked to have to pay £250, the equivalent of about £7500 in 2003, to buy all the uniforms and tropical clothes that the regiment demanded he should have, and once again it must have been Uncle Tommy who footed the bill. In *The Moon's a Balloon* Niv gave the impression that during these years his mother and Uncle Tommy lived mostly apart, she in Bembridge and he in London, but her name appears with his at 110 Sloane Street on the Chelsea electoral registers for every year from 1924 to the day she died in 1932, and two codicils to her will in 1926 and 1931 had them living together there.

In *The Moon's a Balloon* Niv said that he sailed immediately from Tilbury to the Mediterranean island of Malta in January, aged eighteen, aboard a liner, the *Kaisar-i-Hind*, to join the 1st Battalion of the HLI, but his army record shows that he was not posted to Malta until nine months later, on 1 October 1930, when he was nearly twenty-one, and in an article that he wrote in 1945 for the Fleet Air Arm magazine *Flight Deck* he said that his ship had been the *Criterion*. His army record does not say where he was during those missing nine months, but he was probably at the regiment's barracks in Aldershot or Dover training and learning how to command a platoon.

His trip to Malta was the first time he had been further than Switzerland, so at first he was excited, but he soon regretted that he had not been sent to join the 2nd Battalion in India, which was much more exotic and fun. In Malta, where the harbour of the capital, Valetta, was packed with the battleships, aircraft carriers, cruisers, destroyers and submarines of the British Mediterranean Fleet, the HLI's job was a humdrum policing operation at a time when many Maltese wanted to become independent of Britain, and Niv quickly became bored and frustrated. He was placed in 'C' Company and put in charge of No. 3 platoon, a bunch of about thirty rough, tough, streetwise Glaswegians, many with razor and knife scars from old brawls, but most of his fellow officers seemed to be middle-aged deadbeats and few could be bothered to talk to him at first, including his commanding officer, except for one old major who replied when Niv asked when breakfast was served, 'Breakfast? Officers of the Highland Light Infantry never have breakfast. They are generally sick around 11.'

Malta was noisy and smelly, his room stank of donkeys and goat dung, and the only action he saw was when his platoon had to guard a Customs shed at the harbour one night during an anti-British demonstration when some hoodlums threw a few stones. His life in the HLI was so dreary that he claimed in *The Moon's a Balloon* that he served there for two years whereas in fact he was there for only fourteen months. In 1957 he told Lionel Crane that he had spent over three years there. It just *felt* like more than three years.

There were only two bright consolations about that year in Malta: sex and Michael Trubshawe, though preferably not at the same time. Trubshawe was a massive, noisy fellow second lieutenant, 6ft 6ins tall with a huge handlebar moustache, a mischievous twinkle in his eye, an eccentric sense of humour, a bottomless capacity for alcohol and an irresistible talent for getting into trouble. The men thought he was hilarious, the officers shuddered and looked the other way. When Niv met him at a cricket match against the Royal Artillery, Trubshawe produced a bottle of whisky, a soda siphon and two glasses out of a briefcase. 'Come,' he said, 'let us drink to your most timely arrival with a glass of Scottish wine.' Niv took to him immediately and Trubshawe – 'this amazing and wondrous creature', as he called him – was to be his best friend for many years and became a surrogate brother to make up for the fact that Max was so much older and hardly at home.

Trubshawe was himself immediately attracted to Niv's 'wonderful smile, flashing white teeth, very blue eyes and a blue-and-white polka-dot scarf tied around the neck', he told Morley in 1984, a few months before he died. He was twenty-three and lucky enough to have a private income, so it had not bothered him when he had been sent down from Cambridge University after seven terms because he had spent more time hunting than studying. He had a grand piano in his room on which he played medieval folk songs, and instead of wearing a heavy, hot helmet on parade like everyone else he sported a cool, light, papier-mâché replica that eventually turned into mush during a downpour. Niv called him 'an

Elizabethan with a hunting horn' and he certainly galloped to the rescue on David's first regimental guest night, when the daunting guest list included an air marshal and a couple of admirals; the tables glittered with regimental glass and silver, and Niv found himself sitting trapped next to his commanding officer and desperate to go to the lavatory after drinking far too many aperitifs, but unable to move because no one could leave the table before the loyal toast to the king at the end of the meal. After soup and several courses accompanied by glass after glass of wine, David's bladder was bursting by the time the cheese arrived and he was in agony when he heard a whisper in his ear. It was Mr Gifford, the mess steward. 'With Mr Trubshawe's compliments, sir,' he murmured, 'I have just placed an empty magnum underneath your chair.' Gripping the huge bottle with his knees, David relieved himself for several minutes while thanking heaven for the perspicacity and inventiveness of his wacky new friend. Suddenly his CO, who had never yet spoken to him, remarked, 'I have fucked women of every nationality and most animals, but the one thing I cannot abide is a girl with a Glasgow accent. Pass the port.' The colonel never spoke to him again.

Because of his private income Trubshawe could afford to be generous to Niv, who had to survive on his army pay of nine shillings a day – the equivalent of about £95 a week in 2003 – and constantly picked up the bill for both of them, managing to do so without making David embarrassed. They hunted girls together and drank too much and played cricket and polo. In Niv's article for *Flight Deck* he told an hilarious story about one polo match in Malta when he was on a horse called St George and riding off one of his opponents, an admiral, when St George bit the admiral on the buttocks. The admiral roared with pain, Niv lashed out at the ball and implanted the head of his polo stick up the admiral's pony's bum. The pony clamped its tail over the head of the stick and both horses and their riders careered across the field, past the spectators' stand, irretrievably locked together.

'There was really nothing at all to do there except the four Ps,' Trubshawe told Morley, 'polo, piss-ups, parade and poking.' In pursuit of the latter they popped now and then into a brothel in Valetta called Auntie's although neither needed to pay for sex because Malta and especially the posh Marsa Polo Club seethed with available girls: local beauties, officers' wives and daughters, women from England desperately looking for husbands ('The Fishing Fleet'), and the hundreds of lonely young naval wives whose husbands spent months at sea every year. Niv started to pursue rather too openly the wife of an army captain who called him in to his office one day and enquired, 'Niven, are you very much in love with my wife?'

Niv was stunned. 'No, sir,' he stammered. 'Not at all, sir. Thank you very much, sir.'

'Well, if you're not,' said the captain, 'be a good chap, don't go on telling her you are. Upsets her, you know.'

Another close shave that Niv liked to describe was the night that he was in bed and about to ravish the wife of a naval officer who had just sailed off on his destroyer for six weeks of exercises around the Greek islands when she sat bolt upright suddenly and hissed, 'Christ! He's back!' Her husband's ship had broken down just outside Valetta. She bundled Niv into a cupboard, went down to the sitting room, and kept her husband distracted while Niv dived into his clothes and crept out of the house. 'I was impotent for days,' he said. To prevent any similar incident Niv and Trubshawe installed a 'husbandometer' near the harbour that was equipped with a piercing siren so that it could be sounded whenever the fleet was spotted returning to base.

In the summer of 1931 David returned to England, by boat to Marseilles and train to Calais and Bembridge, for his two months' annual leave, and he said later that he was sad and jealous to discover in London that Nessie had given up whoring and gone to Seattle to marry an American. In Bembridge he renewed his friendship with Brian Franks but was horrified to find that his mother was now in constant pain. 'So selfishly occupied was I with my immediate pleasures,' he wrote in *The Moon's a Balloon*, 'that I only dimly realized how serious her illness had become. She herself was gay and vague and wonderful and she pushed it all aside as something boring she had to live with.' Gay, too, but in the modern meaning of the word, was twenty-four-year-old Grizel, David's beloved 'Gump', who was about to give up acting to go to the Chelsea Polytechnic and study under Henry Moore to become a sculptress and who turned out to like girls as much as Niv did. He did not mind that she was a lesbian and referred to her jokingly as 'my sister the dyke'. To brighten Henriette's penultimate summer Max was also home on leave from his South Pacific banana plantation and amazingly persuaded her to lend him £3000, a huge amount that would be worth about £100,000 today. Maybe she knew that she would soon be dead because she told him that the loan need not be repaid until after her death, and it was yet another indication that Etta was not poor at all but extremely wealthy. The other highlight of that leave came when Niv was selected to be a member of the British crew in an international amateur sailing contest for eight-metre yachts at Ryde on 18 July 1931. The British boat, *Severn*, was skippered by his old chum Ralph Gore, and they won the Cumberland Cup by beating the French boat, *L'Etoile*, 3–0 in the final.

Back in Malta Niv and Trubshawe resumed their desperate attempts to brighten their lives. When they went off into the hinterland for manoeuvres and saw that the senior officers' tents all had little wooden signs outside saying 'C.O.' or '2nd I/C' they erected their own that read 'Chief Raspberry Picker' and 'Asst. Raspberry Picker'. Their spirits lifted dramatically when a like-minded lunatic, John Royal, joined the battalion briefly. Royal was a vast and very naughty young man from Sandhurst whose taste for booze matched theirs and who was later to be court-martialled for hitting two officers who were foolish enough to wake him after a party and accuse him of being drunk. At his trial he explained in his defence that because he had been dropped on his head as a baby he tended to lash out if he were suddenly awakened.

'What happens to your batman when he wakes you up in the morning?' asked the prosecuting officer smugly.

'Nothing,' said Royal. 'I have issued him with a fencing mask.'

Sadly he was in Malta for only a few weeks before moving on to join the 2nd Battalion in India.

To spice things up, Niv and Trubshawe got seriously drunk one night and went to a smart fancy dress ball at the opera house in Valetta dressed as goats. They crawled through the fashionable throng on hands and knees with rugs over their heads and backs, football bladders and the teats of rubber gloves swinging obscenely from their crotches, and leaving a trail of little black olives on the dance floor behind them. The snootier guests were appalled, but not as incensed as a gang of Maltese students for whom the goat was a sacred animal. Niv and Trubshawe were jeered, jostled and eventually had to escape from the opera house at a drunken trot, pursued by enraged Maltese. Their superiors were unimpressed by this performance and confined them to barracks. Another day of riotous pleasure occurred when they discovered that Max, passing through Malta on his way back to the Pacific on the liner *Empress of India*, was working his passage below decks as a sweaty, grime-smeared stoker, and the three plunged into a twenty-four-hour drinking orgy.

Such lively times, however, were rare and by now Niv realised that he had made a huge mistake by joining the army. Bored beyond belief, he was heading towards the parade ground in full uniform one day when he came across a dummy that was used for bayonet practice and decided to run it through with his sword, which snapped in two, leaving just six inches of blade in his hand. With no time to find another weapon, he went on parade with the amputated blade. 'Officers, draw your swords!' cried the adjutant. Niv flourished his short, jagged dagger. 'Stick an olive on that, Niven,' said the adjutant, 'and I'll send for a martini.'

He asked to be seconded to the West Africa Frontier Force, which would pay him better and should be much more exciting, perhaps even dangerous, but was turned down. He became transport officer, which gave him the added interest of working with horses and mules, but the novelty soon wore off. What he really needed was the buzz of the theatre: the smell of the greasepaint, an audience, cheers, laughter and applause. During the day he seemed to be the perfect officer, liked and respected by his men and fellow officers, though he must have wondered what the hell he was doing commanding a platoon of Jocks who were so unappreciative of the finer things of life that when he managed to liberate a rare cache of caviar from the impounded cargo of a Russian ship, and had it served to the men, one of them complained: 'This fookin' jam tastes of fish!'

Trubshawe believed that Niv could have had a distinguished military career had he gone to the Argylls or another regiment, but at night in Malta David would sit forlornly in his room reading *The Tatler* and old theatre magazines. He and Trubshawe tried to join the Malta Amateur Dramatic Society but were rejected, and in desperation they put on a show of their own for three nights in a canteen down at the docks. This consisted of a programme of Highland dancing and humorous sketches such as one about a skater who had no ice, which David perfected so well that when he returned to London the Prince of Wales insisted that he should perform it for him at Quaglino's nightclub. The show was hugely successful and gave Niv a wonderful boost, but its main effect was to remind him just how much he missed performing. Already he was gaining a reputation as a raconteur and collecting and burnishing his huge stock of funny anecdotes. 'He was really best, even then, at just telling stories,' Trubshawe told Morley. 'I'd seen him, at some pompous dinner party given by the C-in-C on board ship in Malta, with perhaps twenty-four other guests, gradually manipulate the conversation around until in time everybody was listening to this young man with just one pip on his shoulder. He had this astonishing capacity for anecdote.'

In December 1931 the 1st Battalion returned at last by troopship to England and was stationed at the Citadel barracks in a fort high above the English Channel town of Dover. Most of the officers and men were sent home for Christmas but Trubshawe and Niven were still in disgrace and ordered to stay and guard the fort. Had he known that this was his mother's last Christmas, Niv would have been granted compassionate leave, but he was still a selfish, thoughtless twenty-one-year-old who was bent on having fun rather than worrying about his sick old mother. And there was plenty of fun to be had now that they were back in England. He and Trubshawe would often roar up to London by car, seventy-nine miles, to take a couple of girls to dinner, the theatre or a party, and in March they were in town on the night of the Oxford and Cambridge boat race and with a party of drunken friends became so boisterous at the London Palladium that they had to give their names before they were thrown out. Niv said that he was the headmaster of Eton. Nor did he always have to rely on Trubshawe for wheels: that spring he was able at last to buy his own car, a little Morris Cowley, when his grandmother died in Bournemouth and left him £200, a sum that would be worth nearly £7000 today. Trubshawe was by now engaged to a beautiful blonde whom he had met in Malta, Margie Macdougall, but a young man as handsome, charming and funny as David had no trouble at all in finding girlfriends, and he and Trubshawe were both invited to plenty of parties and debutante dinners in London and to weekends in country houses. He began to enjoy such a busy high society social life, and all of it for free, that he admitted later that he became for some time a terrible snob about money and titles. The only snag was that unless he and Trubshawe had weekend passes they always had to be back at the barracks in Dover for the daily parade at 7 a.m., so one night when they knew that a party at the Coconut Grove nightclub would probably go on until dawn they hired a fast ambulance, equipped it with their uniforms and their two batmen, and after the party zoomed down to Dover at the last minute to arrive just in time for the parade. On the way down the ambulance had a puncture and when eventually they arrived at the barracks the battalion's 800 men were already standing on parade, but the two impeccably dressed renegades simply pretended that nothing was amiss and marched smartly out of the ambulance, carrying their swords, to join their fellow officers. Once again they were given a stern dressing down and a month's detention.

In one major engagement that summer of 1932 the officers of the HLI attended a royal levee to meet King George V at St James's Palace, wearing full regimental dress and regalia with their scarlet tunics, odd squared tartan trews and capes with fringes like old women's shawls, caps with ridiculous little plumes on the top, gloves and swords – and looking, according to Trubshawe, just like a gaggle of Highland postmen. As they queued on a huge staircase leading up to the throne room to meet the king, the Prince of Wales and the Dukes of York, Gloucester and Kent, they passed a line of Gentlemen at Arms, a collection of elderly, very senior, distinguished officers resplendent in Ruritanian fancy dress uniforms and plumed helmets, Niv could not resist prodding one of them. 'Christ, Trubshawe!' he said. 'He's alive!'

The most important party that summer for Niv was a dance in London where he met the vivacious nineteen-year-old American Woolworths heiress Barbara Hutton, who was said to be the richest girl in the world and about to inherit more than £10 million the following year. She was already engaged to a Georgian prince, Alex Mdivani, who became her first husband, but she and David kept meeting at parties over the next few weeks and became such good friends that when she returned to the United States she invited him to join her in New York for Christmas. Niv thought nothing of it at the time but a few months later he was to accept her invitation and take his first hesitant step towards Hollywood.

It was his mother's death that changed the course of his life. In November 1932 he was in Aldershot on a physical training course when Uncle Tommy telephoned to say that Etta was dying in a nursing home in South Kensington. He rushed up to London and was stunned to see how wasted she was by her cancer, but it was too late to say goodbye. Following an operation, peritonitis complications set in, she did not recognise him and she died on 12 November at 5 Collingham Gardens with her beloved husband at her bedside. She was only fifty-two.

She left an astonishingly large estate of £14,169 3s 9d net, the equivalent in modern terms of about £500,000, and to that should be added the £3000 that she had lent to Max, so that her net worth when she died was about £600,000 in modern terms – three times as much as she had inherited from William Niven only sixteen years previously. This huge increase in her wealth was not caused by inflation, which was nil between 1916 and 1932, nor probably by clever investment, since the British stock market index fell by fifty-five per cent between 1919 and 1931 as it was battered by the Great Depression. The only explanation is that Etta left her inheritance from William Niven untouched to grow for sixteen years in some high-earning account, with Comyn-Platt paying all the massive school fees and living expenses – which would be less surprising if he really was Grizel's and David's father.

When Etta died she left a further mystery: in the document granting probate she is described oddly as 'Dame' Henriette Comyn-Platt when her correct title was 'Lady'. After a few small personal legacies she left the bulk of her estate to her trustees to be used for Sir Thomas's benefit so that he could continue to live in their houses for as long as he wished and be paid the entire income from the estate for the rest of his life, after which it would go to her four children. She also appointed him her children's guardian should any of them still be under age when she died – another indication that she loved and trusted him. Among the specific bequests she gave Max some jewellery and most of her family silver, David half of the silver with the Niven crest and a large diamond butterfly brooch, and numerous diamond, sapphire, pearl and platinum rings, brooches and earrings to Joyce and Grizel. Niv's constant claims that she was desperately poor were quite untrue.

He suffered deep guilt about his mother's death. 'I went back to Aldershot,' he wrote in *The Moon's a Balloon*, and 'endlessly chastised myself for always taking her presence for granted, for not doing much, much more to make her happy and for not spending more time with her when I could so easily have done so'. At the age of twenty-two he had become an orphan. His commanding officer told him to take a month's leave and go somewhere completely new. He cabled Barbara Hutton in New York, she told him to come immediately, and he sold his car, borrowed some money from Grizel and the bank, bought the cheapest possible ticket to New York on the liner *Georgic*, and sailed on 14 December in a noisy cabin right above the propellers that he shared with a middle-aged American bootlegger who went ashore when they arrived in New York, where Prohibition still ruled the land and alcohol was illegal, in a baggy suit with huge secret pockets stuffed with bottles of whisky.

He arrived on Christmas Eve and was met by Barbara and a gang of her friends who made him welcome immediately even though they could barely understand his posh English accent. Their openness and friendliness provided the tonic that he needed and he quickly came to love America and Americans for their kindness and generosity, and he was awed by the massive power and beauty of the city, the towering buildings, endless avenues, seething crowds, the glittering Christmas lights and decorations, the sheer vast Americanness of it all. Barbara booked him into the elegant Pierre Hotel, where her family lived in several suites, and for nearly a week he lived like a millionaire and was not allowed to pay for anything.

They attended the Central Park Casino where despite Prohibition everyone was drinking almost as much as Trubshawe, and spent Christmas Day with Barbara's family, who gave David some wonderfully generous presents. They went to Princeton with a party of her friends, including some stunningly beautiful girls, to watch the university play Yale at American football, a game that he came to enjoy immensely. Back in New York, with more of Barbara's friends, among them a tall, shy, quiet millionaire called Howard Hughes, they enjoyed a blur of parties, nightclubs, dives, Harlem joints and the famous '21 Club' speakeasy, where should the police suddenly carry out a raid every glass and bottle of booze would slide down a chute into the cellar and disappear within seconds behind an undetectable two-ton brick door that still guards the wine cellar there today. And they made in the bath their own illicit, dangerous gin with chemist's alcohol, wood chips and juniper juice. Had they got it wrong it could have killed them.

One of Barbara's friends, Phil Ammidown, was about to drive more than 1000 miles down the east coast to Palm Beach in his fast convertible and invited David to join him. On the way they took a 400-mile detour to the west of Florida for a party at Tallahassee, but on their way back south towards Palm Beach, near Jacksonville and driving fast at 5 a.m. they were suddenly blinded by the headlights of an oncoming car, collided in the dark with two black mules and crashed into a swamp. They came round from unconsciousness to find that they were pinned into their seats by the crumpled windshield, the front of their car had disappeared completely, they were covered in blood, and they could hear alligators splashing near them and grunting as they feasted on the bodies of the mules. Niv and Ammidown sat in the wrecked car for ages, paralysed, listening terrified to the dreadful sound of the alligators eating, until eventually at dawn they were able to escape from the wreck.

Ammidown bought a new car and they drove on south that afternoon, checked into an hotel in Palm Beach and soon forgot that nightmare as they revelled in the winter sunshine of Florida. For day after day they played golf or tennis, went sailing and fishing, and for night after night they ate in restaurants, flirted with pretty girls and went dancing. Niv became so hooked on the American way of life and so keen on one of the girls that he missed his return passage and cabled his CO: 'DEAR COLONEL MAGNIFICENT OPPORTUNITY BIG GAME HUNTING WHALE FISHING FLORIDA REQUEST ONE WEEK EXTENDED LEAVE.' The CO replied, 'NO WHALES OR BIG GAME WITHIN A THOUSAND MILES STOP TAKE TWO.'

In the event he was allowed to take two months' leave and it was late February before he sailed back to England on the German liner *Europa*, once again in a tiny cabin in the rumbling depths of the ship, vowing to return to America as soon as possible. He had glimpsed a way of life that seemed so much bigger and richer than the life he was leading in England in the HLI, and he knew now that it would be only a matter of time before he left the army and went back to North America for good. Not only had he had a wonderful long leave at very little expense to himself, he actually returned to England richer than he had been when he left because a generous American passenger on board the ship gave him a share in his daily sweepstake ticket and he won £160, about £5600 in modern terms.

He returned to barracks in Dover on 27 February 1933, by which time Trubshawe had left the regiment to marry Margie Macdougall. While David was away he had been promoted to full lieutenant, but the thought of serving more than twenty more years in the HLI without even Trubshawe to ease the boredom was inconceivable. Nor could he look forward to any further promotion, for unless there were a war soon it would be years before he would be elevated even to captain.

His sweepstake winnings allowed him to buy a sporty old Bentley – 'the complete cad's car', he called it – and he saved money by sticking on his windscreen the label from a Guinness bottle, which looked just like a road tax disc. Several times a week he would escape from the barracks in Dover and drive up to London, to resume his friendship with Ann Todd, whose career as an actress was beginning to take off after making five films in two years. He became increasingly keen on her although she was less impressed by his need always to be in a crowd and to lead the rollicking sort of jolly macho life that he had with Trubshawe. She introduced him to a young actor called Laurence Olivier and for the first time he began to think seriously about becoming an actor himself. One evening he asked her advice. 'I told him he couldn't possibly be an actor,' she said to Morley. 'I'd only ever seen him doing sketches in army concerts and although he was very funny it was always a turn, usually imitating somebody or pretending to skate. I didn't see much sign of him being an actor, so I told him that in my view he was a "ha-ha-ho-ho" sort of person and that he should stick to the army because nobody would ever believe him on a stage. Even if he said, "I love you," they would just laugh. I think that rather depressed him.'

Another of his girlfriends, a bubbly brunette called Priscilla Weigall, who had been voted Deb of the Year, disagreed, told David that he ought to become a movie actor and introduced him to the Hollywood film star Douglas Fairbanks Senior, who was living for a while in Hertfordshire. Fairbanks took to him immediately and they played golf together at

Sunningdale, but Niv was too nervous and awed to ask his advice about becoming an actor, so Priscilla then introduced him to a film producer, Bunty Watts, who was making a film at Sound City, a small studio nearby. Watts took to Niv as well and gave him a part as an extra in the film, *All the Winners*, a thriller about blackmail and race-fixing in the horse-racing world in which David could be glimpsed among the crowd in a paddock at the races. He also tried to land a part in Alexander Korda's epic *The Private Life of Henry VIII*, with Charles Laughton as the king, but had no luck. A film researcher has claimed that David also appeared as an extra in the 1932 film *There Goes the Bride* but there seems to be no other evidence for this.

One consolation that spring was the appointment of a new HLI Commanding Officer, Colonel Alec Telfer-Smollett, who was to become another of David's father figures. Telfer-Smollett brought with him a brisk efficiency and commitment that revitalised the battalion, and Niv quickly came to admire him, and they became friends and often dined and played golf together. 'He was a firm believer in an ancient concept of a regiment – that it should be a family,' Niv wrote in *The Moon's a Balloon*, and a family was what he had sought and needed ever since his father had been killed.

That spring David met Uncle Tommy for the last time in his life. Comyn-Platt invited him to lunch at the Carlton Club but as soon as they met again for the first time in years except for his mother's funeral, Niv claimed in *The Moon's a Balloon*, Sir Thomas 'rose from a chair, ignored my out-stretched hand and said, "The solicitors tell me that, so far, you have paid nothing towards the grave." I did not stay for luncheon and I never saw him again.'

David's disillusionment with the army reached its peak when half his platoon was sent off to India to enjoy exotic Eastern adventures while he was despatched to Salisbury Plain to take a dreary course in machine-gunnery at Netheravon. Deeply fed up one day and raring to get back to the fleshpots of London, he claimed that he was listening to a lecture by a major-general who wound up his talk by asking 'Any questions, gentlemen?' and Niv raised his hand and asked, 'Could you tell me the time, please? I have to catch a train.' Apparently he was placed under close arrest and guarded in his room by another second lieutenant who was armed with a sword but let him escape through a window. Niv claimed in *The Moon's a Balloon* that he drove fast up to London and had dinner at White's Club with two ex-soldier friends, Victor Gordon-Lennox and Philip Astley, who urged him to resign from the army before he was arrested and court-martialled. Gordon-Lennox had recently married a Canadian and was about to sail for Canada and Washington to take up a new job there, said Niv, and in exchange for Niv's Bentley he gave him a return ticket to Quebec and an invitation to stay with them for a week or two until he decided what to do with the rest of his life. It was there and then, said Niv, from the porter's desk at White's, that he sent Telfer-Smollett at the Citadel Barracks in Dover the legendary telegram that he had pinched from Max and that read: 'DEAR COLONEL REQUEST PERMISSION RESIGN COMMISSION LOVE NIVEN.' In *The Moon's a Balloon* he added, 'I sailed for Canada in the morning.'

This was all untrue. In fact his departure from the army was neither sudden nor dramatic and took more than a month to arrange. Telfer-Smollett was not in Dover at all but on holiday in Scotland, and far from receiving a cheeky telegram he had already discussed the resignation with David, who had told him that he wanted to go to Hollywood to become an actor. Telfer-Smollett wrote worriedly to Sir Thomas Comyn-Platt on 4 August 1933:

> Dear Sir Thomas,
>
> I am not sure whether you know that your step-son – David Niven – has applied to resign his commission in the Army – He apparently proposes to take up film work.
>
> If this proposal is with your permission, well and good – and I will forward his resignation to the War Office.
>
> Knowing David as I do, I cant help feeling that it is a mistake his leaving the service so young.
>
> He is very unbalanced, irresponsible etc and the one thing that will save him is discipline, which he wont get in the film world! He has – I am sure you will agree – rather a weakness for the 'flashy' type, man or woman and I dread to think what will be his future if he is film struck. Will you let me know to this address what your views are. He writes 'he has a chance of making big money'. Not so easy without many years of hard work.

Uncle Tommy wrote immediately to David, who was still in Dover, to urge him to think again, but David had made up his mind and replied on 3 September,

> Dear Tommy,
>
> I got your letter this morning.

I am off to Canada on Saturday.

I have thought all this out a million times and I used to talk it over with Mum. We both realised that there was no future in the Army.

I know now that the best I can ever be in the Army is a Major to retire after forty-five years service with a pension of £150 a year! That is no good to me.

I am not like Max – I have got ambitions and I shall not starve.

This is nothing to do with films at all.

I am going over with Victor Gordon Lennox and am going to get in with the big oil people over there. Everything is being paid and I shall be back in a couple of months.

Even if I don't get the job I expect in Canada I shall get some work when I get back.

I am not going to stay on in the Army – its an absolute dead-end and will get me nowhere. I am taking a chance I know – a big chance, but I can look after myself and I shall make good.

Just put your trust in me instead of destructive criticisms.

I shall not let Mum down.

Joyce knows my address.

Hope you are well and happy.

Will get in touch directly I get back.

Yours ever,

David

The third and fourth last lines of that letter – and Sir Thomas's concern that he might be making a big mistake – suggest that they were on much better terms than Niv would have us believe. But Sir Thomas had finally had enough of this difficult stepson and forwarded the letter to Joyce with a pencilled note that read: 'It would appear that both you and Smollett are wrong! It is Oil not Films! I don't understand. Anyhow I have done my best; and now, as I say, I give it up. T.'

Telfer-Smollett's letter disposes of another story about Niv's departure from the army that was quite untrue: many years later there were those (including his literary agent, George Greenfield) who believed that he had behaved so indiscreetly with the wife of a naval officer that he had been ordered to resign or be cashiered, but if that were so Telfer-Smollett would hardly have tried to persuade him to stay in the HLI. Nor would he have given Niv a regimental farewell dinner, which he did, at which Niv made a speech announcing that he was going to Hollywood to become a famous film star – a story that Greenfield was told by one of

Niv's contemporaries, Lieutenant-Colonel Hugh Percival DSO, who was at the dinner. The story about 'the big oil people' was obviously simply a fib to mollify Uncle Tommy.

To raise some money Niv sold to a London hospital the right to dissect his body after his death. They paid him £6 10s 0d for it, about £230 today, when he signed a promise that he would never smoke, and he sailed for Canada on the *Empress of Britain* on 6 September. For the rest of his life he liked to pretend that he became a film star only by amazing accident, but that was quite untrue. From the age of twenty-three he went after it with ruthless determination.

Four

A Swordsman in Hollywood
1933–1937

The Canadian autumn welcomed Niv to his new world with the red and gold of its maple trees, the stillness of its waters, the bracing chill of its clean air. He stayed for several days with Victor Gordon-Lennox, his wife Diana, and her parents, Admiral Charles and Lady Kingsmill, in a wooden guest cabin on the Kingsmills' five-acre island in Lake Rideau halfway between Ottawa and Lake Ontario. They went fishing on the lake, made expeditions into the surrounding countryside and decided that for David to get to Hollywood he needed first to go to New York. In newspaper interviews years later he claimed that he had worked in Canada as a lumberjack and for a bridge-building gang for 18 cents an hour, but he made no mention of these jobs in *The Moon's a Balloon*. He cashed in his return ticket to England and headed for New York but was struck down on the way, in Ottawa, by a very painful throat, had his tonsils removed, and to pay his hospital bill he copied four extracts from a book by Thyrett Drake, *Fox Hunting in Canada*, and sold them as his own work to a local newspaper. A few nights after leaving hospital he collapsed with a terrifying throat haemorrhage, nearly bled to death and had to be rushed back, gushing blood, for transfusions.

It was the middle of an icy October before he made it to New York by train. He took a tiny room in a cheap hotel, the Montclair on Lexington Avenue, and reported in *The Moon's a Balloon* that he found through an agency a few jobs as a waiter at illegal cocktail parties. Many years later he claimed that he had been so desperate for money that he had also worked as a delivery man for a Chinese laundry, but once again he made no mention of this in *The Moon's a Balloon*. Jobs were not easy to find during the Great Depression, when millions were unemployed. 'I saw people lying drunk in the streets,' he told Michael Parkinson on TV in 1981. 'The most awful thing was the marathon dancers. Pathetic. To pick up a first prize of $100 they'd dance for forty-eight hours, in each other's arms, one sleeping while the other kept moving, like zombies. It was absolutely awful, and the spectators were absolute vultures.' The Prohibition law had, however, recently been repealed after nearly fourteen dry years and David landed a job as a liquor salesman for 21 Brands, a wholesale company that was part of the 21 Club at 21 West 52nd Street where Charles Laughton, Mary Pickford, Robert Benchley, Dorothy Parker and Ernest Hemingway were regulars and where he had been a guest so often with Barbara Hutton and her rich friends a year earlier. The 21 was so exclusive that one of the regulars remarked 'the food's so good even the waiters eat it' and the novelist Damon Runyon reported that 'each guest had to present his bank book at the door to prove that he had a worthy balance' and 'the doorman looked him up in the social register before admitting him'.

David made his first sale for 21 Brands, a case of champagne, to Barbara Hutton's rich cousin Woolworth Donahue, but first the FBI took his fingerprints and a mugshot that showed him with a numbered card round his neck, like a criminal – a photograph that hung for many years afterwards in the 21 Club with the caption 'Our First and Worst Salesman'. They paid him $40 a week – about £8 then, or £280 a week today – but to justify that he needed to sell at least $400-worth of booze a week, and although he managed to keep the job for several months he hardly earned his keep, partly because he spent too much time hanging around the 21 Club itself or Rose's bar and restaurant down the road, with Barbara Hutton and her rich friends; partly because he could not bring himself to try to flog liquor to someone who had just bought him a drink or a meal. The area to which he was assigned, which included all the sleazy bars and dodgy restaurants to the west of Lexington between 42nd and 90th Streets, was already the rough territory of some frightening gangsters who made it plain that he was not welcome on their patch, and on one occasion he was the victim of a clever hijack: 'I took a telephone order from one of the lusher night spots in Manhattan for fifty cases of champagne,' he said. 'I pulled up in a truck outside the place and several white-coated characters appeared, unloaded the cases on the sidewalk, and handed me a cheque. I drove happily away. It wasn't until an hour later that I learned that no sooner had our truck moved off than another pulled up in the same spot, the cases were loaded aboard – and never seen again by my clients! And, of course, the cheque bounced.'

To improve his image he pretended that he was staying not at the crummy little Montclair Hotel but at the elegant Waldorf-Astoria nearby, which he would enter every morning through the back door and leave through the front door, nodding genially at the doorman, reversing the procedure each evening. As he strode confidently through the Waldorf in January 1934 he bumped into an old friend from England, Tommy Phipps, the brother of the twenty-three-year-old future actress and comedienne Joyce Grenfell, who invited him to spend the weekend at his mother's and stepfather's house in Connecticut. His stepfather was the champion American athlete and Hollywood actor 'Lefty' Flynn, who liked David immediately and introduced him to the New York hostess and social fixer Elsa Maxwell, who took an immediate shine to him as well and told him that he should do well in Hollywood as an actor 'because nobody out there knows how to speak English except Ronald Colman'.

She was short, ugly, fat and fifty, but she invited him to a party for the German film director Ernst Lubitsch in the hope that Lubitsch might sign him up for a film. Lubitsch ignored him. As his money ran out Niv left the hotel and rented a basement room on Second Avenue, but help seemed to be at hand when he met a fat little cowboy, Doug Hertz, in a bar on 58th Street in March and Hertz persuaded him to join him in setting up a venture to promote indoor novelty horse races during which the jockeys would have to ride several different ways in each race: in the saddle facing forward, then facing backwards, then side-saddle, then bareback, and then change to another horse without touching the ground. David thought it sounded great fun and maybe a money-spinner. He persuaded Lefty to join them, and Lefty and Elsa Maxwell canvassed friends to invest in the venture to buy ponies and hire a bunch of cowboys and Indians as jockeys. Damon Runyon bought $1000-worth of shares and they set up the American Pony Express Racing Association and launched their first novelty race night in May in front of 15,000 people in the municipal auditorium of Atlantic City, a raucous seaside pleasure resort a hundred miles south of New York. 'I recall with a guilty shudder,' said Niv later, 'that I led the grand march billed as Captain David Niven of the Royal North West Mounted Police.' The evening was a huge success – too much so for the local gangsters, who turned up the next day to demand a large share of the action, and when Hertz refused the mobsters put them out of business within a week. Once again David was broke but help suddenly arrived from a most unexpected quarter: Sir Thomas Comyn-Platt. In *The Moon's a Balloon* Niv claimed that he received a letter from Grizel with some excellent news: 'My mother, it appeared, had left everything to "Tommy" in trust for the four of us, but she had stipulated something very important. Max had once borrowed £300 from her to bail himself out of debt, so if either Joyce or Grizel or I were in desperate need, the small estate must try to provide the same amount for us. Within a week, I had collected my share. It came to a little over eight hundred dollars – I was rich.'

In fact Etta's will had said nothing of the kind and had stipulated that her children should inherit none of her money until Sir Thomas's death, so if he agreed to give David cash at all out of the trust it was only because very generously he thought that was fair. But Max had borrowed £3000 not £300, so was it in fact £3000 that Niv was sent – the equivalent of about £100,000 today? If so, it was a stupendous windfall for a young man of twenty-four, and even if it was only £300 that was still £10,000 in modern terms and an astonishingly kind gesture by the much maligned Sir Thomas. If he also agreed to give similar amounts to Joyce and Grizel, which it sounds as if he did, his legacy from Etta would have been seriously diminished.

With a very nice nest-egg in the bank, Niv skipped off to Bermuda to enjoy an idyllic holiday with Lefty and his wife, Norah, in a small rented cottage in Devonshire Bay. For several weeks he swam, cycled, sailed, explored the island and revelled in the magic of the beaches, tranquil sea and glorious flowers, and he had a fling with an eighteen-year-old girl from Virginia. Tommy Phipps joined them after a trip to Hollywood and raved about the place, Lefty agreed and reminisced about his own days there as an actor, and one of Niv's English friends, Dennis Smith-Bingham, wrote from Hollywood urging him to join him there and promising to find him somewhere to live.

'I clearly remember David suddenly grabbing my arm, swinging me around and me thinking I had never seen him so intense,' Phipps wrote for Peter Haining's book fifty years later.

> He glanced around to make sure he couldn't be overheard then he leaned forward. 'Look, chum,' he whispered, 'I've had an idea, but you must swear on your life to keep it between us, because if it doesn't work I'm going to look bloody ridiculous.' And then he said the words I've never forgotten: 'I'm going out to Hollywood to try and be an actor.' I clearly remember standing back and slowly looking him up

> and down. He was wearing bathing trunks; his enormous legs were bright red and beaten up from endless games of rugby and falling about on boats; his nose was peeling, he had a band-aid on his chin where he had cut himself shaving. And in that moment, in the boiling sun, what he had just suggested seemed just about the silliest idea I'd ever heard. 'You must be mad,' I said. 'Nutty as a fruit cake,' he said. And then his eyes crinkled up as they always did when he really laughed hard, and in that instant I suddenly felt sorry for him.

At the end of July Niv sailed aboard an old freighter to Cuba to catch the American liner *President Pierce* a week later as it steamed towards the Panama Canal, the Pacific Ocean and Los Angeles. Havana was a nervous, seedy city in pursuit of every kind of pleasure and perversion, and awash with booze, brothels, casinos, torture and murder, and seething with unrest following a coup the previous year against the brutal and corrupt President Gerardo Machado by the equally brutal and corrupt Colonel Fulgencio Batista, who was later to become President himself and not to be ousted by Fidel Castro for another twenty-five years. Niv loved the louche, twitchy atmosphere of Havana and drank every evening in Sloppy Joe's bar with a dangerous Irishman who tried to persuade him to join a group of mercenaries who were planning to foment a rebellion against the government. When Niv signed his first Hollywood contract the following year, Sam Goldwyn's publicity director livened up his fictional history by claiming that he had joined the rebels and was paid $400 a week to teach them how to use machine-guns, and the legend lived on for years, encouraged by Niv himself, who told the story again and again. But both his sons believed that it was untrue. 'It was just a PR stunt,' said David Jr; Jamie said, 'He never talked about Cuba to me' and Roddy Mann said, 'Of course not. He made it up.' What did perhaps happen in Cuba was that Niv was warned one night by a young man from the British embassy – our man in Havana – that the police were watching him and that he had better get out of town as soon as possible. After that he kept away from Sloppy Joe's and caught the *President Pierce* with relief two days later.

After sailing through the Panama Canal he was met when he arrived in Los Angeles by Dennis Smith-Bingham and Elizabeth Young, a sweet, beautiful twenty-four-year-old actress who had already appeared in more than fifty films under her screen name Sally Blane and whose mother had agreed to put Niv up in their pool house while he looked for somewhere to live. Reporters always met ocean-going liners in those days and as soon as they saw Sally with this unknown young Englishman they sniffed a story, and Niv was only too happy to oblige with another fib. Inspired by his pony-racing experiences in Atlantic City, he told them that he had come to California to buy more than a hundred polo ponies.

Many years later he was fantasising again when he told Lionel Crane of the *Sunday Pictorial* in 1957 that he had landed not in LA but in San Francisco, with just one suitcase, drunk and broke: 'I don't mean I was hard up, old boy. I mean broke, flat, stony. Not a bob. And I was wearing all I had – a dinner jacket.' He went on to claim that he had thumbed a ride south towards Los Angeles on a fruit lorry as far as Santa Barbara, had spotted the British cruiser HMS *Norfolk* in the bay, had gone on board to meet some old friends, been invited by them to a party, and got drunk again. He said he had woken at sea, spotted the replica of an old-time sailing ship, the *Bounty*, to starboard, had been swung across to it on a rope still wearing his dinner jacket, and had discovered on board Robert Montgomery and Clark Gable actually making the movie *Mutiny on the Bounty* – and that, he said, was how he finally arrived in LA. It was absolute tosh but it made a vivid yarn and added to the Niven legend. As for his claim that he arrived with just one suitcase, Sally Blane told Sheridan Morley that Niv had so much luggage that it filled their hallway: 'he seemed to have brought everything he ever owned over from England' and 'we figured it was going to be quite a long stay'.

David was mesmerised by his first balmy glimpse of California as Sally drove him from the harbour at San Pedro into Los Angeles and past the bungalows of Hollywood and the sumptuous film star mansions of Beverly Hills. In those days Hollywood was just a village, the actors had as yet no reason to hide themselves away behind high walls with security men and dogs, and in a grocery or drug store you might well find yourself standing next to Clark Gable or Joan Crawford. For David this was Paradise: the wonderful climate, the open skies, the outdoor life, the palm trees, swimming pools, sailing boats, nightspots, the famous faces, the chance of making a fortune, the girls all stunningly beautiful, even the waitresses and hairdressers, each dreaming of becoming a star too.

David moved in with Sally, her mother Gladys Belzer, and her three sisters in a house on Sunset Boulevard, and discovered that they were all just as sweet and gorgeous as she was. The youngest sister, Georgiana, was only ten, but the other two were also already successful actresses. The eldest, twenty-five-year-old Polly Ann Young, was the most gorgeous of them all, had appeared in more than a dozen movies and was to go on to make twenty more. But the most successful was Gretchen, who was already a famous star at twenty-one after making more than fifty movies under her screen name Loretta Young, and was to make nearly fifty more and to win the Best Actress Oscar in 1947 for her part in *The Farmer's Daughter*. Gretchen had been married at seventeen and divorced at eighteen, and David fell for her immediately. 'She was a big love of his,' I was told by his son Jamie, and although she was a devout Roman Catholic she was no prude when it came to having affairs. 'Every time she sins she builds a church,' quipped Marlene Dietrich. 'That's why there are so many Catholic churches in Hollywood.' But although Gretchen and David became lifelong friends and were to make several movies together, it seems that they were never lovers, certainly not at first. When they met she was deeply involved with Spencer Tracy and early the following year, while making *The Call of the Wild*, she had an affair with Clark Gable that resulted in an illegitimate daughter, Judy, who she pretended for many years was her adopted daughter.

Gretchen/Loretta was making a film at Twentieth Century Fox, *The White Parade*, and when Niv confessed that he wanted to become an actor too she smuggled him into the studio under a blanket on the floor of her car. He was enthralled by the fabulous sets, the vast sound stages, the crowds of actors in all kinds of costumes, the bustling atmosphere of make-believe. As he watched her being made up for her next scene his determination to become an actor was so reinforced that he went to try to register with the Central Casting Office, the employment agency that found film work for non-speaking extras but had a big sign that read: 'DON'T TRY TO BECOME AN ACTOR. FOR EVERY ONE WE EMPLOY WE TURN AWAY A THOUSAND.' He joined the queue but was turned away by a clerk when she discovered that he did not have a work permit.

Despite being completely unknown, Niv had such charm that soon he became close friends with several actors who were already stars. One was fifty-one-year-old Douglas Fairbanks Sr, with whom he had already played golf in England, the dashing athletic star of swashbuckling adventure films like *The Three Musketeers* and *The Private Life of Don Juan*, whose estranged wife Mary Pickford had decided that he was too much of a Don Juan himself and was about to divorce him. Like Niv, Fairbanks was an overgrown schoolboy who loved golf, tennis and practical jokes, and they hit it off right from the start. Another new chum was forty-three-year-old Ronald Colman, the charming, good-looking English actor with the trim moustache and beautiful voice who had a contract with Sam Goldwyn but was about to leave him to freelance after making more than forty films, among them *Bulldog Drummond*, *Raffles* and *The Man Who Broke the Bank at Monte Carlo*. Niv was often considered to be a younger version of Colman and his possible successor, and soon after they met playing tennis they became friends and regularly dined together even though Colman was renowned as a bit of a recluse after his divorce that year from Thelma Raye.

The closest of all Niv's new Hollywood friendships was with thirty-five-year-old Fred Astaire – the dancing star who had made only four films so far but was about to make one of his best, *Top Hat* – and his tiny lisping wife Phyllis, to whom he would stay happily married until her death twenty years later. Niv had met Astaire's sister Adèle in London and knocked on the Astaires' door after a game of tennis nearby. Phyllis opened the door, took one look at him, shut the door again hurriedly and cried out nervously to Fred in the backyard: 'There's a *dweadful* man at the fwont door without a shirt on who says he knows your sister.'

'When I came face-to-face with this individual,' Astaire wrote in his autobiography, 'I detected immediately a rather military-looking Britisher of unquestionably fascinating personality. We had a drink or two and heard all about his stint in the Cuban army since getting out of the Scots Guards, his racing mules in Florida and I don't know what all, and that he was thinking about going in the movies but so far he had had no chance to do anything but think about it. To us he certainly seemed to qualify with that personality. He had us in stitches the entire time . . . How glad we were that he stopped by that day. We gained one of the closest of lifetime friends.' Astaire became another surrogate older brother but even so, despite every effort, he failed to teach Niv how to dance well and gave up in despair.

Most important of all for Niv's career, he became friendly with the powerful thirty-five-year-old MGM producer Irving Thalberg, who had produced *Grand Hotel* and *The Barretts of Wimpole Street*. Thalberg and his thirty-two-year-old Canadian wife, the leading actress Norma Shearer – who had made sixty films and won an Oscar in 1930 for *The Divorcée* – became so fond of Niv that they gave him a breathtakingly generous Christmas present at the end of 1934: a brand new Studebaker car that embarrassed him deeply because his own present to them was six handkerchiefs embroidered with the letters I and N. Later he claimed that he was so hard up that he could not afford to buy even one gallon of petrol for the car and sold it 'to eat and pay the rent'.

David lived for six weeks rent-free with Mrs Belzer and her lovely daughters, and although they made him feel one of the family he realised that he was beginning to outstay his welcome and persuaded a young receptionist at the half-empty Roosevelt Hotel on Hollywood Boulevard, Alvin Weingand, to rent him a room for just $65 a month but not expect to be paid until he had got a job. Lonely for company, he telephoned a girl he had met in New York, Lydia Macy, and spent the weekend with her in Montecito, near Santa Barbara, and it was while he was there that he spotted HMS *Norfolk* in the bay, went on board for a party, drank too much and ended up in his crumpled dinner jacket on the *Bounty.* Thirty-year-old Robert Montgomery was on board, drove Niv back to Hollywood and the MGM studio, and introduced him to the stocky, forty-three-year-old London-born director Edmund Goulding, who had directed sixteen films, most notably *Grand Hotel*. He was to be so important for David's career that Niv was to say later, 'I owe more to him than to anyone else in the business.'

Goulding asked David to do a screen test for the part of a drunken, dissolute young man in his new film, and he felt so nervous and frozen with fear that when the test director, Harry Bouquet, asked him to tell a funny story on camera the only thing he could think of was a naughty limerick:

There once was an old man of Leeds
Who swallowed a packet of seeds.
Great tufts of grass
Shot out of his arse
And his cock was all covered in weeds.

Bouquet was appalled, but Goulding told David that the only decent part of the test had been the limerick because he had been so natural while he was telling it, and he recommended him to another director, Al Hall, who was looking for an Englishman to play the part of a young English aristocrat opposite the tiny, forty-one-year-old, platinum-blonde sexpot Mae West in her next film, *Goin' to Town*. She had become a huge star after making just five movies, notably *She Done Him Wrong* and *I'm No Angel*, and by the following year she was reckoned to be the highest-paid woman in America after earning an incredible $130,000 for *She Done Him Wrong*. She and Hall were impressed by Niv – especially when she asked him to remove his shirt and show his muscles – and many years later she said, 'Niven has charm where other men have only cologne.' But just as he stood on the brink of a breakthrough into the movies after only a few weeks in Hollywood an immigration official caught up with him, reminded him that he had arrived in Los Angeles with only a ten-day visitor's visa and was now an illegal immigrant, and ordered him to leave the country within twenty-four hours or be arrested. David caught a train 200 miles south to Mexico and checked into a flyblown hotel in a one-street border town called Mexicali while he applied to the local US consul for a resident alien visa so that he could work in Hollywood.

It took several weeks for David to get his birth certificate and a police report from England so that he could apply for the visa, and while he waited he earned a small wage working in a bar, washing up in the restaurant and cleaning the guns of American tourists who came to Mexicali on shooting holidays, though typically when he returned to Hollywood he told an English actor, Billy Milton, that he had been in Mexico teaching the local rebels how to use firearms. At last, early in January 1935, he returned to LA with the visa and a new determination to break into movies. He checked into his cheap room at the Roosevelt Hotel again and returned to the Central Casting Office, presented his visa and work permit, and was taken onto their books at last – to join thousands of other extras scrabbling for jobs – as 'Anglo-Saxon Type No. 2008'. As an Anglo-Saxon Type the first part he was offered was to play a swarthy Mexican in a Western movie.

That first job as a professional actor paid him $2.50 a day, for which he had to leave the hotel at 3 a.m., clock in miles away at Universal Studios by 5 a.m., dress in a baggy white suit, sombrero, sandals and a blanket, be sprayed a brown Mexican colour, stick on a false moustache, be driven by bus for an hour to the ranch where the film was being shot, take instructions as to what to do in the various crowd scenes, take a half-hour break at one o'clock for a meagre lunch, continue shooting until the early evening, return by bus to the studio, wash all the make-up off, collect his $2.50, scrounge a lift back to Hollywood with an extra who had a car, sit down to a cheap meal at 10 p.m. and crash into bed for no more than four hours before having to go through the whole routine again if he was lucky, though an extra often worked for no more than one day on any one film. And if shooting were cancelled because of rain the extras were paid nothing at all.

Niv reckoned later that he played in twenty-seven long forgotten Westerns as an extra, probably because he had learned at Sandhurst to ride a horse well, but it seems unlikely to have been so many because it was only six weeks later that he landed an exclusive contract with the Hollywood mogul Sam Goldwyn, who had been one of the founders of MGM but was now an independent producer. Niv also claimed that during those weeks he played a half-naked slave being whipped in the Cecil. B. DeMille epic *Cleopatra*, starring Claudette Colbert, but that too is unlikely because the film was made in 1934, before he had his visa and work permit. To supplement his meagre income during those six weeks he also worked once or twice a week as a deckhand on a charter fishing boat, the *König*, that was based in Balboa. It was a hard, dirty, dangerous, ten-hours-a-day job spearing, hauling, gutting and swabbing, but it paid $6 a day plus tips and one of his earliest clients was a huge star, Clark Gable, who was soon to become another friend.

The big break that led to Sam Goldwyn's and Niv's first Hollywood contract was preceded by a meeting with another Hollywood mogul, Darryl Zanuck, the boss of Twentieth Century-Fox, after Doug Fairbanks Sr introduced them at a Turkish steam bath and told Zanuck that David had played polo in Malta. Zanuck invited Niv to join him for a few chukkas that Sunday afternoon and David's account of that day is one of the funniest set pieces in *The Moon's a Balloon*, in which he described how he was made to ride a vicious white Arab stallion called St George that sank its teeth into Zanuck's buttocks, causing Niv to plant the end of his polo stick up Zanuck's pony's rectum. The story is wonderfully funny but identical to the one he was to tell in *Flight Deck* magazine in 1945, when he claimed that exactly the same thing had happened to him in Malta, where his bitten opponent had been an admiral. Even the horse had had the same name. So did it happen to Zanuck or the admiral? Did it happen at all? Or was it another of Niv's glorious fantasies?

It was Edmund Goulding who finally gave David's career the boost he needed. He suggested to Thalberg that he should give David a part in *Mutiny on the Bounty*, which was about to go into production, and a rumour spread that Thalberg was about to give David a long-term contract – a rumour that may well have been started by David himself. But Goulding had second thoughts and decided that Niv would be better off with Sam Goldwyn. He dug out David's only decent screen test, drove with it to Sam and Frances Goldwyn's house, and persuaded them that if David was good enough for Thalberg it would make sense for Goldwyn to beat him to it by signing him up first himself. It helped Niv's prospects hugely that British actors and accents had suddenly become fashionable in Hollywood movies, that Colman was about to leave Goldwyn's stable, and that David, with his little moustache and impeccable English accent, resembled Colman.

In his office on the Monday morning Goldwyn sent for Niv. 'He sat behind a huge desk in a tastefully furnished office,' he wrote in *The Moon's a Balloon*.

> He was almost entirely bald, very well dressed, with small intense eyes set in a brown face. He was about fifty and looked extremely fit. He spoke without smiling in a strangely high-pitched voice. 'I'm giving you a seven-year contract,' he said. 'I'll pay you very little, and I won't put you in a Goldwyn picture till you've learnt your job: now you have a base. Go out and tell the studios you're under contract to Goldwyn, do anything they offer you, get experience, work hard, and in a year or so, if you're any good – I'll give you a role.'

The contract allowed Goldwyn to cancel it whenever he liked, but David did not notice that and could not believe his luck. The meeting had lasted no more than a couple of minutes and now, dazed, he was giving his personal details to Goldwyn's head of publicity, Jock Lawrence, who decided that for PR purposes Niv had been born in Kirriemuir, his father had been a general, he had indeed been a lumberjack in Canada, and had actually led the rebels into battle in Cuba.

In *The Moon's a Balloon* Niv said that Goldwyn paid him at first $100 a week with twelve weeks unpaid lay-off every year, but the original contract, dated 25 February 1935, shows that he was actually paid $125 a week. In the second year, if Goldwyn kept him on, his salary would increase to $150 a week, in the third to $200, the fourth to $300, the fifth to $400, the sixth to $500, and the seventh to $600. Niv was overjoyed. A Hollywood contract just six weeks after getting a work permit! $125 a week! In modern terms that was the equivalent of £35,000 a year, and he was only just about to turn twenty-five. He went out and bought himself a lavish birthday present, a $500 car, and took Goulding for a celebratory lunch. But when he returned after lunch the head of Goldwyn's casting department, Bob McIntyre, suggested that he had better take the convertible back to the showroom because Goldwyn had just put him on immediate suspension for twelve weeks and he would not be starting work or earning his first $125 until 15 May. After less than a day as a Goldwyn employee he was already unemployed. It was a portent of things to come. Niv had just clamped his wrists into golden handcuffs.

Goldwyn was to become his third surrogate father and as soon as he signed the contract Niv wrote eagerly to J. F. Roxburgh, almost as though he needed his approval. 'I am an actor now, God rest my soul!' he wrote.

'And I find it much more fun, more interesting and definitely more lucrative than being a rather inefficient soldier.' But whereas Roxburgh had been cool, classy and cultured, and Alec Telfer-Smollett had been bluff, military and sporty – and both had been very English – Goldwyn was tempestuous and larger than life.

Now fifty-two, he had been born Schmuel Gelbfisz in the Jewish ghetto in Warsaw, the son of a poor second-hand furniture dealer. At twelve or thirteen he had run away from home, travelled to England and sailed to America. The US immigration official who let him in could not pronounce Schmuel Gelbfisz and told the boy that henceforth he would be known as Samuel Goldfish. He found a job as a glove cutter and became a successful glove salesman before moving to California to make movies in a rented barn in the middle of an orange grove in Hollywood with his vaudeville-producer brother-in-law Jesse Lasky and a Canadian actor, Cecil B. DeMille. Goldfish went on to form a film company with a New York theatrical producer, Edgar Selwyn, combining their names to call it the Goldwyn Picture Corporation, and he liked the name Goldwyn so much that he adopted it legally as his own. In 1925 GPC merged with the Metro and Louis B. Mayer studios to form Metro-Goldwyn-Mayer, MGM, but because Goldwyn was so headstrong, argumentative and bossy he was sacked, became an independent producer, founded Samuel Goldwyn Inc. and was soon the most successful independent producer in Hollywood. By the time that he signed Niv up in 1935 he had made nearly a hundred films in twenty-two years.

He was loud, aggressive, egotistical, stubborn, rude, ruthless and often impossible – a frenzied, dictatorial control freak who was always having rows and feuds, yelling at his cowed employees and pounding his desk, and was once described as 'the only man who can run amok sitting down'. He cheated outrageously at cards, backgammon, tennis, golf and croquet because he could not bear to lose, and Chico Marx once said of him, 'Sam is the only man in the world who can throw a 7 with one die.' Goldwyn even coached his son Sammy to upset the backgammon board 'accidentally' if he was losing. During one game between Goldwyn and Marx, Sammy knocked the board over three times. Marx took the boy out of the room, returned five minutes later, and the game proceeded without interruption.

'How did you do it?' asked Goldwyn, impressed.

'I taught him to masturbate,' said Marx.

During outdoor parties at Goldwyn's beautiful home in Laurel Way up in the hills he had been known to stalk back into the house after a row with one of his guests, locking them all out in the garden and insisting that his butler should bring all the drinks inside too. But he could be dignified and considerate, and was highly admired and respected for his film-making genius, even by his nervous staff. He was at heart a kind man, usually a perfect and generous host who was always dressed immaculately, adored his wife Frances, and was described by Niv in his book about Hollywood, *Bring on the Empty Horses*, as 'like crème brûlée – rock hard on the outside and surprisingly soft underneath'. As Alva Johnston wrote in 1937 in a boldly independent book about him, *The Great Goldwyn*, describing his sudden switches of mood: 'A split second separates Ivan the Terrible from Mr Pickwick.'

Above all, Goldwyn was obsessed by movies, utterly devoted to making quality films, and renowned for his dedication and his magical 'Goldwyn Touch', which ensured that every film he made was in the best of taste and made to the highest standards so that he could be proud of them. He would pay a fortune to acquire the movie rights in the right book and to hire the best writers and directors, and he would throw a fortune away to reshoot a film that was not turning out the way he wanted. The previous year he had been so unhappy with the first version of his film *Nana* that he scrapped it and started all over again, losing $411,000.

Goldwyn was so engrossed in every tiny detail of film-making that he talked to himself, failed to listen to others and could be very forgetful. 'He once forgot his birthday,' Niv told Michael Parkinson in 1981, 'but when he got home his wife Frances met him at the door, told him it was his birthday, blindfolded him, led him into the dining room and left him there while she went to speak to the cook in the kitchen. While he was in the dining room he was full of wind, let it go, and took his coat off and flapped it about. Frances came back, took off his blindfold, and thirty-two people were sitting down for dinner!'

Goldwyn also had trouble remembering people's names and kept calling his unfortunate European PR man, Euan Lloyd, 'Urine Lloyd'. Because he was so powerful and overbearing people took their revenge by joking about him, particularly about his colourful use of the English language. When he resigned from one organisation he told them: 'Gentlemen, include me out.' He once reacted to a proposal by replying, 'In two words: im-possible.' His Goldwynisms became legendary: 'a verbal contract isn't worth the paper it's written on'; 'anyone who goes to a psychiatrist should have his head examined'; 'what we need now is some new, fresh clichés'; 'we've all passed a lot of water since those days'; 'these directors are always biting the hand that lays the golden egg'; 'you're always taking the bull between the teeth'. When one of Goldwyn's directors said that a script was too caustic he replied, 'To hell with the cost. If it's a good picture, we'll make it.' And Edward G. Robinson swore that when he asked Goldwyn if he should accept the part of Shylock in *The Merchant of Venice* Goldwyn exploded: 'Screw 'em! Tell 'em you'll only play the Merchant!'

This was the man who was to become Niv's Svengali and his third and final father figure. He came to love him and then to rebel like a sulky son. As he wrote of Goldwyn in *Bring on the Empty Horses*, 'for half a century he towered like a Colossus above his contemporaries,' but Ronald Colman, who had just left Goldwyn, was horrified to hear that he had hired David. 'He's the best producer by far,' said Colman, 'but watch it, he can be a real bastard!' By joining Goldwyn David had found not only another father figure but also a family to replace those of Stowe, Sandhurst and the army that had kept him protected for the last ten years. 'Hollywood was a kind of giant public school,' said Tom Hutchinson. 'It had a hierarchy and a class structure with its own headmasters, matrons, head boys, monitors and bullies.'

Niv moved out of the Roosevelt Hotel and into a cheap, one-room apartment above a brothel in North Vista Street, and because it was now common knowledge that Goldwyn had signed him up he was welcomed everywhere. He joined the Hollywood Cricket Club, which played every Sunday, and was introduced to its English stalwarts, among them the actors C. Aubrey Smith, Cedric Hardwicke and Nigel Bruce, who played Dr Watson in *Sherlock Holmes* and became a particularly close chum along with his wife Bunnie. Niv met Charlie Chaplin, Basil Rathbone, Cary Grant, Henry Fonda, Boris Karloff and Jimmy Stewart. He played golf with Jean Harlow and William Powell, and joined the West Side Tennis Club because the girls there were much prettier than those at the Beverly Hills Club. In the evenings he would go with Loretta Young, Sally Blane and other girls to nightspots and celebrity haunts such as the Clover Club, with its glass dance floor and orchestra, and the King's Club, the Cocoanut Grove, the Russian Eagle and the Vendôme, and he cut a swathe through the gorgeous starlets and wannabes who twinkled in every corner of LA, Hollywood and Beverly Hills. 'He had an enormous number of relationships,' his son Jamie told me, 'but he never really talked about them because he was so incredibly discreet about his life.'

Many years later Niv's publisher, Jamie Hamilton, wrote in a memo to his editors that it was 'common knowledge that he had practically every star in Hollywood', and Roddy Mann told me: 'He had scores of girlfriends in the Thirties. He was notorious as a swordsman. To be Niven in this town then was extraordinary. Here was this charming, attractive, witty guy who didn't take anything seriously. He used to say that when he started here in Hollywood it was gentlemen trying to be actors, and then it became actors trying to be gentlemen – and now it's neither trying to be both!' He was himself the perfect gentleman and did not tattle about his girlfriends afterwards, though it is said that when Claudette Colbert asked him at a party who was the best lover he had ever had he replied 'your black maid'.

Some of his girlfriends, on the other hand, were quite happy to talk about him, like the blonde, sexy, very young actress Evelyn Keyes, who was to play Scarlett O'Hara's younger sister Suellen in 1939 in *Gone With the Wind*, to marry four times and to become Mike Todd's mistress. She lived with Niv for a while in the late 1930s, even though she was still a teenager, and told Morley that Niv had 'a marvellous sense of humour' and was 'a delightful storyteller, delicious as French pastry, single then and ripe for plucking'. An added bonus for the girls, the British actor Patrick Macnee said, was that 'the width of his member was something to behold. And it's the width that matters, you know.' Macnee once spotted the naked Niven organ when they were filming together, and 'on a very mild, dear, fragrantly light-hearted man a penis of that immensity absolutely staggers you', said Macnee.

'How immense was it?' I asked.

'Well, three times as big as mine.'

'I've never seen yours,' I said. 'Was it also very long?'

'Not very. But that's not important. It's the *width* that matters.'

'So not very long.'

'No.'

'How long?'

Macnee hesitated. 'About a foot?' he said.

Niv's first really serious love affair, with the gorgeous twenty-four-year-old actress Merle Oberon, began in 1935 and was to last for more than a year. Her real name was Estelle Merle O'Brien Thompson, and although she combined her two middle names to inspire her stage name, her family and friends called her Queenie or 'Obie'. What was not known then or for many years afterwards, and had to be kept strictly secret in the racial climate of the 1930s and 1940s, was that she was of mixed race. Her father was English, her mother Indian, and she had been born in Bombay and raised in comparative poverty in India. Her skin was light enough to pass as white, she spoke English beautifully with an upper-class accent, and she looked almost Chinese rather than Indian, but the fact that she was a half-caste would have destroyed her career and position as one of the queens of Hollywood had it been known, so she pretended even to her closest friends that she had been born in Tasmania the daughter of an Australian army officer, and that her dark-skinned little fifty-three-year-old Indian mother in London, Charlotte Thompson, was in fact her maid.

After Queenie had left India for England in 1928, at the age of seventeen, she had worked as a hostess in a London nightclub; had had affairs with the debonair young black West Indian pianist and singer Leslie Hutchinson, who performed as 'Hutch' in fashionable nightclubs in Paris and London, and with the American movie mogul Joe Schenck, the president of United Artists; and had been given small film parts by the Hungarian producer Sándor Kellner, who now lived in England, called himself Alexander Korda and was soon to become a naturalised British subject. By 1935 she had made seventeen movies and her mark playing Anne Boleyn opposite Charles Laughton in *The Private Life of Henry VIII*, the dancer Antonita with Douglas Fairbanks Sr in *The Private Life of Don Juan* and Lady Marguerite Blakeney opposite Leslie Howard in *The Scarlet Pimpernel*, after which Goldwyn had bought a share of her contract from Korda and she had left her embarrassing mother hidden in an hotel in London and had come to Hollywood to star appropriately in *The Dark Angel*, for which she was to be nominated for the Best Actress Oscar. So when she and David became lovers she was already a big star earning thousands of dollars a week, whereas he had yet to make his first film as anything other than a humble extra.

This did not bother Merle at all. She had just emerged from a stressful affair with her sensitive, complicated, intellectual co-star Leslie Howard, and now she basked in the warmth of David's charm and amusing anecdotes, his simple love of life and uncomplicated manly sense of fun, and his pleasure in parties and dinners as well as the outdoors and sport. He had matured hugely since she had first known him briefly in London a couple of years earlier, when Laurence Olivier remembered seeing them together. 'She had this young man with her,' Olivier told Morley, 'who kept putting on silly voices and seemed terribly ill at ease with people who were already making their names as actors, but she was very sweet with him.' He was certainly completely at ease with actors now and smitten by Merle's unusual beauty – her immaculate figure, golden skin, greeny-brown almond-shaped eyes, high forehead, smouldering smile and glorious laughter – and he revelled in her apparently aristocratic elegance, free spirit, and empathy with everything natural, romantic and mystical. Best of all, they both adored sex, especially with each other, and Merle very soon wanted to marry him.

There were those who sneered that Niv was using her because she was a star who could persuade directors to give him parts in movies. Some people called him 'Mr Oberon', Olivier said he was 'Merle's gigolo' and she certainly helped him with his acting, but equally David introduced her to his powerful and amusing contacts in Hollywood, and she soon became Norma Shearer's best friend because of him. Niv and Merle ignored the snide remarks, she bought a house on the beach at Malibu, and they walked the sands together and went swimming, sailing, fishing and riding. They played golf and tennis at the Riviera Country Club. They went dancing at the Trocadero and made the most of the sizzling nightlife of Hollywood. They joined weekday dinner parties, weekend house parties and, as he said in *Bring on the Empty Horses*, Hollywood 'was hardly a nursery for intellectuals, it was a hot-bed of false values, it harboured an unattractive percentage of small-time crooks and con artists and the chances of being successful there were minimal but it was fascinating and IF YOU WERE LUCKY – it was fun: and anyway – it was better than working'. Now and then they would spend several days together at the San Ysidro ranch near Santa Barbara that Ronald Colman and Al Weingand had turned into a discreet hotel resort for illicit lovers. 'I thought that would end up in a marriage,' said Weingand. 'It was a serious affair, not just a shack-up deal – and we hotel men get to know the difference.' And Weingand told Morley: 'It was a very outdoor life and I think David made Merle very happy, taught her not to take anything too seriously.' They became one of Hollywood's golden young couples and were welcome at any party or aboard any yacht, and the affair was so hot that it was soon strongly rumoured that they were engaged.

In the meantime Niv began to appear in movies at last, five in that maiden year of his career. In the first, a murder story entitled *Without Regret*, Goldwyn lent him out to Paramount and he spoke his first line on screen: 'Goodbye, my dear,' he said, and that was all. In the second, *Barbary Coast*, the story of a prostitute during the San Francisco gold rush of 1850, he had just one line again, as a cockney sailor who says during a noisy riot 'orl rite, I'll go', but is thrown out of a brothel window into the mud. In his third, *A Feather in Her Hat*, he was farmed out to Columbia and although it was a very small part he had one scene which focused entirely on him as a young life-and-soul-of-the-party poet. He was so nervous that the director, Alfred Santell, quietly asked the rest of the cast and crew to encourage him by breaking into applause after his first take, no matter how bad he was. They did and he glowed with new self-confidence, but he was terrified again when he made his fourth film, *Splendor*. 'He was terribly nervous and kept coming over to me and reading out his lines and saying, "Do you think that's all right, old boy?" ' Morley was told by the film's male lead, Joel McCrea, who was then thirty, just four years older than Niv, though he had already made more than thirty movies, 'He kept repeating his most difficult line, which was . . . "I'd marry her twenty millions if she had two heads and a club foot." But by the time we got around to shooting that scene, he'd say it so often and was so nervous of the camera that it came out, "I'd marry her club foot." [*He had*] absolutely no confidence in himself as an actor at all.' Even so, his performance earned him his first review in a major newspaper, the *New York Times*, which reported that he had acted 'with poisonous effectiveness'. Finally that year he had a tiny part in MGM's Jeanette MacDonald/Nelson Eddy musical *Rose Marie*, in which he had a whole scene with Jeanette MacDonald as a rich, drunken playboy in vain pursuit of the heroine, and although he was extremely nervous again and completely overshadowed by another newcomer, James Stewart, he had made a start.

To give him some stage experience Goldwyn found a small part for him in a play at the nearby Pasadena Playhouse, *Wedding*, in which he appeared briefly in only three scenes and spoke just two lines in the third, but unfortunately he started boasting about the part and hinting that he had a starring role, and on the opening night he came on stage to a roar of applause and was appalled to see in the front few rows Goldwyn and a horde of his friends, including Gloria Swanson and Charles Laughton. Nervous and terrified, he scuttled back to his dressing room before his next scene, gulped a couple of slugs of whisky, made a mess of his only two lines, was sacked after just one night, and vowed never to appear on the stage again. Goldwyn gave him a rocket and laid him off for his second spell of six unpaid weeks on 22 October – a stern punishment with Christmas just around the corner, though Merle was earning quite enough for the two of them and in due course they celebrated the festive season in style.

At the end of October she had returned from London to New York after two months away from Hollywood during which she had been mobbed by fans at the New York première of *The Dark Angel* and had sailed to England to make two films for Korda that came to nothing. David used his suspension to meet her in New York, where she suggested that instead of taking the train to Los Angeles they should buy a car and drive all the way, 3000 miles. She was by now so famous that when they stopped for the night at an hotel in Chicago she wore dark glasses and a black wig and they called themselves Mr and Mrs Thompson – strangely using her real surname, not his, maybe because she was paying the bill. She had, however, promised to let Goldwyn's office know where she was each evening in case she were needed urgently, and the desk clerk handed Niv the first of a series of telegrams ordering him to call Los Angeles, but he was having far too much fun and in any case wasn't he meant to be suspended? He ignored it. More cables arrived, increasingly urgent and angry, as they crossed the continent, but Niv did not call until they reached California after driving for ten days.

Goldwyn was incandescent. Niv had risked a huge scandal by flaunting his affair with one of Goldwyn's major stars, a woman whose virginal image Goldwyn had spent a fortune trying to promote. He had broken the usual Hollywood morals clause in his contract which specified that he should do nothing to bring himself, Goldwyn or the studio into disrepute. He had risked jail under the law that made it an imprisonable offence to take a woman from one state to another 'for immoral purposes'. What if one of Hollywood's two most famous gossip columnists, Hedda Hopper or Louella Parsons, had picked up the story? In a fury Goldwyn fired him but when he calmed down Merle persuaded him to change his mind.

Despite his passion for her, Niv was never the faithful type and while she had been away he had had a couple of flings with other women. He had even had Marlene Dietrich – 'the most feminine creature I ever knew' – more than once in his bedroom above the brothel, but only because he was ill and she brought him medicine, cooked his dinner, cleaned his room and changed his bedclothes.

Towards the end of 1935 he was having dinner at the Cocoanut Grove with Loretta Young and Sally Blane when an old sailing friend from Bembridge, Anthony Jenkinson, by now Sir Anthony, came in. 'He told me, with justifiable pride, that he had acquired a house in Hollywood,' wrote Jenkinson the following year in his book *America Came My Way*. 'He had been struggling hard to live down the reputation given it by its last inhabitant, a discharged Russian General, who had apparently caused no little comment by maintaining a harem of Oriental proportions.' On the next day Jenkinson went to the house – 'built on a precipitous crag in the heart of the Hollywood hills' – and found its living room decorated with a photograph of the Stowe 1st XI, a Bembridge Sailing Club burgee, an old copy of *The Tatler* and a squash racquet. Niv repeated his false biographical details as though they were true: that he had worked in a Canadian lumber camp and had been a captain in the Cuban Rebel Light Infantry, 'but when hostilities commenced David found, to his chagrin, that his soldiery deserted him on the field of battle, leaving him to face the enemy alone. This he thought it scarcely worth while to do, and accordingly made a hurried departure into the mountains.' Niv even told Jenkinson that he had met Goldwyn in New York, Goldwyn had urged him to go to Hollywood for a screen test and had given him a part in a film opposite 'a famous leading lady'. It was all quite untrue.

Merle and Niv spent Christmas Day at a party at Clifton Webb's house, where Cole Porter played the piano and sang, and New Year's Eve at the Goldwyns', and three weeks later they were sparkling again at Carole Lombard's star-spangled White Mayfair Ball in Beverly Hills. Then it was back to work and he made two quick films: another romantic musical, *Palm Springs Affair*, in which he played a debonair millionaire; and then came his first starring role, albeit in a B-movie to be shown before the main feature, as P. G. Wodehouse's brainless upper-class English prat Bertie Wooster, in the comedy *Thank You, Jeeves*, which gave him his first real chance to show that he could handle a major part and how good he could be at light comedy. He was ideal for the part and his performance was highly praised by the *New York Times*. Goldwyn then sent him off to Warner Brothers to work with another comparative newcomer, the twenty-six-year-old Australian Errol Flynn, who had become a swash-buckling star the previous year with his seventh film, *Captain Blood*.

The new film was *The Charge of the Light Brigade*, another derring-do adventure story that was very loosely based on the suicidal charge 'into the valley of death' by 600 British cavalrymen against the Russian guns at Balaclava in 1854 during the Crimean War. Its director was the aggressive, tyrannical Hungarian Manó Kertész Kaminer, who had angli-cised his name as Michael Curtiz and liked to appear on set wearing riding breeches, boots and carrying a fly whisk. Curtiz, who was forty-nine, was later to direct and win an Oscar for *Casablanca*, but he was deeply disliked by his actors and crews, and renowned for his belligerence as well as his difficulties with the English language. On one occasion he yelled at an assistant, 'The next time I want an idiot to do this I'll do it myself!' But he was impressed when he discovered that Niv had been at Sandhurst and they got on surprisingly well. Best of all, he was to give David the title for his third book nearly forty years later. *The Charge of the Light Brigade* script called for a stampede of riderless horses and when

Curtiz yelled 'Okay! Bring on the empty horses!' that was it: *Bring on the Empty Horses*.

Niv had met the tall, good-looking, rebellious and randy Errol Flynn briefly at a couple of parties and had disliked him for his aggression and arrogance, but they soon discovered that they shared a delight in booze, women and mischief, and became good friends. They delighted especially in taunting Curtiz, particularly when he mangled the English language, until eventually he bellowed at them, 'You lousy bums! You think I know fuck nothing! Well, let me tell you: I know fuck *all*!'

They made *The Charge of the Light Brigade* over eleven weeks in the Californian desert and Sierra Nevada mountains around the town of Bishop, 200 miles north of Los Angeles, and years later Flynn told Niv that physically it was the toughest film he had ever made. A week after shooting started the only hotel in town burned down and they spent the rest of the time on location trying to sleep, freezing, in tents. One scene showed a tiger hunt, for which Flynn and Niven had to sit in a basket on top of an elephant, which suddenly ran amok and rushed around trying to dislodge the basket and them by scraping it against trees and walls.

For some odd reason most of the film depicted military life on the North West Frontier of India rather than in the Crimea. Opening with a wet love story and prissy, affected characters, it struggled on through a barrage of cannon fire and raucous music that doubtless sounded perfect to the wild Hungarian ear. Niv was charming as Captain James Randall and *Variety* said his performance was 'distinguished' but it was a small part and ended halfway through the film when Randall is shot and dies before the cavalry even reaches the Crimea. Even so, for all its stilted hokum, the movie was hailed as a major epic, attracted a huge amount of publicity and gave David his first hint of fame. Before *The Charge of the Light Brigade*, despite *Thank You, Jeeves*, he had been just a bit-part player – 'we were all whores, really,' he told Michael Parkinson on television in 1975 – but after it he began to look like a possible star.

By now Merle Oberon was so keen to marry him that in May newspapers reported they were engaged, but Niv was reluctant to tie himself down to one woman and both issued statements denying the rumour. Thirty years later Merle still regretted that they never married. Niv's son Jamie was to meet her in the 1960s and he told me: 'Every time I ran into her she'd always say "you are the son I should have had". She was a very nice woman.'

She and Niv were still, however, very much an item, and a week later they threw a lavish party for Doug Fairbanks Sr and his new bride, Lady Sylvia Ashley, to which they invited a crowd of stars and Marion Davies, who was herself renowned for throwing the most sumptuous parties of all. She was a beautiful, thirty-nine-year-old comic actress, blue-eyed and blonde, who was about to retire after making fifty films, but more important, she was the beloved mistress of the seventy-three-year-old billionaire media tycoon William Randolph Hearst, whose awesomely wealthy, powerful life was to inspire the 1941 Orson Welles film *Citizen Kane*. David had become friendly with Hearst's four sons, and Marion often invited him and Merle to her fabulously luxurious weekend house parties at Hearst's fairy-tale castle, San Simeon, nearly 300 miles north of Los Angeles, overlooking the Pacific. San Simeon was a palace that had cost him millions of dollars to build, with 165 rooms, including forty-two bedrooms, nineteen sitting rooms, sixty-one bathrooms, a dining hall like a cathedral, two ornate libraries with 5000 books, a billiard room, a cinema, huge indoor and outdoor swimming pools, towers, marble colonnades, cloisters, esplanades and rooms stuffed with antiques and priceless works of art, sixteenth-century Flemish tapestries, antique silver, statues and marble sculptures. There were 127 acres of gardens, terraces, pools and walkways, fifty miles of private beach, a zoo with even lions and elephants, a game reserve sheltering camels, giraffe and kangaroo. There were dairy and poultry farms and a private airfield, all protected by 275,000 acres of surrounding land. Today the house seems hideously garish, vulgar wealth run riot, but the sheer scale and magnitude of the place are breathtaking, and when George Bernard Shaw visited San Simeon in the 1930s he remarked, 'This is probably the way God would have done it if He had had the money.'

Hearst's guests included presidents, politicians, Hollywood moguls and stars, celebrity sportsmen and foreign dignitaries. Some would be flown up to San Simeon on his private plane but most would travel from Los Angeles on the Friday night on Hearst's private train, be dined and wined sumptuously on board and entertained by musicians, and would arrive at San Luis Obispo at midnight and be whisked by limousine up the five-mile drive to the oasis blaze of lights that was San Simeon at night. The weekends were always devotedly casual but with plenty to do: swimming parties, elaborate picnics or barbecues out in the countryside, hiking and horse-riding expeditions, tennis and croquet tournaments. Vintage wines would be served with fabulous dinners and afterwards the guests would watch the latest pre-release film in the private fifty-seat cinema.

Because San Simeon was so far from Hollywood, Hearst built another palace much nearer, on the beach at Santa Monica. He called it 'the beach house' but it was nearly as palatial as San Simeon with more than a hundred rooms, fifty-five bathrooms, an oak-panelled library and thirty-two servants. The thirty-seven fireplace mantelpieces were shipped in from England, the walls were hung with paintings by Hals, Rembrandt, Reynolds and Rubens, and the hundred-foot swimming pool was crossed by a Venetian marble bridge. Almost every weekend Hearst threw parties for fifty or sixty people at the beach house, where his guests would join in the numerous fancy dress parties that Marion loved to organise, and always the guest list included the richest and most famous people in America. Niv, whose charm and popularity made him a regular guest throughout the late 1930s, said later that he spent some of the happiest times of his life at San Simeon and the beach house.

In May 1936 he played a smooth young English seducer in *Dodsworth*, which was directed by the brilliant but infuriating William Wyler. Niv had worked very briefly with Wyler on *Barbary Coast* but Merle warned him that although Wyler was only thirty-four he was a nightmare director, and so it proved. 'I became a gibbering wreck,' he said later. One of Wyler's favourite ploys was to destroy an actor's self-confidence, and he made Niv go through the same scene over and over again while he sat ignoring the performance and reading the *Hollywood Reporter*. 'What do you want me to do?' Niv asked in despair.

'Just do it again,' Wyler would reply, turning the page.

Niv was 'a nice young Englishman who seemed to be in an agony of nerves,' wrote Mary Astor, who was also in the film, in her autobiography.

> He kept a silly smile fastened to his face and constantly patted his pockets, searching for cigarettes, lighter. Lighting up with shaking hands he'd toss the cigarette away, and pat pockets for a handkerchief with which to wipe sweaty palms, all the time keeping up a running, nervous, disjointed conversation. He said his name was David Niven, and he'd never made a movie before. The rest seemed preposterous, and I'm sure he was inventing. It went like this:
>
> 'Bloody hot, isn't it? I *beg* your pardon! . . . I never wanted to be in this silly business . . . wasn't my idea at all . . . they picked me up off a ship.'
>
> 'What do you mean, a ship?'
>
> 'That's right, a ship, a *ship*. It's down in San Pedro Harbour this moment. . . . Whew! Bloody hot . . . I say, what are we supposed to

do? . . . Who's the director? . . . that bloke over there? I jumped ship you know, and look where it got me. 'Twasn't *my* idea.'

'I never did get it sorted out,' she said. 'It sounded as though he'd been kidnapped and brought directly to the studio!'

Despite Niv's nerves, the *New York Times* said that he was excellent in the film, but he was savaged by the reviewer for the *Detroit Free Press* who sneered: 'In this picture we were privileged to see the great Samuel Goldwyn's latest discovery – all we can say about this actor (?) is that he is tall, dark and not the slightest bit handsome.' David framed the review and hung it on his lavatory wall.

His performance was good enough for Merle to persuade Goldwyn to cast him with her and Brian Aherne in her next film, *Beloved Enemy*, a story about an unlikely romance between an upper-class English girl and an Irish rebel leader in Dublin during the anti-British revolt of 1921 that was obviously loosely based on the life and death of the IRA leader Michael Collins. By now Merle was thoroughly fed up with David's philandering and she had a tit-for-tat fling with Aherne during filming.

Niv was gawky and wooden in his role as an English civil servant but he had plenty of lines and won good reviews from *The Times*, the *New York Times* and *Variety*, and Goldwyn was so impressed by his progress that he increased his salary from $150 a week to $250 and rewrote his contract so that during the next five years he would be paid much more each year, until by 1941 he would be on $1000 a week instead of the $600 stipulated in his current contract. Niv wrote him a delighted letter of thanks for the money and encouragement and said in it, 'I hope I may be associated with you for many years and that soon you will be really proud of me.'

While filming *Beloved Enemy* David and Merle were shocked by the sudden death of Irving Thalberg, who caught a chill, developed pneumonia, and died on 14 September 1936 aged only thirty-seven. His widow, Norma Shearer, asked Niv to be an usher at the funeral and was so devastated by his death that she became a recluse for several months.

David made one more film in 1936, *We Have Our Moments*, an undistinguished little movie in which he played a smooth English conman. As a lover, however, he seemed to be as distinguished as ever and Merle told a news agency in October that they were definitely going to get married. He flew to New York to see her off when she sailed for England to spend six months making her next film, *I, Claudius*, for Alexander Korda, and she was so desperate to spend more time with him that she postponed her passage for a week so that they could go to Philadelphia to see Leslie Howard on stage in *Hamlet* and then to Boston to see her old friend Noël Coward, who would soon become a friend of Niv's too.

With Merle away for six months, Niv decided to share a house with Errol Flynn, who had recently separated from his wife, and they rented 601 North Linden Drive, just off Sunset Boulevard, on the edge of Beverly Hills. Today the house, with a black-and-white mock-Tudor first floor, stands in a wide, tree-lined boulevard in a quiet, manicured suburb, but with Flynn and Niven there in 1936 it was the rowdiest place in town and rampant with randy young bachelors, pretty girls, booze, marijuana, mischief and bad behaviour. In later years David admitted that Flynn was mean with money and unkind to his friends, both men and women, but he was fun to be with in those carefree days of their youth. 'You always knew where you stood with him,' Niv told the *Sunday Mirror* in 1973. 'He would always let you down. He really was a shit. It didn't matter at all, once you knew that. You must love people with their faults.' He was less forgiving three years later when he told Clive Hirschhorn of the *Sunday Express*: 'One of the most important things I learned in Hollywood all those years ago, was that only the second-raters allowed success to go to their heads. The giants of the industry – men like Gable and Jimmy Stewart, Bogart, the incomparable Fred Astaire, Ronnie Colman and Spencer Tracy – all remained level-headed about their careers. Only Errol Flynn . . . allowed his fame to go to his head with the result that he became thoroughly disliked in the business.' Five years later Niv was understanding again: 'I really regret saying that Errol always let you down,' he told Michael Parkinson in 1981. 'What I meant was that he'd always discomfort you: if you asked him not to tell someone something he'd tell them as soon as he saw them.'

At the time, though, they had great fun. Flynn bought a 65ft ketch called the *Sirocco* and was later to buy another boat, the *Zaca*, that had a prow proudly decorated with a rampant flying penis. They went sailing every weekend with a crew of floozies and Niv claimed that they introduced water-skiing to California. One water-skiing afternoon, he said, nearly ended in disaster when Flynn mischievously untied the tow rope and abandoned him miles from land while he sailed away to pleasure his latest doxy below deck. As David swam for the distant shore, he said, a big shark appeared beside him and followed him until he reached Ronald Colman's yacht and Colman and one of his crew drove the beast away. When Flynn heard the story he hooted with laughter and bellowed, 'Jesus! I wish I'd seen *that*!'

Sex was a constant pursuit and number 601 echoed with girlish shrieks and giggles, and to add a kick to the proceedings Flynn would sometimes dab some cocaine on the end of his penis as an aphrodisiac. The actor Mickey Rooney recalled in his memoirs one Flynn dinner party that he attended with Clark Gable, Spencer Tracy, Robert Taylor and Wallace Beery: 'When we knocked on the door it was opened by a pair of exquisitely beautiful twins, and they were absolutely nude!' Penises were a constant Flynn/Niven preoccupation, and Joan Collins reported in her autobiography that one wizened little extra, 'OK Freddie', was blessed with such an enormous cock that they often urged him to show it to newcomers, upon which he would grin 'OK' and unveil his massive organ. On one occasion, said Miss Collins, Flynn and Niv persuaded Freddie to dress as a waiter at an elegant garden party and to serve, held low, a silver tray of snacks piled with smoked salmon, quails' eggs, caviar on biscuits, and in the middle a large sausage decorated with thin slices of raw beef and tiny prawns, which turned out – when one of the lady guests stabbed it with a fork – to be Freddie's penis. Freddie howled with pain, dropped the tray and fled, and Flynn and Niv could barely stand up with hysterical laughter.

Flynn's third-favourite hobby, after sex and drinking, was fighting and he kept himself in trim by having regular punch-ups with professional boxers in the garden of number 601. Niv preferred to keep his good looks and fists to himself. He mentioned none of this unseemly behaviour, of course, when he wrote in November an affectionate eight-page letter to J. F. Roxburgh that is so revealing that some of it deserves to be quoted at length:

> I suppose it is pretty poor form if an old boy congratulates a Headmaster. But if you'll not take offence, I would like to do that very thing, from the bottom of my heart.
>
> It was not till many years after leaving Stowe that I realized what a stupendous task you had tackled and what a grand triumph you have had. You have always been so human and you wouldn't be human now if you didn't pause occasionally to pat yourself on the back.
>
> I am still an actor which probably makes you wince. I am being paid very satisfactory sums every Wednesday and hope I am picking up enough experience really to get ahead in the next year or so.
>
> I have no intention of ending my days as a tumbledown actor, so am saving more than half my salary and when I have enough to be independent I shall have a smack at politics.

> The further one gets away from England the more one realizes that it is up to the young men of my vintage to get together and do something for the Empire.
>
> This letter has probably seemed rather pompous, but what I have said is really meant.
>
> I have had my last twinge of remorse at leaving the Army. The Regimental Magazine arrived last week and I noticed that if I had continued in the service, I should now be number twenty-two on the list of subalterns instead of number twenty-five!
>
> I hope to be home for a few weeks in the late spring or early summer and hope so much to see you again.
>
> In spite of what the yellow press says on occasions, as far as I can remember, I am not yet married or engaged.

David's problems with the 'yellow press' were often his own fault because he was not always as discreet about his love life as he should have been. Max sent him a novel Christmas present that year, a letter telling him that he was giving him his body back after redeeming it from the hospital to which David had sold it for £6 10s 0d in 1933, and now that Niv owned his body again he decided to share it as often as possible with a lovely twenty-six-year-old blonde American actress, Helen Briggs, whose screen name was Virginia Bruce. They began an affair in January, the newspapers were quick to report that they were engaged and he admitted that he was 'no longer engaged' to Merle – so they *had* been engaged – and did not deny that he might now be engaged to Virginia. 'I don't know what to say,' he blustered.

But Virginia was just one of many girlfriends in 1937. 'There were a lot of women whom he nearly married in the 1930s,' Jack Hawkins's widow Doreen told me. 'They were all *crazy* about him, even Norma Shearer,' who emerged from her mourning later in the year and was seen so often having dinner and dancing with Niv that the newspapers speculated about them too. Niv's philandering was freer than ever because Flynn's wife had moved in with him at 601 North Linden Drive and Niv had moved out to live on his own in a bungalow at 8425 De Longpre Avenue, where one of his neighbours was the thirty-eight-year-old movie leading lady Kay Francis, who was resting between her fourth and fifth husbands. One night she telephoned him at midnight, very agitated. 'Please come quickly!' she gasped. 'There's a man in my living room and I can't get him out!' Niv went to her house just up the street and found her standing terrified behind a sofa facing a huge man in a black overcoat who turned out to be the Duke of Sutherland, who had thought that Kay Francis's house was a brothel owned by *Lee* Francis.

While Niv was sowing his oats in Hollywood, 1937 was not a happy year for Merle in London. She bought a big Georgian house in York Gate, hired four servants and made secret visits to her mother, who was ill with high blood pressure and diabetes and living in a residential hotel. Merle had always looked after her mother financially and paid all her bills, but the old lady was still distraught that she would not let her live with her because of the colour of her skin: 'Look at my brown hand in your white hand,' she said one day to her friend Sally Sutherland. 'That's the reason I can't be with my Queenie,' and the tears slid down her face. Shooting began on *I, Claudius* in February but the film was never finished, partly because Korda, Laughton and Merle all had doubts about it, and partly because in March she had a bad car crash in London that left her concussed, badly cut over her left eye and ear, and covered with blood. Niv telephoned from Los Angeles, concerned, but she needed four weeks of convalescence, by which time Laughton's contract had almost expired and the film was abandoned. A couple of weeks later her mother died. Merle buried her in an unmarked grave and had a portrait painted of a white woman with blue eyes who she later told friends was her mother. For her 1937 was horrible, but for Niv it was to be the year that he began seriously to climb the ladder to stardom.

Five

A Circus Going on Inside

1937–1939

King Edward VIII abdicated the British throne on 10 December 1936 and David Selznick decided to remake the silent movie classic *The Prisoner of Zenda* to star Ronald Colman as King Rudolph V in a thinly disguised commentary on the abdication. Colman persuaded Selznick to cast Niv as his aide-de-camp, Captain Fritz von Tarlenheim, though Niv later claimed that he got the part only because Selznick won him from Goldwyn in a game of cards. The film was packed with established stars: Madeleine Carroll, Mary Astor, Raymond Massey, C. Aubrey Smith and a grinning, mischievous, chain-smoking Douglas Fairbanks Jr, who would soon become another close Niven chum. The director, John Cromwell, wanted Niv to play his part straight but when Selznick saw the rushes he decided that David was not good enough and would have to be replaced until Niv suggested that he should play the part for laughs, tried one scene his way, with a jaunty flashing smile and a glint of mischief, and both Selznick and Cromwell decided he was perfect. The result was easily his best performance so far. The film itself drags tediously but in it Niv is handsome, sexy, amused and amusing, and quite as charming and debonair as Colman, and he began at last to enjoy the trappings of stardom and for the first time was allowed to choose his own stand-in.

The movie took four months to film and had its moments of drama, notably when Massey's huge black stallion tried during the coronation scene to mount Niv's mare while he was on her back. This delighted Fairbanks, who was as keen on practical jokes as his father, and he and David spiked the extras' bowl of fruit punch in the hope of livening them up. The reviewers generally considered that Niv was pretty good in the film and it raised his profile so considerably that Goldwyn was able to rent him to Twentieth Century-Fox to play his first starring part in a main A-movie feature, *Dinner at the Ritz*, with the up-and-coming French actress Suzanna Charpentier, whose screen name was Annabella and who was to marry his friend Tyrone Power two years later. It was a romantic murder story set in Paris, London and the French Riviera in which he played a smooth undercover detective who tracks down a gang of swindlers, and he sailed to England on the *Normandie* in July to shoot it at Denham Studios. It was his first trip home in four years and he persuaded Goldwyn to give him two months' leave once the film was finished so that he could make the most of that English summer. Trubshawe, who was now the squire of Barton Hall in Norfolk and the father of two little girls, met the ship at Southampton and persuaded him to open his village fête and play cricket for his village team. 'He wasn't at all spoilt by the beginnings of his success,' Trubshawe told Morley. 'He was tickled pink by it and only terrified that it was all too good to be true and might disappear overnight.' Niv stayed with friends near Ascot, looked up others, saw Merle for the first time in eight months and visited many of his old haunts. He went to the Fairford carnival, Bembridge, and stalking in Scotland, but his hopes of seeing Stowe and Roxburgh were in vain because the school was closed for the holidays, and he was disconcerted when he walked into one of his London clubs and was greeted by an elderly member who remarked, 'Good God, Niven, we haven't seen you for a week or two. Where've you been?'

'In America, sir. Making pictures.'

'Pictures? Watercolours?'

Dinner at the Ritz was given lukewarm reviews but the *New York Times* reckoned that David was one of its few virtues and it was the first of many films in which his performance was generally considered to be much better than the film itself. At the end of September he sailed back to New York on the *Queen Mary*, once again denying persistent newspaper reports that he and Merle were going to marry, and his Hollywood friends were delighted to have him back. He spent a weekend at Eddie Goulding's desert home at Palm Springs and was startled to find in the swimming pool the fabulously mysterious Swedish superstar Greta Garbo standing naked in the shallow end. Garbo seems to have made a habit of surprising men in swimming pools in the nude: in later years Niv told journalists that when the Earl of Warwick borrowed Goulding's house, he once ran out and dived naked into the pool, surfacing in the middle cosily chest-to-chest with a topless Garbo. Niv stayed with Ronnie Colman at his San Ysidro ranch, played tennis with Fred Astaire, and enjoyed another lavish weekend with Hearst and Marion Davies at San Simeon, though Hearst, now seventy-four, was heading for bankruptcy with debts said to be $126million.

Goldwyn rented David out again immediately for three months to Paramount to make *Bluebeard's Eighth Wife*, a comedy in which Gary Cooper played a seven-times-married American millionaire, Claudette Colbert an aristocratic French gold-digger, and Niv one of her admirers, a smooth young French bank clerk. His part was tiny but the director, the froglike little Ernst Lubitsch, who was to become one of his favourites, gave him some advice about playing comedy that he treasured for the rest of his life: 'Nobody should try to play comedy,' said Lubitsch, 'unless they have a circus going on inside.' In *Bluebeard's Eighth Wife*, however, the circus had left town and the film is embarrassingly slow, laboured and unfunny. Cooper was cringingly wooden, Colbert deeply irritating, and Niv did little more than look handsome and pull a few comic faces. Undeterred – or unaware – that he had made a bummer, Lubitsch arranged an early private screening of it after a Hollywood dinner party where Charlie Chaplin gave Niv some more excellent advice: 'Don't be like the majority of actors. Don't just stand around waiting your turn to speak – *learn to listen*.'

Unfortunately Goldwyn was beginning to think that Niv was becoming just a bit too cocky and big-headed. 'He was fast becoming a star,' Claudette Colbert told Morley, 'and Goldwyn was already getting irritable with him. "The trouble with that young man", he once said to me, "is that his body has gone to his head," ' though she added, 'I never saw much sign of that. On *Bluebeard* he was divine, very funny and behaved extremely well.' But Niv was indeed so well known by now even in England that Roxburgh asked him if he could use his name to endorse a new fund to raise money for Stowe. David was delighted and replied, 'Please use my name for that or any other reason at any time (except anything to do with the School Certificate!).'

He saw in the New Year at the Californian mountain resort of Lake Arrowhead with Ronnie Colman, Bill Powell, George Cukor and Loretta Young, who was persuading Twentieth Century-Fox to cast him opposite her in her next film, *Four Men and a Prayer*. Back in California he enjoyed yet another Hearst weekend at San Simeon and then spent six weeks on the nursery slopes of a new ski resort at Sun Valley in Idaho for his first lessons in skiing, a sport that was to fill his later years when he lived in

Switzerland. While he was at Sun Valley, Norma Shearer telephoned and sounded still so lonely more than a year after Thalberg's death that Niv invited her to join him and introduced her to Marti Arrougé, a ski instructor twelve years younger than she who was to become her second husband.

Back in Hollywood Niv moved out of the house in De Longpre Avenue and into one of Marion Davies's guest cottages at the huge Hearst 'beach house' at 445 Ocean Front Road at Santa Monica, which he rented with the twenty-eight-year-old English actor Robert Coote and a young Australian fortune hunter, Walter Kerry Davis, who was in California looking for a rich wife. Davis's hunt for a bride was so unsuccessful that he was often unable to pay his share of the rent, but the three young men got on extremely well and became so renowned for their drunken parties that Carole Lombard christened the house 'Cirrhosis by the Sea', a name that they painted on a board and put up outside the house. Flynn stayed with them whenever his marriage went through yet another crisis, Doug Fairbanks Jr moved in as well when his father threw him out of his house further down the beach, the witty writer and actor Robert Benchley was a regular visitor, and Cary Grant lived in the same road, at number 1018, a house that William Hearst Jr said was 'a bachelor's paradise [*with*] girls running in and out of there like a subway station'. It was also a house where David embarked on another lifelong friendship when he met Noël Coward there again in March. Fairbanks, Niven and Benchley once played a wicked practical joke on the fifty-year-old English actor Roland Young when he was suffering from overwork and exhaustion after making five films in one year: they persuaded him to have some treatment from a woman osteopath who turned up in a white uniform and carrying a medical kit but was in fact a prostitute. 'The joke was ruined,' Fairbanks wrote in his autobiography, 'when, like so many idiotic schoolboys, we sought to spy on the two of them and Bob Benchley began to choke out loud with laughter, thus giving the game away. We happy few thoroughly enjoyed each other's companionship for months.'

Niv was briefly involved in a disastrous film with Merle and Gary Cooper, *The Cowboy and the Lady*, from which every one of his scenes was eventually cut, but he enjoyed making *Four Men and a Prayer* with Loretta Young, not least because it was directed by John Ford, who was to become his favourite director. Ford was also an accomplished fellow practical joker and on Niv's twenty-eighth birthday Ford gave him the day off and told him to go out, enjoy himself and get really drunk, and he and Flynn embarked on a monumental pub crawl, boozing in one joint after another until dawn. At 8 a.m. he reported to the studio as usual and was staggered when Ford accused him angrily of being smashed and made a formal complaint to the head of the studio, Darryl Zanuck. Zanuck and a wake of underlings steamed on to the set, looking furious, and ordered Niv to prove he was sober by playing a scene dressed in a doctor's white coat, from the pocket of which he was told to withdraw a stethoscope. He groped drunkenly in the pocket and was horrified to pull out a large snake, which he flung on the floor. Then he was ordered to open a first aid box that produced a colony of little green turtles which he threw into the air with a yell. 'Print it!' bellowed Ford with glee, and he was to show the film at parties for years to come.

In *Four Men and a Prayer* Niv had a straight role for a change as one of the four sons of a murdered British colonel who are determined to prove that he was not guilty of causing the deaths of some of his men. Another of the sons was played by Richard Greene, a twenty-year-old newcomer from England who felt that Niv was jealous of him and resented his being given bigger billing and a better part. 'I always felt he was watching me rather too closely,' Greene told Morley, 'and I remember an ambitious, calculating and very sober man who for some reason wanted to appear to be a cavalier drinker. Behind all that bonhomie and the endless anecdotes and good cheer, there seemed to be a sort of nervousness, as though he was trying to estimate the opposition you might represent to his career. There was always a sting in that tail, and one never really found out what was going on behind the grin.' Niv really had no need to be jealous because *Variety* said that he was 'the best in the cast' and he was signed up immediately by Twentieth Century-Fox for another romantic comedy with Loretta Young, *Three Blind Mice*, about three hard-up sisters who move to Santa Barbara in search of wealthy husbands. David played a penniless playboy pretending to be rich, and although the film was pretty poor his next, *The Dawn Patrol*, was a triumph that was at last to make him an undoubted star after just four years in Hollywood.

It was a very English remake of a 1930 film about the Royal Flying Corps during the First World War, a sad, moving yet stirring anti-war movie, directed by Eddie Goulding, in which Niv co-starred with Flynn, who played the ebullient Captain Courtney to Niv's boozy, happy-go-lucky Lieutenant Scott. Goulding told Niv excitedly that the role of Scott was 'the best part ever written for an actor' and Niv agreed. 'It was a marvellous part,' he said, and he played it to perfection as the drunken but brave, jaunty and sensitive fighter pilot who is appalled by the waste of young lives as wave after wave of boyish Englishmen with only a few hours' flying experience are sent up into battle against German air aces. It was a powerful, provocative film and particularly poignant because when it was made in 1938 another terrible world war was just over a year away. The reviewers were ecstatic and said that he was better than Flynn and Basil Rathbone even though they were excellent too. In England the *New Statesman* raved that 'David Niven emerges as a deeply sensitive, natural actor as well as a potential star of great magnitude', and his performance was so good that Warner Brothers signed him to play the lead in *The African Queen*, Charlie Allnut, opposite Bette Davis but she fell out with the producer, the picture was cancelled, and it was not made until twelve years later with Katharine Hepburn and Humphrey Bogart. When Bogart won an Oscar for it and Niv told him how he had nearly played the part himself, Bogart said unsympathetically, 'Kid, you would have stunk up the screen in that part.'

Even now not everyone was impressed by David. Another actor in *The Dawn Patrol*, Peter Willes, who had been with him at Stowe, accused him of ignoring him and told Morley that Niv 'was an extremely mean and deeply heartless figure. I think perhaps his real tragedy was having less heart than anyone I ever knew . . . I was always surprised all through his life by the contrast between the genial public image and the darker private reality . . . He had a ruthless instinct for survival and self-preservation, and the people he liked best were almost always the ones who could do him a bit of good. There was an odd sort of insecurity always hanging over him, and he often seemed frightened of wasting his charm on the wrong people – as though it was all he had, and it might one day run out.'

Equally unimpressed by Niv was the powerful head of Columbia Studios, Harry Cohn, whose cabin cruiser, the *Jobella*, broke down in rough seas outside Balboa one Sunday evening and was rescued and towed back into harbour by Flynn and Niven as they returned from their usual weekend trip to Catalina Island. Mischievous as ever, Niv persuaded a lawyer friend to send Cohn a letter claiming salvage rights and one half of the *Jobella* for rescuing him at sea. Cohn was not amused and had Niv blacklisted and barred from the Columbia lot for life – a disaster for a young actor since there were only six major studios in Hollywood. Eventually he went to see Cohn and apologised for the joke, but every time Cohn saw him after that he would draw his hand across his throat like a knife, and Niv never worked again at Columbia until Cohn died twenty years later.

Goldwyn rewarded David for his superb performance in *The Dawn Patrol* by giving him a three-month break in April so that he could return to England for another nostalgic summer holiday. First he went to W. R. Hearst's last and most lavish fancy dress party before he went bust, this time for three hundred 'celebrities' for his seventy-fifth birthday at the Santa Monica beach house – where Niv and Flynn turned up as elephant trainers, wearing peaked caps and carrying shovels and buckets marked 'SHIT' – and then he sailed for England, where he visited Stowe and Roxburgh at last as well as Fairford and Bembridge again and joined the smart London club Boodle's in St James's before returning to Hollywood at the end of June.

His success in *The Dawn Patrol* and his burgeoning fame inspired a rumour that Niv had been running Goldwyn down and saying that Selznick had done much more for him than Goldwyn. David quickly wrote to Goldwyn at the end of July to deny it. 'I would like to repeat once more how truly grateful I am to you,' he wrote, 'and to inform you that I have never missed an opportunity of broadcasting my gratitude.' Luckily Goldwyn believed him, and when he gave him more time off to go to New York for several days in October, Niv sent him a telegram that almost trembled with relief. Goldwyn was in fact so confident of his loyalty and talent that he gave him third billing in his next major production, *Wuthering Heights*, after Merle as tormented, demented Cathy Earnshaw and the comparatively unknown thirty-one-year-old Laurence Olivier as her brooding, bitter gipsy stable lad lover, Heathcliff. The film was to be directed by the dreaded William Wyler, who had given Niv such a hard time in *Dodsworth* two years earlier, and he begged Goldwyn not to force him to make the film. Not only did he find Wyler impossible to work with, he also considered that his part, as Cathy's weak husband Edgar Linton, was an actor's nightmare because he was so colourless and wimpish. But Merle and Wyler persuaded him to take the part and shooting began in December 1938, when the location scenes were filmed in a part of the San Fernando Valley that resembled the Yorkshire moors of Emily Brontë's novel once Goldwyn had shipped in and planted a thousand English heather plants.

Wyler turned out to be as tyrannical and sadistic as ever, making Merle and other women in the cast cry and unsettling even Olivier, whose performance was hilariously stagey. 'Look, Willie,' said Olivier in despair after shooting and reshooting one scene over and over again. 'I've done it thirty times. I've done it *differently* thirty times. Just *tell* me, that's all: *What do you want me to do?*'

Wyler gazed at him. 'Just be *better*,' he said.

It was a tense, unhappy film to make. Merle and Olivier disliked and mistrusted each other, which made their passionate love scenes deeply unconvincing, and each walked off the set at times vowing not to return. Olivier had just embarked on a hot affair with the beautiful twenty-five-year-old English actress Vivien Leigh, who was about to land the plum part of Scarlett O'Hara in *Gone With the Wind*, and he sneered that Merle was just 'a little pick-up by Korda' and jeered at some pockmarks that she had on her face after she had contracted a mild case of smallpox as a child in India. She in turn complained several times in front of the crew that he kept spitting in her face during their love scenes. Eventually he shouted at her, 'Why, you amateur little bitch! What's a spit for Christsake between actors, you bloody little idiot? How dare you speak to me like that?' and she burst into tears. She tried to renew her affair with David and was upset when he was not keen. As for Goldwyn, he kept interfering and ranted and raved so much that at one point he shrieked that Olivier was the ugliest actor he had ever seen. 'He's a mess,' he howled, 'dirty, unkempt, stagey, hammy and awful,' and he was furious when Wyler took a fortnight longer to finish shooting and spent $100,000 more than Goldwyn had planned.

David did have one little bit of fun when he called one of Edgar's ferocious dogs 'Trubshawe' – a jest that he was to repeat in one form or another in almost every film he made over the next few years – though Wyler cut the line before it reached the screen. And he took a small revenge on Wyler in the film's final scene, when Cathy was dead, surrounded by mourners, and Niv had to sob at the end of her bed. It was such a ludicrous scene that everyone except Wyler was hysterical with suppressed mirth, and try as he did, Niv could not sob, so Wyler ordered the prop man to puff menthol into his eyes and suddenly a stream of green slime slid out of David's nose. 'Oooh! How *horrid*!' cried Merle, jumping out of her deathbed and bolting towards her dressing room. More than twenty years later, when Niv met the English writer and director Bryan Forbes and told him the story, Forbes found it so funny that from then on Niv signed his letters to him 'Slimey'. 'Niv always called the film *Withering Tights*,' Forbes told me, 'and thought his performance in it was an abysmal embarrassment.'

One happy result of *Wuthering Heights* was that Niv and Olivier became friends. 'He was a great joy to be with on that film,' Olivier told Morley, 'because we both started it with a deep hatred of Willie Wyler.' Less affectionately he added, 'David was always a lightweight, but I think that was probably why we got on so well, because I was no threat to him and he was no threat to me. He couldn't have done a stage classic to save his life, but he had enormous charm and he was very sincere and very good as Edgar, which is a terrible part.' Today the film seems absurdly raucous, melodramatic and overacted, especially by Olivier, but at the time it was generally considered to be a classic – except by the caustic Graham Greene – and David was widely praised for managing against all the odds to make Edgar seem warm, human and not nearly as wet as he was in the novel, though his upper lip did look decidedly trembly without a moustache.

The film raised his profile and self-confidence to such an extent that he started making freelance radio programmes for the Lux Radio Theatre without Goldwyn's permission. By his own later admission he began to get big-headed and to resent the fact that Goldwyn was renting him out to make films for other studios for much more than he was paying him and was making a big profit out of him. He heard that Warner Brothers had paid Goldwyn $175,000 to rent him for *The Dawn Patrol* at a time when Goldwyn was paying him $500 a week, and he consulted the leading Hollywood agent Leland Hayward, who agreed that Goldwyn was making a fortune out of him and promised to make him pay much more. Goldwyn was furious that Niv had consulted an agent behind his back and planted a story in Louella Parsons's daily gossip column in the *Los Angeles Examiner* that reported that success had gone to Niv's head so badly that he was now cutting old friends dead and impossible to work with, and just before Christmas Goldwyn sent Niv a long telegram that was tinged with the regret of a father who was deeply hurt and disappointed by the greed and disloyalty of a favourite son. 'IF YOU ARE UNHAPPY AND DISSATISFIED BECAUSE YOU ARE NOT GETTING ENOUGH MONEY I AM ALWAYS AVAILABLE TO SEE ANYONE WHO HAS CONTRACTUAL OBLIGATIONS WITH ME,' said the cable. 'YOU DID NOT THINK YOU WERE NOT A GOOD ENOUGH BUSINESS MAN TO TALK TO ME WHEN YOU MADE YOUR FIRST CONTRACT NOR DID YOU THINK THAT I WAS A BETTER BUSINESS MAN WHEN I CHANGED MY CONTRACT AND GAVE YOU MORE MONEY . . . DAVID, GET ON TO YOURSELF AND REMEMBER THAT I HAVE DONE MORE FOR YOU THAN MR HAYWARD.'

Goldwyn banned Hayward from the studio and demanded half of all Niv's radio earnings, even though he was entitled to it all under their contract, but Niv was so peeved that when the next radio sponsor gave him one of its hampers filled with cheese, spreads and sardines, childishly he cut everything in half, even the hamper, and sent half to Goldwyn. Goldwyn suspended him for several weeks for his cheek but in February gave him a generous new seven-year contract that increased his salary immediately from $650 to $750 a week, with further regular increases every year that would bring him up to $2250 a week in 1945. He also agreed to give Niv star billing in every film from now on, four weeks' paid holiday a year, and a huge suite on the lot that he said David could have redecorated just as he wished. Niv had finally made it big. After just four years in Hollywood he had become a major star. 'DAVID NIVEN COMES INTO HIS OWN' said the headline in *Picturegoer* magazine in March over a glowing two-page article in which Max Breen wrote: 'It has seemed to me, from the moment I first saw him on the screen . . . that he had all it takes, and more [*with*] a great deal of charm, and an acting skill beyond the ordinary . . . *Dawn Patrol* has given him his long-delayed start. Now watch him fly!'

Goldwyn immediately gave him the male lead in *Bachelor Mother*, the first of his films where his name appeared above the title. His pretty female co-star was twenty-six-year-old Ginger Rogers, who was taking a break from her musical dancing partnership with Fred Astaire to make a straight comedy for a change, and David was so excited about his new exalted status that he drove all around Los Angeles photographing the huge billboard posters of himself looking harassed and nursing a baby. The film told an amusing story about how David – playing a charming playboy – and Ginger, playing a shop assistant, are wrongly assumed to be the unmarried parents of a child that she has found outside an orphanage and end up getting married because of it. It is a delightfully jolly and sweet movie – warm, witty and light-hearted – and was widely applauded as being the best comedy of the year, and when eventually it opened in America at the end of June and in England at the beginning of September, just days before the start of the Second World War, it was hailed as a wonderfully cheerful tonic at a dark moment in history when there was very little to smile about. Trubshawe undoubtedly smiled when he saw it, for in it Niv makes Ginger pretend that she is Swedish and speaks no English, tells her to say 'thank you' in Swedish, and she says 'Trubshawe'. The *New York Times* said that the film was 'hilarious' and Niv was 'perfect', the *New York Post* reckoned that this was the best performance of his career, and in London the *Observer* reported that 'he is growing, film by film, into one of the best romantic comedians in the cinema. He has that light touch, combined with a bewildering courtesy and a faintly dog-like look of sadness, that endears young actors to audiences.'

'My head expanded so much it practically became top heavy,' Niv told

Clive Hirschhorn of the *Sunday Express* years later. 'I was so damn conceited ... at last I was a big star and I positively revelled in it ... I honestly came to believe the publicity handouts they were writing about me.' He co-starred again with Loretta Young in his next film, *Eternally Yours*, but it was a silly little comedy in which he was cast weirdly as 'The Great Arturo', a hypnotist who says at one stage 'take a cigarette and give it to Miss Trubshawe'.

By now Goldwyn was planning to remake a 1930 Ronald Colman film about a stylish English gentleman thief and first-class cricketer, A. J. Raffles, and Niv was desperate to play the part, but Goldwyn punished his cockiness by keeping him on tenterhooks and cast him instead with Gary Cooper in an adventure story, *The Real Glory*, and ordered his latest signing, the up-and-coming thirty-year-old Dana Andrews, who had yet to make his first film, to follow David around while he was making it, accompanied by Goldwyn's official photographer and wearing a white tie and tails, just like Raffles, to remind Niv that even he was expendable if he got too big-headed. Niv kept his nerve and produced an acclaimed performance in *The Real Glory*, in which he played an Irish lieutenant who leads the defence of a fort against an attack by terrorists during a savage revolt against the American army in the Philippines in 1906 but dies heroically at the end. He was 'charming' said the *New Statesman*, 'waggish' according to the *New York Times*, and even Graham Greene agreed in the *Spectator* that he was 'sparkling'.

Perhaps Niv's new star status finally persuaded Merle Oberon to give him up as a lost cause, for she sailed to England in March, went to the French Riviera with Alexander Korda for a preview of his latest film, *The Four Feathers*, and married him in June in Antibes, even though at forty-five he was eighteen years older than she.

Goldwyn finally relented and gave David the part of Raffles, a part that was absolutely made for him, and in July Niv wrote a revealing eight-page letter to Roxburgh that was bursting with pride, humility, flattery and exclamation marks. 'I am at a rather tricky time in my strange career,' he wrote.

> For the last year I have been terribly lucky and have been getting some marvellous parts to play so I simply dare not lose the momentum and consequently have only had four days off not counting Sundays in the last fourteen consecutive months. During that time I have done six big pictures one right after the other and have finally emerged, God knows how!, as a star playing in my own picture – 'Raffles'. I am

> practically a corpse but as soon as I finish 'Raffles' which should be toward the middle of October I am coming home for at least three months and am going to let down every available hair! The awful thing is that the one actor on the screen today that really annoys me is D. NIVEN! I cannot stand the sight of myself in a picture and have only seen two in the last four years!! ... Suffice it to say that I am quite resigned to the fact that I am the luckiest man that ever tried his hand at this peculiar game!

He added, 'It would amuse you to know the number of Stoics past and present who write to me to find out what they have to do to become a film star! ... I hope I have not disgraced the school by becoming a movie actor!' Under the bold flourish of his signature he drew an arrow downwards towards the words 'Movie stars signature!!!'.

Sadly there is no record as to whether Roxburgh ever saw any of David's movies or what he thought of them, though somebody at Stowe kept on file numerous newspaper articles about his career and films. He was now so famous that when King George VI and Queen Elizabeth made a state visit to President Roosevelt in August it was he who was chosen to act as the master of ceremonies on a radio programme that the British of Hollywood – Aherne, Colman, Flynn, Grant, Vivien Leigh and Olivier among them – put together as a loyal tribute to the royal couple.

Niv loved filming *Raffles*. His co-star was the beautiful twenty-two-year-old Olivia de Havilland, who had appeared with him in *The Charge of the Light Brigade* and had just played Melanie Hamilton in *Gone With the Wind*. He was pampered constantly in his big star suite, allowed to recommend old friends as extras, and even when the director fell ill and was replaced by Willie Wyler – the ogre turned out this time to be gentle and helpful. The film itself was slow, unbelievable and just seventy-two minutes long, with a startlingly abrupt end, and the reviews were less than lukewarm, but David's charm was as dazzling as his smile, and Goldwyn was delighted with the film and planned to make him an even bigger star in several big films during the months ahead, including a Raffles sequel.

But Adolf Hitler was about to devastate Niv's Hollywood dream just as he was on the brink of a glittering career. The German army marched into Poland at 4.45 a.m. on Friday, 1 September, Britain and France declared war on Germany two days later and Niv decided bravely that his duty was to return to England to fight for his country. He was aboard a yacht that weekend on a trip to Catalina Island with Doug Fairbanks

Jr and his wife Mary Lee, Laurence Olivier, Vivien Leigh and Robert Coote, with whom Niv had spent the Saturday night drinking far too much rum at a party at the Balboa Yacht Club. When they heard that war had been declared they started drinking gin, even though it was only 6 a.m. 'We began to drink – lightly,' wrote Fairbanks in his autobiography. 'Then more. A very stupid way to cope. But we were fairly young – and probably stupid too. Within a couple of hours we were hiding our utter despondency behind brave talk. Larry, however, was the only one who got really and truly drunk. More than that, he was plainly *pissed*! No longer mixing with the rest of us, he lowered himself over the side into our dinghy and began to row under the bows of the larger and grander yachts anchored in the Yacht Club basin where we were only weekend guests. All had passengers sitting on their boats' afterdecks, presumably as stunned as we. Larry had now cast himself as Cassandra crossed with Henry V. He stood up, a bit wobbly, in his little cockleshell and shouted up, "You're all finished! Done! Drink up! You've had it! *This is the end*!"' Olivier rowed on to several other yachts, giving each his message of doom, and because his little black moustache made him look like Ronald Colman the yacht club's commodore demanded that the quiet, inoffensive Colman should apologise publicly.

Niv told Goldwyn that because he was on the British army reserve he had been called up and had to return to England immediately, but *Raffles* was not yet finished, Goldwyn checked with the British embassy in Washington, was told that nobody outside Britain had yet been called up and that all Britons in the United States should stay put for the time being, and he insisted that Niv should finish the film first. Many British men in Hollywood – Flynn, Grant, Hitchcock – took the embassy's advice and stayed in America, but Niv's patriotic military blood and training told him that it was his duty to return to England even though he would probably never be called up from so far away. He was fatalistic about going to war and told the American actor Tony Randall eighteen years later that he was convinced he would be killed. 'He said that his great-grandfather had been killed in the Crimean War,' Randall told me, 'his grandfather in the Boer War, and his father in World War One, so he was absolutely certain he was going to be killed in World War Two.' Niv got Max, who was now in London, to send him an 'official' telegram ordering him to report to the HLI's regimental barracks immediately, and as soon as *Raffles* was finished Goldwyn released him from his contract until the end of the war and growled that he was going to 'tell that bum Hitler to shoot around you'. He also gave Niv a generous farewell bonus that came to the strange total of $5687.50, for which David wrote to thank him:

> My dear Sam,
>
> I am finding this letter very hard to write but I am just trying to tell you how truly sad I am to be leaving you and your great organization, where I got my start and where I have been so happy working during the last five years.
>
> I am deeply grateful to you for your belief in me at the start and for your help and guidance throughout the rest of the time.
>
> I have been treated most generously and considerately in these last few weeks, and believe me I shall long for the war to be over so that I can come back and repay you by doing some really good work under your banner.
>
> Your personal friendship and the sweetness and kindliness of Frances toward me will always be remembered.
>
> We have had our moments of not exactly seeing eye to eye ! but that I know will be cement that will make our friendship endure all the longer.
>
> If, when I get home, I am told that they definitely have nothing for me to do, then the streak of light half way across the world will be Niven returning to Goldwyn!
>
> In the meanwhile please accept my deepest thanks for everything you have done for me.
>
> I shall miss you all terribly.
>
> Yours ever
>
> David

Goldwyn was deeply moved, called Niv into his office, and said 'this is a very touching note. This letter is so private and personal that I want it to leak out to the Press,' and of course it did, but despite his generous bonus Niv complained nearly forty years later that just before the war he had paid the first premium for a $10,000 life insurance policy, found he could not afford the premiums on a soldier's pay, asked Goldwyn to pay the premiums for him, and Goldwyn had refused. It was a churlish complaint considering that the bonus would easily have covered his premiums for years. Although he was already earning a great deal in Hollywood at the age of twenty-nine, Niv was always to complain that he was short of money, even when he became a multi-millionaire.

On 30 September Doug Fairbanks Jr gave him a lavish farewell party at which David was serenaded by a band of Scots pipes and drums, a stripper, conjuror, numerous sentimental toasts, and copious amounts of alcohol – the guests included Aherne, Bruce, Colman, Coote, Grant, Olivier, and George Sanders – and at the end of October he flew to New York to catch the Italian liner *Rex* and sail to Naples. He hated the thought of rejoining the HLI, and the British ambassador in Washington, Lord Lothian, urged him to stay in Hollywood 'and represent your country on the screen', but Niv's pride and patriotism would not let him sit in luxury in the Californian sun while millions of Britons faced misery and death to save the world from the brutal tyranny of the Nazis. Even so, in later years he often wondered why he had thrown up such a wonderfully promising career in Hollywood so quickly to join an army that at first did not seem to want him at all, and many years later he admitted that part of his motive was to show off and look courageous. Deep down he also felt that he was in danger of becoming insufferably arrogant and pompous now that he was a star, and that some self-sacrifice might be good for the soul. 'I had this sudden, enormous success,' he told the *Telegraph Sunday Magazine* in 1977. 'I believed my studio's ludicrous publicity about me. I think I was saved from being a total shit by the war. Going to war was the only unselfish thing I have ever done for humanity.'

Six

The WAAF, Phantom and SHAEF
1939–1945

When Niv landed in Naples in November 1939 he was met by his Austrian Nazi friend Felix Schaffcotsh, who had founded the Sun Valley ski resort in Idaho and was on his way to Germany to join Hitler's army. They celebrated their new enmity by spending a week in Rome playing golf with Schaffcotsh's friend Count Ciano, Mussolini's son-in-law and Foreign Minister, and drinking each other goodbye. On their last night together they drank gallons, took two girls to St Peter's Square in the Vatican so that all four could kiss a Swiss Guard, embraced, wept and parted, never to see each other again, for Schaffcotsh was to be killed on the Russian front.

From Rome Niv caught a train to Paris, a journey that took four cold, hungry days and blacked-out nights, and there he treated himself to three days in a hotel and a quick fling with a beautiful French model with whom he had gallivanted briefly in Hollywood. Thanks to Noël Coward, who was working in Paris for British naval intelligence, an RAF group captain and the air attaché at the British embassy, he hitched a lift to England in an RAF bomber and arrived at Hendon airfield atop a pile of mailbags on 28 November. He found his way through the London blackout to Grizel's small flat in Chelsea, where she told him that she had joined the Chelsea Fire Service, Joyce was a driver for the Women's Volunteer Service, and Max had joined their father's old regiment, the Berkshire Yeomanry. Max lent him his little flat in Queen Street in Mayfair, and since *Bachelor Mother* was showing in London and David's face was plastered on huge advertisements all over town, Goldwyn's London representative arranged for him to give a press conference for dozens of reporters and photographers at the Odeon cinema in Leicester Square, where he said he would rather join the RAF than the army. 'NIVEN WANTS TO JOIN REAL DAWN PATROL' said the *Daily Mail* headline the next day over a story repeating the old fib that his father had been a general, and he told the *Observer*, 'I'm no hero, and shall probably duck into the first hole when a shell comes along,' so he was horrified to see that Goldwyn's man had had all the *Bachelor Mother* posters plastered with red stickers that shrieked 'THE STAR WHO CAME HOME TO JOIN THE RAF'.

The RAF, however, was not at all keen. He was interviewed by a group captain who made it plain that he thought Niv's application was just a publicity stunt, and he was rejected, officially because at twenty-nine he was too old. He was obviously not qualified to become an officer in the navy and realised that he would have to join the army after all, but he was determined not to go crawling back to the Highland Light Infantry, even if they would have him, and tried to pull strings to join the Scots Guards. In vain. They didn't want a film star, either, and he was further depressed when his old mentor Doug Fairbanks Sr died of a heart attack in Santa Monica on 12 December aged only fifty-six.

Not everyone approved of David's selflessness in returning to England to fight and the English film critic C. A. (Caroline) Lejeune wrote that

> the British film fan does not want David Niven in the army, the navy or the air force. We want him in his proper place, right up there on the screen, helping us to forget this war a little ... He is to us today what Ronald Colman was yesterday – higher than the Gables or the Taylors or the Powers, comparable perhaps only with Spencer Tracy and Deanna Durbin whom all the English love ... There isn't one of us who wouldn't gladly pack him back to Hollywood tomorrow. We like him for being at such pains to come home and fight with us, but we have a feeling that his conscience may have done him wrong.

Depressed and confused, Niv went one night to the Café de Paris in London for dinner and glimpsed among the throng of dancing people the girl he was to marry nine months later, a tall, blonde twenty-one-year-old in the blue uniform of the Women's Auxiliary Air Force, the WAAF. 'I found myself gazing into a face of such beauty and such sweetness that I just stared blankly back,' he wrote in *The Moon's a Balloon*. 'Her complexion was so perfect that the inevitable description, "English Rose", would have been an insult. Her eyes were the merriest and the bluest I had ever seen.' She disappeared into the crowd and he did not see her again for months.

He spent much of his time at Boodle's, asking fellow club members like his latest naval friend, Lieutenant-Commander Ian Fleming, if they could find him a berth somewhere in the forces. He renewed his friendship with Trubshawe, was invited to several country house weekends, and consoled himself with a granddaughter of the Duke of Abercorn, Ursula Kenyon-Slaney, a young Auxiliary Service nurse from Shropshire who was described as 'a Society beauty' when the English newspapers announced at the beginning of January that he and she were engaged – a report that she denied indignantly, though one of her friends told the *Daily Mirror* that it was true. 'I have really lost count of the people who have been reputed at one time or other to be on the point of marrying David,' sighed his sister Joyce. He was also still an enthusiastic 'stage-door Johnny'. His Stowe contemporary Frith Banbury was appearing in a London show, *New Faces*, and told me: 'there was a girl in it called Zoe Gail, and Niven used to come to the stage door and call for her and take her to supper afterwards.'

During his phoney war Niv wrote dozens of letters to his friends in Hollywood, 'gems of hilarious exaggeration and occasional fabrications', according to Doug Fairbanks Jr in his autobiography. 'He would often make wickedly funny jokes at the expense of his "boss", Sam Goldwyn, adding that Sam was so angry with him for leaving that he cut off his salary completely. Actually, few believed this because Sam, infuriating monster that he so often was, was really very fond of Niv and kept him on a retainer "for the duration".'

Thanks to a lieutenant-colonel in the Rifle Brigade, the 'Green Jackets', Niv finally became after nearly three months a second lieutenant in the 2nd Motor Training Battalion at the end of February 1940 and was sent to their barracks at Tidworth on Salisbury Plain to teach the men, most of them cockney conscripts from the East End of London, how to march, drive trucks and do exercises. They grumbled constantly, muttering that it was all right for him, he was a movie star, until eventually he bellowed, 'Right! Now listen to me! You lot have only left your butchers' shops and factories: *I* could be with *Ginger Rogers*, right now!' They got on much better after that, and to escape the boredom and drudgery he drove up to London as often as possible, found himself a tall, blonde Danish model who turned out most conveniently to be an enthusiastic nymphomaniac, and set her up in a cottage in the village.

Often he spent his weekend leaves with Norah Flynn's cousin Nancy

Tree and her husband Ronnie, a Tory Member of Parliament, at Ditchley Park, their beautiful country house near Charlbury in Oxfordshire, fifty miles north of Tidworth. Tree was a friend of Winston Churchill, the First Lord of the Admiralty, who was soon to become Prime Minister and regularly to use a wing of the house to escape the German bombs in London and at his official country retreat at Chequers. One weekend David arrived at Ditchley in uniform to discover that Churchill, his wife and the Cabinet minister Anthony Eden were about to sit down to dinner with a dozen other guests. Churchill loved movies, recognised Niv and stumped the length of the table to shake his hand. 'Young man,' he rumbled, 'you did a very fine thing to give up a most promising career to fight for your country.'

'Thank you, sir,' stammered Niv.

'Mark you,' growled Churchill with a twinkle in his eye, 'had you not done so it would have been despicable!'

After dinner Niv listened agog to Churchill's and Eden's discussions and after church on the Sunday Churchill asked him to walk with him in the walled garden, the first of many walks and chats that they were to share there during the war, and Churchill spoke of how he loved Deanna Durbin, and growing vegetables, and hated Hitler, and asked about the problems of a junior officer nowadays.

In later years Niv was always reluctant to talk about what he had done in the war, and more than sixty years afterwards none of his children or closest friends had any idea about his military activities. His younger son, Jamie, was wrongly convinced that he had been part of the initial British Expeditionary Force that had to be evacuated from Dunkirk in 1940, and some believed that he became a spy behind German lines who infiltrated a *Luftwaffe* air base and inspected German troops. 'Behind enemy lines his job was to distract air base personnel while other agents sabotaged planes,' claimed one of his wartime comrades, Ben Talbot, in the *Daily Mirror* in 1983. 'David took part in many dangerous missions.' But that seems extremely unlikely, if only because his famous face would have been recognised instantly, and had he been outstandingly brave he would have been given a major medal after the war instead of the four ordinary campaign medals he did receive: the 1939–45 Star, the France and Germany Star, the Defence Medal and the War Medal 1939–45. 'I don't think he did anything particularly brave in Europe,' his brother-in-law, Andrew Rollo, told me 'or I would have heard', and Sir Peter Ustinov, who knew him well during the war, told me: 'I don't think there was much derring-do.' Niv's great friend Deborah Kerr's husband,

Peter Viertel, also told me: 'I think the British army was very happy to keep him somewhere out of danger.'

Niv's official service record shows that he spent most of the war training soldiers in Britain, or in administrative jobs, or making official morale-boosting films, and it made sense to keep the famous film star out of danger, since had he been killed or captured that would have given the Nazis a useful propaganda coup. Even so, merely being in London during the Blitz was extremely dangerous, and Niv was openly contemptuous of other British actors who avoided the war by staying in Hollywood. But he never condemned Cary Grant, who was only thirty-six and quite young enough to serve but stayed in California, since Grant did try to join the navy but was told again and again by the Admiralty, the Foreign Office and the British ambassador in Washington to stay where he was and to help Britain by promoting Britishness on the cinema screen. Even so, Grant and others were attacked by the Press, which demanded often that they should 'come home like David Niven', and in 1942 *Picturegoer* suggested that all English actors still in Hollywood should be filmed only in black and white 'since Technicolor would undoubtedly show up the yellow of their skin'. In later years Niv always claimed that he hated every minute of the war, though he told the *Telegraph Sunday Magazine* in 1977: 'I must say I'm pleased about having passed the test of not behaving badly. But, believe me, that's all I really did. I was apt to lie down and wait until it was all finished – but people were watching, and that made me behave a little less like a coward.' Asked why he would not describe how brave he was, he said, 'Because it's not true. I did my best, but it was never better than what I was told to do.'

In April 1940 he was promoted lieutenant and acted as best man at the wedding in London of his thirty-seven-year-old brother Max to Doreen Platt, the beautiful twenty-eight-year-old daughter of a rich South African sugar planter whose youngest daughter was to marry the great English cricketer Denis Compton after the war. Two months later David's forty-year-old spinster sister Joyce was also married in London, to John Mellor, a divorced company director who was two years younger. It was to be a vintage year for Niven weddings and David was to follow them three months later even though he had still not met the girl who would become his wife.

Niv was so bored at Tidworth that he wrote a letter to the *Daily Telegraph* to say it was absurd that during air raids London taxis stopped so that their passengers could scurry into the nearest air raid shelter but the cabbies then left all their lights on and the traffic lights continued to blink. Life was so dull that when volunteers were sought for a secret new force, the Commandos, he put his name forward and was accepted – and the commandos accepted only men who were tough since their job was to undertake quick raids across the Channel, and they had to undergo an exhausting training course at the Irregular Warfare School at Inverailort Castle in the western highlands of Scotland. There, amid wild, demanding countryside and on the rugged nearby islands of Skye, Eigg and Rhum, for three weeks Niv undertook long endurance marches, ran with heavy loads, climbed cliffs, jumped, crawled and swam the loch in full kit under fire. He learned guerrilla tactics, seamanship, how to use landing craft and endure extreme heat, cold and fatigue, and how to shoot a playing card at twenty yards. After training all day he would return exhausted to the castle in the late afternoon only to be given a map and a reference point for some remote glen fifty miles away and told to find his way there by 5.30 a.m. He stalked red deer, slept on a hard wooden floor in a loft with dozens of others, became as fit as he had ever been, and a couple of seriously ugly ex-policemen from Shanghai, Fairbairn and Sykes, taught him unarmed combat and a dozen ways of killing someone silently, from knifing and garotting to breaking a neck. Niv's other instructors included David Sterling, who was later to win three Distinguished Service Orders for making daring clandestine raids behind enemy lines; Lord Lovat, who was to be in the forefront of the Dieppe Raid in 1942 and the Normandy landings in 1944; and Major Charles Newman, who was to win the Victoria Cross when he blew up the dock gates at the German submarine base at St Nazaire in France.

One of Niv's fellow commandos on that course, David Sutherland, wrote in his memoirs that he was one of only two genuine life-enhancers, bubbling with *joie de vivre*, that he ever met. Sutherland was deeply envious when Niv received one day 'a huge coloured postcard of a fantastic Californian palm-fringed beach, and the message: "David, what are you doing over there? Come back soon, love Ginger." ' A week later he received in the post a blue woollen 'willie warmer' to keep the chill out of his nether regions. 'The funny thing is,' chuckled Niv, 'that these interesting things are knitted by an old spinster friend of mine in Memphis, Tennessee, and she doesn't know what they are for!' He reverted to his usual method of warming his willie when he was given a two-day leave, sent a telegram to the Danish nymphomaniac in London that read 'ARRIVING WEDNESDAY MORNING WILL COME STRAIGHT TO FLAT WITH SECRET WEAPON' and was met by MI5 agents who suspected him of sending a coded message to an enemy alien. On the last evening of the Inverailort course the new commandos had a farewell dinner at a local pub where the owner's daughter kept peeping at Niv through the kitchen door. Eventually he marched into the kitchen and kissed her. She fainted. 'Sir,' said Niv to her father, 'you will have to put some backbone into this pretty girl before I take her on as a leading lady!'

Early in August he returned to London, was promoted to acting captain, and posted as a general staff officer to the War Office where his job was to liaise between MO9, the department responsible for the commandos, and the individual commando units themselves. Sharing his desk and ploughing through reams of documents was another captain, Quintin Hogg, who would later inherit the title Lord Hailsham and become a Cabinet minister. Niven and Hogg inspired and processed numerous plans for commando raids on German-occupied Europe, many of them bizarre. One, Operation Colorado, suggested that British commandos should seize the entire country of Denmark, and Operation Attaboy envisaged capturing the huge German headquarters at Knocke in Belgium. As the desperate Battle of Britain between the RAF and the Luftwaffe raged in the skies over southern England, Niv was so excited about the possibilities of the new commandos – and how they were being trained to lead an underground resistance movement should the Nazis invade – that he told Churchill all about them one weekend when they met again at Ditchley Park and went for their customary walk in the walled garden. Churchill, now Prime Minister, was appalled. 'Your security is very lax,' he rumbled. 'You shouldn't be telling me this.'

The first commando raid that David helped to organise was a night assault on the British Channel Island of Guernsey, which had been occupied by German troops on 28 June, in the hope of killing some and capturing others. The leader of the raid was Lieutenant-Colonel John Durnford-Slater, who took a hundred men with him and said in his book *Commando* that he was first briefed by Niv, who was 'a model of what a staff officer should be, lucid, keen, able and helpful'. Niv claimed in *The Moon's a Balloon* that the raid was a success and a few Germans were captured, but it was in fact 'a fiasco', said Durnford-Slater. 'Two launches broke down, another ran onto a rock, one boatful of commandos landed on Sark by mistake, and they captured no prisoners and did no serious damage at all.' Weapons were lost overboard in the heavy swell, three men were left behind and Churchill was furious, said Durnford-Slater, 'and insisted that future commando raids should be serious operations, not amateurish failures'.

Niv's memory was equally faulty when he described how he met 'the

WAAF' again and quickly married her. In *The Moon's a Balloon* he said that at the end of August he wandered into the National Gallery in Trafalgar Square to listen to a lunchtime concert and realised that a woman standing a few feet away was the WAAF. 'She was even more beautiful than I had remembered,' he wrote, 'and so sweet looking and gentle.' At the end of the performance she turned to him, said 'Hello. Wasn't that wonderful?' and he asked her to have a sandwich in a coffee shop, discovered that her name was Primula Rollo, that she worked just outside London as a cypher clerk at the RAF Reconnaissance Squadron at Heston and was living with a family friend in Regent's Park. 'There was never a shadow of a doubt in my mind that this was the one,' Niv wrote, 'but with the whole world flying apart at the seams, there was no time for the niceties of a prolonged courtship.' That night he went to the house in Regent's Park, was invited in and within a week had met both her parents, Flight-Lieutenant and Lady Kathleen Rollo, who were separated, and had asked permission to marry her. 'I can't think why you want to marry her. She can't cook and she can't sew,' said her father, Bill Rollo, a fiftyish divorce lawyer who had won the Military Cross as a lieutenant in the Scots Greys during the First World War and was now in the RAF Volunteer Reserve, and turned out to be such fun that he and Niv were to become good friends. 'War is a great accelerator of events', said Niv in the book, so he and Primmie were married seventeen days later.

He told a different story in the series that he wrote for the *Sunday Express* in 1958: that he had been visiting the RAF station at Biggin Hill, just south of London, when German planes started bombing the airfield and he jumped for safety into a slit trench 'and landed on a white Pekingese which promptly bit me on the behind. It was Primula's dog and we had quite a little argument as to who attacked whom. She was a cypher officer at the station and said she outranked me. I disagreed ... We were married ten days later.' Whichever version is true, when *The Times* on 16 September announced the wedding he fibbed again by saying that his address was still Carswell Manor.

He and Primmie were married soon after noon on Saturday, 21 September 1940 in the depths of Wiltshire in the ancient, tiny parish church in Primmie's little home village of Huish, near Marlborough. It was an unlikely place for a Hollywood film star wedding: a simple, remote little stone and brick church set in the middle of flat, dull farmland, with only sixteen pews, a plain altar, a small font, a timbered ceiling, just six commemorative plaques on the walls and no garish decoration at all, not even one stained-glass window. Niv was thirty, Primmie twenty-two, and it did indeed make sense to marry quickly because who knew how long they might have to live? During the previous week the German *Luftwaffe* had launched wave after wave of terrifying bomber attacks on London, the Blitz, a terrible period of seven months during which London and other great British cities were bombed and set ablaze almost every night and thousands of civilians were killed and buildings destroyed.

Primmie wore a simple blue dress and carried pink orchids. Michael Trubshawe, tall, hugely moustached and wearing the uniform of the Royal Sussex Regiment, was the best man. Niv's sister Joyce signed the register as one of the witnesses, and one of the few guests was Lady Astor, who used up much of her small wartime petrol ration to drive all the way from Hever in Kent in her little red Morris car. It was such a small wedding that only one bottle of champagne was drunk afterwards at the reception, which was held at Cold Blow, Primmie's pink childhood home.

'I liked David very much,' her younger brother, Andrew Rollo, who was in the navy, told me at Cold Blow, where he was still living in 2002. 'My parents approved of him too. He had enormous charm and was great fun, and he made Prim happy. She herself was beautiful and gay in the old-fashioned sense.'

The Rollos were a rural, horsey, dog-loving, aristocratic family. Primmie's father came from a titled Scottish family and her mother, Lady Kathleen, was the daughter of the sixth Marquess of Downshire, a splendid old Northern Irish eccentric whose grandchildren called him Uncle Jumpy because of his devotion to horses, and who did not speak to his wife for half a century even though they had ten children. Primmie's mother was a touch eccentric herself and even in company 'she would fart and make bird noises', I was told by Niv's son David. Primmie's father was a member of the Turf Club and had a very decent income of £5000 a year – the equivalent of about £135,000 a year in 2003 – as well as six horses and a Rolls-Royce, though to pay for their extravagant lifestyle the family also took in a series of 'PGs' – 'paying guests'. As children and teenagers Primmie and Andrew had gone riding, hunting and shooting regularly with their parents, and although they spent every summer at Huish – where they had five servants – they would often have holidays in Scotland and spent every winter in Leicestershire hunting from a house they rented at Melton Mowbray, where their mother hunted six days a week. As a girl Primmie had not been at all academic and had gone to two boarding schools and then to a 'finishing school' in Munich, and in 1935, at the age of seventeen, had 'come out' and been presented to the king and queen as a debutante. 'She was a country girl,' said Andrew Rollo. 'I can't remember her ever having a job.' Grizel told me: 'I approved of Primmie. She was nice and David loved her very much.'

The photographs of Primmie at the time show an upper-class English girl with small eyes and podgy cheeks, but perhaps she did not photograph well and everyone who knew her said she was charming, sweet and adorable. Peter Ustinov, who met her a few years later, said that 'she was like a minor member of the royal family because she smiled a great deal, very generously, and had that slightly mincing talking, rather like the Queen, "*my husband and I* . . ." She was charming and so typical of that class of woman that I saw her in tweeds with a Humber Snipe station wagon with wood on it, and a dog.' Or as Ustinov told Morley, comparing her to a minor English princess: 'She had that same kind of constantly interested expression; you felt that she could make herself frightfully keen on knowing how much underwear was being produced by a certain factory during her visit.' And Trubshawe told Morley: 'She was an absolute darling . . . David always used to say he was the luckiest man in the world, but it was only when he met Primmie that I began to believe him. She was a radiant girl, and at once she gave David something he had never really had before: a sense of purpose and continuity, as well as a sense of what his life was supposed to be about . . . Primmie was England in the 1930s: country cottages and small children and all that gentle, lost world of the upper classes at home.'

The young couple spent their first few married days looking for a house to rent and settled on Halfway Cottage, a four-bedroom, sixteenth-century, thatched, brick-and-timber house with tall Tudor chimneys a few miles to the west of London on the northern edge of the sleepy village of Dorney, near Windsor, which had a post office and just one shop. Primmie had left the WAAF to get married but found a job building Hurricane fighter planes at the Hawker factory two miles away in Slough, to which she would cycle at seven o'clock every morning. She also took in an elderly widow who had been bombed out of her home in London, a Mrs Wisden, who cooked and cleaned for them.

Niv returned to his desk at the War Office in London and wrote to Doug Fairbanks in New York: 'A lot of laughter has gone out of our people, but they are anything but downcast. They all feel rather like knights of old about to do battle against the heathen . . . If we ever go under, at least we will have set a standard that will be hard to beat.' He added, 'I hope nobody sees my face when I'm being bombed. I hate it.' Three weeks later he wrote to Goldwyn from Brooks's: 'Well! I am now married and extremely happy about it . . . She is lovely, Sam. The most beautiful complexion you have ever seen, and you know how our fogs and bombs improve complexion over here. She is about 5'5". GORGEOUS figure. Blonde. Enormous blue eyes and extremely intelligent.' He added,

> London has been a little noisy lately, as you may have gathered from the newspapers. But everything is still running well and people have re-adjusted themselves marvellously to our new way of living.
>
> You really ought to write a scene into one of your pictures between two trollopes on the corner of Bond Street at night – wearing steel helmets!! There are so many great stories being written every day here and I am so happy that even if I missed Dunkirk at least I have not missed a day of the Victory of London.
>
> We will never leave this City, Sam, until pestilence sets in which is improbable even if they could bomb us 100 times as badly, and we'd only leave it then to make room for the fumigators.
>
> The Government are permanently after me to make a picture and one day I might cable you for your permission. After all I came all this way to help all I could and if the Govt. decide that I would be doing something special by making a good picture in the middle of all this, then I'll do anything they say (provided it's a good story!) And also God knows, provided it has your blessing.
>
> I miss Hollywood dreadfully. I never realised how much I enjoyed my life and my work out there until I came home.
>
> However one thing I have never forgotten is how lucky I was to get a start, and above all how lucky it was that the start as well as the rest of it was with you.
>
> I only hope that the end of it will not be underneath several tons of debris without having had a real chance to hit Hitler back first.

In November David's three months at the War Office came to an end and he was sent back to the Green Jackets' barracks at Tidworth, but not for long. He and Primmie spent their first married Christmas at Halfway Cottage, saw the New Year in with the Trees at Ditchley Park, and then on 5 February 1941 David was promoted to acting major and sent to Stourton in Wiltshire, near Shaftesbury, as an intelligence officer to join a secret new outfit, the General Headquarters Liaison Regiment, which was much more commonly known by its nickname, Phantom. Joan Evans, the sister of the soldier who inherited Niv's Rifle Brigade Squadron and later took it to North Africa and Italy, Major James

Lonsdale, told me in 2002: 'He said it was very difficult to come after David Niven because he was such a good soldier and his men all adored him.'

Phantom was a wildly unorthodox outfit, almost a private army, that has been called 'the eyes and ears of the Commander-in-Chief' and went out on reconnaissance, collected intelligence, ensured that its information reached the right people as quickly as possible and was involved in clandestine activities with the French Resistance, the SOE (Special Operations Executive), the SAS (Special Air Service) and in Greece, North Africa, Sicily, Italy, Syria and Iraq. In his book, *Phantom Was There*, Lt-Col R. J. T. Hills, Phantom's first quartermaster, wrote: 'The importance of such a service cannot be overrated. Every commander in the field has always striven to know what lay "on the other side of the hill", or, in other words what his opponent was up to.' Phantom's commanding officer and guiding genius was a squat, cheerful, frighteningly tough, brave and energetic little lieutenant-colonel, G. F. Hopkinson MC, who was known to everyone as Hoppy. He was a man's man who was nervous of women but flirted constantly with death and loved everything military, believing that war was vital if men and nations were not to become feeble and decadent. His idea of a restful leave was to persuade the RAF to take him as a tail-gunner on one of their dangerous daytime raids over Europe, and when one of his Phantom officers, Michael Astor, was about to go on leave himself Hoppy suggested that he ought to spend his holiday having his appendix out. 'When you go into battle you will be a better risk as an officer if you don't have an appendix,' he said. 'I had mine out on leave in India.'

Hoppy handpicked his officers, and the fact that he chose David and gave him command of one of his four squadrons is a tribute to Niv's genuine qualities as a soldier. 'Phantom was renowned for the unusual selection of brilliance, nobility and idiosyncracy, wit, achievement and even criminality exhibited by its officers,' wrote one of them, Peter Baker, in his memoir, *Confession of Faith*. 'The qualifications required for the new officers were in theory high,' wrote another Phantom officer, Miles Reid, in his book, *Last on the List*. 'The work entailed the writing of reports by junior officers which might find their way quickly to the commander short-circuiting the whole of the intervening hierarchy. To do this a definite standard of intelligence and a discriminating judgment was needed.'

Hoppy organised his forty-eight officers and 400 men into four squadrons, each consisting of highly mobile patrol units that had an officer, two radio operators, two drivers and two or three despatch riders, and were equipped with an armoured scout car, radio, Bren gun, three-quarter-ton truck, three motorcycles, and a basketful of carrier pigeons for sending messages back to the regimental pigeon loft in London, at St James's Park, where Lance Corporal G. Starr, assisted by the future champion jockey Gordon Richards, was in command of 500 homing pigeons in the largest loft in the army. All the vehicles were marked with a P – for Phantom – which gave them priority over other vehicles on the roads, and every officer and man wore on his right shoulder a white embroidered P on a black background.

At Stourton Niv was billeted in Stourhead House and his sergeant, Denys Brook-Hart, told Philip Warner, the author of a history of the regiment, *Phantom*, that 'Niven's personality was one which attracted and created amusing and unusual incidents . . . We had some carrier pigeons at Stourhead and one day Niven wrote out a message and sent a bird winging for London. It so happened that a lady member of the Royal family had been invited to inspect our carrier pigeon facilities and she and Niven's bird arrived at St James's much at the same time. This was thought to be a lucky demonstration of our efficiency. The capsule was removed from the bird's leg and handed to HRH who opened it and read out the following message in Niven's hand: "I have been a very naughty girl and so Daddy has sent me straight home!" ' Niv himself told Warner that General Paget was inspecting the pigeon loft when 'a bird slapped in through the intake box. It was from "A" Squadron . . . and the message was ripped off the poor bird's leg and read in an expectant hush as follows: "That beast Major Niven sent me away because he said I had farted in the nest." '

Primmie came to Stourhead for a romantic weekend that spring, Niv took a room for her at the Spread Eagle Inn, and the landlord asked them to scratch their names and the date, 1941, with a diamond ring on a window in the bar that was rediscovered in 1998. Soon afterwards Niv wrote to 'Dear old Fred' and Phyllis Astaire from Boodle's: 'I have managed to be in all the worst Blitz we have had, including three months in London without a day or night off during the worst period.' He was convinced that Hitler was about to invade Britain but despite the real danger that he and all Londoners were facing every night, he was still determined to keep everyone's spirits up and gave an example of typical British army humour:

'I can't, you can't, Hitler can't.'

'Can't what?'

'Milk chocolate.'

But he ended his letter, 'God knows I miss you both terribly.'

In another letter to Hollywood, this time to Nigel Bruce, he said with unexpected venom, 'Thank God we have now got a real government and in Churchill a real leader at last, but there is going to be a little scalp-hunting when the smoke has cleared off the battlefields . . . besides cousins and relations I have now lost practically all my old friends and all in the last few weeks . . . they need never have been sacrificed if the people then at the top had been doing their jobs as well as they said they were doing them. I want to stick a knife into them just as much as I want to fix Hitler.'

In May 1941 Niv was sent to Phantom's headquarters at Richmond Park in Surrey and put in command of its 'A' Squadron, which was preparing for a possible German invasion and learning bomb disposal. He was billeted in a beautiful Georgian mansion, Pembroke Lodge, which had belonged to the nineteenth-century Prime Minister Lord John Russell, had witnessed the signing of the treaty ending the Crimean War and contained a bathroom in which King Edward VII was once heard exclaiming piteously: 'Here I am, King of England, and they don't even allow me a sponge.'

Niv and his men launched into an exhausting dawn-to-dusk training schedule in the park that included motorcycling, Morse code and cyphers, and since Hoppy was determined that his men would be alert and ready at whatever hour the Germans chose to invade he made them train in the middle of the night and sometimes do without a night's sleep altogether. There would be sudden inspections at one o'clock in the morning and vehicles would have to be maintained by torchlight.

Niv 'was very highly respected in the unit for his qualities as a soldier', wrote Philip Warner, 'a dedicated and professional soldier'. One of Niv's comrades, Harold Light, who commanded the training unit, told Warner that Niv brought 'a fresh and exuberant spirit to his duties' and got on well with everyone, and Lt-Col Reggie Hills wrote in his memoir that 'Major Niven had been among our chief delights. He was the morale raiser *par excellence.*' One of his morale-raising jobs was to organise and compère a concert at Richmond Park for all the Phantom squadrons and he rounded up an extraordinary array of talent that included Bud Flanagan and Chesney Allen and was followed by a riotous party where Flanagan and Allen performed a complicated Highland dance. 'As master of ceremonies,' Niv told Warner, 'I was too drunk to be able to assess it properly and afterwards in the officers mess, one of the Crazy Gang asked Hoppy what the sandwiches had inside them. Hoppy pointed to a flag on the pile marked "sardine". Whereupon Jimmy Nervo . . . ate the flag, brushed the sardine sandwiches to the floor and broke the plate on Hoppy's head. They were wonderful days which I would not have missed for anything' – a remark that suggests that he did not hate *every* minute of the war, as he claimed.

Niv and 'A' Squadron were sent to the south coast, attached to General Montgomery's 5th Corps, and stationed behind Poole Harbour, where they assembled a collection of disguises so that they could go underground if the Germans invaded. Niv's own chosen disguise was that if the godless Nazis arrived he would wear a dog-collar and pretend to be a vicar. Montgomery was generally considered to be a fine general but so awkward, prickly and demanding that officers shuddered when they were posted to his command. 'ARE YOU 100% FIT?' bellowed a large notice inside his headquarters. 'ARE YOU 100% EFFICIENT? DO YOU HAVE 100% BINGE?' Nobody had any idea what 'binge' might be but Monty forced even senior staff officers to go on cross-country runs every week – those that he had not already sacked by the dozen as being 'dead wood' – and had recently described one fellow general in an official report as being 'extremely idle [*and*] quite unfit to be a Major-General'. Another elderly officer 'is idle and has taken to drink' – Monty was teetotal – and the commander of the Royal Engineers in the Portsmouth area was 'completely and utterly useless . . . has also taken to drink [*and*] gives the impression of being mentally deficient'. The fact that Niv survived the close attention of Monty is another indication of how good a soldier he was.

When the lease on Halfway Cottage in Dorney expired Primmie rented another house in the village, Flaxford, a 1930s four-bedroom house that had a half-acre garden. 'Prim was charming, awfully sweet and not at all affected,' its owner, Brigit Ames, told me. 'She was well liked in the village but I don't think the villagers knew them much. Food was very short under rationing and you were allowed only 2 ounces of sugar a week, 2 ounces of tea, 2 ounces of butter, 2 ounces of milk, and that was it. If you had meat you had to make it up with rice or spaghetti. They had some ack-ack guns on the common and there was a good deal of noise and shooting going on there at night, and doodlebugs used to come over, and it was quite nasty. There was a time in 1941 when we thought we were going to be invaded by parachutists and they took all the road signs down. It was a real threat and we felt quite nervous.'

Even though Niv was now so happily married, he was still highly susceptible to a good-looking woman, though luckily Primmie never discovered his infidelities. Doug Fairbanks Jr reported in his autobiography that in 1941 he received from Niv an eight-page letter which 'described in hilarious detail a surprisingly uninhibited amorous adventure he had recently experienced in a car, at night, in blacked-out London, during a heavy bombing raid, with a mutual female acquaintance of ours. She was a most attractive lady we had once thought to be far removed from carnal fun-and-games. Niv left nothing out. Every detail of every moment of their mutual lechery was carefully noted.'

Niv was undoubtedly a proper soldier – and that summer he was photographed in full battle kit inspecting Phantom's 'A' Squadron with the Duke of Kent at Richmond Park – but he was still also considered an important weapon in Britain's propaganda war and started making numerous radio broadcasts to the USA. He also joined the Cambridge historian Professor Denis Brogan in *Transatlantic Quiz*, a witty and remarkably intellectual radio programme in which the two of them took on a team from the USA that included the broadcaster Alistair Cooke, and a series of programmes, *Answering You*, in which he and Leslie Howard replied to questions from North American listeners. And Goldwyn was finally persuaded to let him make a morale-boosting movie about the RAF for the British government, *The First of the Few*, at a time when the war was going badly and the British needed an inspiring film.

On 1 September the army released him temporarily to civil employment and he took a week's leave with Primmie at Ditchley Park, where Churchill, who was once again enjoying a country weekend, invited Niv to walk with him again in the walled garden, and talked about how badly the war was going but how he believed the United States would soon be drawn into the war, as it was a few weeks later when the Japanese air force attacked the American naval base at Pearl Harbor in Hawaii. When Niv next met Churchill he asked him how he had been so prescient. 'His reply gave me goose pimples,' said Niv. ' "Because, young man, I study history." '

The First of the Few told the moving story of the inventor R. J. Mitchell and his legendary British single-seater fighter plane, the Spitfire, with which the young pilots of the RAF had foiled a German invasion the previous year. Leslie Howard played Mitchell, Niv a fictional ex-test pilot and RAF station commander, and the film was shot in September on location in Cornwall, and then at Denham Studios, and on an active RAF airfield at Ibsley in Hampshire, where they spent weeks filming real RAF pilots going into action. Niv was at first wary of making the picture in case people sneered at him for going back to films so soon and not being a proper soldier, but he was excellent in the role: brave, charming and insouciant, a roguish ladies' man who flirts with several women including one Elsie Trubshawe. Although much of the film was fiction it was uplifting and defiant, with stirring patriotic music composed by William Walton, and it was Niv's first major British movie and possibly his best performance to date.

During filming Niv met two young British actors who were to become lifelong friends: John Mills and Patricia Medina. Mills was also in the army and making a film at Denham, and told me: 'There's never been another man like Niven. He was a great raconteur and could entertain you for an hour and never repeat himself. If he heard a funny story he wrote it down, so he had a terrific fund of stories.'

In *The Moon's a Balloon* Niv claimed that he spent only four weeks filming *The First of the Few* and continued to command his Phantom squadron via a radio transmitter in his dressing room, but his army record shows that in fact he was 'released to civil employment' for nearly five months and did not return to Phantom until 20 January 1942 – a month after he and Primmie joined Peter Fleming, John Gielgud, Celia Johnson, Edwina Mountbatten and others at a fortieth birthday party for Noël Coward and three weeks after he learned that Alexander Korda had been knighted for services to the film industry, making Merle Lady Korda. Once back at his post Niv led his men from Richmond to Wales on icy roads in dreadful winter weather for a two-month regimental reconnaissance exercise on the Welsh coast to plan a defence should the Germans invade from Ireland.

Soon after Primmie became pregnant in March she gave up working at the aircraft factory in Slough, and followed Niv and 'A' Squadron wherever they were sent, living in a series of rented rooms. 'We were wonderfully in love,' he wrote in *The Moon's a Balloon*, but that did not stop him misbehaving in London that summer when his naughty old friend Doug Fairbanks Jr arrived in England along with thousands of American troops. Niv told Fairbanks that he was dreadfully bored since he had little to do but train his men and kill time while they waited for an eventual invasion of Europe. Otherwise he was spending much of his time in London hanging around his various clubs – Boodle's, Brooks's, Buck's and White's. One night he and Fairbanks wandered through the West End in the blackout and were picked up by a couple of prostitutes: a vast but jolly cockney and a pretty little French girl. Niv suggested going back to their flat for a few drinks, where they paid £5 each and the

Clockwise from left James David Graham Niven at the age of two. (2) Four-year-old David with his father and sisters Joyce *(left)* and Grizel at their Cirencester home, Golden Farm, on the sunny day in 1915 that William Niven went off to join the First World War. (3) David and his father. (4) David's mother, Henrietta, with his elder brother, Max.

Could David Niven's real father have been Sir Thomas Comyn-Platt? Both David and his sister Grizel suspected that William Niven was not their father, and Platt had been writing love letters to their mother for six years before David was born. Judging by these photographs of Platt (*right*) and Niv when they were fifty-four and fifty-three, both had a similar slightly bulbous chin, sensitive mouth, long straight nose and sloping forehead, and both started going bald early.

A sad-eyed David at the age of thirteen – but his unhappy childhood years were nearly over.

A musician at fifteen *(fourth from the left)* playing the drums in the Stowe School jazz band in 1925.

At seventeen, in 1927, Niven (*sitting, second from right*) played cricket regularly for the Stowe School 1st and 2nd XIs.

At Sandhurst in 1929, Niv – now a tough, nineteen-year-old bruiser (*front row, far right*) – played rugby for the Royal Military College's 1st XV.

Nearly twenty and just commissioned as a Second Lieutenant in the Highland Light Infantry in 1930.

Below: Second Lieutenant Niven with his best friend Michael Trubshawe on manoeuvres with the Highland Light Infantry in Malta in 1931, where their senior officers all had little wooden signs outside their tents saying 'C.O.' or '2nd I/C'.

When Niv arrived in Hollywood in 1934 he stayed with four beautiful women: Gladys Belzer *(centre, sitting)* and three of her four daughters, *(left to right)* Polly Ann, Sally and Gretchen. Sally and Gretchen were already stars under their screen names Sally Blane and Loretta Young.

Bottom right: Twenty-five-year-old Niven in Hollywood in 1935 with his first serious love: the twenty-four-year-old Anglo-Indian actress Merle Oberon, who was already a star and wanted to marry him.

Below: Niv's Hollywood mentor Sam Goldwyn, the larger-than-life movie mogul who gave him his big break in films and treated him like a son until their dramatic row.

The cast of *The Charge of the Light Brigade* – not in Russia but in California and the mountains of the Sierra Nevada. Niven is on the far left, Flynn sitting on the right.

Niv *(far right)* with his hell-raising friend Errol Flynn *(second from left)*, director Michael Curtiz *(pointing)* and assistant director Jack Sullivan during filming of *The Charge of the Light Brigade* in 1936.

At the Trocadero in 1937 with one of his many Hollywood girlfriends, Helen Briggs, better known by her screen name Virginia Bruce.

Niv with Fred Astaire, one of his earliest Hollywood friends, at the Santa Anita racecourse in 1937. They were to remain close chums for the rest of his life.

With Joel McCrea and Loretta Young in the 1938 film *Three Blind Mice*.

tarts immediately recognised them as soon as the lights were switched on. 'I have never before or since seen Niv at a loss,' wrote Fairbanks in his autobiography. 'But we shared a silly embarrassed grin.' According to Fairbanks they stayed for an hour, drank whisky, and eavesdropped on the sad performance in the next room of one of the girls' regular customers, an elderly major whose pleasure was to ride her around the room cracking a whip and crying 'Giddyap!' while she made whinnying noises.

In April 1942 David began to help plan the biggest commando operation of the war, a raid on the German-occupied French port of Dieppe. Inspired by Montgomery and the Chief of Combined Operations, the future Admiral Lord Mountbatten, whom Niv came to know well, it envisaged an attack across the English Channel by 6000 Canadian and British commandos who would capture Dieppe, hold the town for twelve hours, take prisoners and secret documents, and retreat across the Channel again. As one of Montgomery's 5th Corps officers, Niv had to assign men from Phantom for this dangerous mission, knowing that many would never return. 'He told me about one particularly hard decision that he had to make,' the British actor John Hurt, who became a friend many years later recalls Niven telling him: ' "I had two radio operators who were excellent but the better one, the best in the regiment, was married with three children." He chose his best man, and he didn't come back, and Niv always felt that he should have chosen the other feller who didn't have a family, but he said "those were the sort of decisions you had to make all the time. They prey on you and never leave your dreams." He intimated that there were many other examples of hard decisions that he had to make, and he had to write all the letters to families when people died.'

The Dieppe Raid was a disaster. It was launched at dawn on 19 August and for more than eight, hours on that hot summer day the commandos were massacred as they tried desperately to land on the pebbly beach. Niv's radio operator was one of 1027 commandos, mostly Canadians, who were killed that day. Hundreds more were wounded and 2340 captured, so that fewer than a third returned home, which explained why Niv hated to talk about the war after it was over. 'There are too many dead men looking over my shoulder,' he said.

But in the midst of death there was also life, and in north London on 15 December 1942 Primmie gave birth to their first son at the Royal Northern Hospital in Upper Holloway a few days before it was hit by a bomb that killed twelve children. They called him David – an unwise decision that Niv came to regret because it cast a long shadow of comparison over the boy in later life. They named him in full David William Graham, and minutes after the birth Niv sent a telegram to Roxburgh that arrived at Stowe within the hour and read: 'SON BORN 9.30 THIS MORNING PLEASE PUT HIM DOWN FOR GRAFTON BOTH DOING WELL FATHER DOING EVEN BETTER.' Hoppy allowed him to spend each night with Primmie in hospital and every evening he borrowed a motorbike, donned a steel helmet and rode from Richmond across London in the blackout, with bombs exploding on all sides and ack-ack guns pounding away at the German aircraft, to sleep on the floor at her side until she and the baby returned home to Dorney.

By now Niv had become almost an official public relations man for Britain and the army, was sent north to Glasgow on a recruiting drive to shake hands and make speeches, and on 14 January 1943 he was seconded to the army's director of PR to come up with ideas for another morale-boosting film, this time to extol the glories of the army rather than the RAF. This did not prevent him having to join the 2nd Motor Training Battalion for more dreary manoeuvres on Dartmoor, where he kept 'A' Squadron on its toes by making the men live for three days off the land without any food or water. There was a brief flurry of excitement when the navy sought help to deal with some German E-boats, and he and the squadron spent several nights at sea with their anti-tank rifles but found nothing, though the cook lost his teeth overboard.

Niv still had plenty of time for a home life with Primmie and baby David, and at weekends, when they were not hobnobbing at Ditchley Park with the Trees, Churchill and Eden they were enjoying parties at Dorney and in the villages nearby. Many of his friends lived in the vicinity so as to be close to Denham Studios – Noël Coward, the Millses, Olivier and Vivien Leigh – and they gathered regularly in each other's houses, bringing their own food and drink because of rationing. 'I remember that once there was a ring at the doorbell,' Sir John Mills told me, 'and there was a soldier in full battledress and a gas mask, a bayonet on the rifle, and it was Niven. He kept doing that sort of thing. He was a great chum and we never stopped laughing. And we all adored Primmie. She was a lovely person and they were a very happy couple. Whenever he told a story she'd roar with laughter even though she must have heard it lots of times already.'

That spring Niv went off on another PR trip, this time to the Midlands for a week to make cheerful speeches in tank and armament factories, and in April the army released him yet again, this time for nine months, to make another morale-boosting propaganda film, *The Way Ahead*. Major

J. E. Dulley took over 'A' Squadron and Niv was never to return to Phantom. *The Way Ahead* was to be directed by Captain Carol Reed and written by Major Niven, Major Eric Ambler, and a twenty-one-year-old playwright, Private Peter Ustinov, who had just had his first success in the theatre with a play called *House of Regrets* – 'Best Play of the War' said the *Daily Mail* – and was now attached to the Army Kinematograph Service. Under army regulations the only way that a private could work closely with officers was for him to be a servant, or 'batman', to one of them, and Ustinov was duly appointed David's batman. At first Goldwyn was reluctant to let Niv make another film without a percentage and some control over it. 'FACT THAT YOU HAVE BEEN IN ONLY ONE PICTURE IN FOUR YEARS MAKES IT MOST IMPORTANT THAT YOU BE PRESENTED PROPERLY IN ANY PICTURE,' he cabled. 'AM VERY FOND OF YOU DAVID AND WANT TO HELP BUT CAN LET YOU GO INTO PICTURE ONLY ON TERMS OF MY OFFER STOP WARMEST REGARDS SAM GOLDWYN.'

Eventually the company making the movie, Two Cities Films, forced Goldwyn to give way by paying him $100,000 and threatening that if he did not release Niv the British army would simply order him to do as he was told. Niv, Ambler and Ustinov were given a room at the Ritz Hotel in London to work every day on the script, and to make life easier for Ustinov Niv gave him a sleeping-out pass that said 'This man may go anywhere and do anything at his discretion in the course of his duty', which deeply upset the first military policeman who stopped Ustinov afterwards. 'I showed him my pass,' Ustinov told me, 'and he said, "Lucky bastard! I've never seen one of these before. *And* you got his fuckin' autograph!" ' The unusual set-up at the Ritz appealed to David's schoolboy sense of humour and whenever a senior officer approached the room Niv would hiss 'Cave-ee!' and Ustinov would swiftly pretend to be doing something batmanlike, such as polishing David's belt.

Niv and Ambler had much more money than Ustinov and often rang room service to order a round of drinks, paying vast Ritz prices, which embarrassed Ustinov because he was earning only fourteen shillings a week and could not afford to reciprocate. To raise some money to buy his round occasionally he sold the only valuable thing he owned, a Derain nude, to a dealer for £60 (about £1500 today). Years later he saw the painting again, by now extremely valuable, hanging on a wall in Niv's house in Hollywood. 'The best bargain of my life,' said David breezily. 'I bought it off a dealer for £65 when we were all working at the Ritz.'

Apart from the script for *The Way Ahead* Niv was also the technical adviser for a War Office instructional film about a gun, *The Seventeen-Pounder*, that was being made in London's Soho by Publicity Picture Productions, one of whose employees, the son of a London policeman, was a fifteen-year-old, £2-a-week teaboy, gofer and trainee animator, Roger Moore, who was to become many years later one of Niv's closest friends and to star on TV as the Saint and in the cinema as James Bond. 'I didn't want to be an actor then,' Sir Roger told me in Monaco. 'I wanted to be an architect or an artist, and I remember the great excitement when he came to visit. I stood around with my mouth open just looking at him on the other side of the office, and the girls were all fainting – and a few of the boys!'

In June 1943 Leslie Howard died when his plane was shot down by two German fighters over the bay of Biscay just as Goldwyn's Americanised version of *The First of the Few* opened in the USA under the title *Spitfire*, but despite all the time that Goldwyn said he had spent trying to improve the film, he wrote to Niv on 2 August:

> To be frank with you, SPITFIRE was a disappointment to me. If I had known the part you were to have, I would never have given my permission for you to appear in it, because such pictures don't help you. I spent two months cutting it and took out about forty minutes, in addition to putting in some closeups of you, which were completely lacking in the picture. I hope that the picture you are about to do for Two Cities has a great part for you. When you left here you had some very good pictures behind you, and it would be a mistake for you to do a number of mediocre pictures just for the money involved. I would much prefer to assist you financially rather than have you do another SPITFIRE.

Goldwyn's offer of financial help was typically generous and his letters to Niv throughout the 1930s and 1940s read as though they were written by a very fond uncle to his nephew. The letter ended, 'I am looking forward to the time when you will be coming back to this country, and we can make some really fine pictures together. Good luck to you, and God bless you. Affectionately, Sam.'

Niv's part in *The Way Ahead* was indeed an excellent one and some believe that the film was the best he ever made. Filming started in August on Salisbury Plain and at Denham Studios, and he played the part of a kind, gentle, genteel young British officer just after the retreat from Dunkirk whose job was to mould a shambolic group of unlikely recruits into a finely honed team of fighting men. He puts them through a tough training programme and sails with them to North Africa to harry Rommel's army after the Battle of El Alamein where they prove at last that they have indeed become fine soldiers. The soldiers were played by some excellent actors – William Hartnell, Stanley Holloway, Raymond Huntley, John Laurie – and Ustinov was the splendidly irritable French owner of a flyblown café in Tunisia. It was a deeply patriotic, inspiring and moving film that can still send shivers down a British spine when the soldiers sing evocative wartime songs such as 'Lily of Laguna', Tessie O'Shea breaks into 'If You Were the Only Girl in the World', and Niv leads a final resolute bayonet advance into the dust and smoke of battle. Today the film leaves a residue of deep regret that the characters of Britain and the British have changed so drastically since then, and many of the performances in it, including David's, were excellent.

Niv's pleasure in making another film at last was marred in September by the news that Hoppy Hopkinson, who had risen to become a major-general and CO of the Glider-Borne Brigade of the 1st Airborne Division, had been killed by a sniper while leading his men into an attack on a German position at Taranto in Italy, but in November Niv, Ustinov and the rest of the cast sailed for the Mediterranean themselves aboard the troopship *The Monarch of Bermuda* to shoot the location scenes in Algeria and Tunisia. They returned to England via Cairo, where Max was also an army major, had just been visited by Doug Fairbanks, and had ridden with him to the Sphinx and the pyramids on camels. Max was possibly even more mischievous than his brother, and as his camel was led away – 'rolling this way and that,' wrote Fairbanks in his war memoir – Max 'shouted for all to hear, "If this keeps up, I'll have an *orgasm*!" ' Afterwards, in true Niven tradition, he took Fairbanks to an Egyptian brothel.

Back in England at the end of November, Niv was promoted to lieutenant-colonel and wrote to Goldwyn's assistant Bill Hebert in Los Angeles: 'I really am rather happy about it as this is a real Colonel in the Field Army and not a sort of "prop" one like so many people from Hollywood have become. After volunteering in 1939 I have served the whole time with the field forces and have held every rank from Second-Lieutenant up.' He added over-optimistically,

> I am sure I shall be eating my next Christmas Dinner in Hollywood. Believe me Bill I think about getting back there and getting on with my work all day and every day. Its funny, on the few occasions that I have been called upon to do anything really dangerous in this war and

> on the many occasions that I have been frightened out of my wits whether things were dangerous or not I have always had the same thought: 'If ever I get through the next few hours, which I know I shan't, I shall be the nicest, kindest, most grateful and uncomplaining man in the world – nothing will ever bother me again!' I wonder how long these fine thoughts would last if I came back and found that Sam had cast me to play Rita Hayworth's drunken great uncle who passes permanently out of the picture in the first reel!

He concluded by reporting that 'my small son, David Jr., is a terrifying human being. He is now eleven months and walks, whistles through his five teeth, bites his mother, roars with laughter all day long and looks faintly Japanese. However, we both think he is the greatest thing on earth.'

Niv's promotion was to give him a suitable rank to sit in on briefings with the American commander-in-chief, General Eisenhower, Monty and other senior officers who were planning the invasion of Europe, and in January he was appointed a high-powered PRO as Assistant to the Director of Broadcasting Services at SHAEF, Eisenhower's Supreme Headquarters of the Allied Expeditionary Force in Europe. There he was to work directly for the American General Ray Barker as a liaison officer to oil the wheels of the great alliance against Hitler and prevent friction and misunderstandings between the British, Americans, Canadians, French and Poles when finally they invaded Europe in June. 'He was a *very* distinguished colonel,' I was told by the British actor Patrick Macnee, who was to star in the TV series *The Avengers*. 'He used to come into the Ivy restaurant in full uniform and women looked at him as if it was God turning up.'

Despite his new job and rank Niv was keen to persuade the army to release him early so that he could return to Hollywood to star in *Coming Home*, a rousing film about soldiers returning to their loved ones at the end of the war that Goldwyn wanted to make before it was over. In a document dated January 1944 one British official reported that Niv had 'said he felt he might give better service to the general cause by returning to Hollywood' and some civil servants supported his argument, insisting that he was not simply trying to dodge his duty so that he could return to 'the fleshpots of Hollywood'. They were still considering his request a year later, but in the end it was refused because they felt that to grant it would create a precedent.

In February he added yet another London gentlemen's club to the four of which he was already a member. This time he joined the Garrick, a notably sociable and unstuffy club whose members tended to be actors, authors, journalists and the jollier lawyers and politicians, some of them verging on the louche. Among the members who signed Niv's nomination page were Laurence Olivier and Jamie Hamilton, who was to become his publisher nearly thirty years later. But it was when Niv lunched in April at his favourite club, Boodle's, that he was nobbled by another old friend, Stephen Watts, and inveigled into playing a part in one of the most bizarre operations of the war. Watts, once the theatre critic of the *Sunday Express* and now a captain in Intelligence, MI5, wanted Niv to impersonate General Montgomery and fool the Germans into thinking that he was in North Africa rather than England and so keep them guessing as to whence the imminent Allied invasion of Europe might come. Niv pointed out that he was far too tall and had the wrong voice, but Watts then found just the man for the job – Lieutenant Meyrick Clifton James, an actor who looked astonishingly like Monty and was serving in the Royal Army Pay Corps at Leicester. It was important to approach James secretly, without telling his superiors, and Niv agreed to inveigle him down to London by pretending that he needed him to appear in his next propaganda film. A few weeks later, just before D-Day, James was flown to Gibraltar and North Africa, and did indeed confuse the Germans. 'Several captured German generals told their interrogators that they had heard of Montgomery's "secret" arrival in the Mediterranean,' wrote Watts in his book *Moonlight on a Lake in Bond Street*. 'One said he never doubted it was a feint – but he never doubted either that it was Montgomery.' Clifton James eventually starred in a film about his exploit, *I Was Monty's Double*.

Niv's own version of this story was wildly exaggerated. 'All his stories were embellished,' said Roger Moore, 'but he said that when James realised that they didn't want him to make a film after all, he burst into tears because he was a bigamist and he was drawing two pay cheques and thought the game was up!' True or not, Niv used to tell another splendid story about British Intelligence. He said he was summoned to a secret meeting, hailed a taxi and gave the hush-hush address. 'Ah, yes,' said the cabbie, 'that'll be MI5.'

In April he wrote again to Bill Hebert: 'Well, here we are, all teed up and waiting for Monty to blow the whistle. I must confess that I am not straining at the leash. But four and a half years of war has long since removed any glamour from the proceedings as far as I am concerned. Nevertheless the boys are all in splendid shape and are all as anxious as I am to get it over with once and for all.' He was impressed that millions of American soldiers were now in England yet 'everything has gone so smoothly between us . . . What wonderful sightseers your people are! I have been dragged off by Americans countless times and literally had my nose rubbed in the Tower of London and Anne Hathaway's cottage. Things that because they always seemed to be around I am ashamed to say I had never bothered to give the once over to before.' He concluded, 'My love to the Swiss Family Goldwyn – and to all my old chums and chumesses.'

Among Niv's friends from America who were now dropping in to see him and Primmie were Bob Coote, John Ford, John Huston, William Wyler and Colonel James Stewart, who spent a weekend leave at Dorney at the end of April, mowed the lawn and posed for photographs with David Jr without telling them that he had been awarded the Distinguished Flying Cross two days previously. Another frequent visitor was American air force Major Clark Gable, who was glad to see Niv so happy as a husband and father, and adored Primmie and the baby even though his own happiness had been destroyed when his beloved wife, Carole Lombard, had been killed in an air crash more than two years previously. One evening Primmie found Gable sitting in the garden on an upturned wheelbarrow, sobbing helplessly.

English friends who visited them in Dorney included Guy Gibson, the bomber pilot who had won the Victoria Cross for blowing up the Eder and Mohne dams, and for David Jr's long delayed christening the guests included his godfather Noël Coward, his godmother Vivien Leigh, and Laurence Olivier. The christening presents were firmly alcoholic. The Oliviers gave the baby a Jacobean drinking mug and Coward had brought a silver cocktail shaker with the inscription:

Because, my Godson dear, I rather
Think you'll turn out like your father.

On 6 June 1944, D-Day itself, *The Way Ahead* was released in London to a chorus of rave reviews from the British critics, Monty 'blew the whistle' at last, and Operation Overlord – the invasion of Europe – began. Before dawn a huge armada headed across the English Channel towards France and the first of 156,000 British, American and Canadian troops landed on five beaches in Normandy. To deliver them there went 2000 ships, 10,000 planes, more than 4000 landing craft and hundreds of tanks. The fighting was fierce and bloody, especially on Omaha Beach, but by the end of the day the Allies had established a bridgehead that marked the beginning of the end of the war at last even though the Germans were to resist for eleven more months.

In *The Moon's a Balloon* Niv said he joined the invasion a few days later: 'I lied to Primmie about leaving after breakfast and at dawn, when she had finally fallen asleep, I slipped out of bed, dressed, looked down at her with the little boy asleep in his cot beside her, and tiptoed out of the house.' He said that he boarded a Liberty ship, the *Empire Battleaxe*, at Southampton, and was landed under fire on Omaha Beach, 'fumble-fingered with fear' as he put it in *Bring on the Empty Horses*, and for weeks, he said, he and his comrades were shelled by the Germans as the Allies pushed inland and vicious battles raged around Cherbourg and Caen. 'Come on, chaps,' he yelled at some soldiers during yet another bombardment. 'It's all right for you. I'll have to do all this again later with Errol Flynn!' The London *Evening News*, however, told a different story a few weeks later when it reported on 18 July 1944 that Niv had in fact landed in Normandy, probably by aeroplane, along with Franklyn Engelmann of the BBC, 'to investigate the BBC programme for the invading forces – what the troops thought of it, what reception was like, whether it could be improved in any way – and that both men were already back in London. During the next few months, as the Allied armies thrust the Germans back, crossed the Seine, liberated Paris, Brussels and Antwerp, and pressed on towards the German border, Niv nipped back and forth to England time and again by plane, almost like a commuter.

At the end of July Goldwyn wrote: 'I can't tell you how anxious I am to have you come back here, as we all have great admiration for you ... I want you to know that we are still loyal to you, and love you.' It is possible that he also sent him some money because Niv wrote to thank him for his 'wonderfully generous gift'. In August Niv escaped back to England again, had lunch with Noël Coward and Fred Astaire, and spent a weekend with the Astors at Cliveden, and in September, back in France and following in the wake of the army to Paris, he received another affectionate letter from Goldwyn that said, 'You have served your country well, and I will always be proud of the way you acted when war broke out. I know that it will always give you great satisfaction to look back on your action. Your child will be proud of you, and your friends are proud of you. A great welcome is in store for you when you get back here, and I shall be at the head of the line.'

In northern France, Niv told his friend David Bolton many years later, some of his soldiers found a building that stank so much they assumed it must be full of dead bodies and blew it up rather than have to bury a lot of rotting corpses, only to discover that the place was a Camembert cheese factory.

In Paris, despite his love for Primmie, Niv began an affair with the leading French film star Yvette Le Bon, I was told by Martine Fields, who was then an eighteen-year-old French girl and was picked up by Niv in a Paris nightclub in September 1944. 'We nice, pretty-pretty young girls of good family were part of something called the Rainbow Corner, where our object was to take out Allied officers,' she said, 'and one day I was assigned to take out a boring Canadian and we went to the '44, a very nice officers' nightclub. It was about ten o'clock at night and the Canadian went to the men's room and somebody came to my table and said "come on, let's get out of here" and it was David Niven. I knew immediately who he was. I was a very, very proper young girl and I'm still astonished that I went with him but he was very attractive and very charming. We went to another nightclub, and we went out several times together after that, and he would take me for lunch or a drink at the Ritz, but he wasn't trying to seduce me and he never tried anything. He was a perfect gentleman. It wasn't even a flirtation: it was a charming friendship.'

There were, however, times when Niv was in real danger. Major Hugh Carey of the 104th Division of the US First Army, who was later Governor of New York from 1975 to 1982, bumped into him at Orly airport and hitched a lift with him to Brussels in a tiny plane that had to be flown over enemy territory by a pilot who 'was a kid who didn't even shave yet', Governor Carey told me. 'Niven said he was on an undercover mission of liaison between Montgomery, Eisenhower and the First Army, and was arranging a face-to-face meeting because there was great disagreement and Montgomery wanted to encircle the Germans and needed more troops. The flight took one and a half hours. He was a real soldier.' Niv also had to try to smoothe over regular rows between Monty and American General Patton that became so personal that when Patton was finally the first to cross the Rhine the following March he telephoned General Bradley and said, 'I want the world to know that the Third Army made it across before Monty.' Niv's job as a peacemaker was not an enviable one.

In Belgium he was wounded when his jeep was blown up and he suffered a whiplash injury to his neck, a damaged right foot, a broken shoulder, and was left with lifelong pain in his lower back that had to be treated for many years by osteopaths in Britain and America. Sometimes his back would become locked if he bent the wrong way, and in later years he had to wear a brace for skiing, and the pain could be so bad that he would have to take to his bed for days at a time. Years later Niv told his daughter Fiona that the explosion had killed 'a lot of his friends' but he made no mention of it in *The Moon's a Balloon* and was soon back in action in November, and even enjoying a spot of duck shooting and wild boar hunting near Bruges, where Roger Moore reported that Niv had a typically Nivenesque adventure. 'He said that he and some friends were ten miles from Bruges and Bruges had fallen,' Moore told me, 'and they decided to go into the town because he remembered there was a rather good restaurant by a canal. The owner of this restaurant was so honoured that he got out his Book of Honour and opened some wonderful vintage wine that he'd kept away from the evil Boche, and then, half-pissed, they got into their jeep on their way back to brigade HQ and were stopped on the road by a Canadian military police patrol who said, "Where have you come from?" They said Bruges. "But Bruges is in German hands."

' "Oh no," said Niv. "It fell two days ago."

' "Well, they retook it!" said the MP.'

In December, while the Battle of the Bulge was raging in Belgium, Niv was back again on leave in England, where Primmie and David had left Flaxford because Mrs Ames wanted the house back and were now living in a lovely rented fifteenth-century cottage, Wheat Butts, at Eton Wick, near Windsor. Flaxford had obviously seen some wild action during parties while they had been living there. 'When they left there was an enormous hole in the carpet in the middle of the sitting room,' Mrs Ames told me, 'and we decided that he'd been practising his dancing steps! I was so thrilled to get the house back that I didn't ask them to replace the carpet. Otherwise they left the house in an excellent condition and they'd kept up the garden.'

Niv spent Christmas with Primmie, the baby and the Trees at Ditchley Park, but despite all his leaves, privileges and comparatively relaxed lifestyle, the war had scarred him. 'Once this thing is over and I have been demobilized,' he wrote to Nigel Bruce in November, 'I hope I shall never have to mention it again . . . I have seen too much misery, horror and suffering ever to want to brag about being even a small part of it all.' He was bitter about having wasted five of the best years of his life while other 'young and healthy men' had evaded their duty. 'They may have made themselves famous and wealthy during the last few years,' he told Bruce, 'but their insides will still be rotten at the end of it. We pity them. I met one the other day in London, an English actor who took out American citizenship papers in 1940 to avoid the war over here. He was now in the uniform of one of Uncle Sam's GIs. I laughed a lot.'

In January he returned to Paris and headed into Germany, where he found among the effects of a German SS Battalion Commander in Stolberg a book containing photographs of beaches in Britain that were said to be just right for a German invasion, including a beach at Bembridge. He posted it to the secretary of the Bembridge Sailing Club with a note saying, 'The enclosed might amuse you and the members . . . It made me quite homesick.' In March he returned to England on leave, Primmie became pregnant again, and back in Germany he crossed the Rhine at Wesel and drove on to Munster, Hanover and Osnabrück. The end of the war was only days away. On 30 April Hitler shot himself in his underground bunker in Berlin as the Allies closed in remorselessly on all sides, and in the first few days of May Niv swept on through Bremen, Nienburg, Hamburg and Liebenau before Germany surrendered on 8 May and the war was over at last after six terrible years.

His main emotion was one not of triumph but exhausted relief. He had survived and so had his closest loved ones. But there was a residue of anger too. 'I didn't only hate the Nazis,' he told Margaret Hinxman of the *Daily Mail* in 1979. 'I hated Neville Chamberlain and his lot because they and Hitler had robbed me of six years of my life and many of my dearest friends.' On a country road near Brunswick he came across an unarmed German general who was trying to make his way home disguised as a farmer. He had almost made it and had just one more kilometre to go. 'I had never seen such utter weariness, such blank despair on a human face before,' Niv wrote in *The Moon's a Balloon*, and he could not bring himself to take him prisoner and consign him to months of captivity and interrogation. He let him go.

It was time for him, too, to go home.

Seven

The Widower and the Model
1945–1949

Niv returned from Germany on 31 May 1945, whisked Primmie and two-year-old David off for an idyllic holiday in Cornwall at the Ferryboat Inn at Frenchman's Creek, and was hugely relieved when Goldwyn offered him a generous new five-year, $3000-a-week contract and told him that he wanted him to star immediately in *A Matter of Life and Death*, which was about to be shot in England by Michael Powell and Emeric Pressburger. The Rank Organisation wanted him to stay in England and make films at their Pinewood studios, but he hankered after Hollywood, accepted Goldwyn's offer, and wrote to say that 'so long as I am in your employment you will have my complete loyalty in all things and that I shall bend every effort to give you full value for your money and I hope you will never regret suggesting our new association together. I know that the last six years have changed me a great deal. I have had a fairly stormy passage at many points and none of it has been fun [*but*] I have been terribly lucky and if I seem to have lost a bit of the carefree attitude that I had towards life before 1939 I hope I shall make up for it by having been up to my eyebrows in worldly experience.' He added, 'For the past six years I have dreamed of nothing else but getting back to Hollywood ... Everybody knows that you are the greatest producer in the business [*and*] it will be grand to get back again.'

Churchill called a general election for 5 July and was devastated to lose to the Labour Party in a political earthquake that gave Labour 393 seats against the Conservatives' 213. Even Niv voted Labour and against Churchill, much as he greatly admired the man himself, because like millions of others he believed that Britain needed a change of political philosophy and maybe a stiff dose of socialism. 'He didn't have strong political views and he said it was the only time he ever voted,' his son Jamie told me. 'Later he regretted voting Labour: they went after him for back taxes.'

Niv was incensed that the British taxman should be hounding him to pay back taxes for the years he had worked in Hollywood. The Revenue claimed that because he had returned to England in 1939 he had become a British resident again and so was liable to pay tax for the years he had been away, back as far as 1934. The fact that he had returned only to fight for his country left them unmoved. They demanded several thousand pounds, gave him three years to pay and he swore he would never live in Britain again.

In the meantime he and Primmie made the most of that English summer, enjoying parties with their actor friends and neighbours, especially at nearby Notley Abbey with Laurence Olivier and Vivien Leigh, where they always played after-dinner games in the library, especially word games, paper-and-pencil games, charades and a game similar to 'Give Us a Clue'. David loved playing games and was soon badgering his guests too to join in when they came to his house. He was still, however, infected by a deep bitterness against actors such as Rex Harrison and James Mason whom he accused of cowardice because they had dodged their duty to fight for their country. 'I have come out of the war with one or two complexes,' he wrote to Goldwyn.

> The chief one is an overpowering distaste for a few actors who have, in this country at any rate, gone to every length to keep themselves out of the Armed Forces and have had a glorious time making themselves wealthy and well known while the rest of us have been sweating it out. I just hope I shall never be asked to work with any of them because I am afraid that for many years to come I would find it impossible. Two of them – Rex Harrison and James Mason – are headed for Hollywood in the very near future; it is a shame that they should be brought over when there are so many much better actors who have not been heard of for obvious reasons during the past six years, but I suppose while war brings out the best in most people it is bound to bring out the worst in a few.

In August the United States dropped atomic bombs on the Japanese cities of Hiroshima and Nagasaki, and the war in the Far East was over at last. That Victory over Japan Day, 14 August, Niv celebrated by playing at the Berkshire Golf Club with three legendary RAF fighter pilots: Max Aitken, Laddie Lucas and Douglas Bader, who played off a handicap of 8 even though he had no legs. The next day Niv was given release leave to make *A Matter of Life and Death* and presented with the customary worsted army demob suit, hat, tie, shoes and two shirts, 'poplin, with collars'. In due course he was awarded his four service medals, none of which he bothered to collect, and in November General Ray Barker presented him with an American decoration, the fourth-class medal of the Legion of Merit, for his liaison work. Niv was out of uniform at last though his name remained on the list of British army reserves for another nine years until he was finally freed of any military obligation in 1954 and granted the honorary rank of lieutenant-colonel. He had done his duty to the utmost.

At the end of August he signed his new contract with Goldwyn, who even gave him a generous indemnity promising that he would pay any tax the British Inland Revenue might levy on Niv's earnings, and wrote to ask which of his friends David would like him and Frances to invite to a welcome home party when he returned to Hollywood. 'You both know my tastes by now,' replied Niv, 'blondes, brunettes, red-heads – anything that moves and talks with a female voice!'

He began shooting *A Matter of Life and Death* at Denham Studios, in Devon and on Lundy Island. The film is a weird, surrealistic fantasy about the afterlife but was made with such passion that it has become a classic and a cult picture. Some consider it the best film David ever made and it is certainly memorably bold and powerful. He played a doomed RAF bomber pilot, Peter Carter, whose burning plane is about to crash on the English coast but who cannot bail out because his parachute has been shot to ribbons. As his aircraft loses height he speaks with brisk courage on his radio to a young American woman operator, June – played by Kim Hunter – who falls in love with his bravery and panache. The plane crashes and Carter is rushed away to have brain surgery. He should be dead, and maybe he is, but when an angel comes to claim him Carter demands to be allowed to live because he has kindled real love in June's heart and surely love should conquer death. Most of the rest of the film depicts a court case in heaven as to whether he should be allowed to live, and against all expectations the result is an extraordinary movie, gripping and fresh as well as touching. Most of the cast are excellent – Marius Goring as the angel, Raymond Massey as the anti-British American prosecutor, Robert Coote as Carter's dead radio engineer – and among the dead in heaven's arrivals hall is a Flying Officer Trubshawe.

During filming 'David had so many stories that were terribly funny that we began to think he was making them up', Kim Hunter told the BBC for its 2003 television documentary *Living Famously: David Niven*. 'The rest of the cast used to joke about it.' Niv had high hopes for the film, which took two months to shoot, was released in Britain amazingly quickly, in November, and was chosen to be the first Royal Command Film Performance, much to the fury of most of the British critics, who were almost unanimously condescending, though the *Daily Telegraph* said quite rightly that 'David Niven has done nothing quite so good as his airman trembling on the brink of a nervous breakdown without ever lapsing into hysteria'. In America, where it was released under the title *Stairway to Heaven*, the reviewers were much kinder: the *New York Post* said that it was one of the three or four best films of the year and according to the *Journal American* it was 'beautifully written, beautifully acted, beautifully executed'. The film's director, Michael Powell, was delighted by Niv's performance. 'I had always admired his work,' he said. 'He seemed so often so much better than the material which he was in. I thought he would be marvellous as Peter Carter, because despite all that surface gallantry there is a sense of underlying strain which is only really perceived by the keen onlooker. It's what always gives his performances that extra dimension of reality. Whatever you think about the film now, I think *he* was quite exceptional.'

While making the film Niv became good friends with the film critic Tom Hutchinson, who was writing for *Picturegoer* magazine. 'Whenever he was in London after that we'd meet and have a drink and he was a great gossip – he loved gossip – and I remember some very bitchy stories that he told about Darryl Zanuck, like the one about how his teeth protruded so much that he could eat an apple through a tennis racket!'

David and Primmie, whose parents had now divorced, spent the last few days of her pregnancy staying in Mayfair with her father at 8 Farm Street, just off Berkeley Square, and a week before *A Matter of Life and Death* opened in Britain she gave birth in London to their second son on 6 November. They named him James Graham – he was always to be known as Jamie – and hired a thirty-two-year-old nanny, Beryl Rogers, who had until the previous month been an army private on an anti-aircraft gun-site in Belgium. 'David was a wonderful man to work for,' I was told in 2002 by eighty-eight-year-old Miss Rogers, who was known to the Nivens as Pinkie because of her pink nanny's uniform. 'He was very nice, always a gentleman, and Primmie was very pretty, very posh, and they adored each other. They held hands and kissed a lot.'

More than 2 million American and Canadian soldiers were trying to return home, every ship sailing to North America was packed, and Niv could find no berths for Primmie, Pinkie and the boys until April, but thanks to General Barker's influence he managed to wangle a single ticket for himself to New York on the *Queen Mary* in the second week of December. Before he left London he threw a farewell party at Claridge's for 200 people, from every stratum of society, who he felt had been especially nice to him and Primmie over the previous six years – generals, titled nobs, actors, nurses, taxi drivers – and he showed a rare streak of ruthlessness when he stood at the door and personally turned gatecrashers away. 'Go away,' he said to one, 'you've never been nice to me in your life.'

He sailed for New York on 10 December, leaving his little family in Farm Street until they could follow him four months later. The ship was jammed with 15,000 soldiers, but Niv was euphoric: he was going back to sunny Hollywood again, away from mean little England with its rationing, low grey drizzle and thin-lipped tax inspectors. In New York he was fêted as a hero at a big cocktail party at his old haunt the 21, and Bill Mooring reported in *Picturegoer* that 'the American Press is all steamed up about his return because, truth is, the American public holds him in higher esteem than any other British actor (with the possible exception of Ronnie Colman) who ever came to Hollywood'. He had not been forgotten. His fears that he might already have been superseded by younger actors were unfounded.

He took a sleeper train across the continent to California, arriving in Pasadena two days before Christmas, the day that Doug Fairbanks also arrived back from the war, and was greeted at Goldwyn's studio by a huge banner that said 'WELCOME HOME, DAVID!' and a lunch for the Press and hundreds of Goldwyn's employees where Goldwyn, Hedda Hopper and others made speeches extolling his courage and character. In his own speech he explained why he was never going to talk about the war. On his way through Belgium the previous year he had found the grave of the son of some American friends who had asked him to look for it. 'It was in the middle of 27,000 others,' he said, 'and I said to myself "here, Niven, are 27,000 reasons why you should keep your mouth shut".'

He was due to attend a stag party that night for a hundred men that Eddie Goulding had arranged for him at Romanoff's nightclub, but during the lunch he felt so ill that he took to his bed with a temperature of 104 degrees and bronchial pneumonia. The dinner went ahead, attended by many of Hollywood's moguls as well as most of his friends – Cooper, Fairbanks, Flynn, Gable, Tyrone Power – and Goulding arranged for a telephone link to his bedside and an amplifier so that Niv could hear all the speeches and listen to the Scottish pipe band. After Christmas he convalesced at Goulding's home at Palm Springs and lived for a few weeks in the Fairbanks' beach house while he looked for somewhere to buy.

Goldwyn decided that the best way to rebuild his career would be to yoke him in his next few films to some big female stars – to tie him to their apron strings, as Niv put it in a disillusioned letter a few months later – and for the first, *A Perfect Marriage*, he was cast with his old chum Loretta Young in a rubbishy movie, about a couple suffering from a ten-year itch and contemplating divorce, that Niv himself called 'a stinker'.

Niv was a stinker himself when it came to his own perfect marriage. His infidelity was constant and compulsive, even though he loved Primmie so much. 'It was innate in him,' I was told by Patricia Medina, who was by now unhappily married to Richard Greene. 'Before she arrived in Hollywood Niv was quite busy with the ladies! He wasn't anybody's angel. He would have been a Romeo whoever he was married to. It was just in him to be unfaithful.' When not in pursuit of crumpet he went after fish with Clark Gable and played a lot of golf, once with Douglas Bader, who liked to put an opponent off his stroke at critical moments by knocking his pipe against his artificial leg. Less fun was Errol Flynn, who was now surrounded by hangers-on and drinking so much vodka that he was starting the day with huge slugs at 7 a.m. even when he was working.

During the eight weeks of filming *A Perfect Marriage* he found the home that Primmie had dreamed of, the first he ever owned: the Pink House in North Amalfi Drive, a rambling old building on a hillside high above Sunset Boulevard in a quiet, stylish, leafy suburb at Pacific Pallisades, next door to the Fairbankses, that he was able to buy thanks to the generosity of Goldwyn, who lent him enough for the deposit. It had been built forty years previously by Vicki Baum, the author of *Grand Hotel*, and had everything that Primmie wanted: plenty of scope for improvement, a big garden and a view of the mountains as well as the sea. Even its colour was the same pink as that of her childhood home in England, Cold Blow, and David paid much less than he expected because the basement was three feet deep in water. Meanwhile, as he waited for Primmie to arrive from England and start doing the place up, he rented a big Spanish house nearby in Beverly Hills at 1721 Chevy Chase Drive.

At the end of March Primmie, Pinkie and the boys arrived in Portland, Maine, on an old freighter after a dreadful transatlantic crossing that took eighteen days instead of seven. Primmie fell in love instantly with California and the house, which she could hardly wait to refurbish and furnish. 'She spent a lot of time with the boys,' said Pinkie Rogers. 'She was a very good mother but didn't spoil them, and David was a great father. The children used to shout with glee when he came home.' The Nivens employed two other staff at the rented house: a woman housekeeper and a male gardener who was also responsible for Niv's clothes. 'They went out a lot,' said Pinkie, 'and I met a lot of film stars.'

In April Goldwyn lent Niv to Universal Pictures to make his second movie with Ginger Rogers, *Magnificent Doll*, and did such a good deal – he was paid $100,000 for just six weeks of David's time – that he voluntarily gave him a bonus of several thousand dollars. David was grateful but beginning to feel twitchy because once again he was being lent to another studio instead of making a film for Goldwyn himself. 'Please remember that I shall not be really happy till I start work at my "home" studio!!' he wrote to Goldwyn. He was right to be reluctant to play the part: *Magnificent Doll* was historical garbage in which he played the traitorous nineteenth-century American Vice-President Aaron Burr and Ginger Rogers his lover Dolly Payne. Niv later described the picture with a shudder as 'gibberish' and 'a stinker', but he needed the money.

Until he started work on *Magnificent Doll* at the end of April he and Primmie enjoyed a hectic social life. He bought a big black Packard car off Laurence Olivier and they were invited constantly to parties and dinners where the guests played games or charades afterwards. Niv loved taking her to all his favourite places and showing her off to his famous friends and she was quickly accepted by them. 'Primmie was unique, quite lovely,' said Pat Medina, 'and she said she'd never been happier in her life.' Phyllis Astaire took her under her wing and showed her around town, and she was welcomed by the Goldwyns, Colmans, Fairbankses and Charles Boyers – even Lilli Palmer and Rex Harrison, who described Niv at this time in his book *A Damned Serious Business* as 'a lovely man, very amusing, and great fun to be with' whom he saw 'a lot', which seems odd since it was only nine months since David had told Goldwyn how much he disliked and despised Harrison, and how he would never be able to work with him. Perhaps Niv's natural good manners overcame his revulsion, for Harrison was one of a small group who went with Niv, Primmie, Gable, Nigel Bruce and Ida Lupino to Monterey and Pebble Beach in mid-May for a week of golf and fishing while Pinkie looked after the children in Beverly Hills. While they were away Primmie wrote to her father to say that she had never dreamed that she could ever be so happy.

They returned to Hollywood on Sunday, 19 May for a party at Tyrone and Annabella Power's house. Many of Niv's friends were there – Bob Coote, Pat Medina, Richard Greene, Lilli Palmer, Rex Harrison yet again – and Niv wrote in *The Moon's a Balloon*: 'as I looked around at them and at Primmie's radiant face, I wondered how it was possible for one man to have so much.' It was a lovely, warm evening and they enjoyed a barbecue by the pool and went indoors afterwards to play a new game that Cesar Romero had played recently at another party, the children's hide-and-seek game Sardines, which was played in the dark. The lights were switched off and 'I was hiding upstairs with Ty Power,' Pat Medina told me, 'when we heard a thud. Ty rushed to put the lights on and we found that Primmie had mistaken the door to the powder room or closet and had fallen down all the stone steps into the cellar.' She had fallen twenty feet, head first, and was lying unconscious on the stone floor at the bottom.

Romero and Oleg Cassini carried her up to the living room where they laid her on the carpet, Lilli Palmer cradled her battered head and Annabella Power dabbed her forehead with icy water. A doctor was called, and while they waited Primmie opened her eyes and murmured, 'I feel so strange. Even when I had babies I never felt so . . .' She closed her eyes. 'We'll never be invited again,' she said. The doctor arrived, reported that she was badly concussed but would be fine after a few days, and he and Niv took her in an ambulance to St John's Hospital in Santa Monica, where more doctors assured him that there was nothing to worry about and told him to go home and relax. He returned at six o'clock the next morning and although she was still unconscious and very pale he was told yet again that she would be fine after a few days' rest. He went to work on *Magnificent Doll* and returned that evening to the hospital, where the doctors told him once again that she would soon recover. He sat beside her bed for a long time, holding her hand, gazing at the face he loved so much, praying for her recovery, and suddenly she opened her eyes, smiled and weakly squeezed his hand. Delighted that she had come round at last, he returned home to Pinkie and the boys, but at eleven o'clock there was a call from the hospital: she had developed a clot on the brain and they would have to operate. Bob Coote accompanied him back to the hospital and they waited for two hours while the operation went ahead, but Primmie never recovered. She died of a fractured skull and brain lacerations. She was only twenty-eight and had been in California for just six weeks.

It was 2 a.m. and the world was suddenly impenetrably dark. His beloved Primmie was dead. He wandered the streets in a daze. In the early hours of the morning, said Pat Medina, 'he came running up our drive crying and screaming. I don't for a second think that he ever recovered from that.' He telephoned her parents in England and Coote took him to the Colmans, who insisted that he should stay with them for several days while Phyllis Astaire took charge of Pinkie, David Jr, who was three and a half, and Jamie, who was six months old. He never returned to the house in Chevy Chase Drive.

The Los Angeles police said that there was no need of an inquest because 'we are satisfied no one was to blame. There had been very little drinking, and we understand that Mrs Niven herself had not had any alcohol.' Primmie was cremated and David flew back to England with her ashes, which he, her parents, her brother and his wife buried just to the left of the entrance to the graveyard of the church in Huish where they had married less than six years previously. Her ashes lie opposite a farmyard under a badly mottled slab of cement that reads barely legibly: 'Here lies Primula, loved wife of David Niven, died at Los Angeles 21st May 1946, aged 28.'

Niv, incoherent with grief, flew back immediately to Los Angeles for a memorial service on 29 May, and another was held the same day in London at the Grosvenor Chapel in South Audley Street, where Grizel, Joyce and her husband were among the mourners and the list of the others read like an extract from *Debrett's Peerage* and included two dukes and duchesses, a marchioness, two earls, a countess, a viscountess, six knights, and twelve titled ladies.

Perhaps Primmie had a premonition that she did not have long to live because on 5 March, just a few days before she had sailed for America, she had made a will leaving everything to David: just £381 19s 9d, the equivalent of little more than £9000 in 2003.

David was utterly devastated by Primmie's death. Grizel, Andrew Rollo, and every one of Niv's friends told me that he never got over it and that the tragedy haunted him until his own death thirty-seven years later. 'He thought he would have been happier if she had lived,' Grizel said, and Jamie said, 'It never went away. He didn't talk about my mother very much, but lots of people wrote to him after she died and he kept their letters in a shoe box in his office where he could go and look at them if he wanted to.' Roddy Mann said that even twenty and thirty years later 'it came up again and again when we'd had a few jars. He'd say how much he'd loved her and how cruel it was, and he was never happy again.'

'He was so sad after she died,' said Pinkie. 'He cried a lot, but never in front of me, and he couldn't bear to be near the Pink House, so I didn't see much of him.' The boys could not, of course, understand but little David must have picked up the atmosphere of misery and wondered where his mother was. 'He loved her but he never cried or said "where's Mummy?"' said Pinkie. One evening he suddenly asked his father if Mummy had gone to heaven. 'Yes,' said Niv. The little boy looked up at a twinkling star. 'I can see Mummy's eye,' he said.

Niv heard that Ann Todd was in New York and although she was married to Nigel Tangye he called her and asked her to fly out to Los Angeles to be with him for a couple of weeks. 'He became very bitter against life and fate,' she said, 'and he was in a very, very bad state.' He moved in with the Fairbankses for several weeks and it was Mary Lee Fairbanks who answered all the letters of condolence because he could not bring himself to do it. 'He was terribly distressed,' said Fairbanks, 'and remained so for a very, very long time.' For decades Niv could not bring himself to tell his sons where their mother's ashes were buried and let them think that her grave was in California until Jamie went to his aunt's funeral at Huish and was startled to discover his mother's grave there.

Work helped a little, even though *Magnificent Doll* was such a dreadful movie. Clark Gable was a rock, having gone through similar misery after Carole Lombard's death. Fred Astaire took him golfing, and the despised Rex Harrison gave him a Boxer puppy called Phantom and visited him at weekends. Phyllis Astaire and Lilli Palmer tried to cheer up the boys by painting Mickey Mouse and Dumbo the elephant on their nursery walls, and Joan Crawford took them and Pinkie in for a while before they moved to Ronnie Colman's ranch up the coast at Montecito until the Pink House was ready for them. Niv 'had the door to the cellar at the Pink House permanently locked and he would never let anybody go down there', said Pat Medina, and although it seems surprising that he did not sell the house immediately, it had no insupportable memories for him since Primmie had never lived there and maybe it comforted him a little to be somewhere that she had loved so much. Work began on it and when one room and the kitchen were finished he moved in, but when the container full of furniture and china that Primmie had chosen so carefully arrived from England almost everything had been smashed –

and then somebody stole a little case containing a few of her most precious possessions: childhood mementoes, bits of jewellery, photographs, the letters he had written to her during the war. 'That night I nearly gave up,' he said.

Eventually he, Pinkie and the boys moved into the house and Bob Coote into the cottage. 'The house wasn't very big, so the boys slept with me,' said Pinkie, 'but there was a lovely pool, beautiful gardens, and a view across the sea. And everything was pink – the house *and* me!' To try to dull the awful pain of being a widower Niv rose early, worked late and the boys saw little of him. He dreaded going home to their eager, trusting little faces and would walk on the beach in the dark for hours, tormented by loss and memories, hoping that the pounding Pacific surf might wash them away, and he lay awake sleepless for much of the nights. 'I looked after the children for two years after she died,' Pinkie told me. 'They were lovely boys. Young David was full of fun and tried to be naughty, but I was strict and made him behave and have table manners. Jamie was my baby, my favourite. They were absolutely different: David was inclined to know it all whereas Jamie was more a baby and a bit clingy.'

Niv had another reason for not coming home. 'He said that he had an incredible, peculiar way of grieving for her,' Tom Hutchinson told me. 'He said that he had an erection all the time and couldn't be satisfied, and it became quite difficult to walk around. "I was insatiable," he told me. "No woman was safe. It was no disrespect or lack of love for Primmie – I was just trying to get something out of my system that was better out than in. I believe I was very ill in a sexual kind of way." And because he was David Niven he could have any woman he wanted. He went to one party where he drank a huge amount and woke up the next morning with a terrible hangover and in bed with a girl: Marilyn Monroe!' Monroe was still an unknown twenty-year-old, recently divorced from her first husband, James Dougherty, and about to make her first film, *Dangerous Years*. 'Niven became quite worried about his condition,' said Hutchinson, 'and went to see a psychiatrist who said he'd get over it.'

He took a long time to get over it. 'He became a womaniser out of desperation,' Lauren Bacall told me. 'He had lots of women. He was in such a state.' Pat Medina became so appalled by his compulsive shagging that she took him for a long walk on the beach near her house at Malibu and gave him a lecture about all 'the prominent young starlets that he was running around with'. She said, 'It's time I talked to you. You're behaving very badly. What are you doing? Everybody's talking about it.' Niv replied, 'I'm anaesthetising myself through certain parts of my anatomy.' One of his lovers was the deliciously merry, light-hearted, twenty-three-year-old Ava Gardner, who had just emerged from an affair with Howard Hughes, and Niv became such a sexual reprobate that he had a one-way mirror installed between the men's and women's changing rooms in the swimming pool cabin at the Pink House. 'You could see through into the ladies' changing room,' chuckled John Mills, 'so the men's changing room was always crowded!'

'When a man is deeply unhappy,' Niv wrote in *The Moon's a Balloon*,

> he brings out the very gentlest instincts in the very nicest women. They want to wrap him up, take him home and look after him. They give all of themselves but he, in turn, can give in only one direction and, inoculated by his unhappiness, rides roughshod far and wide. This happened to me in full measure and I also believe at the same time I went a little mad. I began to resent and avoid the married friends who had showered me with kindness and protection when I had so badly needed it. Perhaps I was jealous of their happiness. Perhaps I was ashamed that they had seen me at my weakest and most vulnerable. This phase lasted several months, and, bewildered and hurt, some wonderful people must have found my coldness most difficult to understand.

Through frenetic sex, hard work and the constant support of those friends whom he did not reject, Niv slowly surfaced from the dark pool of his bottomless grief. At the end of August Goldwyn lent him out again, this time to United Artists to make *The Other Love*, a sentimental romantic tear jerker with Barbara Stanwyck, who played a brilliant concert pianist who has tuberculosis and is sent to a private sanatorium in the Swiss Alps that is run by a doctor, played by Niv, whom she marries before she dies. The reviewers were incredibly unkind in view of Niv's bereavement – the *New Yorker* remarked with stunning insensitivity that 'Niven has a rather mortuary air' – and when I saw the film I found myself on the brim of tears not because of the movie itself but because of his raw courage in playing a man whose beloved wife is dying, just three months after his own had died. At times during the film he seems about to burst into tears and the final love scene, as his wife lies dying, must have been terrible for him.

Yet Niv could be astonishingly insensitive himself. The editor of the *Daily Express* in London, Arthur Christiansen, asked him to write a chatty occasional column from Hollywood in the form of a letter to Trubshawe, who was now running a pub in Sussex, the Lamb Inn at Hoe, near Battle. The first letter, published on 17 September, was a genial series of harmless plugs for forthcoming films starring old friends such as Cary Grant, Vivien Leigh, Laurence Olivier, Tyrone Power and James Stewart – and even the detested Rex Harrison – but in the second, unbelievably, he reported that 'Hollywood is still playing games after dinner and the one that I enjoy most is known as "the drawing game" ' and then devoted the entire column – about 1300 words – to a dreary account of a recent evening playing the game at the Fairbanks's house with Annabella, Jimmy Stewart, Clark Gable, Jennifer Jones, David Selznick, Lilli Palmer and the despicable coward Rex Harrison. At least he did not recommend Sardines. Very sensibly he was not prepared to be bitchy or indiscreet about his friends and colleagues, so the *Daily Express* 'letters' were dull and when the third included a shameless plug about the despised Rex Harrison's future film plans the paper cancelled the deal.

Goldwyn had made $15,000 a week out of Niv when he lent him out to make *The Other Love* and since he was paying him only $3000 a week he sent him voluntarily what Niv called 'a large number of dollars'. 'You have been extremely generous to me this year and I am deeply grateful,' said Niv in a letter of thanks. 'I have had a horrible year in my private life and it has been a wonderful feeling to know that you have been behind me through all my troubles ... I am really grateful to you for your great kindness ... and hope that in the many more years we shall have together I shall fully justify your faith in me ... I don't want to alarm you, but you have a happy actor on your hands.'

Not for much longer. His next film was one of Goldwyn's own productions, a jolly comedy called *The Bishop's Wife*, in which at first he was cast to play an angel who comes down to earth to help a Protestant bishop and his wife – Cary Grant and Loretta Young – to raise enough money to build a cathedral and save their arid marriage. Niv had told Goldwyn that he thought it was one of the most charming stories he had ever read and that the angel was a marvellous part, but Grant was a bigger box-office star and insisted on playing the better part himself. Niv was furious, even though he was excellent as the bishop; the role forced him actually to act rather than to play himself yet again, and the film was amusing and delightful, a sweet, warm-hearted, touching and old-fashioned piece of charming entertainment and rare proof that he could actually act. And among the bishop's congregation, of course, is a couple called Trubshawe.

Despite its lightness of touch the film was plagued by problems and setbacks. Grant was sulky after Goldwyn complained that he was not sufficiently masculine as the angel. Loretta Young was upset when Goldwyn told her she looked too glamorous for a bishop's wife and kept calling her Laurette Taylor. When told that Laurette Taylor had been dead for months he replied, 'That's funny. I was talking to her only a few moments ago.' After two weeks of shooting Goldwyn hated the early rushes, sacked the director, hired another, scrapped the script, ordered the sets to be completely altered and started all over again at a cost said to be $900,000. After all that it was a picture that had most of the critics sneering, yet when it was released in time for Christmas 1947 the public loved it. It was nominated for an Oscar as the best film of 1947, and in Britain was selected for that year's Royal Command Film Performance, the second time a movie of Niv's had been chosen. It also put him firmly back on the map in America and he was signed up to appear in a series of full-page magazine advertisements extolling the power of General Electric television sets and the joys of Friskies Dog Food. Despite six years away from Hollywood he was once again a star.

The Bishop's Wife was the only movie that the two light-comedy English exiles Grant and Niven made together. 'We got on very well,' Grant told Morley,

> though he'd never talk much about himself or his background. He seemed to be terrified of boring or depressing you, felt he always had to be an entertainer. He was more educated, I think more intelligent, than I was but you felt there was always something being held back. I admired him very much for going back and fighting in the war: that was a wonderful thing to have done. When he came back he seemed in some ways to have changed, but I think that may have been because of that terrible accident to Primmie. He was still distraught about that when we were making *The Bishop's Wife*, and yet there was also still that urge to entertain, to tell stories, not always true stories maybe but marvellous rearrangements of the truth. He was a funny man and a brave man and a good man, and there were never too many of those around here.

One marvellous rearrangement of the truth was when Niv told the *Daily Mirror* in February that he had just bought his body back after having sold it in 1933 to no fewer than four hospitals for £4 each. In truth he had pawned it to just one hospital and it had already been redeemed and returned to him eleven years earlier by Max, who had just emigrated to South Africa with his wife to try his hand at yet another job, this time as a stockbroker near Durban. Perhaps Niv told newspapers these fibs and rehashed stories to generate publicity, but he hardly needed to do so. In March he began an affair that lasted longer and seemed more serious than most of his flings – with Rita Hayworth, whom he called 'the super love goddess', and who was very keen to marry him. She was about to divorce her husband, Orson Welles, after only eighteen months of marriage and when the Press heard about her romance with Niv they reported that they were about to marry. Both issued denials. 'All the blather that's being printed about my marrying or being engaged to Rita Hayworth is utter rubbish,' Niv told the *News of the World* in London. 'I'm furious and unhappy about it. Please refute the story and tell the man who first put it around to confine his activities in the future to writing on walls.' He told another newspaper: 'Rita is a darling and probably the only really sweet girl out here, but neither of us want to marry and she will never become Primmie II: I doubt that anyone could.'

Slowly he started to come to terms with his grief and enjoy the Pink House with Pinkie, the boys and his many friends, but then Goldwyn dropped a grenade into his fragile new life: he lent him to Korda to star in an historical epic, *Bonnie Prince Charlie*, which was to be filmed in Britain in the autumn and would take months to make. Niv was appalled. He had just begun to rebuild his life, his children were settled, and the last thing he wanted was to go all the way back to Britain for several months, especially since his earnings would again become liable for British tax if he were there for so long. He begged Goldwyn not to make him go, but Goldwyn was adamant. Korda had agreed to pay him $15,000 a week for David's services for a minimum of ten weeks, and the same for any further weeks that might be necessary, while Goldwyn was paying David $3000 a week, leaving him with a neat profit of $12,000 a week. David refused to go. Goldwyn immediately put him on suspension, which meant that he paid him nothing at all for several weeks, knowing that now that Niv had fat mortgage payments to make he would not be able to hold out for long. To be fair to Goldwyn, it was Niv himself who had first suggested more than a year previously that he should star in a film about Charles Stuart, the Jacobite Young Pretender to the throne of Britain who raised a Scots army in 1745 to try to overthrow the Hanoverian king. In October 1945 David had written to Goldwyn: 'It is the most colourful and romantic story ever told and I have always ... had my heart set on playing it.' He had even shot a colour test of one of the key scenes in the film and had given it to Goldwyn to see what he looked like in the part, so Goldwyn was entitled to insist that he should play it.

Niv had long wanted to learn how to paint, so while he was suspended he went to an art school run by a Mr Finch. 'There was a dilapidated ballerina who was going to hold this pose for five weeks,' Niv told Michael Parkinson on his TV show in 1981. 'I bought a canvas the size of this wall and I started at nine o'clock and by 11.15 I'd finished. So I said to Mr Finch "have you any suggestions?" and he said "make it smaller and move it to the left".' Many years later Niv was to write a novel that at first he called *Make It Smaller and Move It to the Left*.

Painting pictures was not going to pay his huge bills and he surrendered to Goldwyn with a bad grace, and sulked. Korda agreed even to indemnify David for any extra British tax he might incur, but still he sulked. He rented the Pink House to the English actress Phyllis Calvert, sailed to England with Pinkie and the boys at the end of July, refused to move into the suite at Claridge's Hotel that Korda had reserved for them and checked instead into a country hotel just outside London, at Egham, near Shepperton Studios, where the film was to be shot. '*Bonnie Prince Charlie* was one of those huge florid extravaganzas that reek of disaster from the start,' he wrote in *The Moon's a Balloon*. 'There was never a completed screenplay and never at any time during the eight months we were shooting were the writers more than two days ahead of the actors. We suffered three changes of director with Korda himself, for a time, desperately taking over and at one point I cabled Goldwyn as follows: I HAVE NOW WORKED EVERY DAY FOR FIVE MONTHS ON THIS PICTURE AND NOBODY CAN TELL ME HOW THE STORY ENDS.' In fact the film took only five months to shoot, but in a letter to Goldwyn three months after it began he wrote: 'Chaos is reigning supreme at this studio. I started work with exactly 16 pages [*and*] THE SECOND HALF IS NOT YET WRITTEN.' He pointed out that the first cameraman had been fired when Korda discovered that he had never shot a major picture before, let alone one in Technicolor, so that many scenes had to be filmed again and Niv was alarmed that he might still be shooting in England after 21 January, after which 'somebody is horribly liable for an enormous chunk of taxation payable to the British Government!!'. He added, 'Also please remember that I will have been in every shot, every day, bewigged, becloaked, beswordeded, and bewildered since the first day of the picture, and I am going to have to have a holiday this time, and a proper one, not like the one I had before this picture started. This holiday I would also like to have here in England because I have yet to see most of my friends, although I have been in the country for over three months.'

Goldwyn was unimpressed and made it plain that he thought that Niv was whingeing too much. 'You should be pleased over the fact that when the picture is finished, you will have a picture in which you will be proud to have appeared,' he replied, 'instead of something that was just slapped together regardless of whether the director was right, the script was good enough and so on. I don't have to tell you what Alex has done in the past and I imagine that he is aiming to outdo the past by making this picture one of real greatness. It may not be as pleasant over there as you would like it but I assure you that you are probably having it much more pleasant there than I and other producers are having it back here.' Goldwyn listed his own problems: a new British film tax that had all but destroyed his profits outside America; a twenty per cent collapse in the number of people going to the cinema; rocketing production costs. 'This is really the time when a producer would be not only willing but anxious to swap what used to be his prospects for profit for the nice solid weekly check that some actors have their agents pick up for them every Thursday . . . I would gladly exchange my headaches for your problems right now.' He softened his put-down by ending his letter: 'You are still my favorite actor. Fondly, Sam.'

Unfortunately *Bonnie Prince Charlie* was not a film of 'real greatness'. It cost £1 million to make – about £23 million in modern terms – and turned out to be a monstrous piece of historical hokum that is widely considered to be one of the worst films ever made. It was distinguished only by the crassness of the script, the staginess of the acting, the absurdity of many of the scenes and the ludicrous vision of Niv in a series of coloured wigs – blond, red and yellow – and curiously naked without his moustache. He also wore at various times breeches, stockings, a ponytail tied with a ribbon, a kilt, a sporran, a tartan sash, a velvet jabot, a tricorn hat and, not surprisingly, an uneasy fixed grin. 'Jack,' he asked thirty-seven-year-old Jack Hawkins, who was playing Lord George Murray, 'tell me honestly. Do I look a prick?' 'Yes,' said Hawkins, who looked equally penile with his bouffant prototype Teddy Boy hairstyle and a tartan rug draped over his shoulder. The ultimate delight of this ridiculous movie was the vision of Blind Jamie, a sightless seer staggering and crooning across the blasted heath, played to perfection by John Laurie with enough Highland ham to make even his gloriously over-the-top performance twenty-two years later as Private Frazer in the TV series *Dad's Army* taste like prime beef.

Niv's own chosen highlight from all those months of filming came when he was chasing some redcoats across a glen, tripped, and sank his claymore deep into the leg of one of the enemy extras, Bob Head. 'Cut!' shouted the director, but he was wrong: the leg was false; the original had been lost during the war at the real Battle of El Alamein. The only consolation of the entire movie was that Jack Hawkins became a close friend and asked Niv to be his first son's godfather. 'They had the same boyish sense of humour and both were great raconteurs,' Doreen Hawkins told me. 'If you got them at a table together nobody else got a word in!'

Several of Niv's friends believe that about now he had a fling with Princess Marina, the widowed, forty-year-old Duchess of Kent who loved actors and had affairs with several, most notably Danny Kaye, Doug Fairbanks Jr and the band leader Edmundo Ros. Some of them also believe that at some time he had an affair with another royal lady, Princess Margaret. 'It's highly possible,' said Leslie Bricusse. 'They were very fond of each other and, like Princess Marina, Margaret put it about.'

Princess Margaret and her mother, the Queen, both attended the Royal Command Film Performance of *The Bishop's Wife* on 25 November at the Odeon Theatre in Leicester Square. 'The audience loved every second of it,' Niv reported to Goldwyn, 'and the Queen and Princess Margaret told me afterwards and at great length how much they had enjoyed it. So once more many congratulations on a great achievement and enormous personal courage in the early stages of the production.'

Goldwyn's affection for David was such that he sent him a remarkably handsome Christmas present: a cheque for $25,000, which in modern terms would be worth about £135,000. 'As you know,' he wrote, 'conditions are worse now than ever before in the business, but nevertheless I feel that you have worked hard and well this past year. So I want to express my feeling concretely instead of just in words.'

Astonishingly it was while Niv was dressed in his Bonnie Prince Charlie get-up and make-up – looking, according to the *Sunday Graphic* critic, about as comfortable as 'a goldfish in a haggis' – that he met and won the heart of the woman who was to become his second wife, Hjördis Tersmeden. A tall, stunningly good-looking twenty-eight-year-old divorced model from Stockholm, with shoulder-length red-gold hair, she was enjoying a few weeks' holiday in England with friends who knew Anthony Kimming, the director of *Bonnie Prince Charlie*, and had been invited onto the set at the beginning of December. She was sitting in Niv's personal canvas chair when he stalked back after yet another late retake on yet another day of chaos and humiliation in front of the cameras, looking absurd in a white wig. 'Get her out of it!' he snapped at a props man.

'Take a look first,' murmured Hawkins, who had been married himself to Doreen, his second wife, for only a few weeks. 'Take a look.'

Niv did, and was instantly besotted. 'The French have the right word – *coup de foudre*,' he wrote in *The Moon's a Balloon*. 'I had never seen anything so beautiful in my life – tall, slim, auburn hair, uptilted nose, lovely mouth and the most enormous grey eyes I had ever seen. It really happened the way it does when written by the worst lady novelists . . . I goggled. I had difficulty swallowing and I had champagne in my knees. Ten days later, we were married.'

Well, not quite: it was six weeks later, but that was still incredibly fast. Hjördis – whose name was pronounced Yer-diss but always incorrectly by Niv and his friends as Yaw-diss – spoke little English but enough to tell him that she designed and modelled clothes, and had her own fashion page in a weekly magazine. She had been born Hjördis Paulina Genberg, had been raised in the extreme north of Sweden at Kiruna, inside the icy Arctic Circle, and had married an immensely rich yacht-owning Swedish businessman, Carl Tersmeden, at the end of the war but had divorced him after eighteen months, though they remained friends. 'David has a wonderful way of making every woman he talks to feel important and attractive,' she wrote in a ghosted autobiographical series in *Woman* magazine in 1964. 'Among his many virtues he is a fabulous listener. In fact he has cultivated it as an art . . . I was charmed, captivated, enslaved by this man. The funny thing was that I didn't really know anything at all about him. I had never actually seen any of his films and had only rather vaguely heard his name.'

He took her to a riverside pub, plied her with Black Velvet, taught her to play darts, pretending to be good at it, 'and, young as I was,' she said, 'I became conscious that he was showing off in front of me, just like a young lad with his first girlfriend. I cannot deny that I loved him for it.' The next day he took her to Buck's for lunch and was 'so sweet, so gay, so charming' that although both were due to spend the weekend with friends they met for dinner on the Monday and every day that week. One afternoon she met five-year-old David and two-year-old Jamie in Niv's dressing room. 'They were sweet,' she told *Woman*. 'We played all sorts of silly games together, dressing up in fancy hats and clothes we found about the set . . . Yet somehow it never really sank into my consciousness that these were David's children. He was the only person in focus for me at that moment.' The following weekend they stayed with a friend of his in the country, sat up until after midnight listening to jazz records, and he told her that he would have to return to Hollywood in a few days. 'And then, terribly awkwardly and terribly shyly, almost off-hand and detached, like the so-typical Briton he is, he said: "I don't want to leave you behind." Then it all came out in a rush. "Darling, will you marry me?" It was exactly eight days from the time we had first met. I said: "Yes, of course," and . . . I was immensely thrilled and excited, . . . never realizing for a moment what I was taking on.'

Sweetly he introduced her to Primmie's father, Bill Rollo – 'David was very fond of Father,' said Andrew Rollo – almost as though he were seeking the approval of Primmie herself. Rollo gave them his blessing and they were married at South Kensington register office (not Chelsea, as he said in *The Moon's a Balloon*) on Wednesday, 14 January 1948. They told several newspapers that they had known each other for six weeks and that it had been after a month, not eight days, that they had decided to marry, and Hjördis told the *Daily Mirror* that she had recently been to the cinema to see *The Bishop's Wife* 'and I thought he was wonderful'. Niv was thirty-seven, Hjördis twenty-eight, and Trubshawe was again the best man, though he had serious doubts about Niv's choice of bride. So did Grizel, who told me: 'I didn't think much of Hjördis.' On the night before the wedding his friend Audrey Pleydell-Bouverie gave a party for them where Trubshawe met Hjördis for the first time and warned her that she was mistaken if she thought that marrying David would give her an immediate career in films. She was furious and he told Morley that she did not speak to him again for fifteen years, but this is not true: a photograph taken two years later shows her smiling happily while he gave her a big, hairy kiss on her forehead. But his instinct was right. 'She thought that she could be Garbo,' Lauren Bacall told Guy Evans of October Films. 'She certainly was not an actress, but I think she thought that maybe something wonderful would happen to her and she'd have a movie career. Well of course that was never going to happen.'

By now Niv was having second thoughts himself. 'Tomorrow Trubshawe,' he said, 'I am going to get married again, thereby quite possibly making the greatest mistake of my life.' His words were horribly prophetic. 'David was now going through an agony of indecision,' Trubshawe told Morley. 'I was with him late that night when he suddenly decided it had all been too fast and that he was making the most terrible mistake [*and*] it was all going to be a disaster. So I told him that it still wasn't too late, the wedding could still be called off; but he said no, he'd started

Niv as the brave, boozy, happy-go-lucky Lieutenant Scott in the 1938 film that made him a star after just four years in Hollywood, *The Dawn Patrol*, a sad but stirring anti-war movie about the Royal Flying Corps during the First World War in which he co-starred with Errol Flynn (right).

Below: Niv in 1939 in *Raffles*, the film about a stylish English gentleman thief that took him to the brink of a glittering Hollywood career just as Hitler marched into Poland and Niven returned to Britain to join the army.

Niv (*right*) back in England and the army in 1940, reunited with his joky old Highland Light Infantry chum Trubshawe, and 'playing the bagpipes.'

Below: Major David Niven (second from the left) and the Duke of Kent inspecting Niven's Phantom Reconnaissance Regiment squadron in 1942.

David with his beloved first wife, Primula ('Primmie') Rollo, whom he married in 1940 a couple of weeks after meeting her.

Primmie, Niv and their sons David (right, aged three) and Jamie at Jamie's christening in December 1945.

Primmie and Niv at the Stork Club in New York in 1946. Six weeks later, after a stupid accident during a party game in Hollywood, she was dead.

Niv the widower putting on a brave face for his sons at the pool of their house near Hollywood after Primmie's death in May 1946. He was to mourn her and miss her desperately for the rest of his life.

Niv as the Scottish prince in one of the worst films he ever made, *Bonnie Prince Charlie*, in 1948. 'Do I look a prick?' he asked Jack Hawkins. 'Yes,' said Hawkins. On the left, as the seer Blind Jamie, is John Laurie, later famous as Private Frazer in the classic TV comedy series *Dad's Army*.

David and his glamorous second wife, twenty-eight-year-old Swedish model Hjördis Tersmeden, after their wedding at South Kensington registry office in London on 14 January 1948.

Hjördis and David on honeymoon: a portrait in the society magazine *Sketch* a fortnight after their wedding. Hjördis was often photographed for glossy magazines and appeared on the cover of *Life* three months later.

Niv and Jack Hawkins in yet another ridiculous costume epic, *The Elusive Pimpernel*, in 1949. Niven 'makes his first embarrassed entrance like the dame in some nightmare pantomime,' said *The Times* and Sam Goldwyn told the producer Alexander Korda, 'It's the worst picture I have ever seen in my life.'

Niven with Vera Ellen and Cesar Romero in the 1950 movie *Happy Go Lovely*, in one of the many elegant roles that gave him his smooth Hollywood image. It was Romero who had suggested four years earlier the party game 'Sardines' during which Primmie Niven suffered the accident that killed her.

and he'd go through with it and just see what happened afterwards. As you can imagine, it wasn't the easiest of weddings.'

Niv's sons and friends believe that he married Hjördis on the rebound. 'He didn't want to get involved with the actresses he had affairs with,' Pinkie told me. 'He got too involved with Rita Hayworth and I think he married Hjördis on the rebound from her.' Doreen Hawkins agreed and told me that Bob Coote said that after Primmie's death Niv 'was being so chased by women Hollywood stars, with Rita Hayworth heading the chase, that he was terrified he might have to marry one of them, which was part of the reason he was so attracted to Hjördis'. Robert Wagner told me that the only explanation was that 'Hjördis was a *beautiful* woman, very attractive and fun, and David was alone and had the two boys.' Doug Fairbanks agreed: Niv unmarried, he said, 'was a fish out of water; he was lonesome'. David Jr told me that 'she was really pretty and the sex was probably good' and Jamie told me: 'I can't imagine the *verbal* communication was anything that great. She never learned to speak English that well and she always had a heavy accent, and her ability to speak any language other than Swedish was appalling.' After all the affairs that Niv had had since Primmie's death it does seem odd that he should have married Hjördis so quickly instead of simply having an affair with her. 'From the moment I was an adult until the moment he died I asked him about that,' said Jamie, 'and I never got an answer worth repeating.' Roddy Mann was equally baffled. 'I don't know why he did,' he told me, 'I never could figure it out,' even though Niv told him somewhat unconvincingly for his *Sunday Express* column in 1964: 'I was in love, but I *do* believe in quick proposals. I think you should discover each other's faults as you go along. If you're really in love you'll change. Whereas if you stay single, you won't. And by the time you get around to thinking of marriage you've both got a list as long as your arm of things you hate in each other.'

The boys stayed with Pinkie at the hotel in Egham during the wedding, for which Niv wore a dark suit with a flower in his buttonhole and Hjördis looked radiantly sexy in a brown, two-piece suit, feathered hat, ankle-strap sandals, gold brooch, and lush beaver fur coat with orchids on the lapel, and they were mobbed by fans, reporters, photographers and two TV vans.

It was nearly two weeks since the filming of *Bonnie Prince Charlie* had finished but David was still exhausted, partly because he was suffering from flu and partly because he was fighting yet another battle with the British taxman, who was demanding more back taxes because he had returned to Britain without being out of the country for three years. He told Goldwyn he was going to take a decent holiday, a honeymoon, before returning to Hollywood even though Goldwyn had told him he had to be back by 2 February to make another film. Goldwyn sent a sharp letter making it plain that he felt David was becoming arrogant, demanding and selfish, and needed to be cut down to size. The letter deserves to be quoted almost in full because it shows vividly that just a month after sending David a huge bonus Goldwyn had had enough of his increasingly prima donna attitude and was prepared to threaten him. He said he had already agreed to let Niv have a month off following the end of *Bonnie Prince Charlie* and was not prepared to let him have yet another fortnight:

> For the last two years, ever since your return to pictures, I have done everything possible to try to build you up so that you would enjoy a fine position with the American public. David, don't for a minute think that you have reached the stage where you are so big on the screen that you can afford to disregard your contract and your studio's instructions.
>
> While I am doing everything possible to build you up to the position that I would like to see you reach, you should for your own sake be doing your share instead of trying to throw a monkey wrench into what we are doing. Your agents say you are tired, but you should understand that with conditions being what they are, the fight to keep the picture industry going has got us all pretty well tired out, but we must continue to do our best . . .
>
> I am writing this to you in a spirit of friendly guidance and advice because you know how fond I have always been of you personally. But I tell you frankly that if you want to bitch up your career, the very best way you can do it is to disregard directions which come to you from the studio under your contract. I have seen a lot of actors in this town who thought they were so big that they didn't have to pay any attention to their agreements, and I am sure you probably know several of them who are today very sorry about the price they finally had to pay for acting like that.
>
> I have always tried to be as nice as possible in our relations and I want to continue, but I think you know me well enough to know that if I am pushed around I can be very tough. Let's not get to that stage.
>
> You have an order from the Company to report here not later than Monday, February 2. Get all the rest and recuperation that you can before that date but be sure to be here then.

Niv took the warning and three days after the wedding he, Hjördis, Pinkie and the boys sailed for New York on the *Queen Elizabeth*. But rebellion was festering in his breast because he felt that Goldwyn was exploiting him and mishandling his career by lending him out all the time to make bad films for other producers who paid Goldwyn much more than Goldwyn paid him. With resentment building on both sides, a showdown was fast approaching.

Hjördis was always to claim that it was not until they were aboard the *Queen Elizabeth* at Southampton that Niv told her that David Jr and Jamie were his sons and that she had become a stepmother as well as a wife. 'I woke up to reality,' she told *Woman*, 'when ... the door of the adjoining cabin burst open. There were David and Jamie jumping around excitedly to greet their Daddy – with an unsmiling nanny behind them.' The unsmiling Pinkie, shocked by Niv's sudden remarriage, was soon to go. 'Pinkie was terrific, just like a mother,' David Jr told me, but Doreen Hawkins said, 'one thing Hjördis did was to get rid of Primmie's nanny,' and Pinkie told me herself: 'She didn't have much to do with the boys for three months and left me to look after them, but the boys took to her – David Jr liked her because she let him do what he wanted and spoiled him a bit – and I left after five months because I thought I should get out and let her get on with it, and I became a nanny in San Francisco.' Hjördis told Niv naïvely that she wanted to be the boys' best friend or older sister rather than their stepmother, though they did start to call her Mummy. 'It's not easy for any young girl to marry a widower,' she wrote, 'especially if he is the father of two sons whose mother meant so much to him. David often talked to me about his first wife ... "Primmie was a wonderful girl," David told me. "And so are you, darling. Surely it is not given to many men to be so lucky twice." ' But she admitted: 'I was jealous of David's first wife, but it wasn't anything one could fight. He never said to me that he considered her the perfect wife and mother, but I suspect he thought she was. Compared with her, I felt so inadequate. I couldn't cook, I didn't know anything about children, I wasn't even very interested in dressing myself up smartly and I'm most untidy. I'm sure he couldn't help contrasting her and all her wonderful gifts with me.' As Doreen Hawkins put it, 'The trouble with a dead wife is that it's not like a divorce. You can't compete.'

In Hollywood Hjördis was nervous of meeting Niv's famous friends and never felt that the Pink House – where Bob Coote was still living in the guest cottage – was really hers even though Primmie had never actually lived there. 'I don't think I could have gone there if she had ever lived in it,' she said, and she banished all Primmie's initialled towels and linen to the guest house and was never completely happy there. She and David soon had their first row, over the position of a chair that she wanted to move, and she shouted at him. He left the room quietly and later she found him in the cellar 'sadly sorting out some old books'. For the first month of their marriage, she told the *Daily Mail* in 1960, 'I was terribly sulky and irritable because the excitement of it all had been such a strain that I needed to let off steam and have a really good quarrel. He couldn't understand this and got more and more frightened by my sulks until in the end he went and sat in the cellar, reading' – haunted, maybe, by the memory of Primmie and another cellar. Hjördis, with her dark Scandinavian moods, could not have been less like Primmie and he realised it only too soon. As an ex-military man he was also extremely tidy and was soon irritated by her laziness, sleeping late, demanding breakfast in bed, and her habit of leaving her clothes strewn around and the cap off the toothpaste tube. Even so, 'he always loved Hjördis and treated her wonderfully,' said Doreen Hawkins.

Eventually she began to relax a little and enjoy the shops, the warmth, and the laid-back barefoot lifestyle. Bob Coote gave her the teasing nickname that Niv was to call her for the rest of his life: *Nej*, pronounced Nay, the Swedish for 'no', because she said it all the time. The Astaires befriended her and so did several local Swedes including Greta Garbo and Anita Ekberg. So did Pat Medina, who told me: 'Hjördis was very nice and fun in the early days and we were good friends.' The Nivens took tea with Noël Coward and Deborah Kerr, and became close to forty-eight-year-old Humphrey Bogart and his second wife, twenty-three-year-old Lauren Bacall, whose real name was Betty. Bogey had already made *The Maltese Falcon* and *Casablanca* and in 1945 had married Bacall, who had appeared with him in *To Have and Have Not*, *The Big Sleep* and *Dark Passage*. 'The four of us hit it off immediately,' Betty Bacall told me, 'and Niv became one of the best friends I've ever had and one of the most fun. Their marriage was very happy for the first several years and we always had a great time together. He was marvellous, an irresistible man with an irresistible personality. He, Bogey and I were on the same wavelength, and he was crazy about Bogey. They both loved to laugh and sail – Bogey loved sailing more than anything except me – and there's been nobody even close to the kind of man Niv was, and the *fun* that he was, and the *funniness* that he was. He was hysterically funny and a flirt and you just wanted to be in his company.'

One piece of fun that Niv concocted with Tyrone Power was a wicked practical joke on Rex Harrison, whose reputation as a randy seducer was possibly greater even than his own. Harrison was married to Lilli Palmer but having an affair with Carole Landis and still constantly on the prowl for other women, so Niv and Power hired two actresses from Central Casting to play a mother and daughter and planted them at a Hollywood party where they knew Harrison had been invited. 'Sexy Rexy' was duly mesmerised by the 'daughter' and invited to afternoon tea by the 'mother', but when he arrived the 'mother' had been 'called away' and the 'daughter' was on her own and seemed keen to know him better – but just as they got down to 'afternoon tea' in the living room the 'mother' suddenly returned, caught him with his pants down and threatened angrily to ruin his career and his marriage by telling his wife as well as the prim gossip columnists. As Harrison pleaded with her and hopped about trying to pull his trousers on he saw at the window Niven, Power and several other men roaring with laughter. Years later Niv told the actor John Hurt that 'Harrison had a cock like a chicken's neck – long, thin and red!'

As soon as Hjördis reached Hollywood her film star looks earned a full-page photograph in London's *Sketch* magazine that made her look much more glamorous than Niv himself, and three months later her pensive portrait filled the cover of *Life* magazine to illustrate an article that chose her as one of the ten most beautiful women in Hollywood along with Greta Garbo, Ava Gardner, Jean Simmons and Elizabeth Taylor. Several producers, including David Selznick and Billy Wilder, took one look at her and offered her screen tests. 'All those guys were saying "you look fabulous, you should be in movies",' Betty Bacall told Guy Evans, 'and she had herself sculpted, and I knew that being a wife was not her! She wanted to have a career and be noticed more.' Hjördis was sorely tempted by the offers but Niv dissuaded her because 'one actor in the family is more than enough', he told her, forgetting that the wives of nearly all his friends were actresses. In later years she resented increasingly his objection to her having her own career and the fact that she always took second place to him, and by marrying him she had undoubtedly lost something of her independent identity. But maybe he knew already that she was a terrible actress and was trying to save her from embarrassment and failure.

His next picture, *Enchantment*, gave him some idea himself of what no longer being the main attraction might be like when he played a disregarded old codger: an English general looking sadly back on a great but doomed romance when he had been young. He disliked the part because his hair was bleached and he had 32lbs of lead weights sewn into his sleeves and trousers so that he would move slowly, and he discovered that old, slow people are ignored even if they are only playing a part. But because the role was serious and so different from his usual parts it gave him another rare chance actually to act, and Goldwyn indulged him by letting him name one of the characters Trubshawe, the general Rollo, and the niece Grizel. It was a static, sentimental, melodramatic picture, not one of his best, but it delivered a touching little love story and David himself was surprisingly good as the old man. Next Goldwyn lent him out again to make yet another poor comedy, *A Kiss in the Dark*, in which he played a gentle concert pianist whose ruthless agent takes advantage of him until he is saved by the love of a good woman. The *Observer* called it 'one of the silliest and trashiest stories seen on the screen for many a long day', and the *News of the World* asked, 'What on earth are they doing with that fellow's career?' It was a question that Niv was asking himself increasingly. Why was Goldwyn putting him in so many dreadful movies? How was he to stop his faltering career sliding into a pit of mediocrity?

The crunch came quickly. Early in May he was told that Goldwyn was lending him out again to Korda to make another epic costume drama, this time about the Scarlet Pimpernel, Sir Percy Blakeney, the fictional English hero who had saved French aristocrats from the guillotine during the French Revolution. The film was going to be made in England and France, and he would have to return to Europe for six months.

Niv went spare. He had only just returned to Hollywood, his new wife and sons were beginning to feel settled, David Jr was five and about to start nursery school, and now he would have to disrupt their lives again and take them back to England. He refused to do it. They had a fierce row during which Goldwyn said he had picked Niv out of the gutter and could dump him back in it, and Niv replied by accusing Goldwyn of making a fortune out of him by lending him to other producers at a vast profit. Goldwyn suspended him without pay. Niv tried to sit it out, and failed. His lifestyle was lavish and he needed the money badly.

Eventually he crawled back to Goldwyn, simmering with resentment, ordering his agent, the Music Corporation of America, to approach Goldwyn with a string of arrogant demands. MCA was appalled: did Niven not realise that Goldwyn could ruin him if he became too difficult? Niven did, but still insisted that Goldwyn should meet fourteen lavish conditions before he would agree to make *The Elusive Pimpernel*. He wanted Goldwyn or Korda to pay return fares for Hjördis, the boys and the new British nanny, Evelyn Walne, to travel to England by sea, not by air, and fares and living expenses for him and Hjördis when they went to France on location for eight weeks. He wanted a clothes allowance for the boys and the nanny. In England he wanted a house within twenty miles of the studio staffed by 'a housekeeper, servants, gardener, etc.'. In the autumn he wanted two suites or a flat at Claridge's Hotel and Goldwyn or Korda pay all the tips. He wanted a car, an entertainment allowance, British ration books, a $100 food parcel to be sent every week from America and cases of Scotch and gin to be sent each month. He even demanded to be paid compensation for the American radio fees that he would not earn by being out of the country for six months.

'My behaviour during the next few weeks was indicative of an unhinged mind,' Niv admitted in *The Moon's a Balloon*. 'I decided to make life unpleasant for Goldwyn which was tantamount to an eight-year-old with a pea-shooter assaulting Fort Knox.' By contrast Goldwyn behaved impeccably and agreed to everything that was even remotely reasonable, though he did tell David that he would have to fly to England to start shooting on the scheduled date even if the rest of the family followed by sea. Niv refused. Like some sullen child he seemed to want to goad his father figure beyond endurance so that he would punish him and so prove he loved him. During one row in Goldwyn's office in July Niv told him he was ruining his career and stormed out. At the end of the month the Nivens went by slow train to New York, slow boat to Liverpool, and slow train to London, where they looked for a furnished flat to rent in Mayfair or Chelsea and Niv told the *Evening News* that he was appalled by the 'terrific' prices being asked. 'For one of them – a very unattractive place – we were asked a rental of £65 a week,' he complained. 'I am not a millionaire film star who can pay any fantastic price they care to demand – nor am I a "sucker". After six years in the Army one hasn't much left to throw away.' He complained to Goldwyn's representative in London, who cabled Goldwyn: 'NIVEN UPSET BY INADEQUATE HOUSING AND REFUSES TO SEE ME UNTIL HIS FAMILY SETTLED.' One of Goldwyn's assistants in Los Angeles sent Niv a placatory cable only to receive an offensive reply threatening legal action and ending: 'GOOD LUCK YOU WILL NEED IT.' But his masterstroke was yet to come: he cabled Goldwyn to remind him that under his contract he was entitled to six weeks' holiday a year – and he wanted it now. Goldwyn must have been incandescent, but still he agreed. Niv then became absolutely impossible: he insisted that he wanted to take his holiday in California and that Goldwyn should pay for him and Hjördis to return, once again by boat and train. Korda, in despair, offered to lend him his yacht to go anywhere he chose. Niv refused. This was one of the most impressive, self-destructive sulks of all time.

Astonishingly Goldwyn swallowed his anger and agreed yet again. The Nivens returned slowly to Hollywood at Goldwyn's expense and Niv then gave him a two-fingered salute by flying thousands of miles back east again the very next day for a long delayed honeymoon in Bermuda, where he rented a tiny two-room cottage on the beach and swam, snorkelled and fished. Goldwyn must have smiled grimly when a vicious hurricane devastated the island a couple of weeks later, but otherwise the honeymoon was idyllic. 'The more I saw of Hjördis, the more amazed I was at my good fortune,' Niv wrote in *The Moon's a Balloon*. 'The luck, the unbelievable luck that one man should meet, fall head-over-heels in love, marry within ten days and be blissfully happy – twice in a lifetime! I revelled in Hjördis's forthrightness, honesty and laughter and the holiday sped by.'

At the end of six weeks he reported reluctantly back to the studio in Hollywood. Goldwyn refused to see him, understandably, and in later years Niv agreed that he had behaved extremely badly. 'Conduct such as mine, spoiled brat behaviour of the worst sort, was idiotic, conceited, indefensible and unforgivable,' he confessed in *The Moon's a Balloon*, 'the sort of thing that helped bring Hollywood to its knees.' He and Hjördis returned to England at the end of September and went on to France to make some location shots at Mont St-Michel on the coast of Brittany for Korda's long delayed film, which turned out to take even longer to shoot than *Bonnie Prince Charlie* – nearly six months – and to have just as many ridiculous wigs, frills, furbelows and weird stripy costumes. It was also possibly even more absurd than *Bonnie Prince Charlie*. Set in 1792, it was meant to be both funny and exciting but managed to be neither. Niv, as the Pimpernel, was an embarrassingly wooden, unfunny fop, despite all his constant winking and smirking at the camera. Even the usual Niven trademark jokes – a servant called Trubshawe, an aristocrat called the Marquis de Gacher, his mother's maiden name – no longer seemed amusing. Once again the only consolation was that Jack Hawkins – as a choleric, blustering Prince Regent – and Bob Coote were in it too, right up to the neck. Another member of the cast who would become a good friend later was twenty-six-year-old Patrick Macnee, who was long under the impression that he was Niv's nephew because his lesbian mother had once had an affair with Max.

The film was not released in Britain until 1949 and the reviewers were scathing. 'David Niven plays the Scarlet Pimpernel with the sheepish lack of enthusiasm of a tone deaf man called to sing solo in church,' said David Lewin in the *Daily Express*, and *The Times* warned that 'film audiences are in danger of forgetting what a really accomplished actor Mr Niven is. Here he makes his first embarrassed entrance like the dame in some nightmare pantomime.' Goldwyn agreed with the critics. In June 1949 he told Korda: 'Alex, I think it is the worst picture I have ever seen in my life.' He demanded huge changes and even more reshooting, and it was not released in the United States, where it was renamed *The Fighting Pimpernel*, until 1955 because Goldwyn refused to stick to his agreement to distribute it since it was so 'patently bad'. Korda sued him. Goldwyn sued Korda, and for once Niv agreed with Goldwyn. 'It was a disastrous flop,' he said a few years later, but financially it was not a flop at all: the public loved it and it was a huge box-office success.

Despite Niv's complaints about London property prices he could still afford to rent a hugely expensive house in Westminster for two months at 23 Chester Street, which had a drawing room big enough for a hundred guests and was lavishly furnished with Chippendale, Sheraton and Queen Anne furniture, Van Dyck paintings, and Hjördis's bedroom had a gilt bed and an old carved mantelpiece topped with pink marble. In London he caught up with many old friends, among them the Duke of Edinburgh, whom he met for dinner on 27 November 1948, two weeks after the birth of his first child, Prince Charles, when they joined twenty-two fellow members of the Thursday Club, a regular dining club. 'Niv and Doug Fairbanks were among the "Beards" who helped to cover up Prince Philip's dalliances,' Betty Bacall told me. 'Prince Philip always had women and they covered for him and pretended that his women were their women.' When I asked Prince Philip if he would talk to me about Niv, his private secretary, Brigadier Miles Hunt-Davis, said 'no' because according to him the prince met Niv only 'on one or two formal occasions and would not be able to tell you anything of interest'. This was puzzling since Prince Philip later wrote Niv a letter that began 'Dear David' and was signed 'Philip', which he would hardly do unless Niv were a friend.

By now the Nivens were such a golden celebrity couple that they might as well have been royal themselves, and when they returned to California at the end of February the *Sketch* reported their departure with a glamorous, full-page cover photograph of Hjördis. Their arrival in Hollywood was very different: Goldwyn refused to see Niv and issued a brusque order that he was to be loaned out again to appear with the child star Shirley Temple, now twenty, in a film that Niv described as 'a disastrous teenage pot-boiler'. David realised that he had behaved badly over the past few months and wrote to Goldwyn asking to be forgiven:

> Dear Sam,
>
> Eight months ago, when I had the bad manners and lack of humour to walk out of your office during an argument, I started something between us that has since grown out of all proportion.
>
> I would be most grateful if you would see me when I get back from San Francisco; not to discuss me or my future, but to give me a chance to recover the friendship of someone to whom I owe so much.
>
> Yours ever
> David

Goldwyn ignored it. He had finally had enough of this arrogant, selfish, ungrateful actor whom he had treated like a favourite son and who had just finished making one of the worst movies he had ever seen. Niv in turn reacted once more with anger and more arrogance. *OK. Fine, if that's the way he wants it. Why bother with Goldwyn anyway? Who needs him?* Friends in Hollywood, even other producers, told him he was a big enough star now to go it alone as a freelance. Why tie himself to a studio? And what had Goldwyn really done for him? Sure, he had given him his start, and helped him in the early days, and taken him back after the war, but otherwise he had made a huge profit out of renting him out to make crappy films for other producers. For this dreadful Shirley Temple film Goldwyn was being paid $18,700 a week for four weeks for David's services but was paying him only a fifth of that, and he had neglected to guide his career properly, so why should Niv feel guilty? The man had let him down. The time had come to leave, not just Goldwyn but maybe Hollywood altogether. As early as April 1949 he was thinking of going to live in Switzerland.

His attitude towards Goldwyn was partly justified. 'David's misfortune was to have found the wrong employer in Hollywood,' the British critic Alexander Walker told me. 'If he had gone with Irving Thalberg rather than Goldwyn he would have become an MGM contract artist, and MGM would have kept him in business for many, many years so long as he continued to be a star and make money for the corporation. With Goldwyn he was a loan-out for pictures whether they were appropriate for him or not, so there's a sense of his career being dispersed, not building in the way that Cary Grant's was built.'

Simmering with indignation, Niv made the Shirley Temple film, *A Kiss for Corliss*, in which he played a womaniser who is used by the teenage bobby-soxer Shirley to make her boyfriend jealous. His part was tiny and he could not be bothered to take it seriously. 'Because he had joined the company late and desired to finish early, his scenes were compressed into a rushed, lumpy mass, without continuity,' wrote Shirley Temple in her autobiography forty years later. ' "Today we do scene 425," the director Richard Wallace would announce. "Oh, God!" Niven would reply. "I didn't prepare *that* one!" Everything would grind to a halt except the coffee machine. Niven would retreat somewhere to learn the appropriate lines, invariably reappearing with the triumphant clarion call, "I've got it!" Usually he hadn't. The more he fluffed, the more impatient I became. Working over his shoulder and off-camera, I took to smiling superciliously at the crew as he blew over and over again. As he was an experienced actor with brains and wit, Niven's problem was not incompetence. What I neglected to acknowledge with my snide glances was that he detested this job [*and*] may have seen this loan-out as . . . punishment.' Many years later Niv said that acting with Shirley Temple was 'an experience that should really happen to dogs rather than actors'. The critics were sympathetic. 'Poor David Niven!' said the *Sunday Chronicle* and Caroline Lejeune wrote in the *Observer*:

> I sometimes think that David Niven
> Should not take *all* the parts he's given.

Niv finally persuaded Goldwyn to see him in his office on 22 July. 'It was not my finest hour,' he wrote in *The Moon's a Balloon*. 'He sat expressionless behind his desk. I said, "Look, Sam, we don't see eye to eye any more. I have two years left of my contract – how about releasing me?" He never took his eyes off me as he flicked his intercom lever. "Give Niven his release as from today . . . he's through." '

After fourteen years under Goldwyn's wing he was on his own.

Eight

Skating on Thin Ice

1949–1955

Niv's elation at being free of Goldwyn did not last long. Goldwyn's PR people put it about that he had been fired because he had become impossibly big-headed and unreliable, and suddenly the producers who had urged him to go freelance were not returning his calls. He had always lived extravagantly and without the weekly cheque from Goldwyn his savings began to dwindle alarmingly. 'Don't ever do this, Jack,' he warned Hawkins. 'Money! It melts away like butter on a hot stove.' He soon realised that he had been too cocky and overplayed his hand, and later admitted that he was 'terribly frightened' during the 'dreadful, dreadful' days of the early 1950s when he came to fear that he faced the possibility of real poverty, might never work in films again and might lose everything he had. 'To me Goldwyn then was a ruthless tyrant in a tight little empire,' he wrote in his *Sunday Express* series in 1958, but 'he could not have been anything else, I guess. Film-making was not a pattycake kind of game, and the competition was savage. On the other hand – and for this I am eternally grateful – Goldwyn transformed me from a hopeless amateur into a pro,' and he admitted, 'I made an absolute bally fool of myself. I owe old Sam Goldwyn everything.'

Times had changed and although he was only thirty-nine producers were no longer looking for the old-fashioned English-gent actor that was his speciality and were more excited by the new wave of young Method actors, so he grabbed the first film offer that came along: an MGM musical, *The Toast of New Orleans*, that was being made to launch the film career of the latest 'discovery', the twenty-eight-year-old singer Mario

Lanza, in which Lanza played a warbling New Orleans fisherman and Niv an opera diva's manager. It was a very small part but it paid a few bills and kept the bailiffs away for a while. Niv and Lanza got on extremely well, and they and another member of the cast, J. Carrol Naish, started drinking seriously at lunchtime. 'The three male leads drank Scotch each day,' the film's physiotherapist Terry Robinson told Charles Francisco for his book *David Niven: Endearing Rascal*. 'It started out pretty moderately ... but the three of them began having such a good time it started to drive the director nuts. J. Carrol Naish would just curl up and sleep his drinking off. It would finally get to Mario around four and he'd fall asleep, too. On the other hand, David Niven never fell asleep and he looked good all day and evening, as if he'd never had a drop! He outdrank Lanza and Naish – two good drinkers – and his blue eyes continued to sparkle.'

After that months went by without any more work and Niv became worried and depressed. In desperation he sat down every morning in a little rotunda in the garden of the Pink House and started to write a startlingly autobiographical novel, *Round the Rugged Rocks*, in which a randy young English soldier, John Hamilton, leaves the army at the end of the Second World War, becomes a liquor salesman in New York, is involved in indoor horse racing at 'Sea City' and frightened off by the Mafia, goes to Bermuda and then to Hollywood, where he finds a job as a deckhand on a fishing boat and eventually becomes a hugely successful film star. Trubshawe appears in the book as a lanky, 6ft 6ins, boozy, hugely moustached, eccentric joker of a soldier called Oglethorpe who becomes Hamilton's best friend, and together they appear at a fancy dress ball dressed as goats and appal the other guests by scattering black olives on the floor behind them. The book is packed with Niv's favourite anecdotes, including a scene when Hamilton's polo stick gets stuck up a horse's backside, and he manages to include a sneer at a cowardly English actor, Ralph Ridgway, 'idol of millions', who evaded his duty to his country during the war by becoming an American citizen and then pretending to be homosexual so as to escape the army. There is even a Pink House, and plenty of rather coy sex:

> They kissed again and now the tip of her tongue ran round the inside of his lips; when she pulled back her head to look up at him her eyes were bright and wet-looking. He lifted her up then, and carried her to a little grassy slope, lush and inviting, that lay between the azalea bushes. Her arms were about his neck and her lips stayed on his as he

carried her. Later they lay side by side and hand in hand and the shadows crept towards them over the grass.

Like Niv, Hamilton has several affairs but 'never had liked possessive women; they gave him claustrophobia', and there is one scene which seems to have been inspired by David's brief encounter with the sultry sexpot Mae West in 1934 when she had interviewed him as a possible co-star for her next film and admired his muscles. In the novel she is called Marie Davenport:

She flashed her famous smile at him, and her thin peach-coloured silk dressing gown fell slightly apart as she sat down. The inside of a satiny thigh gleamed invitingly until, with an exaggerated flourish, she covered it up again . . . It was not so much her looks, but her walk and the thrust of her breasts. It was the provocative tilt of her head, and, he realized with a sudden quickening of his pulse, the unmistakable fact that he had only to stretch out a hand and take her . . .

Marie Davenport stubbed out her cigarette and stood up, her flimsy dressing gown clinging to her superb figure. 'Come here . . . Let me see how tall you are.' John walked across the room and stood in front of her. She moved close up against him. He could feel the firm curve of her thighs against his, the swell of her breasts warm and firm against his chest. Her skin was flawless, smooth and sun-kissed. She looked up into his face and he saw that her eyes were shining unnaturally. He made no move, but his heart was thumping against his ribs. At length, with an almost imperceptible toss of her blonde head, she moved away from him and spoke over her shoulder, 'Yes, I think we would do very well together.'

As a film star Hamilton becomes impossibly arrogant and selfish, and Oglethorpe has to chide him for his cocky behaviour: 'Hello, old man. I hear you have been making a four-star, first-class, ocean-going drip of yourself.'

Wonderful raconteur though he was, Niv was not a novelist and did not have the necessary creative skills, so *Round the Rugged Rocks* is thin, laboured, amateurish stuff that later he admitted was 'pretty juvenile'. Long after it was published he was so embarrassed by it that when *The Moon's a Balloon* was published twenty-two years afterwards he tried to suppress every copy of *Round the Rugged Rocks* that he could find, and even now there is none even in the British Library, which by law should have a copy of every book published in Britain. Its catalogue has *Round the Rugged Rocks* listed as 'missing' and it is difficult not to suspect that Niv slipped in there in 1970 and pinched it himself. But when he wrote the book it helped to keep his mind off the crisis in his acting career, and in due course, because he was famous, it was published both in Britain and the United States at the end of 1951. And it did include one excellent joke: in the United States Hamilton is much impressed by American advertising slogans, especially one for a deodorant that read 'IT MAY BE DECEMBER BUT IT'S AUGUST UNDER YOUR ARM'.

It was several months after leaving Goldwyn before he was offered another starring role at last, in an English film, *Happy Go Lovely.* He rented the Pink House out for a year and sailed with the family to Southampton on the *Queen Mary* early in March 1950. Despite his constant worries about money he continued to live like a prince, taking Hjördis on holiday to Sweden, moving into Claridge's Hotel, sending David Jr off to boarding school and looking for a house to buy in the country. He threw himself into the club and social life of London, touched base with old friends and at one dinner party sat next to a gorgeous eighteen-year-old, Fiona Campbell-Walter, who had just begun a fabulous career as a top model, was to marry Baron Thyssen-Bornemisza and to become internationally famous as Fiona Thyssen. 'It was my first proper grand dinner party,' she told me, 'and to my absolute *amazement* I was sat on David's left, and there was initial panic, but this wonderful, kind, avuncular man completely put me at my ease and we were lifelong friends from that moment on. Obviously I was pretty scrumptious and very beautiful at that age and he was just wonderful, cosy and adorable, which is how I've always known him. No, he didn't make a pass at me, though he liked young girls and certainly fancied my girlfriend Caroline. We were friends until he died but we never had an affair and he never tried. We were buddies.'

Among the friends he saw in London was Trubshawe, who had just landed a part in his own first film, *Dance Hall*, which told of the ballroom romances of four factory girls – Petula Clark, Diana Dors, Kay Kendall and Dandy Nichols – and in which he played a colonel, and he was about to appear in another, *They Were Not Divided*, in which he was a major. Trubshawe was about to embark on a surprisingly long film career during which he appeared in forty films in the twenty years from 1950 to 1970, often like Niv playing military men and often along with many of the leading comic actors of the time. The following year, 1951, he was in the hilarious Ealing comedy *The Lavender Hill Mob* as the British ambassador –

with Alec Guinness, Stanley Holloway, Sid James, Alfie Bass and Audrey Hepburn – and *The Magic Box*, with Robert Donat and Richard Attenborough. In 1952 he was to make no fewer than six films and during the 1950s was to make twenty-one – exactly the same number as Niv himself, though his roles were of course much smaller. He was even to turn up later in four of Niv's own films: *Around the World in Eighty Days*, *The Guns of Navarone*, *The Best of Enemies* and *The Pink Panther*.

Another chum in London was the Scottish publisher Hamish ('Jamie') Hamilton who paid Hjördis three guineas, about £67 in 2003, to read a Swedish novel and tell him if it was any good. Three guineas was hardly going to go far at a time when David was still spending money with astonishing extravagance. In June he not only rented a house at 12 Catherine Place, a few yards from Buckingham Palace, he also bought a vast, rambling Jacobean mansion and seventy-four-acre estate in Wiltshire, Wilcot Manor, just a few miles from Primmie's childhood home and grave at Huish. The house had been a small monastery during the fifteenth and sixteenth centuries and had three floors, eight bedrooms, a hall, library, numerous other small rooms, and acres of wood panelling. Outside, as well as trees, a lake, lawns and a sweeping circular gravel drive, Wilcot Manor had a round brick-and-flint thatched dovecote and a paddock. It also had a ghost: the spectre of an angry monk who is said today still to haunt the central bedroom on the top floor, because he is still furious with King Henry VIII for turning him out of the house during his purge of the monasteries.

Dark, depressing and cold, Wilcot Manor was a folly which Niv very soon came to hate. At first he intended to live like an English country gent, with a private pew in the village church, a gun in the local pheasant-shooting syndicate, and a rod on the trout-stuffed River Kennet, but 'I don't think he stayed there more than a few nights,' said Andrew Rollo, and Roddy Mann said, 'He didn't know that the local hunt used to meet on the front lawn, and he woke up one morning and there were all these dreadful people in red coats.' Doreen Hawkins told me that

> it wasn't a very good move to go and live at Wilcot with Hjördis. It was gloomy and Hjördis said she saw ghostly nuns rowing a boat on their lake. Soon after they moved in I went for lunch there with Linda Christian, Ty Power's wife. It took us three hours to drive to Wilcot but Hjördis was hopeless with any domestic things and there was no food in the house. She didn't believe in eating. David loved his food but she didn't like it, so Linda and I sat there for hours waiting for

> something to eat. Hjördis had only got gin and I loathe gin but we had gin: we wanted *something* to eat or drink. The kitchens were miles away but finally we went in to eat some cold meat and a very curious dessert and there was this man with white gloves serving us. Hjördis always had this thing, even if there were just the two of you having a snack, there was always a chap with white gloves. It was ridiculous.

To help pay for it all Niv made *Happy Go Lovely* opposite the Hollywood dancer, Vera-Ellen. In the American-style musical set in Scotland but filmed in England he played a Scots millionaire who rescues an American show that is due to be put on at the Edinburgh Festival, and although the picture did not earn wonderful reviews Niv's were the best he had had for a long time. 'Mr Niven, back on top of his form after a series of disappointing pictures, is an excellent light comedian,' said the *Daily Mail*. 'A delightful portrayal,' agreed the *Daily Mirror*, while the *Spectator* reported that his charm 'helps enormously to blind one to the picture's defects'. Much of the film was shot at Elstree Studios, where Euan Lloyd, who was now publicity manager for Associated British Picture Corporation, often bumped into him. After more than two years of his second marriage Niv's eye was roaming again. 'He had this unique ability to chat up a woman,' chuckled Lloyd,

> talking about nothing, really, but he had such a wonderful delivery and open eyes and he'd invite them to lunch, perfectly respectable, and then suggest dinner and a dance. His build-up was astonishing and his conquests were numerous. There was one who has to remain nameless because she's still alive. Madam X and Niv were having this big affair when he went back to Hollywood. She was a major star and he was there on a first visit to her house, and I can see his face now telling me this story, laughing like a drain. He said, 'Don't ever repeat this, old boy, will you? We were well into the third act, having a wonderful time, and she said "David, are you hungry?" and I said, "Oh yes, after that I'm starving," and she said, "There's some caviar and champagne in the fridge," ' and Niv brought this kilo tin of caviar and he said 'Oh, *fuck* it, I didn't bring a spoon,' and she said, 'You don't need a spoon. Use your hand.' He said, 'Where do you want it?' and she said, 'You know where,' so he took a handful of caviar and spread it all over her fanny, and she said, 'Eat, baby.' True story, from his lips! And I said, 'How much caviar can you eat in one session?' and he said, 'Oh

no: more than one session, old boy.' He said, 'That's the only way to eat it. The only thing missing was chopped egg and onions.'

In London Niv had mentioned nervously to Jamie Hamilton that he had almost finished writing a novel, but when he heard no more, his American theatrical agent showed it to a small but reputable British publisher, the Cresset Press, whose editor John Howard, married to the critic Marghanita Laski, took David to lunch and offered him a contract. Hearing this, Jamie Hamilton asked in July if he could see the manuscript too. Niv replied that it was 'appallingly bad' but because Howard had bought him lunch he felt he should let Cresset publish it.

For a few weeks that summer the Nivens rented Winston Churchill's son Randolph's house nearby, in Hobart Place, and the fact that Niv could afford to rent houses in such expensive areas of London, as well as owning a mansion in the country, suggests that all his claims of poverty were as usual highly exaggerated. Even though he was still without any really lucrative work he was living extravagantly, and in September he even bought a young greyhound bitch, Rally Call, which won her first race for him at White City on 7 September. 'I'm a keen White City man,' he told the *Evening Standard*, 'and my wife is crazy about greyhound racing. But I am not a betting man. It's a mug's game.'

The Cresset Press paid him for *Round the Rugged Rocks* a modest advance against royalties of $500 (about £2000 today) with another $500 to come when the book was published. 'My dear Chum,' he wrote to Jamie Hamilton, 'I do not know how to apologise . . . Dear boy, I cannot tell you how miserable I am about it, and I feel that I have let an old chum down, which is not my form, believe me. Probably the novel will be a ghastly flop anyway, and you will feel well out of it . . . So sorry chum. Fondest love, David.' The penultimate clause of the Cresset contract was to cause a major problem when Jamie Hamilton wanted to publish *The Moon's a Balloon* twenty years later, for it gave Cresset an option of first refusal on the next two books that Niv might write. He spotted it himself at the time, remarking glumly in his letter to Hamilton that it looked as if he would be involved for ever with Cresset.

Niv was never going to make a fortune as a novelist but luckily that summer he was offered a part in another MGM movie to be filmed in Hollywood with Stewart Granger and Walter Pidgeon, *Soldiers Three*, and in October he took the family back to California and the Pink House. *Soldiers Three* was set in India in the 1890s and was meant to be an exciting military adventure based on a Kipling story, but it was so shambolic that most audiences thought it was a comedy. Niv had to accept third billing after thirty-six-year-old Granger, a London-born newcomer to Hollywood who was only four years younger than he but had just made his name with *King Solomon's Mines* and was about to make *Scaramouche*. Granger called *Soldiers Three* 'a horror' and wrote in his autobiography: 'what the hell David Niven . . . was doing, I can't imagine. He must have been very hard up.' Granger told Morley that he was astonished by how cheerful Niv remained during filming. 'Well, it may be shit and not very good shit,' Niv shrugged, 'but we have to go through it, so let's just be cheerful about it.' That was typical of his entire character, said Granger: 'He'd describe somebody on the set to me as an utter arsehole, and a moment later the man would be standing there and in almost the same breath David would be saying, "My dear old fellow, how are you?" without turning a hair, and I'd be left with my mouth hanging open, not knowing how he could do it.' Granger added, 'I was always rather jealous about the way that everybody seemed to love David, and the way that he managed to give the impression that he was loving every single minute of every single day. I don't think he was, I don't think anybody could, but he had an enviable knack of seeming to be happy and people liked that.'

Niv grabbed the next film offer too, which turned into one of the worst movies he ever made: *The Lady Says No!*, in which he played a magazine photographer who snaps a feisty bestselling feminist authoress and persuades her to succumb to his male chauvinist charms. The reviews were dreadful, but it paid a few more bills, and at the end of 1950 he landed another film deal, to star in another movie to be made in Britain, *Appointment With Venus*. He sent Hjördis, the children and the nanny ahead of him in February to stay at Wilcot Manor with Grizel, and when he arrived at Southampton a month later on the *Queen Elizabeth* they left the boys with Grizel and the nanny, and went off on a motoring holiday through France, Northern Italy and Switzerland. With *Round the Rugged Rocks* about to be published, he started to write a second more serious novel, *Murgatroyd*, but it did not progress very far after he went off for three extremely boozy weeks on the tiny Channel Island of Sark with the twenty-seven-year-old South African actress Glynis Johns and thirty-six-year-old Kenneth More to shoot the location scenes for *Appointment With Venus*. It was a frothy little black-and-white comedy in which he played yet another dashing young British World War Two major who is landed secretly by submarine at night on a tiny Nazi-occupied Channel Island to kidnap an immensely valuable, pregnant, pedigree cow called Venus.

It was a silly little story and Niv's performance was not much better, but he took the part seriously enough to scent some unwelcome competition in the performance of Kenneth More, a comparative newcomer to movies who was playing a young pacifist painter living on the island.

'He was particularly nice to me,' wrote More in his autobiography, 'and indeed to everyone else in the film [*and*] as far as I was concerned he was Number One . . . a man I admired, almost idolised.' But Niv insisted that More's most important scene was cut altogether because as the star of the movie he had the right to veto anything he did not like. 'Everyone says how wonderful David was, and he *was* to his friends,' More's ex-wife Billie told me at her home in the South of France, on Cap Ferrat. 'He was a most amusing man and a wonderful friend to the people he liked, and at first he and Kenny were bosom friends, but my husband was a beautiful comedy actor, as good as David was, and although he was just beginning his career, he was competition. The director, Ralph Thomas, told Kenny: "I'm afraid David has been watching too many rushes and you're coming over too well." That film mattered to Kenny.' Beneath Niv's suave façade there was still a deep well of insecurity that was deepened by the hiccup in his career.

After Sark they shot most of the film at Pinewood Studios and Niv invited More to Wilcot Manor for the weekend, where he introduced him to Hjördis on the Friday night and kept genially calling him 'dear boy', 'dear bird' or 'dear old thing'. Niv sat him down in front of a lovely log fire in the chintzy sitting room, plied him with numerous Camparis before dinner, glass after glass of wine with the meal, and brandies after Hjördis had gone to bed, and when More was thoroughly drunk, he said, David persuaded him that a chair in the hall was so ugly and vulgar that he should rip its legs and the seat off and throw them on the fire. 'As it began to burn,' said More, 'David did an Indian war dance around me, whooping and shouting "Aah! Aah! Aah!" For some reason, he seemed deliriously happy.' When the chair was reduced to a small pile of charred wood More staggered off to bed but in the morning he came down for breakfast to find Hjördis asking Niv where was her favourite chair. 'Kenny burned it, darling,' said Niv jovially. 'He got high and burned it.'

'You burned *my* chair?' shrieked Hjördis. More had to admit that he had and she refused to speak to him for the rest of the weekend as he crept guiltily around the house. 'David, of course, had never liked the chair,' he said, 'and this had been one way of getting rid of it.'

Appointment With Venus, which was retitled *Island Rescue* in America, was an uneasy mixture of wartime adventure and farce, and did nothing to excite the critics or improve Niv's reputation, and it was to be more than a year before he made another movie. In the meantime he made the most of the English summer and took up painting again so seriously that in June one of his oils, *Fishing Boats*, was put on show at a London exhibition of work by famous amateurs at the Trafford Gallery in Mount Street – along with pictures by Doug Fairbanks, their old girlfriend Princess Marina, Noël Coward, the Duke of Marlborough, the Duchess of Gloucester and Field Marshal Viscount Alexander of Tunis. Niv's painting was described by the *Daily Telegraph* art critic T. W. Earp as 'sensitive and diaphanous' and was auctioned for charity along with all the other paintings.

Noël Coward realised how little work Niv was finding and persuaded his producer friend John Wilson to offer him a part in a stage play that was to open in Hartford, Connecticut, in November and go on to Boston, Philadelphia and Broadway. David had not appeared on stage since the *Wedding* fiasco at the Pasadena Playhouse in 1935 and he was terrified, but he needed the work, thought it might be good for his career to appear in the theatre, and returned to New York with Hjördis in September on the *Queen Mary*. They left eight-year-old David Jr at boarding school in England and five-year-old Jamie at Wilcot Manor with Evelyn the nanny, though by now Niv and Hjördis had decided that the English weather was so awful that they did not want to live there permanently and he resigned from two of his London clubs, Boodle's and the Garrick.

In New York rehearsals for the play, *Nina*, a French bedroom farce that had been hugely successful in Paris for two years, began immediately. The play had only three characters: the fifty-two-year-old, four-times-divorced silent-movie star Gloria Swanson was Nina, Niv was her smoothie lover and Alan Webb her jealous husband. Swanson had just given a glorious autobiographical performance as a has-been silent-movie star in the film *Sunset Boulevard*, but the director was a wild Hungarian, Gregory Ratoff, and an English producer, Toby Rowland, who was there to observe rehearsals for an English theatrical company that had a slice of the action, told Morley that 'it was immediately apparent that Ratoff was mad, that Gloria couldn't do it all, that Alan was going to be extremely good, and that David might just about get by on a wry sort of charm.' He was indeed surprisingly good when *Nina* opened in Hartford on 1 November – so good that the director Otto Preminger cast him for another play that he was to stage in San Francisco the following summer.

But before the first night in New York there was an evil omen. The Nivens checked into the Blackstone Hotel where the twenty-two-year-old English actress Audrey Hepburn was in the next suite and desperately nervous about her own forthcoming Broadway debut in *Gigi*. When one of the guests committed suicide by jumping from his window on the eighteenth floor and bounced off Hepburn's windowsill as he fell, she freaked out and pounded on the Nivens' door, terrified that she was hallucinating and going mad. She was to win rave reviews for *Gigi* but was lonely in New York and she and the Nivens saw a great deal of each other during the next few weeks, beginning a close friendship that was to last for the rest of David's life.

For the first New York night of *Nina* the Royale Theatre on Broadway was thick with the cream of Manhattan theatre when Niv discovered with horror during the first scene that Gloria Swanson had sashayed on stage wearing an absurd new costume that he had never seen, a vast 'black taffeta tent'. When she threw herself into his arms, nestled her head into his chest and he hugged her too hard, there was a crack, a twang, and eight inches of white whalebone shot out of her corset and up his nose. The audience roared with laughter and the show never recovered. The *New York Herald Tribune* critic, Walter Kerr, wrote the next day: 'Miss Swanson has designed her own clothes [*and*] some of them came apart on stage. By that time, however, a similar fate had overtaken the play.' Astonishingly *Nina* was to run until 12 January – for five weeks and forty-five performances – although Niv exaggerated as usual in *The Moon's a Balloon* and claimed that it lasted for three months. He began to relax and enjoy himself so much that he and Alan Webb started to play practical jokes on poor Gloria while they were on stage. 'He used to come in every night and say to Alan, "Well, what shall we do to her tonight?" and they used to devise these terrible practical jokes,' Rowland told Morley.

December 1951 was a good month for Niv because it also marked the publication of *Round the Rugged Rocks*, which he dedicated to Hjördis, both in America and England, where it was praised in a mild two-paragraph review in the *Daily Telegraph* by the future Poet Laureate John Betjeman, who wrote: 'David Niven obviously wrote "ROUND THE RUGGED ROCKS" because he enjoyed doing it and not because he wanted to prove his versatility or literary skill. And he communicates his enjoyment . . . Mr Niven has an affection for real people, he sees the funny side of things, and he sees through shams like publicity. His book is rather too much on the same cheerful note to sustain the story, but it is livelier and therefore better than the journalistic novels which appear at the rate of about 25 a week to be swallowed by the twopenny libraries.' When the book was serialised in a British women's magazine just before publication it was illustrated by a drawing of the hero based on a pose by Roger Moore, who had become a photographic model for knitting patterns, toothpaste, Brylcreem and magazines.

In New York the book was published by thirty-year-old Ken Giniger, the editor-in-chief of Prentice Hall, who retitled it *Once Over Lightly* because 'in America we don't know that British nursery rhyme "round the rugged rocks the ragged rascal ran" ', he told me. 'I thought it was a charming picaresque novel and Niven was a well-known character, but I was disappointed because he did very little promotion for us, so we didn't do very well with the book. The reviews were indifferent and we sold fewer than five thousand copies, which wasn't bad for a first novel in those days, and we made a paperback sale too.'

Years later Niv claimed that *Round the Rugged Rocks* sold 28,000 copies in total in Britain and America, very many fewer than a 'celebrity' author would sell today, which would mean the book earned him little more than £12,000 in modern terms and would have made him realise that it was a great deal easier to make a living as an actor.

Despite his battles with the British taxman and his decision never to live in England again, he remained intensely patriotic and royalist, annoyed some Americans by refusing to take out US citizenship, and always stood to attention when he heard the British national anthem, 'God Save the King'. 'He would always stand even if he was watching a football match on television,' his daughter Kristina told me, so he was deeply affected when King George VI died at Sandringham on 6 February 1952, aged only fifty-six, and he wrote letters of condolence to the dead king's mother, Queen Mary, as well as to Princess Marina and Princess Margaret.

Back in LA and the Pink House, Niv and Hjördis slipped again into their sunny, laid-back Californian routine. Despite his worries about work and money they continued to live extremely well and to give plenty of parties, and Hjördis joined a giggly group of women who regularly played and gambled on canasta. One new friend was a twenty-two-year-old actor who was to become one of Niv's closest chums for the rest of his life: Robert Wagner, 'R. J.' to his friends, who had recently made his fourth film. 'We all loved the water and I met him on Bogart's boat, the *Santana*,' R. J. told me at his home in Mandaville Canyon, not far from the Pink House. 'God, the Pink House was so beautiful then. It overlooked the ocean and was really sensational and we had a lot of good times there.'

To save money Niv brought the boys back to California, cancelled his plan to send them to Stowe or Eton, and sent them to a local Roman Catholic day school. To protect them from the taunts of other children who might jeer that he was a very bad actor, he taught David and Jamie to say that their dad knew he was a terrible actor but just loved making movies, and if people were silly enough to pay him lots and fly him all over the world, why should he say no? 'He was a good, caring father and loved us a lot,' David Jr told me at his home in Beverly Hills, 'but he didn't spoil us or lavish presents on us. He was very strict. He wouldn't tolerate lying and you had to be polite, punctual and tidy. One of his punishments was to make you stand with books on your head facing the corner for maybe an hour. I was beaten once when I was about ten, in 1952, because I changed my school report card and said I hadn't, but unfortunately I'd used black ink and the report card was in dark blue ink. I was beaten because I'd lied about it so many times. I had to go and choose my own stick in the garden and I got six of the best. But he hated that sort of punishment.'

Niv loathed lies and dishonesty, he told Margaret Hinxman in 1979. Honesty, he said, 'is really the same as honour, isn't it? I don't lie, mostly because it's always so difficult remembering the lies you've told. The only time I ever took a birch to one of my sons was when he altered his school marks ... And it hurt me a hell of a lot more than it did him ... Dishonesty must be the worst crime. Oh, you embroider a good story to make it sound funnier. But that's different. You're not harming anyone.' Jamie was never beaten but 'he'd let you know he was displeased', he told me. 'He'd go quiet and sort of cut you out. I don't doubt that he loved me, but I didn't like it if he was distant or rejected me; and I told him so. He was more aloof as a parent than I would have liked. He did the best he could, but I'm not sure he had the best tools, because of the way he'd been brought up himself.' Niv could also sometimes have 'a vicious temper', said David Jr, 'but we discovered that it was actually incited by gin, and Jamie and I pointed out to him that he was really *horrid* when he was on gin and he never drank it again. I never saw him drunk but he drank a huge amount. He had hollow legs and drank all day.' When he was home he often played with the boys. 'He'd stand at the top of the lawn and hit baseballs at me like crazy,' said Jamie, 'and that's why I became quite a good baseball player, and he encouraged me to play basketball, football, tennis, skiing, ice-hockey.' R. J. Wagner told me that Niv was a good father, constantly talking about the boys and concerned for their welfare, but Doreen Hawkins was not so sure. 'He loved the boys very much,' she said, 'but *no* actor's a good father. It's just impossible. They don't see their children enough.' As for Hjördis, 'she didn't do very well as a mother to the boys: we never saw much of them and there was always a nanny.'

David Jr called Hjördis 'The Swede'. 'Daddy and she had a really good time at the beginning,' he said,

> though she was never on time, which used to drive him crazy. She also used to gamble. She'd go off to the racetrack and if she won then there'd be caviar, but if she lost it was baked beans on toast for the rest of the week. My father got very pissed off with this but that was the nature of the beast. She didn't speak very much English and wasn't really a mother, though Pinkie had been like a mother, terrific, and there was a wonderful black laundress called May, who was also terrific, but in the end boarding school was the answer and eventually I went to a number of boarding schools in the States. In the holidays we'd go wherever he was making a film, and if you were in Greece or somewhere unmentionable you wouldn't see your friends and it was rather a bore: he's not there because he's working, you're in a country where you don't speak the language, you don't know anyone, you're eating foul food, and you have to spend a lot of time with your stepmother.

At the Pink House there was always tension between Hjördis and the boys, Jamie told Grace Bradberry of the *Daily Mail*'s *Weekend* magazine in 2002, 'and it never went away. It was really kind of tragic. We did go on family trips and she made an effort, but she just didn't want to deal with the two young boys she'd inherited.' Pat Medina told me: 'She told the boys to stop calling her Mummy. She said, "You have to call me Hjördis, you can't call me Mummy," and I said, "You cannot *do* that. They're very fond of you but you keep correcting them and they can't remember what to call you and they're totally in confusion." Jamie was so upset that he locked himself in his bedroom.'

Niv's attempts to economise were laughable: he reduced the boys' pocket money and insisted that the housekeeper should stop buying bottled water, but otherwise life continued as extravagantly as before. He chartered an expensive boat to take a party of friends to Catalina Island and wafted Hjördis off to Barbados for a two-week holiday, though Jamie told Grace Bradberry: 'It was pretty much wipeout time in 1952, '53 and '54. He was around the house. He had nothing to do. But he was blessed with an enormous sense of humour. He used to come and watch me play baseball, and always said, "Well done." He also came to see me in a school production of *The Haunted Tea Room* that my brother starred in too. I wasn't much of an actor, but he was nothing but enthusiastic.' Young David had parts in lots of school plays too. Because he was fair-haired he was always playing a girl. 'They used to stuff two football socks up my sweater!' he said. 'It was all most embarrassing, and it put me off acting for life.'

It was three years before Niv's luck began to change for the better. He made two live drama appearances on TV in 1952, *The Petrified Forest* and *The Sheffield Story*, and did a couple of guest spots on the Bob Hope and Jack Benny shows, and they were to lead to a crossroads in his career that would save him from bankruptcy and eventually make him rich. The Hollywood moguls saw TV as a dangerous rival and hinted that actors who appeared on it would be blacklisted, but Niv had little to lose now and gambled $20,000 to join Charles Boyer, Ida Lupino and Dick Powell in forming a new company, Four Star Television, to make live half-hour TV films under the title *Four Star Playhouse*. In the first five years they made 1800, from Somerset Maugham and Zane Grey short stories to series such as *The Rifleman*, *Burke's Law* and *The Rogues*. Ida Lupino soon dropped out but Niv, Boyer and Powell each travelled to New York once a month to direct or appear for free in a play, one of which started young Steve McQueen on his road to stardom. Niv became one of the first Hollywood stars to appear regularly on television and 'they made a lot of money', Roddy Mann told me. 'I think that was the main source of his fortune. He always felt that he could produce and make a film as well as anybody.' Betty Bacall told Morley that she and Bogart started watching the shows 'and one night Bogie said, "My God, he can act," and it was true. David's dramas were always the best acted and the best written of the season, and he remains the only leading actor I have ever known whose career was totally revived and turned around as a result of television. He really did begin to do some very good work there.'

'Four Star was very productive for him,' I was told by Jess Morgan, who became Niv's business manager and friend in Los Angeles in 1952 and was to work for him for thirty years. 'The early Fifties were not his best economic times but he was just getting going again. We did everything for him: prepared his tax returns, paid the bills, even the household bills, kept records, helped him with buying and selling of houses and cars, got the proper insurance, and invested his money for him. He wasn't mean but he was careful with money, very respectful of it, very interested in it, and smart about what he did – one of the smartest guys I ever met. He was very canny and understood the business thoroughly – how to function in the entertainment business – and he had a great time doing it. He loved it. He didn't hire me because he was lazy – he could make a lot more money doing other things – and he wasn't extravagant. He never earned superstar salary but he earned star salary and lived comfortably but not wildly. All that first-class travel, for instance, was paid for by whichever studio he was working for.'

A second piece of good fortune came his way in 1952 when Otto Preminger, impressed by his performance in *Nina*, persuaded him to appear as an ageing roué and seducer in another stage play, *The Moon Is Blue*, a slightly risqué sex comedy with just three parts, and then to repeat the role in a film version. Niv was reluctant to go on the stage again but what else was there? He opened in the play with Diana Lynn and Scott Brady at the United Nations Theatre in San Francisco on 8 July, played the part for two months and was so good in the film version – with William Holden and Maggie McNamara – that he won the Foreign Press Association's Golden Globe for the best comedy performance of the year even though the film's distributors, United Artists, had tried several times to persuade Preminger not to cast him because he was 'all washed up'. Some outraged viewers said the film was indecent because it contained words like 'mistress', 'virgin' and 'seduce', and it was banned by the Catholic Church, which ensured that it became a huge success. Bravely Niv had agreed to accept a much smaller fee than usual in exchange for a percentage of the profits, with the result that he said he made more out of that picture than any he had yet been in. 'The money kept rolling in,' he said. His luck was turning at last.

In 1952, however, the money was not rolling in yet. It would be a couple more years before it did because Four Star needed two or three years to show a profit and *The Moon Is Blue* was not released until 1953. In the meantime David continued to skate on thin ice yet live like a millionaire. In November he and Hjördis crossed the continent to spend a weekend pheasant-shooting with friends in Rhode Island, where Hjördis came down to breakfast on the first morning and announced that she would not be going out with them because she had dreamed that someone would shoot her. Niv and the others laughed at her – 'I *know* I am going to be shot,' she insisted – and finally persuaded her to tag along with some warm clothes and a book. She did – and was hit by lead pellets in the face, neck and chest when two guns turned to fire at a low bird. In

The Moon's a Balloon Niv claimed that she was peppered by thirty pellets, her beautiful face was dreadfully swollen and suffused with blood, and that for several terrible moments he feared that a second wife had been killed in a stupid accident, but he was probably exaggerating again because she was left completely unscarred and the *Daily Mail* reported the next day that she had been wounded by only three pellets. Even so, she always claimed to have premonitions of disaster and Niv told Roddy Mann in 1964 that 'she can actually smell bad health. If I'm going to be ill, she knows it, way in advance.' In fact so little damage was done that he soon asked her to appear in a *Four Star Playhouse* production, despite his reluctance to let her become an actress, because he needed a woman to play a foreign spy and she still had a thick Swedish accent and would be cheap. She was delighted and appeared under the stage name Tania Borg. 'I thought I was absolutely divine in the film,' she told the *Daily Mail* in 1960. 'I loved myself, and on the strength of it I was offered a film with Robert Taylor,' but Niv refused to let her do it. 'I married you as a wife,' he told her, 'not as a part-time mistress. I've seen too many marriages break up when both parties film in different parts of the world.' Once again he might simply have been trying to save her from herself because 'she was disastrous as an actress', Betty Bacall told me. 'That she could think she could ever become a star! It was ridiculous!'

But his relentless opposition to her having a career of her own rankled. 'She began to change gradually and became bitter,' Bacall told Guy Evans. 'She was frustrated, and I don't think she knew what she wanted, and she became a serious drinker, which was really bad and very hard on David.' Hjördis also began to carry on with other men. 'She was always flirting with guys, always,' Betty Bacall told me, 'and it was nothing to do with David's philandering because he didn't philander that much when he was with her.' Alastair Forbes, a wartime friend of Niv's, went further. 'Once Hjördis saw that David wouldn't get her any acting jobs,' he told me, 'she started to carry on with other men,' and she told one of her women friends that as a lover Niv was boring and uninventive. 'The problem with David,' she said, 'is that he doesn't like his sex on a bearskin rug on the floor, he likes it very conventionally.' Perhaps she should have invested in a tin of caviar. Hjördis was 'a dreadful, open flirt', said Pat Medina, who had recently divorced Richard Greene and often spent weekends with the Nivens until she married Joseph Cotten eight years later. 'Niv and I never had an affair – we were like brother and sister and had the same sense of humour – but Hjördis was very vain and when he once told her that she was flirting with somebody she said, "David says

I said it with my eyes. Well, I can't help my eyes." She thought that if she left him everyone in Hollywood would be after her, which wasn't the case because part of her attraction was the fact that she was Mrs David Niven. But I think she had a go with an American doctor in Pasadena, a plastic surgeon who was removing a scar. She told me she liked him very much and wanted to meet him, and she met him at *my* place. He was a nice looking man with a nice voice, but I thought "Oh God, what has she got me into?" and she saw him again often. People said Niv called her Nej because she was always saying "no" to him: well, if so he was the only one she *did* say it to!' Betty Bacall remembered the plastic surgeon too. 'That's right,' she said, 'some terrible doctor.' Resentment, alcohol and infidelity on both sides began to infect the marriage, and one of Hjördis's weapons was to feign illness. 'She was a bit of a hypochondriac,' said Pat Medina. 'If anything didn't go to her liking she gave a great performance of being ill and getting better, and I knew they were not always happy. There was a little summer house there and I'd say to Nej, "Where's Niv?" and she'd say, "He's sitting in the summer house," and I'm sure he was sitting there thinking about Primmie.'

Rumours that Niv was really good in *The Moon Is Blue* persuaded two British studios to offer him starring parts in two films to be made in England and Ireland in 1953, but in the middle of March, a fortnight before he and Hjördis were due to sail to Southampton on the *Queen Elizabeth*, he heard that Vivien Leigh, who was in Hollywood making a movie called *Elephant Walk* and at the end of an affair with the actor Peter Finch, was having a nervous breakdown and possibly going mad. It was 2 a.m. and her husband Laurence Olivier was thousands of miles away on holiday in Ischia with William Walton and his wife. Niv telephoned Stewart Granger and they went to her house, where they found her gazing white-faced at a blank TV screen and one of her ex-boyfriends, Gladys Cooper's schizophrenic son John Buckmaster, who had himself recently been held in a mental hospital, naked except for a towel. They persuaded Buckmaster to leave and tried to sedate Vivien with scrambled eggs and coffee heavily laced with sedatives. She insisted that Niv should taste both first, he fell asleep on the sofa, and she stripped naked and sat by the swimming pool. Granger called for medical help and when a doctor and two huge nurses arrived he helped to pin her down on her bed while she was injected with a strong sedative. Olivier arrived from Italy, flew her back to England, and checked her into a psychiatric hospital where she was given electro-convulsive therapy and slowly recovered.

Niv described this tragic episode, changing the names, in *Bring on the*

Empty Horses in a chapter entitled '"Our Little Girl" (Part 2)', but the story is heavily fictionalised, he made no mention of Granger or falling asleep on the sofa, claimed that she had flaunted her body, offered him sex, snarled at him like a caged animal, and that he had dealt with her on his own.

Four days after she was flown back to England, David and Hjördis sailed for Southampton on the *Queen Elizabeth* to film *The Love Lottery*, but while they were at sea they heard the shocking news that the irrepressibly boyish Max had died of a heart attack in South Africa on his farm at Currie's Post in Natal at the age of fifty. In London the Nivens borrowed the Oliviers' house in Chelsea while Sir Laurence was in Italy and Vivien Leigh in hospital, and Niv began to shoot *The Love Lottery* at Ealing Studios, a spoof in which he played the No. 2 star at a Hollywood studio where the No. 1 star is Fang The Wonder Dog, and to raise his profile he agrees to marry the winner of a 'love lottery' for which his women fans buy tickets, only for the winner to find that he is nothing like his image but really rather ordinary and boring. So, sadly, was the film, a dreadfully corny, ludicrous farce, one of the worst that he made.

His next picture, *Happy Ever After*, was much better, but first the Bogarts were in town for the new Queen's coronation on 2 June and the four of them watched the procession together. Then it was off to Ireland to shoot *Happy Ever After*, which was renamed *Tonight's the Night* in America, in which Niv played a part quite different from any previously. This time for a change he was an insufferable villain: Jasper O'Leary, a bounder with a smarmy smile who has inherited an entire feudal village in Ireland from its squire, his great-uncle, and vows to 'squeeze the lemon dry' by refusing to perform his feudal obligations, calling in all debts, cancelling his great-uncle's numerous little bequests, and sacking the drunken butler, village policeman and publican. The men of the village decide to kill him, but this is Ireland and things go wrong – all of which made for a jolly, frothy, harmless little tale, though some of the critics were surprisingly rude.

In October Niv was one of the judges for the Miss World beauty contest – an inspired choice – and he and Hjördis returned to Hollywood and the wonderful news in March that he had won the Golden Globe Award for *The Moon Is Blue* and the tragic news that Fred Astaire's wife Phyllis had lung cancer. Over that Easter weekend she underwent two operations at the hospital in Santa Monica where Primmie had died while Fred and David sat and waited nervously outside. She recovered from surgery so quickly that three months later she seemed as fit as ever, but she had only three more months to live. There was more sadness in May: J. F. Roxburgh died in England of a stroke at the age of sixty-seven. 'We felt just as upset as if our own father had died, or a member of our family,' Dudley Steynor told Guy Evans. 'We were heartbroken. We loved that man.'

In June Niv sailed back to England on the *Queen Elizabeth* to make a film at Shepperton Studios that would earn him great reviews and boost his reputation immensely. In *Carrington VC* he played yet another British major: a noble, selfless, war hero who has won the VC and DSO but is court-martialled for fraud after borrowing £125 from the regimental fund of which he is in charge, even though he borrowed the money quite openly, and only because the army has taken months to pay him £200 that it owes him, and only after telling his commanding officer he was doing so. The film consists mainly of a long, tedious court case during which he defends himself but is betrayed by his cold, neurotic wife (played by Margaret Leighton) because he has understandably had a one-night stand with a pretty woman captain. It is a dull, static and stagey picture but the critics were lavish with their praise in Britain and America, where it was renamed *Court Martial*, and the reviewers for both the *Spectator* and *Variety* judged it one of the best performances of his career.

He returned to Hollywood to face a great sadness: Phyllis Astaire died on 13 September aged only forty-six and leaving Fred with their eighteen-year-old son Fred Jr and twelve-year-old daughter Ava. Fred was devastated. They had had a wonderfully happy marriage and David knew exactly how he was feeling and was himself very upset because he loved both of them dearly. Knowing from experience that work can help to ease grief, he persuaded Fred to return to work on the film he was making, *Daddy Long Legs*, two days after the funeral, and urged him later to start writing his autobiography so as to give him some moments' rest from his unhappiness.

Astaire's grief must have reminded Niv how lucky he was still to have a beautiful young wife, whatever her faults, because when he started that autumn to make his next film in Hollywood, *The King's Thief*, for MGM, one member of the cast, a twenty-six-year-old newcomer, Roger Moore, told me: 'They were always hand-in-hand then. Hjördis was very glamorous and people stood with their mouths open when she walked on the set, though I always thought she wore too much make-up. In fact Tony Curtis once told her so, which pissed her off.'

It is good to know that someone got some fun out of *The King's Thief* because by general consent it is possibly the worst film that Niv ever made – a sword-fighting costume swashbuckler set in the England of Charles II (played by a smirking George Sanders) in which Niv was the king's villainous adviser, the Duke of Brampton, whose evil plan is to persuade the king to execute all his closest friends and allies for 'treason' so that Brampton can steal their estates and money. The plot was absurd, the script dire, and Niv looked so ludicrous in his feathered hat, frilly collars and cuffs, and tiny beard that it is difficult not to cheer when he is hanged at the end. Roger Moore played a highwayman and told me 'I was a long-haired ponce' and no one would argue with that. Yet in the right part Niv could be astonishingly good and at the end of 1954 he was nominated for an Emmy award for the best actor in a single TV performance for his part in *The Answer*, a one-hour episode of *Four Star Playhouse*, in which he had played a Bowery bar-room bum who persuades his fellow drunks that he has discovered the meaning of life. But then it was back to banality for his next film, *The Birds and the Bees* with Mitzi Gaynor, in which he played a smooth cardsharper scheming to rip off the gormless son of a rich tycoon. If it was any consolation, many reviewers said he was the film's only salvation and the *Manchester Guardian* reported that he could be very funny.

In March 1955 David and Hjördis flew to Jamaica for a week's holiday with Noël Coward at his winter home, Blue Harbour, where Niv immediately went down with chickenpox, vicious red spots, a temperature of 104 and a fortnight in quarantine so that they had to stay for two weeks instead of one. 'Hjördis has many wonderful qualities,' wrote Coward's boyfriend Cole Lesley in his biography of Coward, 'but those of Florence Nightingale-cum-*hausfrau* I think she will admit are not among them, though she did her best. Pathetic-looking trays of food and changes of bed-linen were left halfway on the long flight of steps leading to the guest-house, while Hjördis had to wash up the crockery and glass – too infectious to be sent to the kitchen – in their hand-basin.' Niv also managed to pick up a colony of grass ticks that were now breeding energetically in his crotch, but he used his extra week of idleness to paint *Sunday in Jamaica*, a picture that was sold at a charity auction in London three months later for ten guineas – about £170 today.

Back in New York that spring to make yet another *Four Star Playhouse* production and, with Hjördis nearly 3000 miles away in Hollywood, David may well have had a brief affair with the delicious, notoriously promiscuous twenty-five-year-old movie icon Grace Kelly, who had an apartment on East 66th Street, had just made *Dial M for Murder* and *Rear*

Window, and was about to make *High Society*. Some of Niv's friends doubt that he and she had a fling. 'I think she was too busy with other men!' chuckled Roger Moore, and Roddy Mann told me: 'she liked men very much and she was *adorable*, a knockout, and they were huge friends. But it was a brother and sister relationship and I don't think they were lovers.' A biographer, James Spada, however, reported that they did have 'a brief and very discreet affair' in the spring of 1955, and several of Niv's friends – Leslie Bricusse, Bryan Forbes, John Mortimer – told me they thought so too, and Tom Hutchinson told me that Niv had once said to him that Grace was 'a very ardent lover, which made me assume that he'd been to bed with her'. Taki Theodoracopulos, the multi-millionaire Greek socialite and journalist, who knew David well in the 1960s, told me he was sure that they had had an affair, and in 1994 the Superior Auction Galleries in Los Angeles sold a collection of letters that she had written to her friend and secretary Prudy Wise that were said in newspaper reports of the time to refer to several of her affairs, including one with Niv. There was also the story that he told friends in later years about the evening that Grace's husband, Prince Rainier of Monaco, whom she was to marry the following year, asked him after a few drinks late one night, 'Tell me, David, of all the beautiful women you had in Hollywood, who gave you the best blow-job?'

'Grace,' said Niv jovially, and then saw Rainier's horrified expression. 'Ah – Gracie *Fields*!'

Noël Coward's career had faltered briefly but in June he made a triumphant comeback on the first night of a cabaret performance at the Desert Inn in Las Vegas that was raucously applauded by a gang of seventeen friends, including the Nivens, who had been flown in by Frank Sinatra on a chartered plane – among them the Bogarts, Judy Garland, 'Swifty' Lazar, and Gloria and Mike Romanoff. Sinatra paid for them all to have private suites at the Sands Hotel, and after Coward's night of glory they spent three days and nights gambling, seeing other shows, drinking heroically and staying up until dawn, until one morning they all looked so bedraggled and exhausted that Betty Bacall suddenly exclaimed, 'You look like a goddam rat pack!' The name stuck. When they returned to Los Angeles they thanked Sinatra by giving him a dinner at Romanoff's in Beverly Hills and Sinatra's legendary Rat Pack was born. 'In order to qualify,' wrote Betty Bacall in her autobiography, *By Myself*, 'one had to be addicted to nonconformity, staying up late, drinking, laughing, and not caring what anyone thought or said about us.' At the dinner she was jokingly elected den mother, the notoriously rude Bogart became the PR director, and Niv complained that he had not been given a title at all because they were anti-English. A ratty coat of arms was designed and an insignia consisting of 'a large group of rats of all shapes and sizes in all positions', said Bacall. 'What fun we had with it all! We were an odd assortment, but we liked each other so much, and every one of us had a wild sense of the ridiculous.' After that the Rat Pack would meet regularly in each other's houses to sit around talking, drinking, singing, arguing and sometimes fighting. 'We admire ourselves and don't care for anyone else,' Bogart told the *New York Herald Tribune* columnist Joe Hyams, and it was only later that the Rat Pack name was applied to a completely different group of Sinatra's friends that included Sammy Davis Jr, Peter Lawford and Dean Martin.

Sinatra was to become one of Niv's best friends, despite his murky reputation for ruthlessness and his Mafia connections, and David wrote in *The Moon's a Balloon*: 'He is one of the few people in the world I would instinctively think of if I needed help of any sort. I thought of him once when I was in a very bad spot: help was provided instantly and in full measure without a question being asked. It was not, incidentally, money.' Whatever this mysterious episode was, Niv never mentioned it to his sons or friends. Roddy Mann told me he thought that maybe Sinatra had lent David 'some of his strong-arm cronies or recommended some legal muscle to get David out of a contract', and Roger Moore said, 'He could have needed an alibi.'

Some of the Rat Pack came together again on 4 July 1955 to celebrate Independence Day on Bogart's boat, the *Santana*, which was joined by Sinatra in a chartered motor cruiser that had a piano on board. After dinner Sinatra began to sing, fuelled by a bottle of Jack Daniels whisky, and Niv said in *The Moon's a Balloon* that dozens of people from other boats slowly gathered in dinghies and rubber tenders to listen bewitched as 'he sang till the dew came down . . . He sang till the moon and stars paled in the pre-dawn sky – only then did he stop and only then did the awed and grateful audience paddle silently away.' Richard Burton, who was also on Bogie's boat that apparently magical evening, remembered it quite differently. In fact everyone got very drunk, reported Burton in his diary, Sinatra 'got really pissed off' with Bogart because Bogie and Burton ignored him and went off lobster-potting, and Niv kept trying to set fire to the *Santana* to create a diversion because he was so fed up with Sinatra's endless warbling. 'Bogie and Frankie nearly came to blows next day about the singing the night before,' wrote Burton, 'and I drove Betty home because she was so angry with Bogie's cracks about Frankie's singing.' It was a situation that was not helped by the fact that Bacall had started an affair with Sinatra, and Bogie, a heavy smoker who by now had cancer of the oesophagus and was becoming increasingly thin and frail, may well have known about it and was devastated. When Burton read Niv's description of that evening in *The Moon's a Balloon* sixteen years later he was astonished and wrote that it was 'not at all like Niv's description'.

Nor was the next big milestone in his life. In *The Moon's a Balloon* David said that one Sunday afternoon that summer, when they had a houseful of guests at the Pink House, he took a phone call from forty-six-year-old Mike Todd, a loud, brash, vulgar showman who had helped to invent the new Todd-AO system of wide-angle, big-screen cinema photography. Todd had never made a movie but offered Niv the star part in a film that he was later to declare was his favourite of them all, *Around the World in Eighty Days*, and signed him up there and then. Not so, according to David's agent Phil Gersh, who told Peter Haining after Niv's death that Todd had actually wanted Cary Grant for the role, had tried for six months to get him, and when he failed Gersh had to arrange for David to meet Todd three times to beg for the part before Todd agreed reluctantly. It was to be the turning point of his career, to make him richer than ever and to catapult him into a high orbit among the Hollywood stars. After six nervous years of skating on thin ice as a freelance his days in the wilderness were over.

Nine

Around and on Top of the World
1955–1959

Mike Todd wanted to make a vast, spectacular movie to show off his new Todd-AO wide-screen photography and decided to film Jules Verne's epic story of a daring Victorian English adventurer, Phileas Fogg, who in 1872 bets his friends £20,000 that he can travel around the world in eighty days and does so with only seconds to spare with his French valet Passepartout – by train, horse carriage, balloon, ostrich and ship. It was a lavish picture that was to be filmed at 140 locations in thirteen countries and nine studios, with nearly 69,000 extras and fifty brief appearances by major stars, from Ronald Colman, Noël Coward and Marlene Dietrich to John Gielgud, George Raft and Frank Sinatra. Even Trubshawe was in it as 'Man betting at Lloyd's', and in the end it cost £2·5 million to make, about £40 million in modern terms, but on its first release it was to earn twice that and to win five Oscars including the one for the best picture of 1956.

Niv owed his part not only to Phil Gersh but also to his old lover Evelyn Keyes, who was living with Todd and kept telling him how good Niv would be once it was certain that Cary Grant was not available. Gersh negotiated a fee of over $100,000 and the three-hour film, in which David appeared in almost every scene, took six months to shoot, most of it in California but some in France, Spain, Hong Kong, Japan and England, where he found time to play cricket at East Grinstead at the beginning of September for an actors' side against a team of politicians. Making such a big movie inevitably involved a huge number of problems, not least the raising of enough finance, and now and then Todd had to stop shooting while he tried to scrape together a few thousand more dollars. When they came to shoot the scenes in the hot-air balloon Niv confessed that he suffered from vertigo and had to be filmed with the balloon suspended less than five feet off the ground, though one scene had to be shot much higher as the balloon dangled from a crane 180 feet up, so Todd made Niv drink a bottle of champagne first and take another up with him.

Later David said that *Around the World in Eighty Days*, directed by Michael Anderson, was easily his favourite of all his films because the ebullient, cigar-chomping, life-enhancing Todd was such exhilarating fun to work with and so many of his friends were also in it. But he was not very kind to a nervous twenty-one-year-old who was appearing in only her third film: the red-haired, blue-eyed, pale-skinned Shirley MacLaine, who was dreadfully miscast as a poshly-spoken Indian princess whom Niv rescues just as she is about to be burned alive on her late husband's funeral pyre. 'He intimidated me,' she wrote in her autobiography. 'He was bitingly sarcastic about my being cast as a Hindu princess [*and*] for quite a few days [*he*] treated me like an unwanted guest at a garden party. I was so new in the business, so eager to please, and feeling so lonely on location ... that he really hurt my feelings ... I had a terrible time and in many ways blamed his standoffish, detached, droll Englishness for my insecurities. I know he had no respect for me until the picture was over and he saw that perhaps I might make it in the business after all.'

MacLaine was appalled to see how blatantly Hjördis misbehaved with other men, especially when she had had too much to drink, which was increasingly often: ' "Why don't you simply present your entire package, then?" David said to her one evening at dinner when she was embarrassingly flirtatious. He was hurt, and *she* was sarcastic and detached ... We went on to do our love scene the next day and David never missed his marks, was always in his light, was letter-perfect in his lines, but he never looked me in the eye. I could see why Hjördis tried to provoke him.'

Niv was back in California for New Year's Eve 1955, which he and Hjördis spent with the rest of the Rat Pack at Sinatra's house at Palm Springs, where Bogart pushed the tiny, bald agent 'Swifty' Lazar into the pool and Lazar in turn pushed Bogie in, ruining his Cartier watch. 'How are we going to get this dry?' complained Bogart. 'Like this,' said Lazar, tossing the watch into a blazing fire. It was a rare moment of revenge for Lazar, who was often the butt of Rat Pack jokes and a regular victim of Sinatra, who once hired a builder to brick up a cupboard in Lazar's apartment so that he would be unable to get at his clothes. Bogart was on form that New Year's Eve and told the homosexual Noël Coward: 'I think you are wonderful and charming and if I should ever change from liking girls better, you would be my first thought.' Sadly Bogie was now so ill that he was no longer up to loving even girls and was deeply hurt by his young wife's affair with Sinatra, which had become by then common knowledge. Two months later the cancer of the oesophagus that was going to kill him was finally diagnosed and although he underwent a nine-hour operation and radiation treatment it was too late. He had just ten months to live, months during which Niv visited him constantly as he lost a great deal of weight and grew weaker and weaker. Even during Bogart's final weeks his wife spent her thirty-first birthday with Sinatra, the Nivens and the Rat Pack in Las Vegas while Bogart spent the day on his boat with his son at Catalina Island.

Early in 1956 Hjördis was also in hospital, for six weeks, after suffering a miscarriage and subsequent complications, but in the spring she and David returned briefly to England for him to shoot *A Silken Affair* at Elstree and to appear on the TV panel game *What's My Line?*, though when he heard that the TV interviewer Eamonn Andrews was planning to ambush him with his life story for *This Is Your Life* he refused to appear and the programme had to be cancelled. Later that month they flew to Monaco for the wedding of Grace Kelly and Prince Rainier in St Nicholas's cathedral on 19 April, two of the very few from Hollywood on a guest list of 600 people, most of them titled or the mega-rich such as the Aga Khan, ex-King Farouk of Egypt and Aristotle Onassis. Rainier had concocted for himself a chocolate Ruritanian uniform clanking with French and Italian medals, stiff with golden epaulettes and fluffy with ostrich feathers, and was attended by a fanfare of trumpets and Monegasque soldiers, who had never seen a war, with bayonets at the ready, but it was a beautiful Riviera morning and the cathedral was gloriously decorated with cascades of flowers, candles, chandeliers, and television cameramen hanging from the rafters. The sight of Grace as a bride must have stirred Niv's heart and loins because she looked breathtakingly lovely and virginal in a Juliet cap and a long-sleeved ivory gown of silk, lace, taffeta, net and pearls. After the ceremony and lunch in the palace courtyard the guests bizarrely were all whisked off to watch a football match in the national stadium before Grace and Rainier left on their honeymoon cruise of the Mediterranean. It was a puffed-up Toytown wedding but the snob in David, who was always impressed by royalty and titles, relished the make-believe pomp and circumstance. Many people found Rainier vulgar, coarse and dull, but Niv made a point of cultivating his friendship so as to keep alive his relationship with Grace and membership of the small royal circle at the palace of Monte Carlo.

Back in England, he finished *The Silken Affair*, a silly little comedy about a boring, bowler-hatted English accountant who breaks out briefly by cooking the books of a couple of stocking manufacturers, but although the critics damned the film they praised him. It was 'an impeccable and at times brilliant performance', said the *Sunday Express*. 'He has no equal in his own field of precise, polished comedy,' said the *Daily Mail*. He was 'one of the most accomplished light comedians in the business', said the *Financial Times*. Once again he had shown that he was often the only decent ingredient in many of the poor films in which he appeared.

Shirley Anne Field, a beautiful seventeen-year-old, had a tiny part in the film and David duly tried to pick her up and take her to dinner. At first he offered her a lift in his studio Rolls-Royce, but she declined, afraid that people might talk. He grinned. 'I'm sorry, my dear,' he said, 'wouldn't dream of besmirching your reputation.' Later in the week he offered again – 'How do you feel about besmirching your reputation tonight, my dear?' – and she laughed and said 'yes', and accepted a lift on most days after that. Then he sent her a beautiful lace blouse with a card that read 'I hope this won't ruin your reputation any further', and when she thanked him he invited her to have 'a well-behaved dinner' with him. She agreed, and he took her to a very expensive London club, Les Ambassadeurs, where his seduction technique was cruelly interrupted by the drunken arrival of a puffy, blotchy, red-faced Errol Flynn, who tried to flirt with her himself. Niv saw him off and took her home with her virtue intact. Not many seventeen-year-olds can have spurned Errol Flynn and David Niven on the same night.

In May the Nivens flew back to Hollywood for a five-week holiday before returning to London at the end of June to make a film for MGM with two of their contracted stars, Ava Gardner and Stewart Granger, *The Little Hut*, which showed the three of them shipwrecked on a tropical island and indulging in a bit of wife-swapping, which Gardner later called 'a fiasco' and Granger said was 'a bloody stupid comedy', even though it had been a huge success on the stage. Gardner complained that she hated every minute of it and Granger agreed. 'Imagine playing a straight man to David Niven with that bloody moustache,' he complained to his wife, Jean Simmons. 'He's always playing with it or twitching it on everybody else's lines. You can't win against Niven's moustache.' Some of the film was shot in Jamaica but most of it at the Cinecittà Studios in

Rome over more than two stifling months of Italian summer when temperatures reached 140 degrees indoors. Niv's and Granger's tempers were not improved when Ava Gardner kept delaying shooting by taking long lunches with her Italian lover, Walter Chiari, and they agreed to complain to the director, Mark Robson. They approached Robson together but as Granger started to speak he realised that Niv had suddenly disappeared. 'That was typical of Niven,' he told Morley. 'He never liked making trouble if he could get somebody else to make it for him, and you never really quite knew where you were with him. He'd vanish, leaving behind that grin just like a Cheshire Cat.' There were no grins from the critics, who savaged the film, though once again papers such as the *Manchester Guardian* and the *Daily Sketch* singled Niv out as its only redeeming feature.

In England David touched base again with Trubshawe, who was in danger of becoming a bit of a star himself. He had by now had small parts in fifteen films and had just been offered a year's contract with the Associated Rediffusion TV channel to become a 'Personality' and appear in plays and panel games like *What's It All About?*. With his 6ft 6ins height, splendid moustache and silly-ass persona, Trubshawe was to go on to appear in twenty-five more films over the next fourteen years, among them *Doctor at Large*, *A Hard Day's Night*, *Those Magnificent Men in Their Flying Machines*, *The Amorous Adventures of Moll Flanders*, *A Dandy in Aspic* and *The Rise and Rise of Michael Rimmer* – not to mention two episodes of *The Avengers* TV series, in which he played a colonel and a general.

In September the Nivens flew to Sweden for a brief holiday, to Las Vegas to join the Rat Pack at Sinatra's party for Betty Bacall's birthday, and in October to New York for the triumphant Broadway première of *Around the World in Eighty Days*. Todd put them up in the most expensive suite at the St Regis Hotel and stuffed it with champagne, caviar and flowers, and a thousand 'celebrities' in evening dress attended the first night at the Rivoli Theatre in Times Square, and then a midnight champagne supper at the Astor Hotel. The critics were ecstatic. The lively Mexican actor Cantinflas, playing the randy Passepartout, was very funny and stole the film, deservedly winning the Golden Globe award for best actor that year, but Niv's reviews were also raves. 'David Niven is simply perfect,' said the *New York Journal-American*, which called the film 'a fabulous entertainment'. Niv was 'excellent' (*New York Times*), 'superb' (*Financial Times*), 'perfection' (*Observer*), and 'dominates even this gigantic screen with as fine a performance as he has given us for many a long year', said Bernard Levin (*Manchester Guardian*). The *New York Post* said that the film was 'a bubble of delight', the *Daily News* that it was 'sensational' and the *World Telegram and Sun* that the only proper reaction to it was 'wheee-eee-eee!'. The next day Niv sent Todd a cable that read: 'OH WELL STOP BETTER LUCK NEXT TIME.'

Nearly fifty years later the picture seems much less impressive and at times it is actually dull. It is spectacular, of course, with wonderful landscapes, costumes and striking set-piece scenes – a Spanish bullfight, a *suttee* ceremony, a circus in Yokohama, a Red Indian attack, an American election – but as Alexander Walker remarked, 'It is not a film, it is a collection of stars inserted into a travelogue.' Each episode seems disjointed and Niv manages to be little more than blandly smooth, but the movie re-established his name and fortunes, and he was never to look back. From then on he was not only around the world, he was on top of it. And there was more to come: in December he was nominated again for an Emmy award, this time for the best actor in a dramatic TV series for his many appearances in *Four Star Playhouse* that year. And his next film, which he made with Ginger Rogers, *Oh Men! Oh Women!*, a comedy in which he played a psychiatrist whose fiancée seems to be having several affairs with other men, earned him more glowing reviews. There were raves too for thirty-six-year-old Tony Randall, a Broadway actor who was making his film debut and wrote in his autobiography: 'David Niven was the living proof that you don't have to start on the stage and be a stage actor and work hard in repertory and all that in order to become a good actor. He taught himself to be a good actor – and he did know how to act.' Randall told me in New York:

> Niven was a very good actor, and he was so hospitable and enthusiastic, and terribly funny. He could keep you rolling all day. One day on the set he was telling a story and Dan Dailey was laughing so hard that I thought he'd had a stroke. His face had turned purple and his head looked like an egg-plant. I've never seen a man in such paroxysms of laughter. His face was blood red! That's what David could do to you. He was the world's greatest storyteller, and his stories were insanely funny. 'Now promise me, old boy, you'll never repeat this,' he said, 'Rita [*Hayworth*] was the very best there ever was, old boy! You could be in bed with Rita and you might take it into your head that you'd like to wrap a mackerel in newspaper and shove it up her ass, and without your saying a word, old boy, she'd get up and go down to the fridge and get a fish!' When he talked about having girlfriends he said

> 'It's absolutely necessary, old boy, absolutely necessary.' He meant you get bored with your wife and you have to do something to reawaken your libido, and he had the soul of a playboy, though he didn't chase after the girls on the film. He was an enormously powerfully built man, *huge* muscles in his legs, which he was proud of. He pulled up his pants and showed me his calf. His calf was like a football, an *enormous* calf muscle, and I think he was very muscular all over, though he suffered from back problems after a jeep accident. While we were shooting it was giving him trouble again and there were days when he could hardly move and he just stayed stiff on the set and the director moved people around him he was in such pain.

Randall was surprised to see how frugal Niv was – 'he brought his lunch in a paper bag every day' – but that helped to pay off the mortgage on the Pink House after just ten years and to buy a flashy new silver Bentley Continental. But his triumphs were soon to be darkened by tragedy. At the end of November Bogart's cancer was found to have returned and after five days in hospital he was sent home to die. He was now so weak and wasted that the only way he could come down from his bedroom to greet his friends at six o'clock for his evening drink was by being lowered in a wheelchair in a little service elevator, the 'dumb waiter'. They would come in turn, just one or two at a time: Katharine Hepburn, Spencer Tracy and Sinatra often; Niv all the time. Bogie died in the early hours of 14 January 1957, aged fifty-seven. Betty Bacall telephoned the Nivens before dawn. 'My darling husband is gone,' she said. Three days later Niv acted as an usher and bouncer at the memorial service at All Saints' Episcopal church in Beverly Hills, where one of his jobs was to throw out the Press photographers. 'He was wonderful all during Bogie's illness and helped me a lot after Bogie died,' Betty Bacall told me. 'He said, "It's like having a picture on the wall that you've had for ten or twenty years and then suddenly one day you are able to move that picture to another wall. You always have the picture, you never forget the person, but you're able to move it so it's not always a central focus," and I thought that was brilliant, and I in turn have said the same thing to friends who have lost someone very close to them.'

Niv's next movie was a remake with June Allyson of a wacky 1930s comedy, *My Man Godfrey*, in which he played a tramp who is persuaded to become a butler and whose Society-girl employer falls in love with him and discovers that he is in fact an impoverished Austrian count. Niv was brought in to replace an Austrian actor, O. W. Fischer, who had turned out to be so heavily humourless that he would guffaw at the end of every funny line. On Niv's first day in the part the director was horrified to see that he was just as bad and guffawing at the end of every line too, until he discovered that Niv was pulling his leg and winding him up. Once again his reviews reported that he was much better than the film itself – and the same thing happened with his next film, *Bonjour Tristesse*, for which he flew to Paris and the South of France with Deborah Kerr and eighteen-year-old Jean Seberg. The picture was based on the best-selling novel by Françoise Sagan and he played a middle-aged Riviera playboy and philanderer with a taste for pretty young jet-set flesh and an almost incestuous relationship with his seventeen-year-old daughter. 'David is still recognisable as David Niven but there's an edge to him,' said Alexander Walker. 'It was one of his four best films along with *The Way Ahead*, *Carrington VC* and *Separate Tables*.'

While Niv was filming he hired a villa at St Tropez and fell in love with the warm, hedonistic lifestyle of the Côte d'Azur – so much so that four years later he was to buy a villa along the coast on Cap Ferrat and live there for the rest of his life. He was probably seduced not only by the lotus-eating way of life, the balmy Mediterranean and the proximity of Princess Grace but also by the laissez-faire nonchalance of the French policeman who arrested him late one night, when he had forgotten his key and was trying to break in to the villa, and then showed him how to break and enter like a real burglar by inserting a long spoon inside the shutter.

Bonjour Tristesse was the first of five films that Niv was to make with the elegant, thirty-five-year-old, Scots-born Deborah Kerr, who was married to her first husband, Tony Bartley. They clicked immediately, became close friends for the rest of his life, and seventeen years later he told Don Short of the *People* that she was his favourite co-star, 'a marvellous person, with such a tremendous sense of humour. That's what I look for in a woman – femininity and humour.' It was a jokey relationship – sometimes she would adopt the gorblimey cockney accent of a London charlady and he called her Hilda or Hil because of it – but also such a close relationship that it was she who saw through the constant merriment and spotted that he could sometimes be sad and melancholy.

'By now he was very unhappy with Hjördis,' Doreen Hawkins told me, 'and he used to look unhappy, with what Deborah called his "mouse face" look, which seemed to say "I can't stand this any more". Deborah christened him Mouse Face: it had a dark shadow over it when he was unhappy.' In 2002 Deborah Kerr was eighty-one and living in Switzerland but sadly unable to give me an interview because 'she is not well', I was told by her second husband, Peter Viertel, who married her in 1962. 'She has Parkinson's Disease. She wouldn't be able to answer your questions except to say yes or no, and her voice is very weak. She can't move either, but she's somehow bearing up at the moment.' But before the onset of her illness she told Sheridan Morley:

> I loved David very much. Our relationship was one of total fun, because every disaster on the set or off was always met by David as some kind of elaborate joke played on him from above. He never let that mask slip in public, and it was only after years of working with him that I began to see a darker, sadder side to his nature. Most of the time we were like two children in school, crying with laughter over each other's jokes; but there was a terrible insecurity about him when we got near the end of a picture. If he didn't know exactly what film he was going into next, he got terribly neurotic about not being in work. He had to keep working, working, working all the time and I never in all the years I knew him found out why. Was he really so worried about money, or was it an escape from the family, or just that he liked the life of a film studio more than any other? He couldn't bear life if he wasn't actually working: a lot of actors are like that. David didn't have any other life until he started to write again: at this time, the films were really everything.

They never became lovers, her husband told me: 'He did have love affairs but not with Deborah. Not that Deborah didn't have lovers before we were married, but she said she didn't see him that way. They were close chums.' R. J. Wagner told me that he wished Deborah and Niv had married: 'That would have been perfect, a romance made in heaven. They were the most wonderful couple I ever saw together. They had the same sense of humour and such a joyous time together.' Another close but platonic woman friend was R. J.'s own wife, the nineteen-year-old Russian-American actress Natasha Nikolaevna Zakharenko, who called herself Natalie Wood. She had already made twenty-eight films and came into Niv's life when she married twenty-seven-year-old R. J. in December 1957. 'We had some great times together,' said Wagner.

At the end of 1957 David's career was riding high. In London in October *The Little Hut* was playing on one side of Leicester Square, *My Man Godfrey* on the other, and *Around the World in Eighty Days* was on round the corner in Charing Cross Road. At Shepperton Studios he was just finishing the final shots for *Bonjour Tristesse* and about to start filming *Separate Tables*. He was said to be earning £30,000 per film – about £450,000 in modern terms – and since he had made three films that year he must have earned well over £1 million in today's values yet he was still well aware that without Preminger and Todd his career might never have been resurrected. At the end of October he gave an interview to Roy Nash of the *Star*, who asked what he might have been doing now had he failed to make it in Hollywood. 'I should be the lonely and inefficient secretary of a nine-hole golf course, or something equally dismal,' he replied.

As it was, he was about to reach the summit of his career. *Separate Tables*, for which he was to win an Oscar, had been born as two hugely successful one-act stage plays by Terence Rattigan, set in a genteel seaside residential hotel in southern England where most of the residents are old retired people. Burt Lancaster's film company bought the movie rights for Laurence Olivier and Vivien Leigh to play all four leading parts, but when the Oliviers backed out Lancaster himself played the drunken American journalist, Rita Hayworth his beautiful ex-wife, Niv the retired English 'major' who lives at the hotel and lies about his past, and Deborah Kerr the timid spinster who is bullied by her old mother, played by Gladys Cooper, and hopelessly fond of the major.

Shooting began in November and David was delighted to be portraying what he considered to be one of Rattigan's best characters and with such a distinguished cast of English actors, among them Wendy Hiller, Gladys Cooper, Felix Aylmer and Cathleen Nesbitt. 'It was a dream company to work with,' he wrote in *The Moon's a Balloon* although several of the cast would have disagreed. Lancaster and his business partner James Hill, who was to marry Rita Hayworth two months later, kept taunting Wendy Hiller with crude remarks, sniggering jokes, filthy language and suggestive innuendos, possibly because she had rejected a sexual advance. Rita Hayworth was nervous, insecure, overawed by all the celebrated English actors, and drinking too much, and she spoke so softly that there was talk of replacing her. Niv, too, was apprehensive of the other actors, especially when he had to shoot a scene at the end of the film when his 'major' has been exposed as a liar and convicted molester of women in darkened cinemas, and has to walk into the restaurant knowing that the other guests have heard about his disgrace. It took four days to shoot the scene, with long close-ups of David's expressions of embarrassment, fear, guilt and shame, and while he was doing them he trembled with nervous tension. 'There was this whole line-up of the British stage ... all staring at him,' the film's director, Delbert Mann, told Morley, 'and when he'd finished they all applauded. I think that was maybe the best moment of his whole acting career.'

Priscilla Morgan – who was twenty-three and later married Clive Dunn, one of the stars of the TV series *Dad's Army* – played the hotel's cheeky waitress and told me: 'David was very nice and made it happy for everybody. He always made sure that nobody was left out. We English were over in Hollywood for four months and quite lonely, and he was so kind, always asking us over for the weekend. His sons weren't that much younger than me and I used to go there and have Sunday lunch and play croquet with the boys.' Some people claimed that Niv's performance was a shameless copy of Eric Portman's in the stage play but Priscilla Morgan, who was in that production too, said, 'He didn't *pinch* Portman's performance but he'd do bits that went awfully well on the stage the same way in the film. That's fair enough. He admired Portman very much.' Roddy Mann had seen Portman on stage too and denied that Niv had plagiarised his performance: 'They were totally different. Portman's was a much *heavier* portrayal, Niven was rather sad and crumpled. He bloody well deserved the Oscar.'

Niv did not try to seduce Cilla Morgan. 'Everyone said that he would,' she said, sounding almost disappointed,

> but I thought he was an old gent and I already had a liaison in England. When I met David years later at a party he said, 'Oh, Christ, I didn't half fancy you!' and I said, 'Well, you should have said something. I hadn't the faintest idea.' He didn't approach anyone else either – they were all nine hundred years old! – but it's a shame he never married Rita Hayworth. It would have been so good for her because she had such horrible husbands, and David and she got on marvellously well. She was a very quiet person, as shy as anything, and he would bring her out and insist on her sitting with us so she wouldn't be left out. He was absolutely lovely. But I wasn't too keen on Burt Lancaster: he was very rude to Rita and she was so sweet and defenceless against men being rude to her, which I think they always had been.

Another of David's fans was Cathleen Nesbitt, who recalled in her memoirs that 'he made us laugh so much we none of us wanted to go home ... Not only did he tell extremely funny stories, mostly against himself, but he told them so well. And he never was one to hog the scene. He could draw tales from [*another*] eighty-year-old May Hallatt, about her childhood, or from Felix Aylmer about his terrifying attempts to find an exit from the freeways.'

Niv played the 'major' as though he had known him personally – with his blazer, cravat, Trubshawe-length moustache and bogus heroic anecdotes of having been at Wellington, Sandhurst and in the Desert Rats, whereas he had in fact been a humble Supply Corps lieutenant who had spent the whole war nice and safe in the West Indies. It was a comparatively small part yet it trembled with authenticity. 'He kept saying, "God, this is the real stuff, isn't it?," ' Deborah Kerr told Morley, 'and I think he caught that major because in so many ways he understood him . . . as a character and as a person David felt that he was on familiar ground – that he too in his own life had always been acting and pretending, "dressing up for the grown-ups", as he used to say.'

'Why have you told so many *awful* lies?' Deborah Kerr's mousy little spinster asks the 'major' in the film.

'Because I don't like myself the way I am, I suppose,' he replies. 'I've had to invent somebody else. It's not too hard, really. We all have our daydreams. Mine have just gone a step further than most people's. Sometimes I've even managed to believe in the major myself' – just as Niv himself came to believe in the fibs he had told so often about himself. 'David knew all about the weak character of the major keeping up a front,' said Alexander Walker, 'because he had to keep up a front himself in life, so he was excellent in the part and deserved the Oscar for that very reason.' Like the 'major', too, Niv feared all his life that one day he would be exposed as a fraud. 'He always used to say he was scared of being found out,' his son Jamie told me, 'that he'd wake up one morning and someone would tap him on the shoulder and say "you know you're not any good".'

He was in fact superb in *Separate Tables*. 'NIVEN'S MASTERPIECE' ran the *Daily Herald* headline. 'The finest role of his career,' said the *Daily Sketch*. 'Excellent,' said *Time*. 'A shining performance,' said the *Evening News*. 'Beautifully characterised,' said the *Sunday Times*. It was a powerful and deeply poignant performance, the best of his career, that proved that he was not just a lightweight comic actor. 'He won the Oscar deservedly,' Bryan Forbes told me. 'Lesser people have won it for much less.'

Yet he was still so insecure that just before the film was released he told his agent, Phil Gersh, 'Nobody wants me. I guess I'm finished and perhaps I should return to London where I feel there is employment,' and instead of waiting for just the right film to follow it he grabbed the first two that came his way. As soon as *Separate Tables* was released, he told

Tom Hutchinson: 'I got some wonderful films offered to me but I couldn't take them. I had already contracted to do two more of the usual crap.' Michael Parkinson asked him on his TV show in 1981 why he had not had much better roles after winning the Oscar. 'I suppose I dropped the ball,' he replied. 'You do the next film for the scratch. I never expected to get the Oscar and I was booked for two more films after that.'

Shooting of *Separate Tables* was finished by the first week of January 1958 and briefly there was a chance that he might be cast as James Bond in the first of the films about the British secret agent 007. Bond's creator, Niv's old friend Ian Fleming, was keen that he should have the part but eventually it went to Sean Connery.

In the middle of March the Nivens spent a jolly weekend at Palm Springs with Mike Todd and his twenty-six-year-old wife of just a year, Elizabeth Taylor, and they got on so well that Todd invited them again for the following weekend, but tragedy was only days away. On 22 March his plane crashed in New Mexico and he was killed. He was only forty-eight, the same age as David, and two months later one of Niv's oldest friends, Ronnie Colman, died in Santa Barbara of a lung infection at the age of sixty-seven. He had a third shock just a few months after Todd's death when Liz Taylor embarked on a scandalous affair with the singer Eddie Fisher, who was married to Debbie Reynolds, and married him the following year. David was appalled, and though he and Liz 'had been fast friends, he cut E. dead for seven months', wrote her next husband, Richard Burton, in his diary nine years later. 'Though we were still friendly it could never be the same again.' Niv's disapproval of Taylor and Fisher was decidedly hypocritical considering his own sexual rampage after Primmie's death.

At the end of March he and Hjördis tried to repair their battered marriage by going around the world in a hundred and eighty days – six months – during which they visited Japan and Hong Kong with Shirley MacLaine and her husband Steve Parker and Thailand, India, Turkey and Venice on their own. When they reached Greece David Jr and Jamie, now fifteen and twelve, flew out to sail with them around the Greek islands on a chartered ketch. They flew home via Sweden, to see Hjördis's family, and back to the Pink House in August. Niv treasured his memories of that long trip: the beauty of Jaipur, where everything was painted a shocking pink, even the elephants' accoutrements; the tiny, dainty, lemon-coloured women of Bangkok, whom he called 'the loveliest people in the world'; the jewel-like little Italian *palazzi* of Venice; the glittering sparkle of the Aegean Sea. But the long break did nothing for his marriage. Hjördis was as unappreciative as ever and increasingly irritated and jealous to find that David was recognised everywhere, even in the backwaters of Third World countries. 'He gets all the attention,' she complained in her series in *Woman* six years later and added, 'Then there is the question of other women. It would be terrible if they didn't flirt with David for it would mean he had lost his charm. But I think they make fools of themselves when they overdo it. I used to get mad when they overdid it.' The storm clouds over their marriage were growing darker, and Hjördis's own behaviour with other men was just as outrageous as that of her husband's women admirers.

'We first met her and David in 1958 in La Jolla, California, when we went to dinner at a friend's house,' I was told by Valerie Youmans, who later became friendly with David when they lived in Switzerland.

> David was a gentleman, gracious and hilariously funny. As an opener he said, 'I've got this sister who's a marvellous dyke in London,' and then he told us her description of the male appendage! I will not quote it because I was a bit shocked and hadn't heard quite such vulgar language, but it was very, very funny – and this was why his sister was a dyke! But his wife was impossible and very much on the make. My husband was sitting in a wooden chair with arms and she sat on the floor and put her arm over my husband's legs and started fondling him. I was young and naïve and I watched this, sort of fascinated, when all of a sudden our hostess said, 'Would you kindly stop playing with my best friend's husband's leg,' – whereupon my husband took his arm away from the wooden chair arm and her head, which had been on his arm, went *clunk* onto the wood. My husband was a very good-looking man and I think she found him very attractive, but it was rotten manners, just vulgar and horrid.

That summer of 1958 Niv assessed his life so far in the series he contributed to the *Sunday Express* and said he thought that maybe he was growing up at last – and about time too at forty-eight. He had been 'a man strolling rather casually through life, and not taking any of it very seriously', he said. 'I find nothing dynamic or sensational in my character, and that is a pity. But if I find a man who so far has not accomplished anything very startling, I also see a man who hasn't really done much harm. It is not an electrifying portrait.' Nor was it a fair one, for he had made a few excellent movies as well as many dreadful ones, had brightened millions of lives and whenever he walked into a room he cheered people up, all of which is a great deal more than most of us achieve.

Separate Tables had yet to be released but word of Niv's performance reached one of Hollywood's most powerful agents, fifty-nine-year-old Bert Allenberg, who approached him at a party one night towards the end of November and said he would like to handle him and had several ideas for giving his career a major boost. David's current hard-working agent, Phil Gersh, had become a good friend but Allenberg was in a different league and Niv's contract with Gersh was about to run out. He 'carefully weighed his ambition and greed against his integrity', he wrote in *Bring on the Empty Horses*, decided to tell Gersh he would not be renewing their contract and 'was surprised at how easy it must have been for Judas Iscariot'. Gersh was deeply hurt to be dumped. 'You were the first actor I ever *really* liked,' he told him. 'Now I know you are just the same as all the rest.' David felt bad about it but on the Monday morning told Allenberg he had done the dirty deed and Allenberg promised that he would be seeing two major movie moguls the next day and would have good news for him on the Wednesday. Tuesday dragged by and with mounting excitement Niv called Allenberg's office first thing on the Wednesday morning. 'Mr Allenberg died last night,' said his secretary.

Separate Tables opened in December and was showered with sparkling reviews. 'One of the year's finest achievements,' said the *New York Herald Tribune*. The New York critics circle gave David their award for best actor and in due course he was nominated too for the Oscar. One of the New York critics, however, announced belligerently that he had voted against him, and David was so curious to find out why that he took him out for lunch and asked him. 'Because,' said the critic aggressively, 'some British army ex-lieutenant fucked my wife in Bermuda, that's why!'

'Say no more!' said Niv.

He earned more excellent reviews for another romantic comedy, *Ask Any Girl*, this time with Shirley MacLaine, in which he played the prissy boss of a research agency who tries to play Cupid for his brother and a naïve young country girl but ends up winning her himself. The reviewers loved both him and the film, which 'seems to confirm him as a captain and *chef du protocol* of Hollywood's British colony for the next twenty years or so', said the *Daily Mail*. The critics were much less enthusiastic about *Happy Anniversary*, a risqué little domestic comedy about premarital sex which he made in New York with Mitzi Gaynor after Doris Day backed out because she thought it might damage her pure, virginal screen image, and the film did cause a stir in America because although the main characters have been married for thirteen years, it was considered scandalous that they should admit that they had been lovers long before their wedding. 'David said he slept with unmarried people all the time!' the film's producer, Ralph Fields, told me.

So did Hjördis. 'She started to look around for men,' Betty Bacall told me. 'Getting older did not agree with her and she had several affairs and that was bad news. She should never have done that.' Not even when Niv was himself so often unfaithful? 'No, I don't think you can blame him for that. I think she brought it all on herself. I'm sure he was not always easy to live with but *nobody*'s easy to live with.'

In February 1959 the Nivens were due to go to the Berlin Film Festival and then visit Hjördis's family in Sweden again, but they had grown so far apart that she changed her mind at the last minute, preferring to stay in California, perhaps because of a boyfriend, and David went on his own. Peter Ustinov, who was also suffering an unhappy marriage, was living mostly in Paris at the time and 'occasionally Niv would ring up and we'd go out to some small restaurant where nobody knew us', he told me, 'largely because we knew that neither of us was very happy because of our unhappy marriages. I remember him saying, "I told Hjördis that in order to be loved you should try to be lovable." I don't think he was to blame for her behaviour. I think she was intrinsically flawed in some way. She was very Scandinavian, very doomy and gloomy, and under the pressure of his second marriage he became a melancholy, introspective man. He found out what it's like to be unloved, and to be making the effort but no effort is visible on the other side, so is it worth it? I'm sure he never really recovered from Primmie's death and I think he had quite an unhappy life.'

As the night of the Oscars approached, Niv became increasingly nervous. He was up against Tony Curtis and Sidney Poitier for their performances in *The Defiant Ones*, Paul Newman in *Cat on a Hot Tin Roof* and Spencer Tracy in *The Old Man and the Sea*, and he thought he had no chance against such distinguished actors. To reinforce his pessimism the *Hollywood Reporter* quoted one producer as saying that he would not vote for Niv because he had merely copied Eric Portman's stage performance, which he claimed Niv had seen forty times. David made the paper print an apology, insisting that he had seen the play only once, but he was convinced that now his chance of winning was zero, even though he received an encouragingly naughty letter from Bing Crosby two days before the Oscars ceremony. 'Dear David,' wrote Crosby. 'I have committed a heinous breach of Academy discipline. I voted for you without ever having seen the picture "Separate Tables". I'm glad I did though, because last night I got a chance to see the movie. Your performance is the most delicate, sensitive portrayal I've ever seen on the screen – a truly accurate delineation of a pitiable phony. Congratulations, David – win, lose or draw, Monday night.'

To add to the tension Niv was not only a nominee but also one of the three compères at the Oscar ceremony at the Pantages Theatre in Hollywood on 6 April 1959, and for nearly an hour, in front of an estimated television audience of 80 million, he went through the motions, self-conscious in his white tie and tails, sweating, loosening his collar, tugging at his ear, only too aware of the TV cameras perched on the walls like vultures watching for the slightest weakness, as the speeches and awards went on and on. Wendy Hiller won the Oscar for best supporting actress for *Separate Tables*, so surely he could not win as well. Burl Ives was best supporting actor for *The Big Country*, Susan Hayward best actress for *I Want to Live*, and then it was the Oscar for the best actor. Irene Dunne opened the big white envelope, hesitated a moment and read out his name. Astonished, euphoric, he kissed Hjördis, jumped up and blundered through the applause towards the stage, running down the aisle, tripping on the steps, falling on his hands and knees. Irene Dunne gave him the golden Oscar statuette and a kiss, and flushed with pride he approached the microphone. 'The reason I just fell down,' he said, 'was because I was so loaded . . .' He meant to say 'loaded down with good luck charms' but the audience roared with delight, assuming he meant that he was drunk.

Sam Goldwyn was unwell and watching at home on TV, but as Niv left the stage he saw Goldwyn's son sitting at one of the tables and went over to him. 'Sammy,' he said, 'I want Sam and Frances to know how much a part of this they are. I wouldn't have had this if it hadn't been for them.' That night was the unforgettable peak of his career and he kept every one of the 230 telegrams of congratulation that arrived the next day, including one from Sam and Frances Goldwyn, who finally ended their ten-year estrangement by inviting him to dinner a few days later. When he reached their house Goldwyn hugged him and in the drawing room Niv saw his own framed photograph standing on the piano. 'Sam never took it down,' said Frances fondly.

And then, at the moment of his greatest triumph, Hjördis left him.

Ten

Château d'Oex and the Côte d'Azur
1959–1962

Hjördis left him to find herself. She had just turned forty, was terrified of old age and losing her looks, deeply depressed after several miscarriages and a hysterectomy, and now that Niv had won the Oscar she was more jealous than ever, desperate to rediscover her own identity and assert her independence. She was still having an affair with her doctor and drinking far too much, and for more than a year had been telling Niv that she was going to leave him. When finally she went in the summer of 1959 he looked 'like a pathetic and bewildered small boy', she told *Woman*. 'We said goodbye and parted, in a terribly adult and matter-of-fact way, and I moved into a house I had taken not far away.'

Niv was as gentlemanly as ever, blaming himself publicly and later admitting that after the Oscar he became big-headed and took Hjördis for granted, but Peter Viertel, who was then a scriptwriter and living nearby with Deborah Kerr, told me that Hjördis was 'a very neurotic, mixed-up woman'. Even so, he said, Niv wanted to save the marriage, mainly for the sake of the boys, who were now sixteen and thirteen, and both at fashionable St Paul's boarding school in New Hampshire. Niv told Viertel that Hjördis had not let him sleep with her for a long time and 'was flirting with someone else, so I said, "That's a big mistake. If you want to *keep* her take the boys to Hawaii or some place where she'll know there are other pretty ladies," and he said, "You may be right." Frank Sinatra had a house in Hawaii and he went there.'

In Honolulu Niv and the boys 'had a terrific time', David Jr told me. 'He went through the girls of Honolulu like a machete through a pineapple!' Neither of the boys could understand later why he did not grab his chance then to get divorced. 'When she moved out and was having a relationship with this doctor,' Jamie told me, 'he tried to get a divorce and I never could understand why he didn't go ahead and do it. Everyone has stories about bad stepmothers but she has to rank right up there with the worst. I can't imagine how she could behave the way she did toward my brother and myself. When you're a young kid and you've lost your mother you crave affection and warmth from the woman in the house. To go out of her way to deny us that on purpose and to make us feel so rejected was almost inhuman.'

What Niv really thought of Hjördis may well have been indicated in a revealing interview that he gave to the *Evening Standard* a year later when he said, 'Beautiful faces are often the dullest ones of them all because there's nothing behind the eyes,' and as for make-up, 'I don't care how much a woman uses so long as I don't know . . . But I do hate loads of that pale blue eyeshadow or those graveyard lipsticks.' Hjördis was notorious for caking her face so that it looked like a mask, and one of the actors in Niv's next film, Richard Haydn, told Sheridan Morley that 'she was wonderfully decorative and always smelt gorgeous, but there was something odd about her. She always looked like a perfectly decorated house in which nobody ever actually lived, and David treated her rather like a precious toy that might get broken if you were too rough with it.'

Pat Medina was appalled when she visited Hjördis at her new house and discovered the sort of people she was entertaining there. 'She had a few people to lunch and they were drinking an awful lot, and I didn't like any of them,' she told me. ' "Where did you find this lot?" I asked her, and she said one of them was very fond of her, and I said, "Let me get out of here, I can't take this." She was a friend of mine but that upheaval was entirely her own fault.'

Niv was not the sort of man to sit at home and mope because his wife had left him, and he soon found other women to amuse him. 'One was a lovely friend of mine called Caroline Kirkwood,' Fiona Thyssen-Bornemisza told me. 'She was a sort of model, about twenty-seven, and came from a good English family, and she was small, blonde and very pretty – not a spectacular beauty but very sweet and enchanting. He was madly in love with her and we all knew about it.'

Niv also tried to forget his marital problems by going back to work. He teamed up with the wholesome Doris Day in a jolly family comedy, *Please Don't Eat the Daisies*, for which he broke two basic actors' rules – never to appear with children or animals – by taking on both: a wonderfully wacky infant with a huge, wicked grin, and a big, shaggy, cowardly dog that was terrified of cats and squirrels. Both threatened to steal the film and although the critics hated it Niv and Doris Day played their parts with genial panache, although his accent veered from English to American and back.

Hjördis's declaration of independence lasted for three months. She returned to him so quickly, she told *Woman*, because Niv kept dropping by and bombarding her with red carnations and roses, and because the boys missed her so much and kept calling by too. 'I could see they longed to have me back,' she claimed, and added, 'He finally broke me down when he started to bring along his lunch in a parcel from the studio when he visited me. This really touched my heart more than any words from him could have done . . . this human, small-boy gesture made me want to cry. It struck a maternal chord in me and made me worry about whether he was being properly fed, and, indeed, it brought home to me as nothing else could the loneliness of his life as a bachelor-husband.' Since she told *Woman* that if she had nobody to cook for her she would open a tin of baked beans 'and eat out of the tin', and since she had never previously worried about Niv's diet or loneliness it seems unlikely that she did now, and Pat Medina gave me a very different reason for her return: 'She knew he was making a lot of money from Four Star and thinking of going to live in Switzerland, and she wanted the money. That was another thing that she and I had a disagreement about, and towards the end we didn't see much of each other.' Her return was well timed, for Niv told Pat Medina: 'Hjördis came back *just* in time because by then I was very nicely tucked in with someone else.'

Amazingly and foolishly he took her back and they flew down to Rio for him to be presented with a vast gold key to the city. 'What about me?' demanded Hjördis. 'Can't I have a little one too?' A small replica was made for her that afternoon.

Back in Hollywood Niv met another president, Khrushchev of the Soviet Union, who was visiting Los Angeles, and sat next to the fat, homely Mrs Khrushchev at a big lunch packed with hundreds of stars where Frank Sinatra was the master of ceremonies and sat on the other side of the Russian First Lady, who was excited to see so many famous faces and proudly showed Niv and Sinatra photographs of her grand-children. 'She smelt of hot velvet,' said David afterwards.

The 1950s ended with a double sadness: on 14 October Errol Flynn died in Vancouver of a heart attack at the age of only fifty, and on Christmas Eve Niv's old mentor, the director Edmund Goulding, was so depressed at the collapse of his career and the lack of offers of work that he committed suicide at the age of sixty-eight. Goulding had asked for Niv to be one of his pallbearers, and his description of the funeral in *Bring on the Empty Horses* is so hilarious that the tears roll down my cheeks every time I read it. No one could possibly retell the story as well as he did, but it involves a grim Niven hangover, a very hot day, a very heavy mahogany coffin, a steep hill, and a gloriously bizarre team of pallbearers: a giant young body-builder, a midget, an ancient with only one leg, another with only one arm, and an extremely fat, wheezy businessman with a sweaty, purple face. The story is probably hugely exaggerated – and Niv said it happened in August whereas it was in December – but who cares? It is very funny.

Now that Hjördis was back Niv made valiant efforts to heal their marriage and tried pathetically to buy her affection by showering her with gifts. 'It's the only recipe for a successful marriage,' he told a journalist, Paul Grant, unconvincingly in 1977. He would tuck a piece of jewellery under her pillow, or pretend to have found a hidden locket, or smother her with vast bouquets. 'It's been the basis for our staying so much in love,' Hjördis told Grant cynically. Niv also tried to make her happier by suggesting that they ought to adopt a baby and eventually, after encouragement from women friends like Betty Bacall, she was to agree so long as the child was a girl and Swedish. 'Children are necessary to any marriage,' he told the *Daily Express* five years later. 'Without them it's like eating an egg without salt.' And finally he decided that the marriage had more chance of success if they left the shallow hothouse of Hollywood and returned to live in Europe.

'I think he would have stayed in the Pink House much longer if Bogie and other friends of his hadn't died,' said Betty Bacall, 'but his heart wasn't there any more.' He certainly felt that Hollywood was not nearly as much fun as it had been. 'The old camaraderie . . . was gone,' he wrote in *The Moon's a Balloon*. 'The mystique had evaporated . . . the lovely joke was over.' Los Angeles was increasingly polluted by smog and violence, and a neighbour's teenage son was shot and killed when four junkies broke into his house. And although Niv was now earning about $200,000 per film – the equivalent of about £700,000 in 2003 – and Four Star was making good profits, he was paying a huge amount of US tax and had just been reassessed for the previous four years and forced to hand over such a big chunk of his savings that he told his sons that after years of playing starring roles he could not afford even to have the Pink House repainted. 'He told me that he had to leave because he hadn't got any money, which I thought was extraordinary,' said Roddy Mann. Deborah Kerr and her second husband Peter Viertel had already moved to Switzerland and persuaded him to join them and become a Swiss resident like several other friends: Liz Taylor and Richard Burton, Noël Coward, Peter Ustinov. 'In Switzerland he was able to keep ninety per cent of his earnings instead of giving ninety per cent to the government,' said David Jr.

He sold the Pink House to a friend, the agent Phil Kellogg, early in 1960, sent the boys back to their boarding school and flew with Hjördis to Switzerland to look for a new home. They drove down through the Ardennes, visited Deborah and Peter Viertel in Klosters, celebrated Niv's fiftieth birthday by having lunch with Noël Coward at his home at Les Avants, and started to look seriously for somewhere nearby in the French-speaking part of Switzerland because, Viertel told me, 'he could get by in French although he spoke it with a thick accent.'

While Hjördis looked at properties Niv flew off to the Greek island of Rhodes to start work on *The Guns of Navarone*, Carl Foreman's spectacular blockbuster of a wartime action thriller about a small group of Allied commandos who land secretly in 1943 on a tiny Greek island that has been heavily fortified by the Nazis, and blow up their two huge guns. The cast included several old friends: Gregory Peck, Anthony Quinn, Anthony Quayle, Stanley Baker, Richard Harris and even Trubshawe, who had a small part as a pompous hairy soldier. This was 'a lovely bonus for me', wrote Niv in *The Moon's a Balloon* but in fact their friendship had soured because, Trubshawe told Morley, Niv seemed embarrassed by him, resented having him in the same movie and avoided him.

Niv's role in the picture was as one of the commandos, an explosives expert who would destroy the massive German guns, and he gave one of his very best performances, though once again his accent kept slipping. At first there was a lot of tense rivalry among the starry cast. Peck was suspicious that Quinn would try to upstage him, Quinn was wary of Niv because of his Oscar, and Niv was wary of everyone else because they were all such good actors, but the tension evaporated when Quinn produced a portable chess set. 'There was David Niven, the Errol Flynn of the chessboard, charging around with his queen, crying, "Idiotic move, what, eh? Well never mind, on we go. Charge!"' Quinn told Michael Munn for his biography of Gregory Peck, who said that Niv 'was always so incredibly cheerful that when you asked why he was, he'd just say, "Well, old bean, life is really so bloody awful that I feel it's my absolute duty to be chirpy and try and make everybody else happy too."' His irrepressible cheerfulness, however, was not always appreciated. Quayle became a good chum of Niv's but told Morley: 'After a while it became almost unbearable to hear him telling the same stories time and time again.' None of Niv's other friends would ever admit to me that sometimes his stories became tedious because he had told them so often.

Niv hated Rhodes, where he said there was nothing to do and the food was terrible, but it did give him yet another anecdote when he picked up a copy of the *Hollywood Reporter* and was stunned to see on the front page a splash headline shrieking that Four Star had gone bust and that he, Boyer and Powell were bankrupt. In a rising panic he read the report, in which his partners attacked him bitterly for selfishly leaving them to bail the company out while he was lying on a Greek island beach. Then he looked at the date: April Fools' Day. Powell and Boyer had bought the entire front page for an advertisement and had run the story as a practical joke.

Hjördis found a wooden chalet in Switzerland and David bought it – a house he always called his Swiss 'cuckoo clock' in a very English little Alpine valley village, Château d'Oex, near the skiing village of Gstaad and an hour's drive from Geneva. Built in 1946, it was not especially pretty but it had a tennis court and from its three balconies a spectacular view of the mighty mountains across the valley – a view that some might find claustrophobic, even threatening. 'The chalet was awful,' Roddy Mann told me. 'It wasn't comfortable and it didn't have much land, just a dreary bit of ground in front of it,' and the Dutch couple who bought it after Hjördis's death in 1997, Jan and Coco Wyers, told me that the decor was very depressing and it was very dark and gloomy, with lots of poky little rooms. 'They had separate bedrooms,' said Mrs Wyers, 'and the three little servants' rooms at the top were amazingly small. The doors were very cheap plywood – what you'd pack your oranges in! – and the furniture very unstylish. Nothing matched. And in the basement, where he had a little cinema, a billiard room, a sauna and a wine cellar, all the walls and ceilings were dark grey!'

Niv decided to live in Château d'Oex – which is pronounced 'Day' – rather than Gstaad, where the skiing is much better, because it was in the canton of Vaud rather than Berne and the tax was a little lower, I was told in Gstaad by seventy-five-year-old Hedi Donizetti, who owned and ran the Olden Hotel, where David ate almost every day when he was at Château d'Oex. The Nivens moved into the chalet that spring and sent the boys to a school in Lausanne, the Lycée Jacard, which was on Lake Geneva in the suburb of Pully, twenty-five miles away. The change of school came at exactly the right time for David Jr since he had just been expelled from St Paul's in New Hampshire for buying beer. 'Daddy was furious,' David told me, 'because he thought it was a stupid thing to be expelled for' – apparently forgetting that he had himself been expelled for sending dog droppings through the post.

Sadly the move to Switzerland failed to repair the marriage. 'Hjördis was a pest,' Mrs Donizetti told me.

> If I ever hated somebody it was her. David had a most amazing, sweet character and was always smiling, and was really a friend, but by lunchtime she was already really drunk, right from when I first knew her and all through the marriage. When she came to lunch at the Olden she was always gone and very loud. The Olden used to be the melting pot of Gstaad. We had King Constantine of Greece, Prince Rainier, Princess Grace, the Queens of Holland, Sweden and Denmark, King Hussein and his wife, and lots of jet setters – the Burtons, Liza Minnelli, Gunter Sachs, Peter Sellers – and Hjördis would always sit at the second table to the right when you come into the restaurant so that she could see everybody coming in, and it was always 'Whoa! Whoa!', a big show. David suffered a lot and he never complained one word, and she was really bad to him. She had lovers and she was always flirting around, and she danced very sexily with other men at parties, and he was sitting there and he never complained. That's why I hated her, because he was such a nice man and he did everything he could to be good to her and she was behaving like a very cheap lady. She was just living for herself and David just didn't deserve that kind of woman. I think he had a rotten life, something he just didn't deserve.

As Jamie said to me about Hjördis, 'This was a woman who didn't love him, who didn't think he was funny, who didn't try and be helpful with his friends, who was constantly fighting with his children, who was just very difficult and resented his success.'

Hjördis gave the *Sunday Mirror* an interview the following month and remarked with astounding condescension about David, 'He is a worrier. He worries about little things, like catching a plane or having people to dinner. He worries about his future, about money. He is a good husband – because he worries.' He seems to have had a lot to worry about. In September she gave another interview, this time to the *Daily Mail*, in which she admitted that he was 'the most even-tempered man imaginable, but I can always start an argument if I dare to criticise his friends'.

She added, as though surprised, 'I often feel that women don't like me.' Yet Niv tried so hard to make the marriage work that when he was offered the starring role in *Lolita* that year he consulted Hjördis and then turned it down because she disapproved of him playing a middle-aged lecher obsessed by a twelve-year-old girl. The role would have stretched him as much as the 'major' in *Separate Tables* and could have given his reputation a huge boost, but he rejected it for the sake of a woman who did not love him and knew nothing about acting. The part went instead to his wartime *bête noire* James Mason.

With the marriage as miserable as ever, Hjördis mainly in Switzerland and Niv filming *The Guns of Navarone* in England that summer, he compensated for his unhappiness by having an affair with a beautiful young English model and seriously thought of leaving Hjördis to live with her. 'I thought then that he was going to leave Hjördis for sure and get divorced,' Jamie told me, but he refused to tell me the name of his father's new love 'as she is very much alive and it could cause some harm in her current relationship'. One beautiful young English girl with whom Niv later claimed to have had a fling that summer was Sally Croker Poole, who had married Lord James Crichton-Stuart the previous year but whose marriage was already a failure. She was only nineteen, Niv was fifty, and nine years later she was to marry Karim Aga Khan and become Princess Salimah, the Begum Aga Khan.

Sally denies having had an affair with Niv. 'I absolutely adored David,' she told me at her sumptuous home in Switzerland overlooking Lake Geneva. 'He was the sweetest man, very kind, and I hero-worshipped him. He was such terribly good company, not a bit like an old fart, but I was just a kid.' They met when she was shown around the Shepperton Studios set of *The Guns of Navarone* and he joined her, her husband and several of their young friends for dinner. 'I went to watch him filming six or seven times and we'd go back to London in the evening and go to the Mirabelle – here, there and everywhere – in a gang of young people, and he was adorable to everybody.'

Sally also met David Jr and Jamie, who were seventeen and fourteen, played tennis with them at Hurlingham and took them for walks in the park. 'It was like having a couple of younger brothers,' she said. As for Hjördis, 'there was this terrible iciness and tension between them and they never talked to each other. She'd walk into my tiny mews house in Cromwell Gardens and there'd be lots of people, but as she walked in everyone froze and she made the whole thing fall apart. She was this beautiful ice lady, very frozen, with thick make-up. The men did look at her because she was so beautiful, but she never gave anything. I think he could be pretty sad inside. He talked about Primmie with such love, about what a tragedy it was. He adored her, and I think he never got over it.'

So was it Sally that Niv wanted to marry? 'I don't think so,' said Princess Salimah, 'but I think the boys would have liked that. He never asked me to marry him and we didn't have any naughty weekends together. I wish we had! I *wish* we *had*!' She saw him only once more, for lunch in New York in the late 1960s, just before she married the Aga Khan. In the meantime 'he wrote me the most lovely, adorable letters', she said, 'so funny – I could *kill* myself for getting rid of them – and he called me Sal-Pal and always signed them with some absolutely ridiculous name, like Fogworthy.'

In November Noël Coward lunched with the Nivens at Château d'Oex and wrote in his diary: 'Oh dear, I fear Hjördis will *never* make a good housekeeper. The lunch was fairly dreadful and the house *could* be made charming but I doubt if it will be.' Coward obviously brought out the best in her because when he went for lunch again nine days later he described them in his diary as 'the dear Nivens', and after another visit for lunch during the summer he wrote: 'Hjördis very gay and charming, but fairly silly as usual.'

Later in November Niv returned to England to shoot some dangerous sea scenes for *The Guns of Navarone* in a huge tank of icy water. The water was filthy, he cut his lip, it turned septic, and he had to be taken to Guy's Hospital in London where he became so ill with general septicaemia that the doctors thought he might die. Executives from Columbia flew in from the States to discuss just how they might handle such a disaster with the film still not finished. Niv struggled bravely out of bed against doctors' orders, completed the last three days of shooting, and then went down again, seriously ill, and was out of action for seven weeks. It was a hugely expensive movie for those days that cost $6 million – about £30 million today – took nine months to make, attracted a vast amount of publicity and the critics loved it. 'The film is absolutely superlative of its sort,' reported the *Sunday Telegraph*, and the *New York Post* said, 'The picture grips you with an astounding power.' In London the *Evening News* said that 'Gregory Peck, David Niven and Anthony Quinn give brilliant performances', and the *New York Herald Tribune* thought David was 'superb'.

Niv spent his weeks of convalescence at Château d'Oex. 'He was very ill,' Doreen Hawkins told me, 'and we were terribly worried about him, but Hjördis wouldn't have anything to do with him and moved into a separate room.' When he had fully recovered he began to establish an alpine routine that he was to follow every winter for the rest of his life. He would rise early, do his daily exercises and drive the eight miles to Gstaad to ski with his instructor, François Masson, who was to become a good friend. He would lunch every day at the Eagle Club perched high on nearby Mount Wasserngrat, where he was soon elected onto the committee, or the Olden Hotel, where Mrs Donizetti painted a personal glass for him and hung it behind the bar. 'Practically every day for years he had curried veal with rice and chutney,' she said. 'Sometimes he'd eat it every day for three months!' After lunch he would ski again, or walk across country for several miles, and then drive home to Château d'Oex to change, and return to Gstaad or one of the nearby villages, Saanen or Rougemont, for a cocktail or dinner party, usually alone because Hjördis was drunk or could not be bothered. Mrs Donizetti remembered that because he found himself driving several times a day to and from Gstaad he said, 'Why did I ever buy a chalet in Château d'Oex? I must have been crazy.' No, she told him, 'it was because you were stingy about tax!'

'Gstaad was a tiny community in those days,' I was told by Taki Theodoracopulos,

> and it hadn't become the jet-set mecca that it is now. Gianni Agnelli made a couple of derisory remarks about David being too smooth but I never met anybody who didn't like him. He was never a good skier and I got him into cross-country skiing and he did that all day long. Hjördis didn't ski but she used to play gin rummy every afternoon with three other women at the Palace Hotel, but whenever they went out there was always a lot of tension. She would kiss everybody on the mouth and she used to massage complete strangers to make David jealous, and I think she had a lover. I think he was deeply unhappy. When they came to a party they'd separate. My first wife once said to him, 'You want to be liked by every single person,' and Hjördis yelled from the end of the table, 'You're absolutely right!' People who want to be liked very much by everyone have an insecurity complex.

There was, however, one woman in the area, another Swede, who liked Hjördis, maybe because she was very young and perhaps too naïve to understand what was going on: Sussie Kearley, the twenty-one-year-old wife of an American financier. She was twenty-two years younger than Hjördis and told me: 'I don't know why people didn't like her. I loved her company and she was so amusing in the Swedish language. It was the sort of words she used – not slang but full of humour in the way she spoke.'

In Switzerland David started painting and collecting pictures again, and was about to buy an expensive Miró when the dealer remarked how amusing it was that six months after painting it Miró had forgotten which way up it was meant to be. Niv was not amused at all. 'If the artist didn't know which way up his original idea should be, then I didn't want to fork out my hard earned cash to buy it,' he wrote in a letter to *The Times* twelve years later. 'The picture, needless to say, was snapped up by someone else and now is valued at 10 times the original figure.' Numerous readers replied and he wrote to the paper again to say that he had recently spent a whole day studying a Miró one-man exhibition at St Paul de Vence and 'I still harbour a sneaking suspicion that he is frequently laughing at all of us.'

A cheaper addition to his household came onto the scene soon after he bought the chalet: an Italian called Bernardo turned up at the door, announced that he had come to work for him and became the Nivens' resident butler/cook. 'He wore a long, white, buttoned jacket to his knees, like those worn by milkers in a dairy,' David Jr told me, 'and Daddy found this so amusing that he bought several of them for him.'

Niv's first job after his illness was to make an Italian multinational movie, *I Due Nemici*, which was filmed in Rome and the Israeli desert near Eilat, released in English as *The Best of Enemies*, and told of the constantly changing relationship between two officers in Ethiopia in 1941, one British, one Italian, who keep capturing each other. During shooting he was nearly shot himself when an Arab extra fired an old wartime rifle by mistake and the bullet missed his head by inches. While filming *The Best of Enemies* he was briefly reconciled to Trubshawe, who had once been the best of friends. Trubshawe was in the picture too, fell ill in the desert and Niv moved him into his own air-conditioned hotel room to recover. 'But the friendship was really over,' Trubshawe told Morley. 'In the thirty years after the war I think he came down to lunch in Sussex maybe twice, bringing with him a bottle of whisky and a pot of caviar. There'd be a few brief reminiscences and then he'd be off back to London and that was that. A few letters, more towards the end when he began to get ill, but no real contact. I think he began to regard me, probably rightly, as rather a dimwit who could only talk about the past and somehow he didn't want to think about our past, only the Hollywood past which I hadn't shared. I think our past meant Primmie and the war, and he really wanted to forget all of that: his was now a quite different life.'

On 18 March 1961 Niv's stepfather, Sir Thomas Comyn-Platt, died in hospital in London at the age of ninety-two. *The Times* and *Daily Telegraph* both printed brief obituaries and his lifelong fib about his age was so successful that both newspapers reported that he was only eighty-five. In a tribute in *The Times* his Turf Club friend Henry Maxwell, who the club barman Jimmy Holland told me was 'a lovely man', wrote of Comyn-Platt: 'Of his qualities the one which I think was outstanding was his courage. Old age, infirmity when it came, enforced isolation, and physical suffering, he fought them step by step to the end.' Niv did not go to the funeral, but Joyce and Grizel attended the memorial service at St James's, Piccadilly, along with more than forty mourners, among them three earls, a countess, two knights, three titled ladies and two Queen's Counsels, so 'Uncle Tommy' was not nearly as unpopular and unloved as Niv would have had us believe. He left a gross estate of £55,539 10s 0d, which in modern terms would be worth about £777,000, an extremely respectable sum for a man who had lived for so long. Not a penny went to any of the Nivens: apart from two small £500 bequests the entire estate was left to a niece in Somerset, though it is possible that Niv, Joyce and Grizel did benefit financially from Sir Thomas's death because under the terms of their mother's will the income from her own estate should now have been passed on to them.

That summer Niv, Hjördis and the boys went off for an extended holiday in a villa in the South of France on the exclusive, expensive little Côte d'Azur peninsula of Cap Ferrat, near Nice, that Niv rented from a French ex-Member of Parliament, Jacques Bounin. The house was called Lo Scoglietto and although it was a dilapidated mess inside and the garden a jungle of overgrown trees and dark, soggy grass, they loved it so much that he bought it six months later, renovated it, painted it the same colour as the Pink House and was to spend most of each year there for the rest of his life.

Lo Scoglietto – Italian for 'Little Rock' – was built on a small peninsula that juts into the Mediterranean between Beaulieu and St Jean-Cap Ferrat, and had its own little green-water harbour, a big garden with fig trees, cedars, cypress, pines and two 2000-year-old olive trees that had been planted by the Romans, and a sweeping view of Beaulieu, its green and white cliffs and the sparkling blue bay towards Cap d'Ail. It had six bedrooms, three bathrooms, marble floors, a library, two salons, an office, a kitchen, a laundry, and three rooms for servants. Not everyone loved

(From left) Shirley MacLaine, George Raft, Marlene Dietrich and David Niven (as the Victorian adventurer Phileas Fogg) in the sumptuously extravagant film that rescued his faltering career in 1956, *Around the World in Eighty Days*.

. . . and Niv in the same movie with his randy French valet Passepartout, played by the lively Mexican actor Cantinflas, who went on to win the Golden Globe award for best actor that year.

David's old lover Merle Oberon, now Lady Korda, with her film producer husband Sir Alexander Korda at the Stork Club in New York.

Niv with another old lover, Ava Gardner, in the 1956 film *The Little Hut*, in which they and Stewart Granger were shipwrecked on a tropical island. The film was 'a fiasco,' she said, and Granger called it 'a bloody stupid comedy' and complained to his wife, Jean Simmons: 'Imagine playing a straight man to David Niven with that bloody moustache. He's always playing with it or twitching it on everybody else's lines. You can't win against Niven's moustache.'

David with Jackie Kennedy, the wife of the future President of the United States, at a gala dinner at the Waldorf-Astoria Hotel in 1958. Five years later President Kennedy was to seduce Niv's wife, Hjördis, aboard the Presidential yacht the *Sequoia*.

Niv disguised as a cinema usher with two of his best friends, Lauren Bacall and her husband Humphrey Bogart, at a charity show in 1958.

David with one of his closest but platonic friends, Deborah Kerr, in the role that won him the Oscar for Best Actor in 1959, as the bogus 'Major' Pollock in *Separate Tables*.

The only time in his life that Niv ever smoked a cigarette, in a scene for *The Guns of Navarone*, the 1961 wartime adventure in which he played an explosives expert, Sergeant Miller.

Niv and the winner of the Best Actress award, Susan Hayward, with their Oscars at the Academy Awards ceremony at the Pantages Theatre in Hollywood on 6 April 1959.

With Sophia Loren in *Lady L*, a 1965 comedy directed by his old friend (and army batman) Peter Ustinov.

In the summer of 1959 Hjördis left him for another man, and to make her jealous Niv took his sons David (left, aged sixteen) and thirteen-year-old Jamie for a holiday in Hawaii, where, according to David Jr, 'he went through the girls of Honolulu like a machete through a pineapple!'

When David's autobiography *The Moon's a Balloon* was published in 1971 this picture appeared over the caption 'With Hjördis in Spain, near Malaga.' In later editions he changed it to read 'Hjördis in Malaga resting outside hotel with encouraging name' – a sad alteration because their marriage had become a sham and she was locking him out of her bedroom.

Another misleading family photograph that belied the truth of the Nivens' unhappy marriage: Niv and Hjördis at their home in the South of France in the late 1960s with his sons Jamie (*left*) and David and adopted daughters Fiona (*left*) and Kristina.

The Nivens' 1970 Christmas card: a cartoon by their artist friend Willie Feilding showing Hjördis with Kristina (*left*), Fiona and her dogs, with Niv as a grumpy water spout.

the South of France, even then. As Sam Goldwyn put it in one of his classic Goldwynisms, 'Nobody goes to the South of France no more: it's too crowded,' and Noël Coward wrote in his diary the previous summer that 'the whole of the Côte d'Azur has become one vast honky-tonk. Millions of cars, millions of people, thousands of "motels" and camping sites. The coast, viewed from the sea, is still romantic and beautiful, but once ashore it is hell. . . . The whole place was filled with ghastly tourists augmented by hordes of gormless American sailors with vast Adam's apples and rimless glasses . . . the South of France, as far as I am concerned, has had it.' But out of season, even today, the Côte d'Azur is delightful and Niv loved its warmth, sunshine, swimming, sailing, fishing, the wonderful food and wine, the laid-back southern-French lifestyle. The Rainiers lived a few miles along the coast in Monaco and his neighbours included Somerset Maugham. Véronique and Gregory Peck had recently bought a villa nearby on the Cap, though Niv and Peck soon found themselves in trouble with the police when they sailed a boat to Italy, called their wives at home by walkie-talkie radio, and joked, 'We'll be back with the loot at eight. Keep the harbour open.' Their conversation was intercepted by *les flics* and five armed men turned up at Lo Scoglietto with a search warrant.

In June Niv and Hjördis at last adopted the little Swedish girl he had promised her, a blonde, blue-eyed infant just a couple of weeks old. She had been born in Geneva on 4 June, the illegitimate daughter of a Swedish woman in her early twenties who lived there, Mona Gunnarson, who named the child Eva Charlotte before the Nivens changed it to Kristina. Before the adoption they had to get the formal permission of eighteen-year-old David Jr, who was soon to start his first term at the London School of Economics, and Jamie, who was now fifteen. Jamie said, 'Under Swiss law if one of the parents is over the age of fifty and has two children by an original marriage, and that child is over the age of fourteen, that child can say no. I didn't say no because he asked me not to. He said, "I know that you want to say no because she's been a terrible mother to you, but you mustn't do that to me. Please don't." Well, that was it, but had I been eighteen or nineteen I would probably have said, "You've got to be out of your mind. This woman is a horrible person. This is a dreadful soul. You can't have another child brought up by this person." But she was fine with the girls and he was terrific and loved them very much.'

Kristina, who was still living in Switzerland in 2002, told me she was convinced that she was not just adopted but was actually Niv's real daughter, the result of an affair he had with Mona Gunnarson. 'I think she was a model,' she said. 'I found out that he really was my father after he died, when I had to get a birth certificate to become Swiss, and I think my real mother went to the school right next to the chalet in Château d'Oex, the Clos des Abeilles, and I believe she had a son too. There must have been a lot of subterfuge for me to be passed off as adopted rather than my father's daughter. I think Hjördis knew this and that's what created a lot of the disagreements between her and my father. Everybody used to say how alike my father and I were and that we had the same look in our eyes. I always had a little suspicion about it because we were very much alike, with a great sense of humour and always laughing. Maybe it was finding out about me that made Hjördis drink, but she wasn't particularly faithful herself. I think David and Jamie knew and it's bothered them since I was born. It must have been heavy for my father to keep the secret for so long. My real mother came to his funeral and was so covered up that she had a veil over her face, because apparently the resemblance between her and me is so great that it would have stuck out like a sore thumb. She married an Egyptian but is now widowed or divorced. She'd be about sixty-five or sixty-six now, and was in London at the Connaught Hotel a couple of months ago, and I sent her some flowers but she's never been in touch with me.'

Is it really possible that Niv could have duped or persuaded Hjördis to adopt his own child by another woman, maybe a pretty girl whom he had spotted at the school in Château d'Oex? It seems preposterous, an example perhaps of the common poignant delusion of many children, especially orphans or those who are adopted, that their real parent is someone rich or famous, but Kristina was adamant. 'David Niven was my real father,' she insisted, and showed me two Swiss birth certificates, both relating to her, with the same date of birth and reference numbers, but one names her as Kristina, adopted daughter of Niv and Hjördis, while the other, probably the first, calls her Eva Charlotte and lists her surname already as Niven and her nationality as British even before she was adopted, which Kristina believed is evidence that she was born with the surname Niven and was therefore the real daughter of someone called Niven. It certainly seems strange that Niv and Hjördis kept the adoption secret for more than three years. 'David and I made a pact,' she told *Woman* three years later. 'We wanted Kristina to lead a normal life without fuss and the inevitable publicity she'd receive if the press were to hear about her. So for three whole years, although she has been with us in London, Paris, Rome and even Hollywood, her secret has been kept. We have landed at airports and walked through groups of waiting pressmen to the customs followed by Kristina and some good friend and no one ever suspected a thing.' But why bother to hide it? An infant would hardly be upset by photographers and many famous people adopt children without any great fuss from the media. 'Although the three men in the family tend to spoil Kristina,' Hjördis told *Woman*, 'I spank her a little when she is naughty. I could not do this if I felt she was another woman's child, but David and I both think of ourselves as her real parents.' Maybe he was.

Sadly the Clos des Abeilles, a finishing school for girls aged sixteen to eighteen, no longer exists and in 2003 its head, Madame Simone Favey, was in an old folks' home and 'cannot remember anything', her son Benoit Favey told me, 'and I'm afraid that there are no school records that might refer to Miss Gunnarson.'

To pay for their two homes, three children and several servants, Niv started to accept every film that was offered. In the next seven years he made fourteen movies, most of them pretty dreadful, and in the twelve years after that another fifteen, usually just for the money. The first was a Bing Crosby/Bob Hope picture, *The Road to Hong Kong*, in which he made a mercifully brief appearance as a Tibetan monk. Then came a much better movie, *Guns of Darkness*, a thriller in which he played a British planter in a South American republic who rescues the country's wounded president after he has been overthrown in a coup. It was an unusually serious part for him and the reviewers were impressed. 'The planter is such a convincing figure,' said the *Daily Mail*, 'a man in agony because he sees and asks too much, that you never think of him as David Niven until the film ends.' The *Financial Times* agreed: 'David Niven . . . seems continually to improve as an actor,' it said.

His co-star was Leslie Caron, who played his disgruntled wife and was one of the few women who did not like him. 'He was not my kind of gentleman,' she told me, but refused to say why. 'He did not particularly like her either,' said Jamie, 'so perhaps they were just not suited to each other or perhaps there is more here than you or I will ever know.' When I asked Princess Salimah for an opinion, she grinned. 'Maybe he tried to jump her bones!' she suggested. 'Or maybe he *didn't*!'

The script for *The Guns of Darkness* was written by John Mortimer, who was to become one of Niv's closest friends. 'He found Leslie Caron slightly irritating,' Mortimer told me. 'It was filmed in Spain and we spent a lot of time together. We went to see things like the Alhambra, which was not really his thing because it was a bigger star than he was! He was very funny. We drank a lot of cheap Fundador brandy, so he called me Fundador. Afterwards we would always meet when he came to

England. He'd come to lunch in the country and was very sweet because we used to ask him for one o'clock and people would see him walking about the lanes because he thought it would be rude to arrive early. And he once brought a beauty queen whom he'd picked up at London airport!'

The Nivens returned for Christmas to Château d'Oex, where he was now to spend every winter skiing and enjoying the mountains and the social life of Gstaad, and he started an annual Christmas tradition that he was to keep up for many years: he invited Noël Coward and his companions Graham Payn and Cole Lesley to spend Boxing Day at Château d'Oex. Coward and his chums would arrive at noon on the little mountain train from Les Avants wearing mink coats and carrying three pillowcases full of presents, and the Nivens would meet them at the station with bullshots – glasses of beef soup heavily laced with vodka – before walking round to the chalet, where they would join other friends such as the Burtons or Blake Edwards and his wife, Julie Andrews. One Boxing Day Niv hired a local oom-pah-pah band in traditional costume to play 'Rule, Britannia' as Coward and Co. stepped onto the platform, much to the delight of the stationmaster and the crowds of skiers, while the white-coated butler presented them with drinks on a silver salver.

Niv rarely went to the Côte d'Azur in winter but he did in January 1962 to clinch his purchase of Lo Scoglietto for a reported £50,000, though he told several friends that he paid much less for it. Today the house is worth at least £12 million and maybe much more, but 'he bought it so cheaply because he claimed that the sewers of both St Jean and Beaulieu emptied right outside the house', Leslie Bricusse told me. 'In fact he made his offer only after he had some frogmen go down to check that it wasn't true.'

One of the first improvements Niv undertook was to build a swimming pool. 'He wanted a beautiful figure-eight pool,' said Bricusse, 'at least seventy feet long, and they had to blast into the rock to do it. He went away, made a movie, and came back four months later and there was this vast hole in the garden: he had told the guy he wanted it eight feet deep but they had made it eight *metres* deep. You could have put a submarine in there!'

Niv relished Château d'Oex and his winter life in Switzerland but Lo Scoglietto became his favourite home and he was to spend more time there than anywhere, though he told the French tax authorities that it was merely his summer holiday place. He loved America and Americans, but in his heart he was still European, and after twenty-one years in the States he felt that he had come home.

Eleven

Shampoo, Beakers and Fernet Branca
1962–1969

On April Fools' Day 1962 Hjördis was skiing with David Jr, Jamie and her Swedish niece near Gstaad and was so disconcerted by a strange man who kept staring at her and murmured 'I love you' that as she sped down the mountain she glanced nervously over her shoulder to see if he was following her and crashed, knocking herself out and breaking her leg in fifteen places. Niv flew her to the Nuffield Orthopaedic Hospital in Oxford and checked her into a private room before flying back to Rome to shoot two more Italian films. Later she claimed she was in hospital for nine months and that he flew back to London to spend every Sunday with her, but her absence still left him with plenty of time to enjoy the pretty girls of the Côte d'Azur that summer.

He was amused to discover that Lo Scoglietto had once been a convent, which gave an extra spice to his infidelities. 'He was an attractive man and women threw themselves at him, so you can't blame him,' I was told by Kathrine Palmer, who was Jamie's sixteen-year-old girlfriend and spent that summer with them. 'He was a little flirty with everybody, even me, and once when he had a girlfriend there with him he gave Jamie some money to take me to the cinema so that they would be on their own.' His social life was full and he spent a great deal of time with the Rainiers and often with Grace alone. 'I was staying at Cap Ferrat once when Hjördis was away,' Roddy Mann told me, 'and David said, "We're going out to dinner in Monte Carlo but I want to pick a chum up." A chum! It was Grace and I fell instantly in love with her. She was *adorable*, a knockout, and they were huge friends. So we were charging around

Monte Carlo in the dark and he gets lost and goes up a one-way street, and Grace says, "David, you'll get into trouble, it's a one-way street!" and he said, "How can we get into trouble? You *own* this place!"'

Another good friend – and a friend of the Rainiers – was the American journalist and novelist Paul Gallico, who lived a few miles along the coast in a lovely medieval house on the ramparts overlooking the sea at Antibes. 'David was a snob and loved mixing with titled, rich or famous people, but he was such fun to be with,' I was told by Gallico's widow, Virginia, who was thirty years younger than her husband, still lives in the same house and has been for many years Rainier's *Dame d'Honneur* at the palace in Monaco. 'He lit up a room and was very much on stage even with his friends and rather fancied himself as this dashing chap with the twinkle in his eye, and that rather worried Paul because he felt that David never relaxed in public.' Sometimes, though, Niv's attempts to be jolly could backfire. When John Wayne's wife Pilar gave birth to their son John that year Niv sent them a telegram that read: 'CONGRATULATIONS STOP I THOUGHT IT WAS WIND.' She had in fact had a very difficult labour and Wayne was furious.

The two Italian films that David made in Rome that year were *Il Giorno Più Corto* with Stewart Granger, Marcello Mastroianni and Walter Pidgeon, a spoof of the wartime epic *The Longest Day*, which was released in English as *The Shortest Day*; and *La Città Prigioniera*, which was retitled *The Captive City* in Britain and *The Conquered City* in the United States, and told another Second World War story, this time about a British major who is trapped by Greek partisans in an Athens hotel. The critics were sniffy about both and it was becoming increasingly obvious that with two houses, a non-working wife, three children and staff to support Niv was taking on too many movies just for the money. Fortunately his next, *55 Days at Peking*, was much better: a slow but colourful, spectacular two-and-a-half-hour epic about the anti-European Boxer rebellion in Peking in 1900, in which he played the British ambassador to China with Charlton Heston as an American marine, his old squeeze Ava Gardner as an improbable Russian baroness, and Flora Robson as the Chinese dowager empress. The movie took six months to make, was shot in Spain, and 'David was a lovely actor, terribly engaging and very funny', Heston told me in Hollywood. 'The Brits tend to be better than Americans at acting and he was one of the good ones. There's a scene where he and I are trying to blow up an ammunition dump, we were a hundred yards away from it, crouching down, and he said, "I'm getting a bit long in the tooth for this, so don't run too fast and leave me behind," but then he ran very fast like a fucking rabbit.' One of the film's main problems was Ava Gardner. 'She was still extraordinarily beautiful,' said Heston, 'but the problem was liquor. After three in the afternoon it was not easy to get anything out of her.' To make matters worse, she was afraid of Flora Robson, frightened of the thousands of Chinese extras, and often locked herself in her dressing room to drink, so that many of her scenes had to be shot over the shoulder of her stand-in. Not surprisingly the director, Nicholas Ray, had a heart attack halfway through the film.

While Niv was filming in Spain he was saddened to learn that R. J. Wagner and Natalie Wood were divorcing after four years of marriage, and in the autumn that Primmie's father, Bill Rollo, had died in England when he fell from his horse and broke his neck while out fox-hunting. He was seventy. Niv had always been very fond of him and returned for the funeral in Rutland, where the Duke of Beaufort asked him what he was doing the next day. 'I have to go back to Spain,' said Niv. 'I'm shooting in the morning.'

'Ah!' said the Duke. 'I hear they've got a nice lot of birds down there this year.'

Rollo was buried in the churchyard at Huish beside Primmie and her mother, who had died two years earlier, and another old friend of Niv's died in January of cancer: Dick Powell, one of his Four Star partners, who had spent much more time running the company than either Niv or Boyer. Death had become a neighbour and was fingering his friends, and as he told Roddy Mann two years later: 'Never resent growing older. Millions are denied the privilege.' But the good news was that R. J. moved to Europe to get over his divorce and joined David in his next movie, Blake Edwards's farce *The Pink Panther*, in which Niv played the aristocratic jewel thief Sir Charles Lytton, 'The Phantom', a Sixties Raffles who preys on rich women. R. J. was his nephew, Capucine his mistress, Claudia Cardinale the princess who owns the Pink Panther diamond, Peter Sellers was making his debut as the bumbling French police inspector Jacques Clouseau, and Trubshawe appeared briefly as a novelist. Unfortunately the film was dreadfully unfunny except for a couple of scenes, Niv's performance was stilted and unconvincing, and his love scene with Cardinale was excruciatingly embarrassing. Even so, Miss Cardinale told me, 'we had such fun during the shooting of that film in London and at Cinecittà in Italy. Peter Sellers was so funny when he was shooting but off the set he was totally different, a very sad person, very serious, very unhappy, a lonely man. He never relaxed. But David had so much energy and sense of humour and he was very sexy and elegant. I knew he had an unhappy marriage and I could understand women having affairs with him, but not me: I've never been an easy woman and he never pursued me because he knew it was impossible. But I'm surprised Leslie Caron didn't like him. Perhaps they had a history of some sort.'

It was a harmonious movie to make except that Sellers and Edwards disagreed so often that at one time they communicated only in writing, and R. J. told me: 'Niv gave me so much when I went to Europe. He took me to his tailor and shirtmaker and he was a warm mentor for me in many ways because I loved the way he styled his life. I loved the way he left Hollywood and moved to Europe. That was a very courageous thing to do at that time.'

Niv did suffer one terrifying crisis when they had to shoot some skiing scenes in the Italian Alps and they went out on the slopes to practise on a day that was so cold he quickly realised that his ski suit was much too thin. Halfway down the mountain he became aware that his penis was freezing. He and R. J. rushed to the nearest hotel, yelling for a glass of brandy, and scuttled into the lavatory where Niv plunged his penis – by now 'a pale blue acorn', he said – into the alcohol to thaw it out and save it from agonising frostbite. 'He put his unit into the brandy,' R. J. told me, 'and this guy came out of one of the cubicles and said, "My God, what are you doing?" and Niv said, "I always give it a drink now and then." I laughed so hard I wet my pants. I've had such great times with Niven. Roddy Mann and I got so pissed with him one night it was unbelievable. We drank bottles and bottles of *vino*, continually laughing, and stayed up until the early hours.'

Another famous penis that was exposed in March was that of Douglas Fairbanks Jr, whose cock was the major focus of a scandalous divorce case in Edinburgh when the Duke of Argyll accused his wife Margaret of having had at least eighty-eight lovers during their marriage, including three royals, two Cabinet ministers and several film stars. Among the evidence was a cache of Polaroid photographs of the duchess, wearing only a three-strand pearl necklace, fellating a naked 'Headless Man' in the bathroom of her Mayfair flat. The photos showed him only from the neck down, but in some circles it was common knowledge that he was Fairbanks – and another of the duchess's eighty-eight lovers, given her taste for film star flesh, may well have been Niv since she was to be a surprise mourner at his memorial service twenty years later. They had known each other since the 1920s, when as a girl she had often spent the Easter holidays at Bembridge and confessed in her autobiography that she had had a schoolgirl crush on him. He was not, however, the second unknown man who appeared in some of the photographs: he was later identified as the Secretary of State for Defence, Duncan Sandys. The photos were so explicit that Sandys was thereafter nicknamed Sunken Glands.

At the end of April Niv and Hjördis flew to Hollywood for him to make another awful farce, this time with Marlon Brando in his first comedy, *Bedtime Story*, in which they played two rival playboys conning rich women in the South of France. David was relieved to discover that Brando was not nearly as moody and difficult as people said, and Brando said later that 'working with David Niven was the only time I ever looked forward to filming. I just couldn't wait to wake up each morning and go to work so he could make me laugh.' He was intrigued by Niv's constant good humour and kept looking in vain for cracks in his bonhomie. 'Why are you always laughing?' he asked. 'I wanna see the *real* Niven.' The film itself was much less amusing and when Noël Coward saw it he wrote in his diary that it was 'a common, vulgar movie' in which David was 'dull throughout'.

Several years previously the Nivens had met Jack and Jackie Kennedy, and now that Kennedy had been President of the United States for more than two years they were invited to dinner at the White House in March and got on so well with them that Jackie asked them to join a much smaller, mainly family party two months later to celebrate JFK's forty-sixth birthday on the evening of 29 May. It was held in Washington aboard the Presidential yacht, the *Sequoia*, on the Potomac river, and a three-piece band played all evening while the yacht cruised up the river and the guests feasted and played the boisterous games that the Kennedys loved, during one of which a leg of Senator Teddy Kennedy's trousers was torn off. The President's trousers also came off that evening. He was renowned for grabbing any woman he fancied, dragging her into a corner, yanking her skirts up and having his way with her, and that night he bundled Hjördis below decks and ravished her. Senator George Smathers of Florida, who witnessed the genesis of this speedy courtship, told Kitty Kelley for her biography of Jackie Kennedy, who was five months pregnant, that Kennedy asked him to keep a lookout while he was with Hjördis and returned about ten minutes later: 'It was like a rooster getting on top of a chicken real fast and then the poor little hen ruffles her feathers and wonders what the hell happened to her ... No one was off-limits to Jack – not your wife, your mother, your sister. If he wanted a woman, he'd take her.' The story has been repeated by at least two other

Kennedy biographers, but more serious than a cheerful romp was the fact that for many years Kennedy had suffered from a chronic venereal disease, chlamydia or non-specific urethritis, and might well have infected Hjördis – and if a woman is infected by chlamydia she may produce fewer hormones than normal, which can make her deeply depressed, so that quick romp with President Kennedy may have caused or worsened the dreadful depression that Hjördis was to display increasingly through the 1960s and 1970s, and that was to make Niv's life so miserable. Nor was that evening necessarily the only time that Kennedy and Hjördis coupled, for the Nivens spent that weekend with the Kennedys at Camp David, where maybe they fornicated again. Niv probably had no idea that his host had cuckolded him, for he wrote glowingly about him and that weekend in *The Moon's a Balloon*, but he would have found out eventually when Kitty Kelley's biography was published in 1979.

Back in Hollywood Niv found a letter from Ian Fleming, who told him that his next James Bond novel, *You Only Live Twice*, included a cormorant called David Niven because its owner, a beautiful Japanese girl, Kissy Suzuki, says that 'you were the only person who was nice to her in Hollywood!'. The heavy-smoking, hard-drinking, rich-eating Fleming was to die of heart failure just over a year later, aged fifty-six – another of Niv's friends to die young.

That summer of 1963 was the first that Niv and Hjördis spent together at Lo Scoglietto. Peter Ustinov told me that he didn't like the house at all 'because it looked impermanent, like a Hollywood set', but Niv revelled in it and kept extremely fit by exercising for thirty minutes every morning, swimming every day in his pool or the sea, waterskiing, walking for miles every day, and playing golf. He bought a catamaran and speed-boat which he kept in his little private harbour and used for fishing. He loved eating in little bistros and cafés, like the African Queen in Beaulieu, as well as smart restaurants like the Colombe d'Or in the medieval hill village of St Paul de Vence, where the walls were lined with pictures that Picasso and Matisse had painted to pay for their meals. 'He loved wine,' Jamie told me, 'but stopped drinking hard liquor in the Fifties and ate flat food – food close to the plate, like grilled fillet of sole and spinach rather than steak and *frites*.' Most of all Niv enjoyed visiting and entertaining friends: the Rainiers over at Monaco, the Gallicos in Antibes, the Pecks on the Cap, Greta Garbo, and visitors such as the Roger Moores, Dickie Attenboroughs, Bryan Forbeses, Ustinovs. Lunch at Lo Scoglietto was always served by a man wearing white gloves and when Grace came to dinner once she was startled to find the Nivens' eccentric butler wearing his white, ankle-length milkman's coat and thought he must be a doctor. 'Niv loved that house,' said R. J. Wagner, who often stayed at Lo Scoglietto and tried to forget his beloved ex-wife Natalie by marrying an old girlfriend, Marion Marshall. 'He loved the garden and flowers, and he'd help the bees and wasps out of the pool to stop them drowning. And he loved his little sailboat, *Foxy*.' Niv regularly went fishing for sea bass and snorkelling for sea urchins, which he ate by the bucketful, and early every evening, his younger daughter Fiona told me, he relished a glass or two of wine before dinner: 'Evening Beakers, he called them. EBs.' Such was to be the summer pattern of his life for more than twenty years, and to enjoy his Côte d'Azur lifestyle he refused to agree to make any movie unless it fitted in with his hedonistic leisure timetable. One that he turned down that year was *My Fair Lady*, a film that like *Lolita* eventually went to one of his *bêtes noires*, this time to Rex Harrison.

Kenneth More had a holiday home on the Villefranche side of Cap Ferrat, and his first wife Billie was still living there in 2002. 'David was a dreadful snob, very shallow and conceited, but he was also very witty and attractive,' she told me. 'He was always charming and sweet to me, but he was false and I never knew whether he was going to cut me or not when I saw him. I used to see him a lot around Beaulieu and on some days he wouldn't even recognise you, but on other days he would greet you and you'd think you were the only woman in the world. Once I went to buy a paper and noticed a strange man who nobody liked hanging about, and suddenly I was goosed. I thought, "He's just lost his head, do nothing," but then it happened again and I thought "he's gone too far now!" and I turned round and there was David having hysterics. "You thought it was *him*, didn't you?" he said.'

The one big flaw in Niv's idyllic life was Hjördis, who was becoming increasingly alcoholic, remote and unloving. By the end of 1963, David Jr and Jamie told me, she was quite impossible in private at home though for most of the Sixties she could keep up a public façade of cheerful normality when she chose. 'It was pretty terrible,' said Jamie. 'You were an unwelcome guest in your own home. My father would be making a movie somewhere in Europe so he'd go away on Sunday night and come back on Friday night. She would be perfectly OK to me from Monday morning till about Friday noon, but then she'd pick a fight so by the time he arrived, exhausted having flown from wherever he was, there'd be a full-scale war going on. And she'd do that on purpose, every time, to wind him up.'

David Jr, who was now twenty-one, had left the London School of

Economics and was working as an agent with the William Morris agency in Los Angeles, got on better with her but told me that Hjördis was drinking so much that she started to have blackouts 'so she couldn't drive. She was always drinking: vodka, then she went on to Fernet Branca, and Daddy hated the smell of it. Often they had lunch parties at the house and she would decide that she wouldn't even come down. And he'd find any excuse to get out of the house: he'd go out to get the newspaper and that might be a three-hour excursion! She was such a pain in the ass and so *moody*. I once went to the South of France to see her and she said, "I'm not feeling very well, I'll see you later," and she didn't appear for another day, she just stayed in her room. Things like that.'

Hjördis used to lock Jamie out of the house and he would have to break a window to get in. He said 'She was moody and volatile, but I never saw her throw something at him. I don't think she would have tried that. You don't ever want to get that kind of man angry at you. He was powerful, and an intimidating personality.' Yet it was Niv who had to run the household with the help of the servants. 'She couldn't cook even an egg. She'd have starved to death if she'd had to cook anything. She was on the telephone all the time, and she arranged flowers beautifully, and she drank: Fernet Branca and vodka, half and half. Fernet Branca is an almost medicinal aperitivo and it tastes horrible.'

When Jack and Doreen Hawkins once stayed at Château d'Oex, Niv wanted to take them to Lausanne to see Jamie playing hockey but Hjördis stopped them because she insisted they would be bored even though they were keen to go. 'David had on his Mouse Face, as Deborah Kerr used to call it,' Mrs Hawkins told me. 'It was something to do with the mouth, sort of hurt, but he wouldn't go with us on his own because he never wanted to hurt her. He really loved her and was determined to make a go of his marriage. Jack said to me, "I don't know why David puts up with it."'

Jamie escaped the horrible atmosphere at home by leaving the Lycée Jacard in Lausanne – where he rowed on Lake Geneva to help the school win the Swiss Junior Championship Crew race – with a couple of A-level exam passes, and he went to a crammer in London to pass a third subject so that he could go to Trinity College, Cambridge, where generations of Primmie's family had been. 'Jamie was much brighter than Daddy and me,' David Jr told me. Jamie was now sixteen and growing up so quickly that in London he lived alone in a little basement flat in Mayfair. His Aunt Joyce, who was living in Onslow Square in South Kensington, was supposed to be keeping an eye on him, but he avoided her because he was not keen on her husband. Just a few streets away, too, in Chelsea, was his Aunt Grizel, now a highly praised but hard-up sculptress, who had a long-term girlfriend but lived alone in a cheap council flat in Jubilee Place even though Niv had generously bought her a house in the Fulham Road that she did not like.

In public Hjördis could sometimes still be outgoing and fun, and Princess Grace was particularly fond of her. 'I never used to understand it,' said Roddy Mann, 'because Hjördis was boring and totally stupid. She would say the most stupid things and didn't know anything about anything. But I think Grace was lonely for friendship in Monaco, and Rainier was a dull man.' Betty Bacall told me that she thought Grace's friendship with Hjördis 'was all to do with men because Grace Kelly was very active with men and I think that's what Hjördis wanted'. Pat Medina agreed: 'I'm not sure that Grace didn't catch a little of Hjördis's infidelity,' she said.

The Nivens and Rainiers often made up a foursome. 'David enjoyed the pomp and ceremony of Monaco, which I thought was the biggest joke I'd ever seen,' said Betty Bacall. 'I couldn't believe it, all these trumpets blaring, "the Prince and the Princess!", *dum-da-dum-da-dum, da-da-da-da-da-da*.' Grace introduced the Nivens to the film director Ken Annakin and his wife Pauline, who lived nearby at Vence, and although Annakin never liked Hjördis they would often be invited to Lo Scoglietto to play the charades and word games that Niv enjoyed so much. 'The moment he opened the door he'd say "shampoo?" because he loved champagne,' Annakin told me in Los Angeles. Another of Hjördis's friends was the novelist James Clavell's wife, April. The Clavells lived in Antibes in the early 1970s and bought a house later on Cap Ferrat, where Mrs Clavell told me: 'Hjördis was very wrapped up in herself, and even when she was young in Sweden I believe she had a very bad reputation for alcoholism before she ever married Niv. I don't think it was Niv who drove her to drink. She got pretty bitter with everybody and I don't think she had many friends, but before that she was always extremely pleasant and my kids *loved* her. She'd have them over and chat and they'd dance, and they thought she was super.'

Yet almost all of the Nivens' friends and acquaintances told me that Hjördis was a cold, unpleasant woman. 'You couldn't get to know her very well,' Bryan Forbes told me. 'If you went to lunch there she would very often leave the table and disappear. She was a very cold Scandinavian who didn't exude any warmth and was always immaculately turned out and made up, almost like one of the women in my film *The Stepford Wives*.'

Roger Moore said that Hjördis resented Niv 'and would act very bored and raise her eyebrows when he was going to tell a story which she'd obviously heard a hundred times' – an understandable reaction, though every one of David's friends told me that his anecdotes were still hilarious even if they had heard them a dozen times before because he would change them slightly every time. Forbes said Niv's anecdotes often were very funny and 'usually had a particular point to them, like the one about the King of Siam who came to visit Hollywood, and Jack Warner, who fancied himself as a tennis player, played against the king in a doubles match and when the ball came over the net towards Warner he missed it and screamed at the top of his voice, "Slam it into the Chink!" You couldn't be bored by stories like that.' It was Jack Warner, too, who once stunned a formal dinner in honour of the wife of the Chinese leader Chiang Kai-shek by concluding his speech: 'So, folks, if you have any laundry you know where to take it!'

Doreen Hawkins remembered that 'Hjördis used to have a late breakfast upstairs in bed, but only when she rang the bell, and she was *hopeless* domestically. She couldn't cook anything and didn't want to. She used to say to me, "What are you doing all that cooking for?" and I said, "You have to if you're married," and she said, "You're a fool to do it." So they had a butler, a cook, an upstairs maid who did all Hjördis's clothes and things, a cleaner, a washing woman, a gardener who also did the pool, and an assistant gardener.' Pampered by all these servants, Hjördis 'was always on the phone', said Mrs Hawkins.

'Hjördis used to lie by the pool making endless telephone calls,' John Mortimer said, 'and she'd say, "I'm so tired. Telephoning is so exhausting. I must have a holiday. My fingers are too tired." ' He once asked her if he could see the kitchen at Lo Scoglietto. 'With some difficulty Hjördis found the number of the kitchen – a place, it seemed, with which she was not familiar – rang it up and announced that a visit would not be possible,' he wrote in his autobiography *Murderers and Other Friends*. 'Niven took us out for drives and to small restaurants. Hjördis stayed at home, a martyr to the telephone.'

'She used to do the flowers so beautifully but then she did nothing all day,' said Mrs Hawkins. 'David was willing to do anything to get her doing things, and when she got this thing about painting he built a studio in the garden where she could paint, but she only did a couple.'

Peter Ustinov told me that Hjördis 'always had some absurd desire. She would suddenly say things like, "Vy don't ve all run naked in ze garden?". She was also uncanny rather than beautiful. She had greenish eyes which were flecked with all sorts of colours and they didn't look quite human, and she had a huge *mane* of hair.' The hair was in fact a wig, of which Hjördis had several. 'She always had an enormous wig, like a lion,' Hedi Donizette told me, and Ustinov said, 'I imagine Niv married her because she seemed extremely erotic, but she wouldn't turn me on. I'd run a mile. She wasn't sexy to me at all: she just looked false, as if she was the creation of a make-up man. She wore an enormous amount of make-up, and she was *big*, and with all those Swedish complexes she worried me no end. She was always sulking about something. You always had the impression you had arrived in the middle of a row. Dancink naked in ze garden! What rubbish!'

Hjördis fought with the servants as well as Niv and the boys. 'He came to collect me at Nice airport once,' Pat Medina said, 'and as we drove back to Cap Ferrat he said, "Oh God, Nej's having a row with Evelyn," – the children's nurse – "and she wants to get rid of her because she told Kristina off and Nej got angry. Well, if it's a question of Evelyn or Nej," he said, "I'll take Evelyn and Nej can go back to Sweden!" So I wasn't joining a very happy couple.' Every one of the Nivens' women friends, as well as the men, blamed Hjördis for the marriage's problems. 'She was very difficult,' said Virginia Gallico, 'beautiful and cold, and she cared only about her looks, and was terrified of getting old', and Billie More said, 'Hjördis was the most difficult lady. If David was unfaithful I expect she drove him to it.' Another woman friend, who asked not to be named, said, 'Hjördis would lock him out of the bedroom to get her own way. It went on for years and made him deeply unhappy. He told my husband once that when she locked the bedroom door she wouldn't let him in even to get a shirt.'

Six months after Hjördis's brief encounter with President Kennedy on board the *Sequoia* he was assassinated, on 22 November 1963. Niv went to the funeral in Washington, kept the black-rimmed funeral photograph card among his papers for the rest of his life, and in later years Jackie visited the Nivens in Switzerland and France.

Now that Kristina was two and a half Niv and Hjördis decided that she needed a playmate and in December they adopted another little blue-eyed, blonde, Swedish girl, a four-month-old orphan whom they named Fiona, who told me thirty-eight years later that she had no interest in tracking down her real parents because it was not important.

It was more than a year since Niv had finished making *Bedtime Story* but in 1964 he made up for lost time by working on two films simultaneously: *Where the Spies Are* at Elstree Studios in England and in the Lebanon, and

Lady L at Castle Howard in Yorkshire and Paris. He had missed out on James Bond but in *Where the Spies Are* he played another British secret agent, Jason Love, who is sent to the Middle East to prevent the assassination of an Arab prince. The critics loved it. 'Mr Niven's sure-fire comedy instinct and perfectionist timing are a source of perpetual joy and delight,' said the *Sunday Express*, and the *Sunday Times* reckoned that he 'simply doesn't give a performance which is less than excellent'.

His was easily the best performance in *Lady L* as well, even though he did not appear until halfway through. Written and directed by Peter Ustinov, it co-starred thirty-year-old Sophia Loren and thirty-nine-year-old Paul Newman, and told in flashback the story of an eighty-year-old English aristocrat, played by Loren, who has risen from being a Corsican laundress in a Paris brothel to a position of wealth and influence thanks to her marriage to an impotent old duke (Niv) and despite having several children by a French anarchist (Newman). The costumes and scenery for this frothy nonsense were gloriously colourful but the reviewers rightly felt that neither Loren as a crone nor Newman as a Frenchman came up to scratch and that Niv's performance was as usual the best of the lot, and as soon as he came on the scene the whole picture perked up and became quite jolly. The atmosphere on the set, however, was sometimes unpleasant. 'Loren and Newman couldn't stand each other,' Ustinov said. 'It was like when a dog passes another in the street and ignores it, but suddenly sees another on the opposite pavement and goes mad. It was exactly that: they were snapping at each other. Eventually I said to them, "*Do* make an effort, for Christ's sake, this is *so* childish. You're supposed to be in *love* with each other." ' After that Loren did make a big effort to be sociable, said Ustinov, but when she enquired pleasantly one day, 'Paul, how do you stick the moustache on your face?' he glared at her and snarled, 'With *sperm*!'

Niv 'was very good and very funny in *Lady L*,' said Ustinov. 'He played himself in every film, but because he was a man of many facets he could play a crook quite easily because the same qualities went into deceiving people as to charming them. There's really no difference. He was highly intelligent and understood very quickly what you were up to. I asked him to do impossible things in *Lady L*, for an ordinary British actor, like having Burmese servants and saying, "Tung hak tung tun hai you-ho?" but he did it with absolute conviction. Nobody knew whether it was Burmese or not but it sounded pretty authentic.' Niv liked to give the impression that acting was terribly easy and almost a despicable way for a grown man to make a living. 'They all do that,' said Ustinov. 'All these actors, Paul Newman, people like that, are *embarrassed* by their success and the enormous amount of money they can make. To act well is difficult but it is *intrinsically* much easier than writing, for instance. There are very good actors who give you *exactly* what they rehearsed, and there are better actors who keep fresh enough in order to give you the impression it has never happened before or even been rehearsed before, and David was like that, fresh and spontaneous even on the fortieth take.'

At the end of May 1964 Niv was driving through the St Bernard tunnel in Switzerland when he spotted a pedestrian in the gloom, swerved to avoid him, crashed and inflamed his old wartime back injury. He was flown in agony to London to see his osteopath, whose treatment was so successful that two weeks later he was best man in Geneva when fifty-one-year-old Stewart Granger married his third bride, a luscious twenty-three-year-old Belgian beauty queen, Viviane Lecerf, and able to bend over to help with the exchange of wedding rings. He spent the rest of the summer at Lo Scoglietto, where David Jr and Jamie joined the family for a holiday, and he learned to be a father again with his tiny new daughter, Fiona. Now older, richer, more relaxed and secure, and working much less, he was to be a much better father to the girls than he had been with the boys. 'Dad loved the girls and they gave him a whole new lease of life,' David Jr told me, 'and he treated all of us equally.' Hjördis 'adored the girls too', Doreen Hawkins told me, 'but she treated them a bit like dolls. As they grew up they were dressed up to the nines in the best French clothes.'

That summer Niv was able to rediscover his sons when Hjördis and the nanny took the girls up to Château d'Oex in August to escape the ferocious heat of Cap Ferrat. David Jr was now working in William Morris's office in New York and would soon spend two years at their branch in Rome, and Jamie, now eighteen, had decided he would rather go to Harvard than to Cambridge and had been offered a place there to read history and economics. Because he had three good English A-levels already, Harvard let him take his degree in three years instead of four, but Niv 'had hardly a word of congratulation', Jamie said. 'He expected his children to do their best; nothing less was acceptable.' Niv's attitude hurt Jamie because he never went to see him in all his three years at Harvard. 'He'd always tell people that I was there,' said Jamie, 'but when I asked him later why he never came he couldn't answer me. It still bothers me today. I shouldn't even talk about it because it's a long time ago, but at times he wasn't that great a father. He was very busy making one movie after another, and very interested in making money, and he was a sole parent and had been brought up by a single parent, and looking back I think that made a huge difference. Had he been brought up by two parents I think he would have had a different attitude about how he handled his children.'

Early in September 1964 Niv flew to New York to play yet another gentleman crook when he joined Charles Boyer, Robert Coote, Gladys Cooper and Gig Young in launching a new Four Star TV series that was to become hugely popular, *The Rogues*, in which they played members of an international family of conmen who prey on the rich all over the world. The first episode was set on the French Riviera but Niv appeared in six more over the next seven months that were set in places as far-flung as London and Rio with actors as varied as Larry Hagman, Sally Kellerman, George Sanders, Telly Savalas and Walter Matthau.

In November he flew to Beirut to shoot the Lebanese scenes for *Where the Spies Are* and was nearly killed by an Arab when a huge crowd turned out to watch the filming, armed riot police were called out, shots were fired and someone hurled a rock which just missed his head. 'It's the first time that I've ever been stoned,' he told the *Daily Sketch*. That Christmas Noël Coward and his retinue came over to Château d'Oex as usual on Boxing Day and Coward wrote in his diary: 'Everybody kissed everybody else, exchanged presents, drank too much and ate too much and it was also lovely. We played games and giggled and David was dearer than ever. The snow lay all about, deep and uncrisp and uneven. Hjördis, the two boys and the two little adopted girls were enchanting and we staggered off the train at Les Avants giggling like idiots and feeling fine.' Now and then Hjördis could still make an effort for the right people.

Another old friend arrived for New Year's Eve: Natalie Wood, whose life at the age of twenty-six had become an emotional mess since she and R. J. had divorced two-and-a-half years previously. Since then she had lived with Warren Beatty, had flings with several men including Tom Courtenay and Frank Sinatra, and although she had had great successes in *West Side Story*, *Gypsy* and *Love With a Proper Stranger* she had tried to commit suicide with an overdose of sleeping pills a month earlier after bumping into R. J., whose second wife had just given birth to his daughter. Now Natalie was having a fling with David Jr, who was four years younger but whose reputation in the bedroom at the age of twenty-two was beginning to rival his father's. 'David and David Jr once challenged each other as to how many women they could have,' Ken Annakin told me, and although David Jr denied this, other friends believed it was true. It must have been a nerve-racking visit for Niv since Natalie was still obsessed by R. J. and constantly on the telephone to her Californian shrink, who was not too keen on David Jr as psychiatric therapy. He did not last long and she went on to audition an entire cast of English actors – Michael Caine, Alan Bates, Albert Finney, Richard Johnson – before marrying the British agent Richard Gregson in 1969.

Three new friends who were to become close came into Niv's life in Switzerland that winter when he met the fifty-seven-year-old American economist, author and ex-US ambassador to India, J. K. Galbraith, who had a house in Gstaad. The Galbraiths introduced him to the influential thirty-nine-year-old American conservative thinker, columnist, *National Review* editor, TV talk-show host and novelist William F. Buckley Jr, who was about to run for Mayor of New York and had rented a house in Gstaad for a few weeks. Niv was to build strong friendships with Buckley and his wife Pat, another woman who liked Hjördis until she discovered how horrible she could be to Niv in private. 'He was my best friend,' Pat Buckley told me, 'and I still miss him,' before refusing to say any more because she was so upset to think of him even nineteen years after his death.

'David and my wife had a tremendous attraction to each other,' Bill Buckley, now seventy-five, told me at his house in New York, 'and at the end of his life he wrote to her to say she was his closest friend on earth. He was witty and a wonderful, wonderful friend, and there wasn't a negative aspect to him.' The following year the Buckleys began renting a château at Rougemont, near Château d'Oex, where they would spend six weeks each winter for the next twenty-seven years while Buckley worked on his latest book, and Niv often joined him to ski, lunch and paint. 'Between 1965 and 1970 I must have seen him five hundred times,' said Buckley. 'He was quite a good painter and conscientious – I'm abominable – and there was a very nice painting that he did which reflected his melancholy: he kept changing the shade of the colours above the Swiss mountain that he was doing and it turned darker as he worked on it, feeling wretched. He was very proud of the fact that he had the same eight brushes that he had had since he took up painting years before in Hollywood. He washed them fastidiously in just the right temperature of water and stored them very neatly. His paintings are mostly country scenes in oils with very few human beings.' In later years the Buckleys also visited Lo Scoglietto. 'I was at the helm of his little boat one day,' said Buckley, 'and there was this huge 400ft yacht that was owned by a rich Brit called Guinness, and we were coming up to say hello and there was a wind shift and I tapped the belly of the boat, and out of the window right above sprang the head of Truman Capote. This delighted David and we used to joke that if you hit the Guinness boat just right Truman Capote would pop out!'

If it seems unlikely that Niv could have become so close to such political intellectuals as Buckley and Galbraith, Buckley explained, 'No, he wasn't an intellectual but he was thoughtful, serious, and a very good listener, a sort of inertial liberal who would have said he was a Democrat if he'd had to fill out a form.' He was also 'amusing, sensible and highly literate', Galbraith said at his home in Boston, 'and one of my most cherished friends. He never bored you, he entertained you.' As for Hjördis, Buckley said she was still 'good company. She smiled, laughed and enjoyed everything, and was very coquettish.' It all depended on who you were.

According to Buckley David did not drink a great deal – 'never more than two glasses of "shampoo" ' – but other friends disagreed. 'He drank a huge amount,' said Roddy Mann. 'He could put away more booze than anybody I've seen. Niven, Bob Wagner, Natalie and I once sat in a little bistro in Villefranche and afterwards I counted fifteen empty bottles. He loved it, but never got drunk and was always jolly. He had a theory that if you drank as much water as wine you would never get pissed. In London we had late-night drinking sessions in a lot of little trats in Soho. We used to sit and drink ourselves stupid.' In the pool house changing room at Lo Scoglietto there was a sign that read 'if one night we all get very merry and beg you to stay over for a few days – we don't really mean it', and even towards the end of his life Niv admitted in an interview that he was still drinking two bottles of wine a day, which some modern doctors will suggest is enough to make you an alcoholic. Certainly he was seriously hung-over one Monday morning towards the end of January 1965 when he was still filming *Lady L* in Paris. Peter Lennon interviewed him for the *Observer*, and Niv confessed that he had just enjoyed a seriously boozy weekend, and a week earlier he had told James Green of the *Evening News* that after lunch he always slept for an hour in his dressing room. He also told Green that in the coming year Four Star would be producing forty one-hour episodes each of *Burke's Law* and *The Rogues*, in total 'the equivalent of sixty-two feature films – a figure worth noting since MGM at their peak produced around fifty films a year'. He reported that the company was now worth $11 million, so it was no wonder that he started referring to the money he was earning from it as 'The Fortune'.

When he finished *Lady L* at the end of March he began to toy with the idea of transmuting some of his golden hoard of anecdotes into a collection of short stories. Friends, especially Roddy Mann, had been telling him for ages that he ought to publish them. 'Noël Coward told me that David was the greatest raconteur he'd ever heard,' Mann told me, 'and he *was*. I would sit with him, pissing myself with laughter, as everybody else was, while he told a story, and then I'd think "wait a minute: I was *there* and it wasn't *that* funny", and then I realised how he was able to take *nothing* and make it wonderful.' Niv wrote to his old friend Jamie Hamilton, the boss of the publishers Hamish Hamilton, to ask his advice. 'As you know, I am a frustrated writer,' he wrote. 'I loathe autobiographies by actors – particularly movie actors. But do you think there is any market for a book of short stories, each one autobiographical – so that one can capture the high and low lights without all that smug self-satisfaction in between? If you encourage me . . . I'll start – slowly. And of course you get first hack at the result.' Hamilton was enthusiastic but remembered that Niv's first book, *Round the Rugged Rocks*, had been published by the Cresset Press, so they probably had a legal option to publish his next book, and asked him to clarify the situation. *The Moon's a Balloon* had been conceived – as fiction, a collection of autobiographical short stories.

Back at Lo Scoglietto in the spring, Niv gave the British journalist Mike Tomkies an insight into the way he intended to raise four-year-old Kristina and two-year-old Fiona: TV for no more than an hour a day and lots of advice never to become actresses 'because if you are lucky enough to be at or near the top, it's a marvellous existence, but if you're not, it is terrifying because by the time you realize you're not going to get there, it's too late to do anything else'. Kristina was already going to a nursery school in London when they were there and was about to be sent to the Swiss village school at Château d'Oex each winter and a French school near Lo Scoglietto each summer, 'and when we go to California,' said Niv, 'she will go to a local school, too. Going to four different schools is terribly good for a child, if the schools are good ones. We cart them round wherever we go, none of that leaving them home with a nurse.' With such nomadic childhoods it is surprising that neither girl became an alcoholic, drug addict or criminal, though several of Niv's friends told me that they were difficult girls to raise but probably only because Hjördis was an alcoholic. Niv confessed that Hjördis was as 'moody as hell, of course, as all Scandinavians are. The black moods come on and I go to hide in the cellar for a couple of days.'

In May Niv gave another interview, to Peter Evans of the *Daily Express*, in which he was unnecessarily cruel about Trubshawe. 'I hate having the same bunch of chums and never changing them,' he said. 'It must be awful, all getting old together, decrepit together, and finally dying together. We have tons of changing chums.' Trubshawe was deeply hurt, framed the article, and hung it in his bathroom to remind himself of what he called Niv's 'heartlessness and thoughtlessness'. R. J. Wagner believed that Niv became fed up with Trubshawe because he kept nagging him to help him get parts in his films, and Niv told Roddy Mann that Trubshawe had just become boring: 'He kept reminiscing and saying "remember when" and Niven was doing his own remember when. You outgrow people, and he became tiresome.' Trubshawe tried to revive their mutual running joke when he appeared that year in the film *Those Magnificent Men in Their Flying Machines* as a character called Niven, but the friendship had gone cold.

At the end of July Niv embarked on *The Eye of the Devil*, a horror movie about witchcraft and Satanism in a French château that was filmed in Bordeaux country near Limoges and in which there was a maid with magical powers, cowled monks, and he played the aristocratic owner of a vineyard who has by ancient custom to be sacrificed for the failure of the grape harvest. In due course the *Sunday Times* reported that the film was 'hilariously bad' and it seemed to be cursed from the start when it was initially entitled *13*, Niv's co-star Kim Novak – 'a horrid lady,' he wrote to Jamie Hamilton – had a riding accident after eight weeks of shooting and had to be replaced by Deborah Kerr, which meant that the first eight weeks had to be filmed all over again, and a low-flying jet upset Niv's horse and he was thrown off. Much worse was to come: Sharon Tate, who played a sinister witch, was to be murdered horribly by the Charles Manson ritual witchcraft gang four years later.

Niv was earning so much now that he started being incredibly generous to both his sisters. In October 1965 he sent Grizel a cheque for £1000, which would be worth about £12,000 today, followed by another for £500 just before Christmas and another £1000 in April – a total in modern values of £30,000 in just over five months. In April he gave Joyce £1000 as well, and from now on he was to send them both huge cheques every year and sometimes twice a year. In November 1966 he sent Grizel £1000 and another £1500 a month later – another £30,000 in modern values in just a month. At the end of 1967 she got £2000 (about £23,000) and Joyce £1000 (£11,500), and so it went on: in 1968 he sent Joyce £2000 and Grizel an astonishing £4000 (about £65,000 today); in 1969 he gave Grizel £5000, which would be worth more than £50,000 in 2003. It was an amazing demonstration of fraternal affection that went on every year for nearly twenty years. 'David was always very, very generous to me,' said Grizel. 'We didn't see a lot of each other when we were grown up but we always remained very good friends and I stayed with him sometimes in France and Switzerland.'

In December he had another close encounter with death: he was driving with Hjördis along a Swiss mountain road when his Mercedes sports car skidded on ice and crashed into a post that stopped it plunging into a deep ravine. Death was sniffing too that month around Jack Hawkins, who had contracted cancer of the larynx and underwent a laryngectomy in January 1966 in London. 'David was wonderful all through Jack's illness,' Doreen Hawkins told me, and in his autobiography Hawkins wrote that Niv had 'an infectious gaiety, and an extremely colourful sense of humour, both of which buoyed me up immensely'. Hawkins was to have a device implanted in his throat to help him to speak in a 'strange Dalek voice', as his wife put it, but the operation gave him another seven years of life.

In March, a year after Niv had first suggested writing a book for Jamie Hamilton, the publisher wrote again to ask if he would dig out his old contract with the Cresset Press 'to verify whether you are under option to them for your stories. If not, we would love to publish them.' He was to have to keep nagging David about it for five more years before the situation was sorted out. As Niv looked back over his life for incidents to turn into stories he was reminded of how lucky he had been to break into Hollywood and wrote a long letter to Sam Goldwyn to thank him for taking him on more than thirty-one years previously. 'My dear Sam,' he wrote. 'I start a new picture next week (they still seem to invite me to make those same six expressions!). Each time I start a new one – I think with so much gratitude of you . . . So, after thirty years of incredible good fortune . . . I just had to sit down in my Swiss cuckoo clock after a good days skiing and thank you once again from the bottom of my heart for all you did for me when it really counted . . . Best love and endless gratitude. David (Niven).'

Goldwyn replied, 'Thank you for that warm and charming letter. To me you are still tops and I have been pleased to watch your career over the years and see the great success you have made. If you didn't have it, you couldn't give it.' He ended the letter 'Your devoted fan, Sam'. The days of animosity were over. Or were they? 'Niv didn't like Goldwyn at the end,' said Roddy Mann. 'I remember him being quite bitchy about him.'

The movie that Niv was about to make was the lavish slapstick farce

Casino Royale, which let him play James Bond at last – an elderly, retired *Sir* James Bond – a spoof that took the mickey out of 007 and spy films in general. It was a frenetic, plotless shambles involving six scriptwriters, seven directors (John Huston, Kenneth Hughes, Val Guest, Robert Parrish, Joseph McGrath, Richard Talmadge and Anthony Squire), three far-flung studios and no fewer than five Bonds apart from Niv: Woody Allen, Peter Sellers, Terence Cooper, and even Ursula Andress and Daliah Lavi as female 007s. The public adored it, but despite an extraordinarily starry cast that included Orson Welles, Deborah Kerr, William Holden and Peter O'Toole, it was savaged by the critics, though many singled out David's wry, amused, twinkly performance yet again as being the only one worth watching. 'He was like a fox in a hen house, surrounded by pretty girls,' grinned David Jr, but the picture was plagued by problems. It was shot at Mereworth Castle in Kent, Killeen Castle in Eire, and Shepperton Studios, but after four weeks of filming there was still no proper script, the paranoid Sellers had a punch-up in his caravan with one of the seven directors, Joe McGrath, and accused Orson Welles of casting an evil spell on him and despising him for being fat – a case of pot and kettle if ever there was one. It was a welcome diversion when the soccer World Cup was played in England that summer and Niv bought thirty tickets to give to the film crew. 'The crews *loved* him,' said Jamie. 'Almost everyone got to see the World Cup and he and I saw the England against Germany final.'

Niv finished *Casino Royale* at the end of August and gave Roddy Mann yet another interview for his column before flying back to Cap Ferrat. 'Something I've never been able to understand,' he said, 'is why one never gets credit for light comedy performances. They're the most difficult things in the world to do, yet nobody ever got an award for them. Look at Cary! I won my Oscar for being highly dramatic in *Separate Tables*, which I found much easier to do than comedy. If you're nervous while playing in drama it adds something to your performance. If you're nervous in comedy you might as well shoot yourself.'

At the beginning of September 1966, when Kristina and Fiona went back to school after the summer holidays, Niv began at last to make a valiant effort to start writing the book that eventually became *The Moon's a Balloon*. He found it so difficult that he wrote to Jamie Hamilton for advice: 'The movie biz is now a complete shambles and like everyone else I am more or less on the shelf. When your readers come across a good potential movie story please for God's sake tip me off . . . it really is do-it-yourself time with all the major studios going or gone broke.' He added, 'My so called "book" is driving me mad. You do realize that dont you? There are so many characters bobbing up and they all seem suspiciously alike in the way I describe them,' so obviously he was still writing the book as fiction. Later the same day he wrote again to Hamilton:

> My dear Jamie
>
> I need your advice. I ask for it shamelessly because if I ever finish the damn thing I do want to offer you the first hack at saying No to my book. (I am sure we can take care of Cresset et al).
>
> I vacillate between being all buoyed up at the thought of writing a full autobiography complete with (I hope) rather fascinating moments with some greats such as Jack Kennedy, Winston and of course Flynn, Bogart, Gable, Garbo, Cooper, Sinatra and Co – and feeling that it would become just another actor polishing his ego at the expense of those sort of people.
>
> Would it ever go into paperback?
>
> Would it be possible to write it as a novel and while lacking the loss of direct confrontations with entertaining friends make up to the reader by adding all sorts of little spicey and scandalous happenings that could not be mentioned 'in truth', and would probably amuse a far larger public?
>
> I also feel that it is terribly conceited unless one is a great statesman or author to write a straight autobiography. SOS please. Glorious weather!
>
> love
>
> David

Jamie Hamilton, sniffing the birth of a big bestseller, replied immediately, 'Autobiography every time! Yours could not possibly be "just another actor polishing his ego" – you have far too much sense of humour, and of proportion, for that. Furthermore, as the book Cresset did was a novel, any option thereon might not apply to non-fiction,' and he added long-sufferingly, 'Did you ever unearth that contract?!' Niv had not, but by the middle of November he had actually written two and a half chapters and wrote to Hamilton: 'All that has emerged so far is the fact that I was undoubtedly the most poisonous little bastard that God ever put breath into.'

In April he flew to the wilds of Mexico to make *The Extraordinary Seaman* with twenty-six-year-old Faye Dunaway, Alan Alda and Mickey

Rooney, an anti-war satire in which he played the ghost of a British Royal Navy lieutenant-commander who has been forced to return from the beyond to redeem himself after besmirching the family honour in battle. It was made around the tiny, poverty-stricken village of Coatzacoalcos, on the jungly northern Gulf of Mexico coast between Veracruz and Tabasco, where the temperature could reach 110°F in the shade and the interiors were filmed in a tin shed oven. 'The cockroaches, which were huge – three inches long on average – would move in herds so thick that the ground would look like it was alive,' wrote Faye Dunaway in her autobiography. 'Being stuck in your room waiting out the nearly daily tropical downpours could drive anyone to the brink of madness ... As soon as David was finished with his scenes each day, he would head to the nearest Mexican bar and start on the margaritas, ordering a pitcher of them, and then I would come and meet him there. He sort of took me under his wing platonically and we chatted on and on. He told me all these stories about his days in Hollywood [*and*] that each time he made a movie, when it was over, he always felt as if he would never work again. That staggered me.'

The margaritas were not always a good idea. 'One night we were really pushing them down,' Niv told Don Short seven years later,

> when I suddenly began to attack Faye. I heard myself saying the most awful things about her. 'You're not Faye Dunaway – you're Fake Dunaway!' I rounded on her: 'Look at your hair, your nose, your teeth, your bosom ... haven't they all been fixed?' Faye was absolutely stunned. I mean, I was her friend. It was madness. I sat bolt upright all night, asking myself what had I done. I really adored Faye. Next morning I went to work with the most dreadful hangover and conscience. I knew that I would have to face Faye. To my amazement Faye ran to me with tears streaming down her face, flung herself into my arms and said: 'Will you ever forgive me for the terrible things I said to you last night?' I'm afraid I was a bit of a cad. I suggested she shouldn't drink tequila in future.

Life was primitive. 'Horses would wander riderless through the streets,' wrote Ms Dunaway, 'and chickens would squawk and scratch in front of the lean-tos made of scraps of tin, with palm leaves for roofs, that housed half the population. There was an oil refinery on the edge of Coatzacoalcos that belched soot into the air day and night ... But the beach was still pristine ...' In one scene Niv had to fall from a mast into the ocean and was terrified when he splashed down and saw a dorsal fin heading towards him. 'Sharks!' he yelped. 'Dolphins!' shrieked the director, John Frankenheimer – but Niv refused to shoot another take. The critics tore the movie to pieces. It was 'a disaster', said Ms Dunaway. 'The studio was livid at the results [*and it*] never had a real theatrical run.'

Niv's next film, *Prudence and the Pill*, which was made in England at Pinewood Studios, was equally awful despite a cast that included Deborah Kerr, Robert Coote and Edith Evans. It was a tacky farce about adultery and contraception in which Niv has a mistress, his wife has a lover, and their eighteen-year-old niece is pinching her mother's birth control pills and replacing them with aspirins, with the result that all the women become pregnant. It was 'a leering, tasteless mess', reported the *Saturday Review* and the *New York Times* considered it to be 'nauseating' and said in despair of Niven and Kerr: 'Because their parts are unendurable they give the worst, worst performances of their lives.' Considering Niv's own disastrous marriage he deserved an award for the next performance he gave when he told the *News of the World* po-faced that by making the film 'we're striking a blow for freedom for married couples who hang on and on together and are too frightened to do anything about a dreadful situation. I am happily married; but how many couples are there hanging on and on in England alone?' The picture was notable only because Niv normally got on well with everyone but this time was constantly at loggerheads with the director, Fielder Cook, who walked out after shooting more than half the movie and had to be replaced by Ronald Neame.

In October David flew to New York and lunched with Jamie, who was now nearly twenty, and the nineteen-year-old girl he wanted to marry, Fernanda Wanamaker Wetherill, the daughter of a very rich Philadelphia department store owner, a lively young woman whose 'coming out' party on Long Island in 1963 had been such a riot that eighteen guests were arrested for trashing the house and causing the modern equivalent of £15,000-worth of damage. 'I was very nervous meeting him,' she told me, 'but he put me at ease immediately.'

The following year, 1968, Niv made yet another dreadful film, this time in Hollywood, about the generation gap, *The Impossible Years*, in which he was a psychiatrist who specialises in teenagers but cannot control his own seventeen-year-old daughter. The *People* called it 'his worst ever film' and John Mills told me that Niv 'was in a lot of very bad films, but we all were. We had to go on earning a living and they couldn't all be good. I made several and burnt the negatives when I could get them!' yet Niv's next film, which he made the following year, was to be one of his best and showed what an excellent actor he could be when he chose the right script. It was a serious movie about wartime duty, loyalty and betrayal, *Before Winter Comes*, in which he played yet another British officer, this time a tough but fair major who is running a refugee camp in the spring of 1945 in occupied Austria on the edge of the Soviet-occupied zone and has to decide which refugees are sent to the American zone and which returned to the Russians and certain death. He appoints one of the refugees, played with wonderful exuberance by Chaim Topol, as his official interpreter, but when they both fall for the same girl and the Soviets insist that the interpreter is a deserter from the Red Army, the major sends him back to them to face a firing squad.

The picture was shot in Austria and included several excellent performances, among them one by twenty-eight-year-old John Hurt, who was superb as a naïve lieutenant with a conscience. 'It was one of my first movies,' Hurt told me, 'and David was very helpful because Chaim was being quite difficult and tricksy. We got on enormously well and became lifelong friends and we'd often meet in Soho in the 1970s. He was incredibly generous – with his spirit and his spondulicks – and funny funny funny. We were stuck in a little village up in the hills, but we went out and ate together. He liked his wine – he probably drank a couple of bottles a day – and the odd scotch, but he wasn't a boozer. He loved being naughty and was very flirtatious. When I said, "What do you miss about Hollywood?" he said, "The girls cos they were all so pretty and all wanted to play. In modern Hollywood they're all twisted and neurotic." But he was a total gentleman and never played at home: if his wife were to catch him in bed with a girl he would deny it; to do anything else would be rude!' Hurt met Hjördis but 'didn't take to her at all. She was tall and monumental and pretty difficult, but he was very romantic with her. I remember him booking a private room when she arrived, with candles and so on, for a romantic dinner for two. He made it his business to adore her because he was a gentleman, but the love of his life was Primmie. Behind that mask he was quite melancholy.' Hurt was surprised at how big Niv was, 'much bigger than you'd think, with very thick legs and extremely well endowed'. As for his acting, 'he was pretty good, but he said, "I know exactly what my position is, old cock: I'm a second-rate star," and he was right. He wasn't the greatest actor but he was more than adequate, a very good light comedian – so long as the writer wasn't on the set. He couldn't work at all if the writer was anywhere near it. He was very self-conscious and got quite nervous.'

Natalie Wood came to stay at Lo Scoglietto that summer with her latest lover, the British agent Richard Gregson, whom she was to marry a year later, and he introduced them to the songwriter Leslie Bricusse and his wife Evie, who spent every summer nearby at St Paul de Vence. 'We hit it off right away,' Bricusse told me, 'and for the rest of David's life we had lunch with him, Hjördis and the girls a minimum of twice a week all summer long. We'd sail our little wooden speedboat into his dock' and Niv 'always used to stand there with a bottle of champagne in one hand and a glass in the other', said Evie Bricusse. They took to Hjördis as well: 'She would come down to lunch with a big towelling turban round her head,' said Bricusse. 'That was her trademark. I know a lot of Swedish people don't get jokes at all, but she could laugh and was fun. If you'd known her before she got into the vodka bottle she was a devastatingly attractive woman, and we had a lot of fun in the late Sixties and early Seventies.' So, now and then, did David Jr, who was twenty-five. 'They used to play cards and swear like fiends and have a good time,' Fiona told me. 'Oh, God, the swearing that went on in that house! Ohhhh! Even Daddy sometimes: "oh shit!" and the c word. Mother and David didn't have any problem using the c word and he would call her "you bitch!" but it was just fun, not being nasty.' But during the 1970s, 'as Hjördis got deeper into the vodka bottle, she retreated more and more until towards the end we hardly ever saw her,' said Bricusse. 'There was a dark side to her that we never saw in the early days. Niv's goodness was shown best for me in his protection of her.'

Another new friend that summer was the Hon. William Feilding, a twenty-eight-year-old English painter who was cousin and heir to the Earl of Denbigh. Niv commissioned him to paint a vast mural on canvas, a 4ft high, 15ft wide acryllic view of Cap Ferrat and the coastline, which took him a month to complete in the garage at Lo Scoglietto and was then erected beside a little classical rotunda in the garden. 'David was a very enthusiastic painter himself,' Feilding told me. 'His pictures were quite rough and primitive but he had a real pictorial sense. He always drank wine at lunchtime and lots of it, at least two bottles a day, and was always offering you "a beaker" – "a beaker of shampoo, old boy". He had a huge tolerance for alcohol and after drinking with him at lunchtime one day I fell asleep on the top of a ladder while I was painting and woke when he came in with some people to hear him saying, "Ssh! Drunken painter!" '

'We all drank a lot in the South of France in those days,' Doreen Hawkins told me. 'We were always getting a bottle out of the fridge. It was difficult to draw the line.' Feilding recalled one memorably boozy lunch when Princess Grace came over from Monaco on her own and she, Feilding and the Nivens had lunch at the African Queen in Beaulieu. 'We got a bit pissed,' said Feilding, 'and afterwards we were all walking arm-in-arm around the marina and singing, like children, when we came to a yacht that was owned by some millionaire whom Grace and Hjördis hated because whenever he was talking to them he would play with himself through a hole in his trouser pocket. So Grace and Hjördis got hold of one of the boat's ropes, and David got hold of the other, and they pulled it in, and I pissed all over the back deck! He once said to me "a day without a laugh is a day wasted".' Niv could make a joke out of almost any situation. One day when he and Feilding were naked in the swimming pool changing room Feilding noticed that Niv 'had a pretty big tonk. The girls were aged about six and seven and they ran into the room and one of them grabbed his cock and swung on it, and he said, "better get them used to a decent size at an early age!" '

They used to have lunch at Lo Scoglietto at the end of the garden, and one day when they saw an enormous yacht in the bay with people on the bridge looking at them through binoculars David said, 'Quick, under the table!' and 'we all dived under the table,' said Feilding, 'along with the nanny and the children, and he said, "That's Richard Burton and Liz Taylor," and sure enough the Burtons sailed over in a speedboat and we could hear them talking to the butler, whom David had told to say we were out. They went back to their boat and we continued our lunch and could see that they were still looking at us through their binoculars. "Don't you like them, then?" I said, and David said, "Yes, if they telephone first"!'

Feilding was one of the 600 guests at Jamie's marriage, which some American newspapers inevitably called 'the wedding of the year' and took place in July 1968 at the First Presbyterian Church at Southampton on Long Island. David Jr, who had now moved to the William Morris London office, was best man, and Kristina and Fiona were bridesmaids. Niv wore an extraordinary outfit: a pearl-grey Edwardian morning suit with a flared, knee-length jacket and a top hat. 'What the *fuck* has the old man got on?' asked David Jr, and Jamie was extremely irritated because he felt that his father was trying to upstage everyone. The young couple flew off to Jamaica on honeymoon and when they returned to New York Jamie went to work on Wall Street for the investment bankers Lehman Brothers. 'I didn't go to Harvard Business School because my father told me that he'd spent enough money on my education and he wasn't going to pay any more,' Jamie told me. At times Niv could give his sons the impression that he resented how much they had cost him. Once when they were skiing in Switzerland Jamie did four right turns and said proudly, 'Isn't it amazing, Father, that I can still turn like that after all these years?' Niv gave him one of his old-fashioned looks. 'You bloody well should be able to,' he said. 'Each one of those turns set me back $50,000.'

Niv flew to Paris to make a French comedy, *Le Cerveau*, which was released in Britain and America as *The Brain*, in which he was yet again a British officer, this time a colonel, a sort of military Raffles, a gentleman crook who has masterminded the Great Train Robbery in Britain and now plans to steal $12 million from NATO. He had to play each scene twice, in English and French, and again the critics reported that except for him the picture was a mess.

In September Jamie Hamilton wrote yet again to ask whether Niv had discovered if he was legally bound to offer his next book – which he was still calling a 'novel' – to the Cresset Press, and Niv replied ingenuously to say that Cresset could not possibly insist on publishing his next book, despite his contractual agreement to give them first refusal, since 'I am under contract for everything to a Swiss Company (I wonder who could control that!!) so any Publisher would have to deal with the Swiss Company and Cresset would have to be able to match the Swiss Company's offer . . . get it?!!' This devious ploy would have been decidedly underhand since the Swiss company, Marulto AG, was his own, which he had set up to avoid tax, so that any offer it made to publish his book would be a spurious one designed to cheat Cresset out of it. He apologised for having written so little of the book, explaining that he was always working or having fun, but 'it will get done tho' – I promise'. He added, 'I said to Noël the other day . . . "Christ! I'm now at the age when all my chums are dying like flies." To which he replied – "Personally I am delighted if mine last through luncheon"!' It was to be another year before he finally got down to work on the book in earnest.

Another new friend in Switzerland was Evan Galbraith, a Wall Street investment banker who had a holiday home near Château d'Oex, in Saanen, and was to become Ronald Reagan's ambassador to France from 1981 to 1985. 'He wasn't a very good skier,' Galbraith told me,

> but we got quite chummy. We'd have lunch at the Eagle Club and he'd go to the Buckleys almost every night, or we might watch a movie in his little studio for about twenty people in Château d'Oex, but you

almost never saw Hjördis. She was such a pain in the ass to him and I'm surprised they stayed together. His skirt-chasing was only because she was not very affectionate. He knew she had lovers, and rather than break the marriage up he'd just go away. He was also acting as the girls' father all the time, driving them to and from Gstaad and always organising something for their amusement. She did nothing but was always dolling herself up and her make-up was always a foot thick. You'd go there for dinner and it would appear difficult for her to pitch in. Her only redeeming feature was that she did have a sense of humour and would laugh at a joke, but she got bored with his stories. She'd roll her eyes and say, 'Oh my God!' He'd see something during the day and that night he'd tell about it and it wasn't the truth but he'd exaggerate it to make it funny.

Niv told Sally Chrichton-Stuart that he was still thinking of divorcing Hjördis, but was worried about what would happen to his two adopted daughters. 'He said that Hjördis was very fragile.' Another friend in Switzerland was Valerie Youmans, who had met the Nivens in California ten years earlier when Hjördis had been reprimanded for fondling her husband at a dinner party. 'He was adored by everyone but was clearly lonely and unhappy,' said Mrs Youmans, 'but he would never say anything against her. He was too much of a gentleman.'

Kristina, Hjördis's favourite daughter, who was seven, told me:

I don't know if she loved me. She was very difficult to get to know and I never did in all those years because she always told a different story. She was very moody and if I went into the room at the wrong moment, *ooops*-a-daisy! She would *make* herself unhappy and make a mountain out of a molehill. She never learned how to cook – just corned beef hash and a boiled egg – and she didn't like eating much and was so skinny. She had a lot of health problems and had epileptic fits that were brought on by her drinking. She drank Fernet Branca because I think she was trying to cleanse herself out, thinking it would help, but it's foul stuff with a bitter taste and it's forty-two per cent alcohol! She did nothing all day except read and talk on the phone. She had telephonitis but I never knew who her friends were. She did a bit of swimming, or painting in the winter, but she said to me often, 'I prefer being alone.' I think she loved me, deep down, somewhere, yes, and my father, but she was jealous of him and his popularity and jealous of his girlfriends, even though she had lovers too. I don't know how many

Niv's friend Lesley Watson, *née* Rowlatt, now Viscountess Hambleden, in 1982. 'If Niven's friends were urging him to marry somebody else at the end of his life I think it must have been her,' said her ex-husband, Peter Watson. 'She really adored him and she'd have made him happy.'

Prince Rainier with Hjördis (drunk as usual) and her daughter Kristina behind them after Niv's funeral service in Château d'Oex in August 1983.

At Christmas 1983, four months after Niv died, his friends Evie and Leslie Bricusse went to his grave to pay their respects. As Bricusse took a photograph of his wife beside the cross 'into the frame flew a multi-coloured hot-air balloon going down the valley,' he said. 'Not only was it *The Moon's a Balloon*, it was also *Around the World in Eighty Days*. I told Niv Jr about it and he shivered.'

> lovers she had: I'm very bad at math! But I didn't have an unhappy childhood because Daddy was great fun, easygoing, very affectionate, a really good father. We always used to giggle together and when I was older we used to look at each other at about 11 a.m. and he'd wink and say 'time for a beaker?' and we'd go to the Clipper in Beaulieu and have a kir, and the African Queen for pizzas. He never got cross and I couldn't ask for a better childhood. Later we were encouraged to join in with his famous friends and he was always there at school and for skiing races. He called me Kristabel, Fiona was Pooh, Jamie was Squeak and David was Nigger – I don't know why. My mother used to call my father J. C. – short for Jesus Christ. When Fiona and I were baptised I was meant to be called Kristina Maria Patricia Henriette Niven, but I think Daddy had had a lot of fun the night before and when he got up from kneeling he bumped his head and gave my name as Juliet instead of Henriette!

To be fair to Hjördis I asked Kristina to list her mother's good points. 'She had a sense of humour,' she said, 'and was very patient, and had good taste in clothes as well as decoration. We played Canasta very often, or gin rummy, and backgammon, just the two of us, and she'd have a beaker, but it was a pity that she never wanted to go out of the house. I think maybe her health scared her so she didn't feel too secure if she went out even though when I was older I offered hundreds of times to take her out for lunch. I think she might have had a very sad childhood herself, so that part of the shadows of her childhood came out on us. I never knew about her childhood and I've no idea even what her father did.'

Fiona, who was five in 1968, was not fond of Hjördis at all. 'She was an alcoholic and when I was five or six she fell down the stairs,' she told me, 'so she was already out of control. And she was terribly vain. She had five passports, all English but with different dates of birth, and I found one in which she had *forged* her age by changing the date of birth. She was twenty-nine for most of my life!' Kristina told me that Hjördis pretended to have been born in 1924 but had in fact been born in 1919: 'She wasn't a great believer in telling the truth.' Niv, on the other hand, 'was a great father', Fiona said, 'and I spent more time with him while Kristina spent more time with Mummy. He adored Kristina and me, and he'd try to be there for us as much as he could. I used to go walking and sailing with him, and I had a great childhood. He didn't need to be strict because all he had to do was look at us and that was enough said. He never had to raise his voice. He spoilt us with affection and love but not with money though he was very generous at Christmas and birthdays.'

'They were very nice kids, pretty and fun,' Jamie told me, 'and my father did the best he could to give them a happy life, but Hjördis ruined their upbringing: when you have a drunk staggering around the house, what kind of advice are you going to have? He tried to shield these kids from all this and he was around a lot for them, much more than he was for us, and that was great.' Betty Bacall said that 'he was a wonderful dad' and the American actress Jane Del Amo, whose screen name was Jane Randolph and who lived near the Nivens both in Switzerland and Cap Ferrat, agreed. 'He was an exceptionally good father to the girls,' she told me.

> He was the one who did everything with them and took care of them, and he was always very, very considerate of her. I think he felt sorry for her and thought that was his responsibility. But she was very difficult to like and so self-centred that I don't think she cared about anybody. One day a whole group of us were invited for Sunday lunch on his birthday, and we were all there playing ping-pong and out in the garden, and he came in at about two o'clock and said 'Hjördis, don't you think it's time we ate?' and she said '*ate*? What do you mean?' and he had to go off with his oldest son down to the hotel in Château d'Oex and they brought back a lot of cold cuts and everybody helped themselves. Then I saw her on the street in Gstaad one day – she always had these long black eyelashes on, even in the morning – and she said 'the cook just left' and I said 'well, I guess you'll have to cook', and she said '*Me*? I'm not cooking. We'll eat out of cans.' God knows what she did all day. It wasn't a very nice chalet and the furniture was terrible – old tables, old sofas, plastic chairs – and the house in Cap Ferrat was pretty much that way too.

In March 1969 Hjördis fell over and broke her leg again. Niv flew with her to London and decided to take an extended break and make a serious effort to write the book. *The Moon's a Balloon* was about to fly.

Twelve

The Moon's a Balloon

1969–1972

At first Niv called the book *Five Sides of a Square* and began to dictate it into a tape recorder but was put off by the monotonous drone of his voice when he played it back. He tried to dictate it to 'a sour-faced lady from Nice' but she disapproved of his four-letter words and risqué anecdotes, so in the end he wrote in longhand in Kristina's school exercise books.

He began with a bang. 'Nessie, when I first saw her, was seventeen years old,' he wrote, 'honey-blonde, pretty rather than beautiful, the owner of a voluptuous but somehow innocent body and a pair of legs that went on for ever. She was a Piccadilly whore. I was a fourteen-year-old heterosexual schoolboy and I met her thanks to my stepfather.' He wrote first about his childhood and although some of his stories were untrue and some inaccurate because he could not be bothered to check the facts, at his best he was wonderfully entertaining and hilarious. For three weeks he scribbled away and by mid-April had finished the first two chapters, gave them to Roddy Mann to take back to London to be typed by the Connaught manager's secretary, Mrs Faulkner, and then sent them off to Jamie Hamilton. 'I would love you to wade through these first 50 pages and see if you think there could be anything in this thing,' Niv wrote to him modestly. 'I feel that the style is pretty schoolboy, but I believe I can improve that quite a bit.' Four days later Hamilton cabled to say he was delighted with what he had read and sent an ecstatic letter that began: 'Those first two chapters are hilarious. Not only did I laugh aloud, but later heard my secretary splitting her sides. I shall jump in the Thames if you find you are still committed to Cresset . . . You are a bloody marvel.'

Instead of being encouraged to get on with the book as quickly as possible, Niv relaxed, flew to New York and Los Angeles for two weeks in May, and then went into neutral for most of that lovely Côte d'Azur summer, writing only when the weather was bad, which was extremely rare that year. Hamilton wrote more encouraging letters. Niv replied, 'Have finished CHAP. 3 – ghastly! . . . It's a slow game as I have no discipline, am easily distracted by a robin and am not broke thank God . . . but it will get done.' The old Cresset contract of 25 September 1950 was finally unearthed and found to have granted Cresset first refusal on Niv's next *two* books, so he suggested yet again that he could cheat Cresset – and his previous American publisher, Prentice Hall – if 'one of those strange Swiss companies that we know so well could offer an enormous sum as an advance against this second book and you could then ask Cresset and Prentice Hall . . . if they would care to match it!!'

The problem was that Niv was lazy, relished playing with his pretty young daughters, and was easily led astray by the hordes of guests and visitors who turned up at Lo Scoglietto, among them Noël Coward, who came for two weeks. Not that Niv stayed up late at night: when Coward wanted to go to the casino he went with Jamie because Niv liked to rise early and be in bed by eleven at the latest. Other friends who dropped by and distracted him that summer included Lord Hanson and his wife Geraldine, whom Niv teasingly nicknamed 'Ugly' as he did almost every good-looking woman he was fond of, including beauties like Bryan Forbes's wife Nanette Newman and their daughter Emma. 'God, you've got some ugly women!' Niv told Forbes, and he called other favourite women and girls 'Double Ugly', 'Beast' or 'Beastly'.

By the middle of October, nearly six months after he had finished the first two chapters, he had written little more and the book was delayed even further when he flew to England in November to make an epic picture with Peter Finch, Liv Ullmann and Max von Sydow for MGM, *Man's Fate*, but after three weeks' rehearsal the film was cancelled because of industrial unrest at the studio. He flew back to Nice, furious, and he, Finch and von Sydow sued MGM for more than £500,000, a claim that took nearly four years to settle. He feared that this was the end of his career and that he might never be offered another film, so after a gala tribute to Noël Coward in London on his seventieth birthday, Niv sat down seriously to write that winter at Château d'Oex in his first-floor study overlooking the valley and facing the vast mountains opposite. He produced two more chapters in six weeks, but was finding it so difficult that 'I'm just shoving everything down', he wrote to Hamilton. 'It's pretty bad and you must be truthful.' He was so disheartened that he thought of abandoning the book altogether, and his mood was not improved when he turned sixty in March – a glum day for anyone, let alone a vain actor.

In April he took a break from the book and flew to Rome to make one of the very worst films of his career, *The Statue*, in which he played a professor whose sculptress wife produces a huge nude statue with genitals that are obviously not based on his. The critics were appalled. The film was 'a sniggering comedy carried to such extremes that it becomes difficult to tell which is more offensive: its prissy hypocrisy, its blatant banality, or the clumsily-fashioned "double entendres" that sit in the script like flies in the soup', reported Anita Seales in the *San Francisco Chronicle*.

By the end of May Jamie Hamilton was seriously worried that he was never going to finish the book and Niv replied that he was still bogged down on chapter 5. 'I am bitterly ashamed of myself,' he wrote. 'Dammit! I find so many excuses NOT to sit down and write!' Yet even now he flew off to New York for a week of carousing with friends that upset his son Jamie as much as it would have annoyed Hamilton. Jamie and Fernanda were living in New York and kept reading in the society columns of the newspapers about the fun he was having with his chums, and it was not until Niv's last day in town that he rang Jamie and asked to meet for lunch at Le Mistral. Jamie, now twenty-four, was incensed. At the restaurant he ordered his meal, told David how hurt and upset he was, and when his father took exception to being criticised Jamie threw his napkin down, stood up, said loudly, 'I think you'll need both plates of food – one for you and one for your ego,' and stormed out of the restaurant. It was a vital turning point in their relationship. 'From then on we were friends,' he told me, 'and became really close. For the last twelve years of his life I was his best friend and he relied on me for lots of things, financial advice and so on, and I don't think I let him down.'

Back at Lo Scoglietto that summer Niv tried to force himself to write for at least an hour a day 'but it's AGONY!' he wrote to Hamilton. 'Oh this dreary little piddle of output! I'm so sorry but . . . the children came home for the holidays and that was that . . . I have too much fun with them . . . I cant work!' He also took Hjördis to Sweden on holiday in August and was constantly distracted by the usual summer stream of friends and guests. 'God its dull,' he wrote to Hamilton. 'I've just read it through.' Hamilton battled valiantly to bolster his confidence. 'Everyone who has read the samples so far has found it hilariously entertaining, so you simply must press on,' he wrote, and Niv was sufficiently encouraged to take on Roddy Mann's literary agent, George Greenfield of the John Farquharson agency, as his own. Greenfield promptly came up with another possible obstacle to publication of the book by Hamish Hamilton: he discovered that the Cresset Press not only had a legal right to first sight of the book but might also sue Niv for plagiarism of his own earlier book because the new book contained many of the same anecdotes as *Round the Rugged Rocks*. But he soon extricated him from his Cresset option clause. 'Niv, Greenfield, Hamilton and I,' said Roddy Mann, 'concocted a letter from Greenfield to Cresset that went something like this: "I have received a very long manuscript from the veteran actor David Niven full of rambling reminiscences. It is written by hand" – which it wasn't – "and I understand that you published his first book and are obviously entitled to have a look at this one. Shall I box the pages up and send them to you?" It was hysterical! Cresset said "No way!" so Hamilton became his publisher.' Niv celebrated his freedom by sending huge cheques to Joyce and Grizel for Christmas, the modern equivalent of £52,000 between them.

He finally finished the book at the end of February, nearly two years after he had started it. Hamilton was delighted and drafted a telegram 'TO CONGRATULATE YOU ON FUNNIEST WITTIEST MOST OUTSPOKEN MODEST WARM HEARTED TOUCHING MEMOIRS FOR AGES'. In an internal memo to his senior editors Roger Machell and Christopher Sinclair-Stevenson he reported that the book was 'excruciatingly funny and chock full of libel ... and extremely vulgar with a great many 4-letter words thrown in'. Greenfield negotiated an advance of £7500 – about £77,000 in 2003, much less than a 'celebrity' author would be offered today – and the typescript was handed to Machell for some serious editing. Sinclair-Stevenson took to Niv immediately, 'and he had abundant charm,' he told me,

> but I felt that he was a bit too smooth by half – and he wasn't quite as nice as everyone seems to think. As his publisher I saw the nervous, twitchy side of him, and he was a very difficult author. He was very articulate and amusing but far more complex than one might have thought. Later I got to know him quite well and he was *tremendously* insecure, which was probably why he made things up all the time. One never actually knew whether any of these stories were true or not. I would guess a good sixty per cent were elaborated at least, but they had a germ, a kernel of truth, and why not? He thought they sounded better with this twiddle and that twiddle and I'm sure an enormous

number were embellished. I suspect he wanted to be loved – lack of security again – and he wanted adulation. If people recognised him in the street he was absolutely thrilled.

Surprisingly for an author who admitted openly that he was an amateur, David hated accepting editorial suggestions to improve the book. 'Roger was an extremely good editor,' said Sinclair-Stevenson, 'and he would say, "I think we should take this story out because it doesn't really fit," and Niven would grumble away. He was very bad indeed at being edited, very tetchy and very difficult, and he'd say, "No, no, absolutely not," and get rather sulky, but Roger knew how to deal with people like that and Niven eventually, grumbling, agreed to the cuts.' Niv did, however, eventually give Machell 'tremendous credit' for the changes that he suggested and told Patrick Macnee that 'without a good editor he wouldn't have had a success at all'.

The book's original title, *Five Sides of a Square*, was soon dumped 'because it was ludicrous and boring', said Sinclair-Stevenson, and when Niv came up with an alternative, *The Moon's a Balloon*, a quote from an E. E. Cummings 'poem', nobody liked that either. Buckley and Galbraith both told him it was a dreadful title and tried to persuade him to change it, in vain. 'We all look back and think "what a wonderful title" because it was a big success,' said Sinclair-Stevenson, 'but it didn't mean anything. But he had very strong views over the title and the cover, and we had to produce *enormous* numbers of roughs of the jacket because he didn't like them. When it came to doing the jacket his prima donna side was really beginning to show, which is why I think Roger didn't like him very much. David could be quite brusque and was not very good with people like waiters, and I could imagine he could be quite unpleasant. Incidentally, I never saw him pick up the bill in a restaurant even though *The Moon's a Balloon* eventually sold about 4 million and millions out of it.'

The title was bewilderingly fey and came from a piece of doggerel by the pretentious E. E. Cummings, who avoided capital letters or even spaces after punctuation and called himself 'e.e.cummings'. Why did Niv choose the title? Search me:

who knows if the moon's
a balloon,coming out of a keen city
in the sky–filled with pretty people?
(and if you and I should

get into it,if they
should take me and take you into their balloon,
why then
we'd go up higher with all the pretty people

than houses and steeples and clouds:
go sailing
away and away sailing into a keen
city which nobody's ever visited,where

always
it's
Spring)and everyone's
*in love and flowers pick themselves**

The significance of this twee drivel eludes me, but Niv liked it so much that when he came to write his fourth book he wanted to take the title for that from the final line and call it *Flowers Pick Themselves*. His dedication in *The Moon's a Balloon* was equally bizarre: 'for Kira Triandpyllapopulous'. Kira was the Greek name of one of Hjördis's Afghan hounds, and Niv explained bafflingly in *Smith's Trade News* two years later that 'Kira piddles on everything so I invented a Greek sounding challenge to her – KIRA TRI AND PYLL A POPULOUS. (I don't know what a "populous" is but she has filled everything else in my house.)' Perhaps 'pyll' was a misprint and should have been 'fill', but it was in any case pretty silly. He may not have wanted to dedicate another book to Hjördis, but why not to his sons or Roddy Mann, who had nagged him to write it?

In retrospect, knowing how hugely successful *The Moon's a Balloon* was to be, it is astonishing how much trouble Greenfield and Machell had selling the American rights and finding a company to publish the British paperback edition. In Britain the editorial director of Pan Books, Clarence Paget, said dismissively that the first third of the book, about David's childhood, schooldays and army experiences, was 'quite interesting' and he was prepared to pay a paltry £500 advance for that, but the stuff about Hollywood was 'terribly boring' and ought to be junked. In the end British paperback rights were sold to Coronet, but they refused to pay

* From *Complete Poems* by e.e. cummings – US title *Poems 1923–1954* – copyright 1923, 1925, 1931, 1935 by e.e. cummings (© Marion Moorhouse Cummings, 1968) and published by MacGibbon & Kee Ltd, London and Harcourt, Brace, Jovanovich Inc., New York.

an advance of more than £800 – about £7000 in modern terms – or subsequent royalties of more than seven and a half per cent. Niv, who was used to earning $150,000 for a film that might take just a few weeks to shoot – £610,000 today – could hardly believe such a derisory offer. In New York it was just as bad. In his autobiography Greenfield claimed that the editor-in-chief of Simon and Schuster, Michael Korda, the nephew of Sir Alexander Korda, refused to read even the first few pages, telling Greenfield that Niv was a boring old British ham actor who had never been a major star and had not made a decent film for years, but Korda told me that this was quite untrue. 'I always admired and liked Niven and did not think he was a has-been,' said Korda. 'In fact I loved the book and tried to buy it, but it went for more money than Simon and Schuster was willing to let me pay.' Even so, Greenfield was horrified that only four publishers were prepared to make an offer for the book and that the highest, from G. P. Putnam's Sons, was for only $17,500. He had made the mistake of assuring Niv that he would be able to sell the US rights for an advance of at least $35,000 and had flown to New York especially to do it, and although he managed to push Putnam's up to $22,500 (£83,000 today) 'he was pretty nervous of telephoning Niven to tell him because Niven was pretty tough,' recalled Greenfield's assistant, Vivienne Schuster, who went to New York with him. David was incensed at such a 'piddling' bid – 'His screams of rage penetrated my skull,' said Greenfield – and although Greenfield eventually persuaded him that that was simply the best offer there was, Niv threatened to sack him if ever he fouled up again. This was a very different Niven from his screen image. The British newspaper serial rights were bought by the *People* for another £10,000 – £97,000 today – but even then he was annoyed because he had been expecting a much bigger bid from Roddy Mann's paper, the *Sunday Express*, but its editor, John Junor, understandably refused to buy yet again a bunch of anecdotes for which he had already paid handsomely when he had published Niv's ghosted autobiographical series in the paper thirteen years previously. To avoid tax all these literary contracts, like those for his films, were signed by his Swiss business manager in Zurich, Dr Bill Staehelin, who was now collaborating on Niv's financial affairs with Jess Morgan in Los Angeles, on behalf of Niv's Swiss company Marulto AG, which was described inventively as 'the author'.

David turned out to be one of the most difficult authors Hamish Hamilton ever published. He complained constantly about suggested cuts, jacket designs and publicity, and was at first unwilling to help to sell the book. When Jamie Hamilton asked him to attend an important lunch in London for his sales reps he replied airily, 'I am afraid there is no hope as we are going yachting in early July . . . so sorry.' He said he was 'delighted' about the projected green book jacket, which showed a horse race – 'it could be really great' – but later changed his mind and said he hated it. When he corrected the proofs and then flew off to Hollywood to sing 'Hello, Dolly' with Pearl Bailey at a 5200-seat charity gala in June no one in London could understand his corrections, and when Hamilton sent him a series of urgent cables because the book was overdue at the printer he ignored them all. By now Jamie Hamilton was angry and wrote:

> I am concerned over your attitude towards the book. To begin with I both telephoned and wired asking you to speak to me about your corrections. Instead you ring Greenfield and get him to pass on messages. Now I can understand your using him for contractual arrangements, as you don't like to do business with friends. But after all you and I have known each other for many years and I would have thought it more courteous to deal with me direct over proofs. Again I invite you to our semi-annual lunch, which would have done much to raise enthusiasm amongst our representatives, who are very important in launching a book [*but*] you can't do it. In fact the impression is now prevalent that you are very casual about the whole thing, and if you don't come to London when the book is published, to be interviewed on TV etc. this will be confirmed. We have paid a large advance on the book, and I imagine that you are as keen that it should be a success as we are. In that case I hope you will give me an assurance which I can read to my colleagues that you intend to help.

Niv hit the roof and replied with grim typed formality: 'Dear Hamilton, When I first read your letter of June 18th I very nearly blew a fuse. Then I reflected that I have in my time been insulted by champions including Samuel Goldwyn and Field Marshal Montgomery, so I decided that you must have suffered a crise de foi. Even so, I must ask you never again to give me the Dr. Allington to Scroggs Minor treatment, or the explosion will be heard by the Russians in their space lab! . . . Of course I have every intention of doing everything I can do to help but we are to be realistic about this: I am not just sitting on my ass waiting for publication day, I am working on at least half a dozen movie projects . . . So eat a lot of veg soups and yoghurts and don't write any more "Dr. Allington's".' Before sending the letter he changed 'Dear Hamilton' to 'Dear Jamie' by pen, made corrections to eight garbled words, added 'Bloody drunken French secretary' and 'love David', and promised to attend the reps' lunch in London after all.

Hamilton cabled him to say 'GOOD BOY SEE YOU MONDAY IN MY STUDY ALLINGTON' but the lunch was not a total success because Niv was by now so touchy about the book that he thought he overheard one of the reps say 'I hate it' and the unfortunate fellow was forced to write to the paranoid author to say that he loved the book and the jacket. Niv, however, decided now that he hated the jacket himself and demanded another. Even when he had his photograph taken for the jacket he objected to the photographer, Beverly Lebarrow. 'Coming to London to pose for Mr. Lebarrow was one of the most horrible experiences of my professional career,' he wrote to Jamie Hamilton. 'It's quite possible that I do look like an elderly baker but I should have thought any professional photographer worth his salt would have taken special pains to disguise the fact and do something better for the author.' When the final hurried jacket was produced it did indeed look a dreadful mess and showed an emaciated, unhandsome Niv holding four coloured balloons, each stencilled with one fashionably uncapitalised word that together read *the moon's a balloon*.

Jamie Hamilton begged Niv to do a signing session at London's most fashionable bookshop, Hatchards, when the book was published in October, and to agree to be the guest of honour at the influential Foyle's literary lunch. He refused both and eventually agreed only reluctantly to make a BBC TV programme about his old movies, a half-hour *Aquarius* programme, and to spend two nights in London to give some Press, TV and radio interviews. More trouble was to come when he was finally sent a finished copy of the book: he still hated the jacket, and then discovered to his fury that the index called Primmie Primrose, not Primula, that the caption to a photo of their wedding was dated 1941 instead of 1940, and that another caption said wrongly that Jamie's wedding was in 1969. Hamilton wrote to apologise but added insensitively that 'they are, after all, comparatively small errors and unlikely to upset anyone except yourself'. Niv hit the roof again: 'Nobody sent me either the photographs or the index to check and I find it very humiliating to be a man who knows neither the year of his own wedding or his son's wedding, or even the name of his first wife.'

He became a grandfather when Jamie's first daughter, Fernanda Jr, was born on 24 June, and towards the end of September he flew to Munich and then to Nice to film *King, Queen, Knave* with Gina Lollobrigida, whom he came to dislike intensely, but he was back in London early in October for the publication of *The Moon's a Balloon*. Jamie Hamilton gave a launch party for literary editors, columnists and booksellers where Niv cannily homed in on the booksellers, realising that they were the people to charm and impress if the book was to become a bestseller. 'For the next twenty minutes and more, there were roars of laughter coming from that corner as he poured out jokes and anecdotes and flattery,' wrote Greenfield in his autobiography. 'You could see them swelling with pride. Roger Machell told me the following week that the buyers present at the party had more than doubled their orders in the next few days.' Another huge boost to sales came when Niv was interviewed on TV on the *Michael Parkinson Show*. 'He was a nice man,' Parkinson told me,

> the most naturally good-mannered man I've ever met in my life, with effortless charm, and there was a hinterland to him. When he came on the show that first time he said, 'I'm desperately nervous, I still can't get over my nerves, even when I'm acting,' and I heard him being incredibly sick, puking in his dressing room before the show. 'I have to do it every time I go on,' he said, and then he came on and delivered the best one-man show I've ever done. He was wonderfully entertaining, highly intelligent, and that insecurity was part of his charm, like Hugh Grant, that public school type that makes a virtue out of being slightly *distrait*. The book was unknown on the Saturday night and on the Monday morning they had to reprint, and it went on and on and on. It doesn't matter if half his stories were untrue. I don't care! It's the way you tell 'em, and Niven was masterful. God, he was funny.

The Moon's a Balloon was published at last on 11 October 1971 at £2.50 and Niv was still so unsure about it that he gave Roddy Mann, his press agent Theo Cowan, and several other friends £100 each to go round key bookshops and buy forty copies each. 'He was really quite nervous about it,' Mann told me, but there was no need to be. The reviewers raved about it and when I praised it in my weekly books column in the *Sunday Express*, saying that it was 'the funniest volume of reminiscences for ages . . . forthright, bawdy and often hilarious', he wrote an astonishingly humble and modest letter that very day to thank me:

> Dear Graham Lord,
> I am dazzled that out of the hundreds of possibilities each week you

should have reviewed my book . . . and I am blinded by the generosity of your praise!

I am as nervous as a bride about the whole thing because I misjudged the amount of time and money which the publisher was prepared to spend so that I could rewrite it several times to my satisfaction.

In the event he ripped it out of my hot sticky hands before the ink was dry and was extremely upstage when I complained, so I feel that I rushed it all horribly.

Anyway a few old friends might get a laugh or two, and as it is impossible to be an actor unless you are also an egomaniac, my egomania has received a glorious boost from you for which I am hereby thanking you very much indeed.

Few famous authors would take the trouble to thank an unknown young critic for a good review.

The literary editor of the *Daily Telegraph*, David Holloway, queried the truth of many of the stories in *The Moon's a Balloon* and Roddy Mann told me that he actually challenged Niv about a lot of the stories in his book 'and he said, "Of *course* they're true", and although I think all the anecdotes were fictionalised I couldn't say to a friend, "I don't believe you". He exaggerated only to be more amusing. "That's my greatest joy," he said, "making people laugh." ' Peter Ustinov, a wonderful raconteur himself, told me that all great storytelling needs a degree of fictional embellishment – 'you're not really telling a lie, you're just concentrating something into a nugget' – and David Jr told me: 'Daddy was known to exaggerate and then suddenly he'd start believing his own stories. Every year each story got a bit better, so I can no longer remember what is the really *true* true story, or whether it happened to him or a friend of his, or whether it was just a good story that he'd heard. One of his stories had actually happened to *me* but he said it had happened to *him*. I was in a rage. I thought, "How can you *do* that sort of thing? *I* told you that story." ' Rex Harrison claimed after reading *The Moon's a Balloon* that 'they're all *my* stories!' but Jamie Niven said, 'It was the wonderful imaginative additions to the stories that made them great. I remember sitting on a beautiful terrazzo in the South of France with Alec Guinness, my father and Jack Hawkins – *that* was a late night! – and it got funnier and funnier and Hawkins and I were laughing so hard because these two giants were going *at* it with stories neither of them had heard. Hawkins said to me, "Don't you *ever* forget this night." '

In a way *The Moon's a Balloon* was almost a novel, albeit a much better one than *Round the Rugged Rocks*, though a book that purports to be a factual autobiography should not be flawed by quite so many inaccuracies about dates, names and places. Niv even managed to get wrong Primmie's age when she died. Loving her as much as he did, how could he possibly get it wrong? Was his memory really that bad? Was he just too lazy to check? Or did he say that she was twenty-five rather than twenty-eight simply to make her death even more poignant? The chronology of *The Moon's a Balloon* is also wildly inaccurate: some things are said to have happened years before or after they did, and there are some odd omissions. He makes no mention at all of *Round the Rugged Rocks*, for instance, and the end is so rushed that while he devoted 259 pages to his first thirty-nine years, i.e. six and a half pages per year, he gave only forty-five pages to the next twenty-one years, just two pages per year, and very disjointed they are too. His compulsive fibbing had become such a habit that he even claimed in an interview with William Hall of the *Evening News* that the book had taken him only four months to write 'and I swear to you that everything in that book happened to me. It would be unforgivable – and very foolish – to steal anything. Someone would catch you out.' He told Hall that the disapproving secretary to whom he had initially tried to dictate the book 'was a tight-lipped Swiss lady', but a year later wrote in *Smith's Trade News* that she had been 'a sour-faced lady from Nice'. One wonders whether she existed at all.

Within a week the book shot to the top of the bestseller lists, where it stayed at number one for weeks, and had to be reprinted again and again. Most of his friends loved the book and Laurence Olivier wrote ecstatically: 'Dearest beloved Niv, ... Darling Boy Oh how I do congratulate you and rejoice for your glorious and so completely deserved success. I don't think I ever enjoyed a book so much – funny, fascinating, always interesting and yet possessing a not unwelcome seam of intense sadness, and at times dreadfully moving. Dearest Boy its really first rate and lovely. My God your life makes mine seem like a well protected piece of boring organ music. All my love dear heart to you and yours Always your own L.'

Not everyone approved of the book. For some reason it did not appeal at all to the Teutonic mind and nearly twenty German publishers turned it down, and even in Britain there were voices of dissent. 'You'd think from reading *The Moon's a Balloon* that here is the most superficial bounder in the whole history of civilisation,' wrote Bart Mills in the *Guardian* three years later. 'All those anecdotes and so little substance. Never a nasty word about anyone.' Soon after publication Niv received a package that contained a jacket of the book wrapped around more than 200 blank sheets of paper with a note that said, 'I have removed all the filth,' and when he read the book on BBC radio four years later Mrs Mary Whitehouse, the leader of the British National Viewers and Listeners Association, attacked the book's 'foul language and indecency'. Little did the puritans realise that Niv had in fact left out all his filthiest and most scurrilous stories, like the one about the Hollywood actor who loved to sit naked on a large cake and masturbate: as Niv said wisely, 'You can't have your cake and have it too!' Another reader who might well have been angry – or even have sued for libel – was the RAF group captain who had rejected him when he had tried to join the RAF in 1939, a Group Captain Fletcher, whose name had been removed from the text to avoid a libel writ but unfortunately not from the index. 'OUT,' wrote Niv urgently and it was hurriedly removed.

In November he returned to Munich to finish filming *King, Queen, Knave*, a black comedy in which he and Gina Lollobrigida played a rich Anglo-Italian couple whose nineteen-year-old nephew becomes her lover and plots with her to murder him. Niv would quite happily have murdered Lollobrigida if he had had a chance. He was infuriated by her rudeness, temperamental outbursts and unpunctuality, and took great pleasure in one scene in which he had to smack her playfully on the bottom with a tennis racket. He whacked her as hard as he could and said, 'I've been longing to do that all through this picture.'

Jamie Hamilton was already urging him to write another book and suggested a comic biography of Trubshawe, a novel, or a second volume of autobiography, and begged David to let him republish *Round the Rugged Rocks*, but he was determined to suppress his embarrassing old novel.

Boxing Day was sadly muted that year. Noël Coward, Cole Lesley and Graham Payn came to Château d'Oex as usual but Coward was subdued and suddenly announced, 'I will not be here next Christmas.' He was only seventy-two and not particularly ill but he took to his bed and died three months later to the day.

In January 1972 David flew to New York for his granddaughter Fernanda's christening and a triumphant tour of the States to promote the American edition of *The Moon's a Balloon*. He travelled proudly for the first time with a passport that gave his occupation as 'Writer' rather than 'Actor'. Most of the American reviewers were genial except for a sarky critic in the *New York Times* who wondered whether Niv saw anything at all when he looked into the mirror each morning, but the book still shot into the paper's bestseller list and stayed there for three months. The tour was a huge success and 'he got a great kick out of it', said Jamie Niven. He appeared on the top TV talk shows, Putnam's sold nearly 200,000 copies in hardback, the book became a Literary Guild book club choice, and Dell paid $350,000 (£1,140,000 today) for the US paperback rights. In the end he made about $750,000 from the American editions of the book, the equivalent of about £2·5 million today.

At the end of February the Nivens flew to Budapest for the weekend to join Princess Grace, Fred Astaire, Marlon Brando and 200 other guests for Elizabeth Taylor's lavish fortieth birthday party at the Duna Hotel, which cost the Burtons an estimated £50,000 – about £400,000 today – and Niv returned to Château d'Oex to revel in his own cascading new wealth. 'It's the first time in my life that I'm making a lot of money,' he told Hedi Donizetti, and Ken Galbraith told me that he, Niv and Buckley 'used to stare in the bookshop window in Gstaad to see which of us had the most books on display' – a foregone result since Galbraith's had solemnly unsexy titles such as *American Capitalism*, *The Affluent Society* and *The New Industrial State*. Niv was so chuffed by his huge unexpected success as an author, said Kitty Galbraith, that when a pretty girl in chartreuse ski pants passed them on the snow he goosed her with his ski stick.

Life at home with Hjördis, however, was becoming increasingly unpleasant, and unusually for Niv he confided in a thirty-one-year-old Welsh divorcée, Sue Bongard, an ex-model who lived in Gstaad and whose three daughters went to the same small school as Kristina and Fiona, the Marie-José, where she and David dropped their children off each morning and picked them up in the afternoon. 'I never saw Hjördis do it,' Mrs Bongard told me, and they began to meet regularly for an 8.30 a.m. coffee at the Rialto Café. 'I was very flattered by his attention,' she said, 'but I was fairly young and innocent and it was never a flirtatious relationship, just a friendship. A love affair never occurred to me. He was thirty years older than me, the same as my father. He seemed to like me for my mind! We'd laugh and giggle and tell each other the latest jokes, but now that I know how many girlfriends he had I feel a bit upset that he *didn't* make a pass at me! What was wrong with me?!' Niv confided in her only once, but what he said devastated her: 'I said to him one day, "You really are universally adored," and he laughed rather ruefully and said, "Except by my wife." I said, "What do you mean?" and he said, "Well, my wife has a lover. She's had a boyfriend for years." I was stunned. He never dwelt on it, but although he was the best company imaginable there was always a bit of sadness, and I think that was the reason.'

Because her eleven-year-old eldest daughter, Gaynor, was the same age as Kristina, Mrs Bongard and her girls were often invited to the Niven chalet:

> There was no real warmth between Niv and Hjördis. It was not a happy home to go to. The chalet was hideous, a lot of the furniture was very ugly, and there was an awful lot of plastic and plastic covers. It wasn't lived in and it didn't have flowers or magazines, but then Hjördis was a bit plastic-y herself. Her face had no animation and it wasn't wrinkled, either. People used to tell me she was very beautiful but I never actually saw it. She was always perfectly pleasant to me and would tell me about parties at the palace in Monte Carlo, and her friendship with Princess Grace, but I always felt she lived in her own little world. There was an older woman there, Madame Andrey, a housekeeper, who seemed very much part of the family and the children seemed very fond of her, but Hjördis was cold and never smiled, and I always had the feeling her girls didn't like her. Kristina suddenly said at dinner one night in a very loud voice, 'Sue, do you know Mummy's got disgustingly hairy legs?' – the sort of thing a loving child would not do. It was hugely embarrassing. So I said, 'All mummies do,' and Kristina said, 'But she hasn't got any hair at *all* except on her legs! Look at this!' and she whipped of Hjördis's wig. She was right: Hjördis's legs were very hairy and she always wore wigs, but I was *mortified*. Fiona was a sweet, very introverted little girl and I don't ever remember her laugh. Kristina did laugh and was much more feisty and outgoing, but I never felt they were relaxed, happy children, though they were more relaxed with David. They used to come over quite a lot to our chalet in Gstaad, too, because the girls got on quite well.'

Mrs Bongard's daughter, Gaynor Mazzone, confirmed that the Niven chalet 'wasn't a happy house. It was a very dark house and although David was a sweet man – we called him Fishface because he would do fish faces for us – Hjördis wasn't a happy Mummy and Kristina and Fiona weren't happy little girls. At eleven and nine they were already reserved about something. Hjördis stayed very much in her own room and she was very weird with them. She was never *with* them. It was not a normal family.'

Even though *The Moon's a Balloon* was now selling in huge numbers on both sides of the Atlantic and constantly being reprinted, David kept sending long letters to Jamie Hamilton to complain about 'the meagre publicity' for the book in Britain and to say that he was not spending enough on advertising and there were no copies in several bookshops he had visited. 'He was always nagging and he got worse as time went on,' said Sinclair-Stevenson. 'He was not easy to please. Even if you sold five thousand in a week he thought it should have been ten.'

On 26 March Noël Coward had a stroke and died at his home in Jamaica. He left his estate mainly to Cole Lesley and Graham Payn but Niv inherited an oil-on-glass painting by Salvador Dali, *Pegasus*, and was one of twenty-seven of Coward's friends – along with Sinatra, Gielgud, Dietrich and Liz Taylor – who Coward said should choose suitable mementoes. Niv picked one of Coward's own paintings of a beach in Jamaica.

In April he flew to Jersey to open a new gorilla house at Gerald Durrell's Jersey Zoo and to be the 'best man' at a 'wedding' of two gorillas that proceeded to consummate their 'marriage' prematurely behind his back while he made his best man's speech. Back at Lo Scoglietto he started to write a novel, *Make It Smaller and Move It to the Left*, the suggestion of his art teacher in Hollywood decades earlier, but it was even more difficult than *The Moon's a Balloon*. 'I'm on chapter three and already I have thirty-two people stuck in a lighthouse,' he told the *Daily Express*. 'Every time I sit down to write more, another three turn up in a boat. I just don't know what to do!' He thought of writing a biography instead, or a book about the Chinese Opium Wars, but told Jamie Hamilton at the end of May that both would need too much daunting research. He had actually written two chapters of the novel but Putnam's were now offering him a huge advance if he would write about the golden age of Hollywood from the 1930s to the 1950s. 'I don't fancy this too much,' he wrote to Hamilton, 'in spite of the current spate of nostalgia, because I feel it has all been done too often and could only be a series of anecdotes. Advice please – I badly need it (and I don't really need the advance). The second effort is almost bound to flop . . . which is the least risky?'

Hamilton replied immediately, 'For God's sake don't let Putnam's coax you into writing about the great days of the movies. The subject has been done over and over again . . . and as you say you don't need the huge advance mentioned, I really must beg you to keep off the subject . . . I'm sure you trust me.' It was a letter that Niv was to gloat over for the rest of his life, for he decided to ignore Hamilton's advice, accepted Putnam's cheque, and wrote the book – and it became an even bigger success than *The Moon's a Balloon*. At first he gave it the uninspiring title *PS*, but later he was to call it *Bring on the Empty Horses*.

Thirteen

The Grumpy Bestseller
1972–1977

Despite the huge success of *The Moon's a Balloon*, which was still in the British bestseller lists an astonishing eight months after it was published, Niv was worried that he had not had a decent movie offer for ages and that his acting career might be over. 'This is important,' he wrote to Jamie Hamilton. 'I do have another profession! and now more than ever it is the story that makes the film . . . PLEASE tip me off in the very early stages if you come across something that could make a different sort of picture.' He still worried endlessly about money, and when he asked Hamilton to send eight autographed copies of *The Moon's a Balloon* to Stowe and was charged £13 for them, about £100 today, he refused to pay and claimed they had been advertisements.

In June there was wonderful news from Hollywood: R. J. Wagner and Natalie Wood remarried after dumping their second spouses, and from now on would visit the Nivens whenever they were in Europe. 'We had many wonderful times together and huge laughs,' Wagner told me. On the financial front there was good news too when Niv earned £40,000 – nearly £350,000 in modern terms – making a series of TV commercials that summer for a Japanese deodorant called 'Who's Who'. In one of the ads he was chased along the Promenade des Anglais in Nice by a gaggle of Japanese girls shrieking 'David! David!', turned round, said, 'Girls, girls, how did you recognise me?' in dubbed Japanese, sniffed his armpit, and declared, 'Of *course*. *Now* I understand. It's "Who's Who"!' In London soon afterwards he was mobbed by a crowd of Japanese tourists who recognised him, raised their arms, dabbed at their armpits and laughed hysterically.

In July he was nagging Jamie Hamilton yet again to spend more to advertise the book – 'GOING ABROAD? TAKE A BALLOON', he suggested – though he did have the good grace to thank Roger Machell at last for all his hard work on the book, nine months after publication. He did not do it himself but wrote to Hamilton: 'I never really thanked Roger Machell for all the excellent suggestions he made about editing the original. May I do so now officially through you? A lot of the book's success is thanks to his careful and most helpful guiding hand. Bless you dear friend. Love David.' For Christmas he suggested headlines for yet more ads – 'GIVE PROVEN PLEASURE FOR CHRISTMAS!' – and Roger Machell forwarded his letter to Hamilton with a weary memo that said, 'Niven again. No reply needed, I think.' Niv was also constantly making suggestions for small changes to the book whenever it was reprinted. The saddest was when he asked that an eleven-year-old photograph of him and Hjördis sitting in front of a hotel in Malaga should be recaptioned "With Hjördis resting outside Spanish hotel with encouraging name'. It was called the Hotel Sexi.

In September *The Moon's a Balloon* was still in the British Top Ten, had sold 50,000 hardbacks in Britain and 85,000 in the States, and he told 'Atticus' of the *Sunday Times* that it had given him more pleasure than all his eighty-five movies. It was also beginning to earn more than any of his films and inspired a new career as a public speaker, and in October he flew off to the States for the first of a series of lucrative lecture tours on which he crossed the continent to regale colleges and clubs with his anecdotes about movie stars and Hollywood. On one tour he gave twenty-seven talks in a month and made so much money that for Christmas he sent Grizel £3000 and David Jr £2000 – a total of £40,000 in modern values – even though young David was now thirty, an extremely highly paid executive of Columbia Films in London and soon to become the head of Paramount for the world outside the US. Jamie, too, who was now twenty-seven and doing extremely well with a small investment company in New York, would open an envelope from his father and find $10,000 or $20,000 in banknotes. '"Just a little folding money" he'd call it,' said Jamie. 'I was very successful and had a good living, but sometimes at Christmas I'd get a huge cheque, maybe $50,000 [£160,000 today],' and Niv kept sending both of them bundles of cash for the rest of his life.

He was less charitable that Christmas towards Cole Lesley and Graham Payn, who had for so many years spent Boxing Day with Noël Coward and the Nivens at Château d'Oex. Now that Coward was dead Lesley rang Niv and asked, 'Shall we see you on Boxing Day as usual?' but he made an excuse and they never heard from him again. His own Yuletide was a merry one: for the second Christmas running *The Moon's a Balloon* sailed to the top of the British bestseller lists, an unprecedented resurrection for a hardback.

That winter Niv persuaded another new friend, the eighty-five-year-old painter Marc Chagall, to stay at Château d'Oex. They had met when Niv had spotted an old tramp sitting on his private dock at Lo Scoglietto, told the butler to tell him to beat it and discovered that the old guy was the famous painter. When he arrived at Château d'Oex David told Bill Buckley that Chagall wanted to see his chateau but begged him not to show him any of his own dreadful paintings. Buckley promised, but as soon as Niv and Chagall arrived Buckley produced a canvas 'covered in some catshit yellow excrescence', Niv said later. Chagall gazed at the painting with a tragic expression. 'Oh!' he sighed. 'Oh, ze *poor* paint!'

In March *The Moon's a Balloon* was still in the top four British bestsellers and about to get another huge boost when Niv flew to London to promote the paperback edition in April and lunched with Michael Parkinson at the Savoy Grill. 'It was like a one-man show,' Parkinson told me. 'He never stopped talking and we had a hilarious lunch and drank a lot of marvellous wine. When we came out he said, "Have you ever seen Nelson holding his dick?" and showed me that if you stand in the Strand about halfway between the Savoy and Trafalgar Square and look up at Nelson's Column it looks just as if he's holding his dick in his hand! We were a bit pissed and howled with laughter, and eventually a crowd gathered round and looked as well. It was a wonderfully funny moment.'

Niv travelled all over Britain to promote the Coronet paperback, making speeches, giving interviews, signing books, and it worked wonders. 'Paperbacks weren't selling huge amounts yet in those days,' Alan Gordon Walker of Coronet told me, 'but David was probably the first author who was prepared to promote the paperback as well as the hardback and although he hated doing it he was the first to sell hundreds of thousands in paperback.' During the campaign he nagged Jamie Hamilton yet again to buy more ads for the hardback, yet grumbled to George Greenfield that it was quite wrong that Hamish Hamilton should take a share of his paperback royalties when he had done all the work. 'What have they done to earn it?' he asked. Greenfield persuaded Hamilton to spend another £1000 on Christmas advertising but Hamilton pointed out to Niv that because of the paperback 'our own hard-cover sales have inevitably dropped, for as a fellow Scot you will realise why people prefer paying 40p to £2.50'.

In the first week of May he returned to Lo Scoglietto and gave an interview to a reporter from the *Sunday Mirror*, lunched with him in Villefranche and was distressed to see in the harbour the rotting hulk of a boat that turned out to be the sad remains of Errol Flynn's old yacht, the *Zaca*. They climbed aboard and David was visibly moved by this memory of his riproaring old chum. 'It's all gone,' he said unhappily. 'Even the famous old flying cock on the bow has dropped off! Flynn would have loved the irony of that!' There were more sad memories a couple of weeks later when he returned to London for Noël Coward's memorial service, where more than a thousand friends and admirers crammed into the church of St Martin-in-the-Fields and the eulogy was delivered by the Poet Laureate, Sir John Betjeman.

June was much happier. The legal case that Niv, Peter Finch and Max von Sydow had brought against MGM four years earlier after the cancellation of *Man's Fate* was settled out of court for £335,816. Equally welcome financially was an astonishingly generous gesture by the new editorial director of Coronet, Philip Evans, who was embarrassed to find that the paperback of *The Moon's a Balloon* had sold 470,000 copies and was making a great deal of money yet Niv was still being paid a measly royalty of only seven and a half per cent per copy and under his contract would never earn any more, even if it went on to sell millions. Evans raised his royalty to twelve and a half per cent voluntarily – something quite unheard of in publishing – and even backdated the rise to the date when sales had reached 200,000. This amazing generosity gave Niv and Greenfield eventually an extra windfall of about £60,000 – more than £400,000 today – and earned David's undying affection for Evans and Coronet for the rest of his days. But then he behaved remarkably meanly towards Jamie Hamilton, who had done so much to coax the book out of him and had given him so much help and advice. He made Greenfield write to Hamilton to insist that the increase in the Coronet royalties should not be shared with him, as per contract, but should go entirely to Niv 'because of all the strenuous efforts he made to help publicise and promote the Coronet edition'. It was not the first time that he had tried to move the legal goalposts when money was involved: he had tried it with Goldwyn, and succeeded with the Cresset Press and Prentice Hall, but Jamie Hamilton was made of sterner Scots stuff and refused to agree. David was 'very upset', Greenfield wrote to Hamilton, even though it 'may not be at all logical for an author whose publisher has sold over

70,000 copies of his book to adopt such an attitude'. Hamilton 'hated parting with money', said Christopher Sinclair-Stevenson, 'and he would have suggested some compromise. He might have promised to pay him more for the next book.' The rift did not last long: a month later Niv was once again sending Hamilton his love.

July brought the death of another good old chum, Jack Hawkins, who had been ill for some time. 'David was marvellous,' Doreen Hawkins told me. 'He was filming in England and he'd ring me two or three times a day, and he came to the funeral. He was very good about anyone who was in trouble.'

The film that Niv had just started to make in England was *Vampira*, a spoof horror movie in which he played a stylish, witty Count Dracula who sips the blood of pretty girls from crystal glasses and grades them like vintage wine. Most of the critics sucked their teeth and the director, Clive Donner, got it in the neck, but David enjoyed himself immensely. To publicise the picture he gave a strikingly honest interview to Quentin Falk of *Cinema Today* and admitted that most of the films he made now were pretty poor. 'I would love to be stretched,' he said, 'but . . . people do not offer one stretching parts . . . I get offered piles of scripts all the time, but it is usually muck.' He gave another interview, about wine, to Maggie Burr of the *Evening News*, and confessed that he drank on average one and a half bottles of wine a day, 'probably more, but then I don't touch spirits'.

Kristina, now twelve, joined the fashionable Swiss boarding school Le Rosey, where Niv – who was now a grandfather again after the birth of Jamie's daughter Eugenie – was delighted to find himself meeting two other parents who were old friends: Audrey Hepburn and Fiona Thyssen, both now divorced. 'We became good old buddies again,' Fiona Thyssen told me, 'and although we never had an affair and he never tried to have one, he was very fond of me and I adored him and we had fun together. He was a good father but those kids were never happy campers. I suppose they suffered from the burdens of having a drunken mother.'

That autumn he flew to the States for another lecture tour and returned to tell Sue Bongard at their first school-run coffee meeting in Gstaad that in one obscure Midwestern town he had met Nessie, the prostitute he had loved as a teenager. She had heard he was in town and arranged to meet secretly in a coffee shop out on the highway. 'He sat there full of anticipation, he said, and in came this stout little middle-aged lady with a very tight grey perm and plonked herself down in front of him and said, "I've married an American who's done extremely well and I'm head of the Women's Institute." But he knew it really was Nessie because he said "we relived what we had done. But she was a respectable grandmother, extremely boring, and there was no spark of friendship." '

That Christmas he took Hjördis and the girls for a holiday in Kenya and a month after their return another old friend and enemy died in Los Angeles: Sam Goldwyn, of heart failure, aged ninety-one. Niv's father figures were all gone and at nearly sixty-four himself he began to feel the years closing in. 'I can't bear the thought of dying,' he told Don Short. 'I'd like to live another forty years [*but*] on the law of averages I haven't got a lot of time to go.'

He was working seriously now on *Bring on the Empty Horses* but found time to fly to Hollywood in April to compère the Oscars, where he was about to introduce Liz Taylor, who was to present some of the prizes, when a thirty-three-year-old advertising agent, Robert Opel, appeared naked behind him and streaked across the stage and millions of TV screens. Niv glanced at his retreating buttocks and sniffed contemptuously: 'The only laugh that man will ever get is by stripping off his clothes and showing his shortcomings.'

Niv was pouring some of his new wealth into paintings and in June had them valued. Those at Lo Scoglietto were valued at $851,000 [*£2·5 million in 2003*] and included three oils by Max Ernst and pictures by Vasily Kandinsky, Paul Klee, Edward Seago and Toulouse-Lautrec. At Château d'Oex the paintings were worth an estimated Swiss Fr. 147,000 and included a Miró, Braque and Chagall. To pay the huge annual insurance premiums he popped back to England for a week at the beginning of July to record Oscar Wilde's play about a mischievous medieval phantom, *The Canterville Ghost*, with Flora Robson for Harlech Television in Bristol, and then flew off to Malaysia to earn $250,000 [£825,000 in 2003] in ten weeks making *Paper Tiger*.

It was a movie many believe was his last decent one, in which he played a character similar to the bogus major in *Separate Tables*, this time an elderly English teacher and apparently gallant ex-soldier who becomes the tutor to an eleven-year-old Japanese boy on a Pacific island and turns out to be a liar, fraud and coward when they are kidnapped by guerrillas but finally finds strength through the boy's own bravery. He much enjoyed the role and told the *Daily Express*: 'We've all got phoney chunks in us. He tells lovely lies.' Asked what were his own phoney chunks, he replied, 'Well, perhaps the word is not phoney but fantasy.'

The film was shot in Kuala Lumpur, Malacca and the Genting Highlands of Malaysia. 'He came First Class to Kuala Lumpur,' the film's producer, Euan Lloyd, told me, 'and during the flight some smartarse had a few drinks too many and got fresh with the gorgeous Swedish stewardess and started groping her from his aisle seat, and David in one of his rare moments of anger knocked this feller back in his seat. The idea of David actually *hitting* someone! In KL he booked her into the room next to his suite in the Hilton and introduced me to her. I said, "Could we have breakfast around eight?" and he said, "Make it ten, dear boy. I need a good night's rest!" He was like that throughout the film. He'd be talking to you about something serious but he'd be looking at some gorgeous creature sitting nearby, and pretty soon you'd find him wandering off and talking to her, "Good afternoon, my dear," and he was off again.'

The movie's director, Ken Annakin, and his wife Pauline chuckled to remember Niv's rampant promiscuity in Malaysia. 'He was a very sexy feller,' said Annakin. 'Every woman he met practically fell to her knees in front of him,' and Pauline Annakin told me: 'He was very very sexy and I'd say he had hundreds of girlfriends in his life. He had a minor crack at me, and if it had been more serious I might have said yes! The ladies in Malaysia adored him and I know he had at least two of the local British wives.'

'He also spent a lot of time with two Australian air hostesses, twins,' said Annakin. 'In the last couple of days his back went, he collapsed suddenly, couldn't walk, and had to be flown home flat on the floor of the plane. He told Hjördis that I had made him climb some mountains and this was the result. Well, we know damned well his back didn't go because of *that* because we never made him climb anything much. His back went from indoor exercise. Maybe he'd had both of the twins at the same time!'

Annakin was impressed not only by Niv's rampant libido – at least five women, and maybe more, in ten weeks at the age of sixty-four – but also by his professionalism. 'At seven o'clock every night he'd spend an hour with the Japanese boy, Ando, who couldn't speak a word of English at first, and taught him billiards and played games with him, anything to make him feel at home, and that shows tremendously in the picture. I don't know of many actors who would have done that, and the boy became absolutely devoted to him.'

David's version of events in Malaysia was typically dramatic and he claimed to have been threatened by terrorists. 'The chief of police in Kuala Lumpur said it was so dangerous there that he was going to put a twenty-four-hour guard on the actors,' he told Parkinson on TV the following year, 'but the day we arrived they killed the chief of police! It was 137 degrees and ninety-seven per cent humidity. One fellow in the crew came from Battersea and he'd never been out of England before, and he appeared in this terrific heat with a sweater on and a cap and looked round and said to me, "Turned mild, 'asn't it, David?" The heat finally got to this feller and one day he said, "I think I'll take a little zizz in the jungle, David. There's quite a nice little 'ole behind that tree. Keep an eye on things," and he came out of his hole about two hours later and he'd aged fifty years. "Oh my God!" he said, "there's been a dreadful incident, David. I woke up with a dreadful weight on my chest. There was an anaconda right across me," – that's the snake that eats the *pythons*, you know – and he said, "It took 25 minutes to go past"!'

In between filming and fornicating Niv was scribbling frantically to try to finish *Bring on the Empty Horses* in time for the book to be published before Christmas the following year. It was not going well. Malaysia was 'this FOUL part of the world', he wrote to Sinclair-Stevenson. 'Nice people – Malays, Chinese, Indians – all hating each other and some really ghastly relics of our Imperial Past, and a climate of undiluted steamy horror, plus raging epidemics of cholera and Dengue Fever topped off by cobras, pythons, voracious ants and mosquitos! ... The new book is DISASTER! I am now reading through the 110,000 words I have written and, at a rough estimate, 105,000 are useless senseless and shaming. Is Roger M. still with you? (he will be horrified at how bad it is).' Worse was to come. While they were filming in the jungle of the Genting Highlands the film unit's production office burned down in the Holiday Inn in Kuala Lumpur and he lost a lot of his diaries and notes for the book. 'He was distraught,' said Lloyd. 'It was in such a moment that he would turn to the bottle. He drank a lot, usually when he had a bit of pressure, but he never got drunk though I saw him tipsy.' In September Niv flew back to Lo Scoglietto and wrote the next day to a friend in London: 'I just got back last night from the most miserable two months in the Far East,' and to John Mortimer that he was hugely relieved to have returned from 'the foul Far East full of raging epidemics and rampant terrorists, one of whom shot the chief of police, some others slaughtered twenty soldiers very near us and a third group, in a burst of good taste, put a match to the Holiday Inn!' When I told Annakin about this letter he laughed. 'It wasn't terrorists,' he said. 'It was somebody smoking in bed. We had no contact with any terrorists.'

In October Niv and Hjördis attended a charity ball in Leeds, organised by Roger Moore, where the MC said how grateful they were to him for coming all that way when he was so busy and Hjördis called out drunkenly, 'What about me? I've come as well.' By now she was wearing around her neck a gold disc engraved with the words 'I am always allergic to penicillin and sometimes also to my husband'. Then he flew back to Malaysia where he gave another interview, to Bart Mills of the *Guardian*, and told him that 'an actor always has a huge inferiority complex. With good reason. It's nine-to-one against a hit.' Even so, 'you press on, you do your best. Stomach in. Chest out. The best I can.'

Finally he went to Bavaria to shoot some wartime scenes for *Paper Tiger.* Although I found the film silly and pedestrian, with dreadfully intrusive music, and Niv's acting wooden though his relationship with the boy is touching at times, several critics thought differently and most were impressed by his performance. 'David Niven plays with his unfailing elegance and that touch of pathos which is his especial gift,' Dilys Powell reported in the *Sunday Times*, but 'I wish only that someone could find the perfect role for Mr Niven. A Dickens character, perhaps? Something out of Thackeray or Meredith? I don't know. I know only that I long to see him recapturing and enlarging the qualities I saw in his tiny role in *Lady L.* He is an actor far more delicate, far more easily damaged by wrong treatment in the medium, than his insouciant air might suggest. I can't help feeling that, lying around somewhere, there is a small masterpiece for David Niven.' He was never to find it.

That Christmas of 1974 he sent not only £3000 to Grizel and £1000 to Joyce but also £300 to a new friend of whom he had become very fond, a twenty-seven-year-old English girl, Lesley Rowlatt, the daughter of a London police sergeant, who worked in PR and advertising, and was to remain a close friend until he died. 'She was very beautiful,' I was told by her first husband, Peter Watson, who was to marry her eight years later, in 1982. '*Spectacularly* beautiful: statuesque, tall, very prominent cheekbones, very deep-set eyes, wonderful eyelids, fantastic figure. I think she met him in Hollywood, where she hoped to become a star. Her friendship with Niven was a long one.' Niv sent her another £300 in January, which made a total in modern terms of nearly £4000 that he had given her in less than a month.

At sixty-five Niv's love of women was irrepressible. 'I can't have dinner with you tonight,' he told Leslie Bricusse, 'because Miss Rhodesia is in London!' His marriage was by now a complete sham. 'Hjördis was often whispering on the telephone,' said Roddy Mann, 'and she even told me once that there was somebody else in her life. We all urged him to leave her. It was an appalling marriage. She was just a lump and he was bored with her. What's worse than being stuck with a woman who drinks and has nothing to say? Niven used to find bottles of Fernet Branca all through the house and she pooh-poohed all of his writing – "oh, boring book", everything was "boring".'

'He loved having lunch or dinner with buddies,' said Jamie, 'but she used to say, "It's so boring to chew. Do we have to have dinner tonight? Can't we have nothing?" '

'Niv told me she was either pissed or on pills,' said Mann. 'He took a flat in London behind Peter Jones and came to London a lot by himself and misbehaved. The girls were always about twenty-five.' April Clavell told me that Niv once propositioned a friend of hers in London – 'she was rather taken aback' – but he told Mann he would never leave Hjördis because if he did 'she'd end up a drunk in the gutter'.

Hjördis became so unpleasant in the late 1970s that I could find hardly any of her former friends to say a good word about her. 'Daddy would leave Alcoholics Anonymous leaflets and subtle little messages from doctors lying around in the hope that she would see them,' said Fiona, 'but she never caught on,' and Buckley told me that he thought Hjördis took drugs as well as drinking heavily. 'She became darker and darker and eventually vicious,' said Leslie Bricusse, and Taki Theodoracopulos told me that 'slowly over about twenty years she went through a very strange metamorphosis and became a bore and an embarrassment. There was always tension and it got worse. She used to stare, and at the end we used to run away. Eventually she became a total recluse.' Several of the Nivens' friends mentioned that she refused to read any of his books. 'That makes colossal sense,' said Ustinov. 'That would be part of her revenge.'

Even Hjördis's women friends ran out of patience with her. 'I used to invite them for dinner,' said Kitty Galbraith, 'but Hjördis would say they couldn't come. She had to be somewhere that she could slip out and have a drink in secret.' Jane Del Amo told me that 'Hjördis became very difficult. Every time she was coming to dinner she'd say, "Oh, I can't come because I'm going to the dentist." I'd say, "Hjördis, dinner is not until nine," but she wouldn't come. He'd come on his own and she'd call at about 9.30, when we were all eating, and he'd have to get up and talk to her for about twenty minutes and he'd be very nice and soothe her – 'yes, darling, yes, darling' – because he cared and was worried about her. And there was one evening at the Olden when she got into a fight on the dance floor with an English woman and it came to shouting and then to blows.' Martine Fields said that 'she was horrible. Nobody liked her. He was very popular but always alone.' On the rare occasions that Hjördis did go to the Olden Hotel, said Hedi Donizetti, 'she came with somebody else, like the old Spanish prince Gonzalo Bourbon-Parma, who I think could have been her lover.'

At Cap Ferrat 'David used to be in despair about Hjördis's drinking', Evie Bricusse told me. 'More and more when we were with him she was in her room. When we were all going out to dinner he would say, "Nej isn't joining us tonight. She's not feeling too well." And she'd say, things like, "How *boring* sitting there eating. Oh God, all you can do is sit there and eat." It was almost a relief when she wasn't going to join us because we could let our hair down. She had a beautiful Saluki dog with long hair that looked like her, but it died and she went into *such* depression that it appeared that she loved the dog much more than she loved David.'

Doreen Hawkins told me that 'David used to come over most evenings in St Jean when I was alone and we'd take a bottle of champagne down to the sea at the end of our garden and sit and talk, and he was very unhappy. I said, "Oh, David, why don't you go off and have an affair?" and he just went silent. They were really unhappy for the last few years and Hjördis had a couple of lovers.' Another woman friend who did not want to be named told me: 'He never showed her up in front of people except once when he was in despair and we went over and you could see he'd been crying. When he opened the bathroom cupboard under the sink bottles fell out and he said, "Oh, darling, what am I going to do?" He was really, really distressed.'

Considering their home life it is not surprising that several of the Nivens' friends told me that Kristina and Fiona were difficult children, 'but then they got no love from their mother,' said Mrs Donizetti. Evie Bricusse told me that Hjördis 'was a distant mother and never warm or affectionate with them', and another woman friend who did not want to be named said 'they were strange little girls, not evil but naughty and a problem', and Bryan Forbes remembered that when the Nivens came to dinner in England one of the girls set fire to a carpet with matches.

At Château d'Oex Niv escaped Hjördis by working on the new book, skiing, lunching and painting with Buckley. In his wine cellar den, which was stuffed with racks of champagne, he painted several vivid murals of bullfighters and bulls with enormous testicles that were still there in 2002, when I was told by the present owner of the chalet, Coco Wyers: 'When we first came into this house in 1997 I thought "I'm not going to live here" because it was such an unhappy house. I thought, "oh my God, what happened here?" I felt that something was really not OK. In the end we bought it only because they couldn't sell it and let us have it very cheaply.' Niv also began to see a lot of Roger Moore, who bought a chalet in Gstaad and told me that when his wife Luisa once put on a blonde wig and Hjördis opened the door, 'Niv, who was coming down the stairs, did not recognise Luisa, thought "oh God, this is somebody I've had", and went straight up the stairs again!'

In March at last he finished *Bring on the Empty Horses* – the order that Michael Curtiz had barked while filming *The Charge of the Light Brigade*. 'I was going to London,' said Evan Galbraith, 'and David asked me to take the book to his publisher, and Hjördis said, "That's another pack of lies". She wouldn't give him any credit for it and she had nothing but contempt for it.' Niv wrote to Jamie Hamilton: 'I am only too well aware that your original doubts may yet turn out to be very right indeed but lets pray that we are both wrong.' As soon as he had read the script Hamilton realised that he had another bestseller on his hands and ordered a huge hardback first print run of 120,000 copies, but pre-publication orders for the new book were so vast that even that was not enough and it had to be reprinted two months before publication.

Despite Hamilton's initial reluctance, *Bring on the Empty Horses* was not just another book about Hollywood but one by a brilliant raconteur who had known the place as an insider for forty years, and it was packed with anecdotes, insights and pen portraits of old friends such as Bogart, Colman, the Fairbankses, Flynn and Gable as well as four fictionalised chapters. In it he called Goldwyn 'the greatest independent producer the world has ever seen'. He reported that when Greta Garbo came for lunch at Lo Scoglietto and he asked her why she had retired from movies so young she replied, 'I had made enough faces.' He described Cary Grant spaced out on LSD, and a suicidal Errol Flynn sitting up all night with a bottle of vodka in one hand and a loaded revolver in another and ending up as a 'boozing bum ... puffy and blotchy'. Above all he depicted Hollywood as a brutal, meretricious place full of shallow, selfish, snobbish people and alcoholics, addicts, attempted suicides and nervous breakdowns. He quoted Wilson Mizner as saying that working for Warner Brothers was 'like fucking a porcupine – it's a hundred pricks against one', and despite all the fun that Niv had had there himself he wrote of it now with shame and sometimes dislike, and lamented the deep unhappiness of many of its biggest names, from Gable to Scott Fitzgerald.

The book was edited again by Roger Machell and needed so much work on it that four years later Niv told Patrick Macnee that half of it 'wasn't his at all, it was written by the editor'. Yet this time Niv was even less keen to accept changes. 'All the stories that Roger had taken out of *The Moon's a Balloon* were there again,' said Sinclair-Stevenson, 'and Niven became quite difficult on the basis that if we told him what to do George Greenfield could easily find him another publisher.' One casualty of the editing process was a section about Marilyn Monroe that accused her of being unprofessional, ungrateful, exhibitionist, 'short on humour about herself', and described her 'bad temper, hysterics, thoughtlessness and dedicated love of self. When she was at the top, she thought nothing of keeping huge casts waiting for hours till she was ready to work. "Go fuck yourself!" she screamed at a quivering young assistant director who had been dispatched to enquire when her presence could be expected on the set.' Niv even wrote that she was 'not beautiful unless her mouth was slightly open' – one of the few occasions that he was ungallant about a woman with whom he had had a fling. The deleted section also included a revealing paragraph admitting that 'actors are notoriously insecure; many have feelings of guilt because they enjoy their work too much. Some keep their feet on the ground by reminding themselves that at best they are playing children's games and are being wonderfully overpaid for getting up in the morning, dressing up and showing off in front of the grownups. They realise that they are not building irrigation dams, researching incurable diseases or improving the standard of living and that nobody is going to put up a monument to them when they die, so they laugh at themselves and through their laughter, provide their own therapy when things get tough.' It was an eloquent statement of his own philosophy.

Coronet snapped up the paperback rights for £15,000 [*£80,000 today*] but David's thirty-two-year-old benefactor there, the editorial director Phil Evans, had a terrible car crash on 14 February that left him in a coma for four months, crippled and barely able to speak for the rest of his life, and although he was mentally alert he had to be replaced by Alan Gordon Walker. 'David came to see me in hospital,' Evans told me, 'and then again in this house when he was in England, which was wonderful of him,' and Niv wrote him numerous affectionate letters over the next eight years.

In July David flew to Hollywood to make a film for Walt Disney 'about two children and a skunk', he wrote to Ken Galbraith. 'I have a nasty suspicion that I am the skunk, but I have no alternative as the French tax authorities have just nailed me for five years back taxes!!' He told Leslie Bricusse a different story: 'He said he got a letter from the French tax authorities which said, "It's come to our attention that you are a Swiss resident but we have noticed that you have been in St Jean

Cap Ferrat seven or eight months in each one of the last four or five years. Would you please care to explain the situation?" David said he went back up to Château d'Oex and had his lawyers there send a closely typed six-page letter in Switzer-Deutsch, which is the most impenetrable language on the planet, and he never heard from the taxman again!'

The Disney film, *No Deposit, No Return*, was a comedy thriller in which he played an elderly millionaire whose eleven- and nine-year-old grandchildren are dumped on him for the holidays and pretend to be kidnapped and held to ransom, but he refuses to fall for their ploy and they nearly die. Niv's main memory of the movie was that every time he suggested even a small change in the script the director would say 'Walt wouldn't have liked that' even though Walt had been dead for nine years. The reviewers did not care for the picture much but it did well at the box office, and while he was in Hollywood he made a sentimental journey back to the now-computerised offices of Central Casting, where he found on the wall photographs of the only three of their extras who ever made it to the big time: Clark Gable, Alice Faye and himself. 'I've been bloody lucky,' he said.

Fiona joined Kristina at Le Rosey in September and Niv returned to England to publicise *Bring on the Empty Horses* when it was published on 24 September 1975. It was about to be reprinted yet again and he made another TV appearance on the *Michael Parkinson Show*, where he was as modest and self-deprecating as ever, telling Parkinson: 'I'm an actor, not a writer,' though he had yet another unkind crack at Trubshawe when he said, 'the trick is not to live in one cocoon of friends who get older and bored together.' At the end of the interview he reduced Parkinson and the audience to hysterics when he told a shaggy dog story about a prawn and a crab: 'A prawn fell in love with a crab and it went back to its family and it said, "Look, I'm mad about that crab that lives behind that big rock at the end," and the prawn's father was furious: "You're not going to be seen with a crab. Ridiculous animals. They go sideways. No way! Go to the crab and say it's all off. Tell the crab it's finished." So the prawn went back to the crab and said, "Crab, I'm terribly sorry. It's off, because my father says you look rather stupid because you go sideways." The crab was furious and said, "That does it! I'll be down this evening and I'll have seaweed and soda with your father," and went off. At six o'clock in the evening the prawns are all sitting around their rock and the seaweed opened and in came the crab, but he came straight, and the prawn said, "Crab! Crab, you're wonderful! Crab, you're going *straight*!" and the crab said, "Shut up, I'm pissed!" '

This time the British reviewers were dismissive. The book was no more than a 'hodge-podge of material', said *The Critic*, 'mostly second-rate – leftovers from the first book, perhaps', and I described it in my *Sunday Express* column as 'something of a disappointment'. Niv was furious and railed that the British critics were 'patronising bastards'. The reviews were kinder in America when he flew to Hollywood at the end of September to make *Death by Murder*, a poor spoof that took the mickey out of great fictional detectives like Philip Marlowe, Miss Marple and Hercule Poirot, five of whom have been invited to an eerie mansion by a cringingly camp American multi-millionaire (Truman Capote) to solve a murder that has not yet been committed. The cast list was impressive – Alec Guinness, Peter Sellers. Maggie Smith, Peter O'Toole – and many critics were amused but I found the picture utterly unfunny except for the fact that Jamie Niven invested a great deal of money in it for a company that wanted to show a tax loss, expecting it to flop, only to find it becoming a huge success and making a profit of $27 million. Less amusing was the fact that this was the first of Niv's films in which he suddenly appeared to be old, thin and drawn. He was only sixty-five but he looked exhausted. On top of finishing the book, worrying about Hjördis and the girls, and travelling a great deal, he had also made two TV series that year, a travelogue called *Around the World* and a wildlife *Survival* series, which had taken him to Africa, Mexico and Nepal. Was it all too much? 'I have had a sinister letter from my doctor insisting that I take it more easily this year,' he wrote to Ron Read, the sales director of Coronet, and although he was not to fall seriously ill for another five years, in retrospect it seems like an evil omen.

From Los Angeles Niv wrote to Sinclair-Stevenson to report that 'here the reviewers, with one exception, have been fabulous', and asking, 'What the hell do I do next?' Sinclair-Stevenson replied that both he and Machell felt his next book should be the novel.

Bring on the Empty Horses stayed at the top of the *New York Times* bestseller list for an astonishing eighteen weeks and sold a huge number of copies all over the world, though once again six German firms turned the book down and his Italian publishers rejected it because they had done so badly with *The Moon's a Balloon*. Mischievously Niv thought of sending Christmas cards that year which reproduced Jamie Hamilton's two old letters begging him not to write an autobiography or a book about Hollywood followed by the mammoth sales figures for both books, but was persuaded that that would be cruel.

On 3 January he started again on the novel *Make It Smaller and Move It to the Left* and wrote a new first line: 'Charlie Ammidown had an erection – and it hurt.' So, still, did his bad reviews and he wrote to Sinclair-Stevenson that the book had received 'uniformly ecstatic reviews in the US as opposed to the patronising and dismissive shit the dear British accorded us!' One ecstatic review, in the *New York Times*, was by Bill Buckley, who wrote: 'This might easily be the best book ever written about Hollywood.' Buckley's own spy novel *Saving the Queen* was due to be published in Britain a few months later and he asked Niv to endorse it. David replied cheekily, 'How about this? "The best book ever written this year." Change this in any way you want.' Buckley took his revenge when they met in London a few weeks later and he said, 'I changed that quote because you said I could. I've made it "this is the best book about fucking the Queen written this year".' Niv looked horrified, and then realised it was a joke.

'He liked acting,' Buckley told me, 'but he was never so happy as he was when he had written his two books. He was *blissfully* happy at having accomplished that.' It was possibly now that Niv wrote a one-page first-person short story about a businessman whose wife and children seem to have forgotten his birthday but his secretary Liz has remembered, invites him out to lunch, asks him back to her apartment for another drink and tells him she is going to go to slip into something more comfortable. 'She went into her bedroom and in about five minutes she came out of the bedroom carrying a big birthday cake, followed by my wife and children, all of them singing "Happy Birthday", and there was me sitting there with nothing on but my socks.' He called the story 'Why I Fired My Secretary'.

Fiona, who was now twelve, bright, and much more academic than Kristina, started to do very well at Le Rosey, where she was to earn a string of good reports over the next seven years. Niv was very popular with the girls' friends 'and the minute we sat down in a café in Gstaad the table would fill up with young people and he'd tell stories', said Fiona. 'Some would actually sit on his knee! He liked having young people around, and he was fun, and they loved him. He was such a loving person, and wanted to be loved too, and he got a lot of pleasure out of people coming up in the street and saying, "Your book is wonderful, thank you for giving us so much pleasure." ' The British reviews for *Bring on the Empty Horses*, however, still rankled, and he wrote to Coronet when they were choosing critics' quotes for the cover of the paperback: 'Remember what B. Behan said about British critics! "They are like eunuchs in a harem ... they know how its done, they see it being done every night, but they cant do it themselves."'

'He was *tremendously* insecure,' said Sinclair-Stevenson, who lunched with him at the Eagle Club two weeks later. 'He said, "Would you consider that our little book has been a success?" and I said, "Yes, it's been number one in the *Bookseller* bestseller list for the last eight weeks and the sales are huge," and he said, "Ah, but you haven't seen the new *Bookseller*. It's no longer number one, it's sunk to number two, so it must be a failure." You could tell from that how *deeply* insecure he was, and I think it was because his acting career had stopped and suddenly nobody wanted him or romantic light comedy leads any more.' When Sinclair-Stevenson returned to London he tried to bolster Niv's confidence by telling him that he was ordering yet another reprint of 15,000 copies of *Bring on the Empty Horses* and that the book club edition had now sold nearly 180,000 – 'THIS IS A RECORD'.

In fact Niv's acting career was far from over for he was about to make three thirty-second TV commercials for Maxwell House coffee for a huge amount of money and then another film for Disney, *Candleshoe*. Nor did Sinclair-Stevenson's reassurances mollify him when Hamish Hamilton were three weeks late in paying his latest paperback royalties – £70,000, more than £315,000 today – so that he lost more than £1300 (£6000 today) due to a sudden fall in the value of the Swiss franc against the pound. Even worse, their latest royalty payment for *The Moon's a Balloon* failed to include the Coronet bonus. 'I really don't think we will want to do business with H. H. any more,' Niv wrote angrily to Greenfield. 'Remember that little effort of trying to extract a percentage of the purely voluntary adjustment of Coronet on "Moon"? – UGH! ... We always thought Jamie was a "creep", but I am deeply surprised at Roger and Christopher.' Sinclair-Stevenson tried to settle the dispute by agreeing to make up the difference in the exchange rate, but Niv then wheeled on his Swiss lawyer, Dr Staehelin, to demand £849.98 more and to insist that Greenfield should repay commission that he had deducted from Niv's BBC fee for reading *The Moon's a Balloon* on radio because that was for a broadcast, not a book. Niv then told Greenfield that he should sack his foreign rights assistant, Vanessa Holt, because he did not believe she was trying hard enough to obtain the best deals for foreign translations of *Bring on the Empty Horses*. Greenfield defended her, agreeing that the foreign sales were disappointing but pointing out that it was hardly her fault if 'these damned Continentals' did not understand or appreciate his sense of humour. A month later Niv was complaining again, this time because Putnam's hardback edition of *The Moon's a Balloon* seemed to be out of print in New York. Greenfield discovered that Putnam's had pulped a large number of copies. 'What fools! (or crooks),' Niv fumed, and was not appeased when Putnam's explained that US hardback sales had dwindled to just twenty a month now that the paperback was out. Then it was Coronet's turn: their paperback edition of *Bring on the Empty Horses* was not nearly as stylish as the American one, he grumbled, and had an 'incredible number of mistakes'. Once again he had been too lazy to read his own proofs. Despite his huge success he had become irritable, curmudgeonly, demanding and suspicious that everyone was either useless or trying to cheat him. Perhaps he had been spoiled as a film star by earning so much so easily for so long.

He was also becoming a control freak at home. 'I went to see them in the South of France,' said Fiona Thyssen, 'and David took me sailing but was quite different in the boat, rather fierce, and instead of the usual charm I thought, "My God, he's become a complete bloody admiral, very much Bossy Flossy." ' He was, however, about to be terrified himself when he saw the shark horror film *Jaws* and according to Peter Ustinov dived into his bottomless pool for a swim very early the next morning 'and suddenly saw beneath him an enormous figure moving very slowly. Seized by panic, he leapt out of the pool and ran for safety until he realised that it was a man cleaning the pool in an exaggerated rubber uniform. He told me it gave him a terrible shock.'

In August he flew to England and travelled up to Warwickshire to make *Candleshoe*, in which fourteen-year-old Jodie Foster played a feisty, confident, streetwise kid from New York who is persuaded to pretend to be the long-lost, lookalike granddaughter and heir of an English aristocrat, the Marquis of Candleshoe. Niv played several parts – a blimpish old colonel as well as the Candleshoe butler, Irish chauffeur, Scottish gardener and bosomy Cockney cook, Miss Oglethorpe – the surname that he had given to the Trubshawe character in *Round the Rugged Rocks*. It was a silly, unfunny movie but he was hugely impressed by Jodie Foster and told Roger Moore that she was 'a most *extraordinarily* talented child who knew more than the director or cameraman!' She told Niv sternly that she preferred to work with adults rather than children 'as long as they remember their lines'.

He was fed up with one of his own children that autumn when Le Rosey suggested that Kristina, who was now fifteen, ought to leave the school. 'She was always more interested in boys than her studies,' said Fiona, so Niv sent her to an all-girls finishing school in Lausanne, the

Institut Château Mont-Choisi, where 'she attempted to do some O-levels and A-levels but didn't do very well. She was never very academic.' Even so, Kristina did pass her French O-level exam with an A grade the following summer.

By now *The Moon's a Balloon* had sold 4½ million copies, *Bring on the Empty Horses* 400,000 in hardback, the royalties were cascading in and Putnam's were offering another fortune for any book he cared to write, but Niv still insisted that an Edinburgh author, Gordon Smith, should pay him a £5 copyright fee because he wanted to include one paragraph from *The Moon's a Balloon* in a patriotic Scottish anthology that he was compiling, *This Is My Country*. Such ridiculous meanness was a startling contrast to his stunning generosity towards his family. 'He was pretty close to the chest with a buck,' said Betty Bacall but Jess Morgan denied that Niv's insistence on being paid £5 was an example of his meanness. 'That was just another Niven joke!' he said. ' "Let's make the bloke pay a bit, just for the fun of it!" '

He finished *Candleshoe* at the end of October, flew back to Nice, complained to Greenfield that the bookshops at Heathrow airport had none of his books but plenty of Rex Harrison's, and resumed his struggle to write *Make It Smaller and Move It to the Left*. He was daunted by the fear of writing a disaster after two such huge successes and could be distracted for ten minutes by a 747 flying overhead or a bird on a tree. In desperation he wandered along Cap Ferrat to Somerset Maugham's old villa to seek inspiration by sitting in the little summer house where Maugham had used to write, only to discover that it was now a lavatory for Algerian workers who were building new houses on Maugham's estate.

In November he flew to New York by Concorde to promote the Dell paperback edition of *Bring on the Empty Horses* with TV appearances and interviews that helped to sell 1½ million copies in just two weeks. On the plane too was Bryan Forbes. 'It was a hilarious trip because we both got legless on free drink,' Forbes told me, 'and I told him a story about Larry Olivier that he thought was the best he had ever heard and immediately wrote down, as he always did with a good story. Larry said he was once in a production of one of the Shakespeare histories and an actor called Dan Cunningham was playing a messenger, and one matinée with Olivier on stage Cunningham was standing in the wings having a fag and thought, "It's bloody quiet on stage. Oh, shit! I've missed my cue!" So he stubbed the fag out, rushed on stage, flung himself at Larry's feet, and said, "My liege, the Duke of Buckingham is slain this hour." Now that presented problems because the Duke of Buckingham hadn't even been on yet and had an awful lot of plot. So Larry said, "I gripped him very firmly by the arm and said, 'Thou liest, sirrah!' " So Cunningham thought, "Christ! Larry's dried!" so he started to make up Shakespearean doggerel and said, "Nay, my liege, I swear, by yonder thicket he lies all covered in gore." So Larry then applied a real tourniquet on his arm and said, "Is't positive, sirrah?" and he said, "Yea, my liege, I swear by all that is holy, the Duke of Buckingham is slain this hour," whereupon Larry said "I gripped him by the throat, turned him upstage, and said, 'Then, by my troth, thou hast fucketh the entire play!' " And Larry said nobody in the audience even realised!'

Buoyed by this addition to his hoard of anecdotes, Niv chatted up the air hostess and 'I expect when he got off the plane he asked her for a drink,' said Forbes, 'and laughed her into bed.' His bonhomie vanished again, however, when he suffered a very painful attack of sciatica down his right leg and then flew back to Nice via London and found that there were still no copies of his books in the Heathrow shops. He complained again to Greenfield and a fortnight later was irritated even more when Greenfield seemed to have broken one of the basic rules of agenting by giving his address to a complete stranger, who wrote to ask if he would collaborate on an illustrated cocktail recipe book. 'STOP IT DAMMIT,' he wrote furiously to Greenfield, and was angered again five days later when he suspected that Greenfield or his assistant had given his telephone number to a French publisher. 'I have an agent to defend me from trap-baiting creeps like this!' he wrote sarcastically. He recovered his good humour sufficiently by Christmas to send Grizel her biggest present yet, £5000 (about £22,000 today), and Joyce £1500 (£6700 today), but he was to excel even his own remarkable generosity in 1977 by sending his sisters cheques that totalled £13,000 (£49,000 today).

In February 1977 Niv forced himself to interrupt his skiing and return to England to undergo yet again the grind of promoting another book, this time the British paperback edition of *Bring on the Empty Horses*, of which Coronet already had a million copies in print. 'He hated doing it,' Alan Gordon Walker told me, 'and at times he wasn't terribly happy. There was a hard centre behind the twinkle in his eye, and if things didn't work he would let people know pretty quickly.' During the tour he recorded a *Desert Island Discs* radio programme for which he chose eight favourite records: 'You Are the Sunshine of My Life' by Blue Mink, 'Amazing Grace' by the band of the Royal Scots Dragoon Guards, 'Never Say Goodbye' by Gloria Gaynor, Verdi's 'Celesta Aida', 'Rock Your Baby' by George McCrae, Maria Callas singing the 'Bell Song' from *Lakmé* by

Delibes, 'There Is Nothing Like a Dame' from *South Pacific* by Rodgers and Hammerstein and Laurence Olivier delivering the 'Once more unto the breach, dear friends' speech from Shakespeare's *Henry V*. Asked to choose one luxury for his desert island, he chose – of course – a double bed.

He delighted his crippled ex-editor Phil Evans by going to see him out in the London suburb of Chiswick, and after he returned to Château d'Oex wrote to say: 'I cannot tell you, dear friend, how impressed I am with your recovery and please keep up with those dull exercises because they seem to have done miracles for you already.'

Back at Lo Scoglietto he gave an interview to a reporter from the *Telegraph Sunday Magazine* who found the house 'slightly cold and stiff, as if taken too directly from magazine pages', and who recalled the dismissive remark of a colleague who had sneered about Niv: 'Can anyone still fall for that oh-so-British, jolly-grand-sport line of his? Niven is the quintessential sham: so greedy and unsure of himself that he switched his own personality, whatever that really is, for a phoney one.' But he was quickly seduced by David's graciousness and generosity, came to like him very much and was disarmed by his modesty when he said: 'I'm not a writer. I've just had two accidental successes [*and*] my acting talent is extremely moderate ... I've made a wonderful living out of very, very little.' Niv added engagingly, 'The key to actors is that they want to be liked ... If a little old lady from Ghana were to walk in now, I'd hope she'd like me. I'm sitting here hoping *you* like me. And anxious that you don't, that I'm not being what you want me to be, not telling you what you want to hear.'

Niv's difficulties with writing the novel were to continue for several years and often he nearly gave up. Apparently he still had 'thirty-two people stuck in a lighthouse at the moment and every time I sit down to write some more another three arrive by boat', he told the *Sunday Express*. Greenfield urged him to write a book about his war and call it *Niven at Arms*, saying he could easily get advances totalling £250,000 – £1 million today – for it, but Niv had sworn never to talk about the war. His American publisher John Dodds, editor-in-chief of Putnam's, urged him to write a novel that David had himself once suggested, about a highly decorated war hero who knows that the act of great courage that won him his medals had in fact been one of cowardice. Niv had imagined that after the war the hero would go into a seedy decline on the French Riviera, and Dodds now suggested mischievously that he could make the hero 'a second-rate film star'.

Much as David liked the popular and respected Dodds his relationship with Putnam's was about to end in tatters. In June he heard that in America a Mrs Vera Amey had threatened to sue for libel because of a passage in *Bring on the Empty Horses* that described a brothel in old Hollywood where the madam's little daughter had sat playing with her dolls at the foot of the stairs while the clients went up and down. Mrs Amey claimed to have been the little girl and demanded damages. Niv had mentioned no names or an address but Putnam's decided it would be cheaper to settle out of court, paid Mrs Amey $6000 [*£14,000 today*] without consulting him, deducted half from his next royalty payment and told him to write her a letter of apology as part of the agreed settlement. He was enraged. With huge reluctance he wrote the letter, telling her that he had mentioned no names and had intended to offend no one, but he never forgave Putnam's for not giving him the chance to fight the case. Fairly or not, he blamed the company's President, Walter Minton, whom he called 'he of the slippery sneakers and smelly socks', and swore that Putnam's would never publish another of his books even though they had an option on his next. 'I recall very little contact with Niven, have never had a pair of slippery shoes and change my socks daily,' Minton, now a lawyer, told me in 2002. 'But it is not unusual for the head of a publishing house to be the fall man if anything goes against an author's wishes.' He also pointed out that Niv had wanted an advance of $1 million for his next book and since Putnam's would never have paid that much he would in any case have had to go to another publisher. 'David had a very considerable regard for money,' said Minton, and a fortnight after hearing about Mrs Amey Niv was lining up yet another possible source of income by agreeing in exchange for commission to let the British aircraft company Hawker Siddeley Aviation know if he could come up with potential purchasers of their new $3½ million HS 125–700 business jet. 'Will keep eyes and ears peeled,' he promised. The millionaire film star bestselling author and lecturer was now an aircraft salesman too.

Putnam's were not the only people that summer to anger him. At sixty-seven he was becoming decidedly grumpy and told the *Evening Standard* that his life at Lo Scoglietto was being ruined by gin-swilling dentists from Dresden and other vulgar types who had taken to roaring across the bay of Beaulieu in their powerboats. He was not delighted either when Rex Harrison bought a villa nearby on Cap Ferrat. Harrison was jealous of Niv's popularity as well as his success with *The Moon's a Balloon*, and Niv had come to dislike him deeply – like everyone who knew Harrison – because he was so rude, arrogant and selfish. 'Rex was kind of an asshole,' Charlton Heston told me – 'one of the top five most unpleasant men you've ever met,' said Patrick Macnee – and Roddy Mann told me: 'Noël Coward said, "When you realise Rex's real name is Reg it tells you everything." '

John Mortimer had to go once to see Harrison on Cap Ferrat about a film script and rang Niv first to arrange to meet for dinner afterwards. Moments later, Mortimer recalled, 'the phone rang and Rex Harrison's voice said, "I just want to say something to you before you come. I just want to make it clear that you're a complete *shit* and you always have been." My eyes misted over with tears and then there was a great big laugh and that was Niven impersonating him. It was so exactly the sort of thing that Rex Harrison *would* do. Nobody liked Rex. He *was* a shit, an appalling man. He once called his agent's wife a "clockwork cunt" because she thought a play he was in was a little too long!' Leslie Bricusse once asked Harrison if he and Niv had fallen out because they had to compete for the same roles. 'Oh no,' sneered Harrison. 'Niven was always a *light* comedian and I'm a *high* comedian.'

'When Rex came to live in Cap Ferrat he was very offended that David didn't welcome him with an amazing lunch,' Evie Bricusse told me at her home in St Paul de Vence, 'so we had a lunch here and I put them opposite each other. They declared undying love to each other and never saw each other again! They just didn't like each other.'

In October 1977 Niv flew to Egypt to join Peter Ustinov, Bette Davis, Maggie Smith, Mia Farrow and Angela Lansbury in making *Death on the Nile*, an Agatha Christie Hercule Poirot murder mystery – apprehensively because he was wary of Egyptian food and ordered a series of Fortnum's hampers to be sent out to Cairo. In vain: the entire cast went down with stomach trouble, Niv himself inconveniently while riding a camel. He was appalled by the flies and 130° heat but kept his cool. When Maggie Smith arrived exhausted, harrassed and bedraggled after a long three-leg flight from Toronto to Luxor during which her luggage was lost, David greeted her at the airport, 'cool, smiling and immaculate as always, with a large bunch of flowers in his arms and a bottle of champagne on ice!' she told Peter Haining. 'It was *so* typical of him! . . . I simply burst into tears!'

The film was one of the most enjoyable he made: elegant, amusing, vividly atmospheric and beautifully photographed. Ustinov was splendid as Poirot investigating the murder of an heiress on a Nile river steamer in the 1930s, Maggie Smith and Bette Davis were excellent playing themselves, and Angela Lansbury was wonderful as a drunken writer who dances a hilarious tango with Niv. He played himself as usual, as Poirot's bland English-gent lawyer and assistant, but halfway through the film he suddenly looks much older, gaunt and stressed, with haunted eyes. The reason was that in the middle of shooting the film, on 4 November, Kristina was nearly killed in a terrible car crash in Switzerland. Niv rushed to the hospital in Lausanne. For eight days she lay in a coma, for months she was dangerously ill, and he was desperately distressed and worried. In a few days he lost a great deal of weight and much of his sparkle, and was never the same again. Kristina's accident marked the beginning of the end of his life and may have triggered the dreadful disease that was to kill him.

Fourteen

'Wodehouse With Tears'

1977–1983

At sixteen Kristina was too young to drive but had persuaded her law student boyfriend to let her try out his BMW as they returned to Château d'Oex on an icy mountain road and crashed into a tree that saved them from plunging 700 feet into a reservoir. The boy was barely scratched but Kristina had smashed her skull, eye socket, sinus and cheekbone, and had broken a leg and punctured a lung. She was helicoptered to Lausanne General Hospital but her kidneys stopped working, marrow from the broken thigh bone seeped into the bloodstream and headed towards her brain, and she nearly died. She was in a coma for eight days and had an operation to relieve the pressure on her brain followed by twenty-two more ops over the next few years to reconstruct her face.

Niv was devastated – 'a broken man,' said Sue Bongard. For weeks he did not know whether she would survive or be crippled, and the accident 'made him for the first time seem very frail', Ustinov told me. Patrick Macnee reckoned that the trauma suddenly turned him into an old man, and Jamie agreed: 'It affected him dramatically, and from then on he always treated her like she was damaged.'

'After the operations,' said Kristina, 'I used to repeat myself a lot, and Daddy used to come every weekend from wherever he was working to see me in hospital, and he helped by speaking to me, being by my side and listening to me. I know I was ever so difficult to deal with and I'd become very impatient.' Even after she returned to school nearly a year later Niv was terrified that she might have an epileptic fit at any time and did everything he could to avoid upsetting her. Hjördis, however, seemed hardly affected even though Kristina was her favourite daughter. 'We spoke to them in the lobby of the Beau Rivage Hotel in Lausanne the night after the accident,' said Valerie Youmans, 'and he looked drawn but she was drunk, of course,' and Bill Buckley told me: 'When we saw him again in February he looked a lot older, but I didn't see any change at all in Hjördis: she was very painted up.' To add to the stress, said Buckley, Niv was bitter that Kristina's boyfriend's father refused to accept any responsibility for the crash or to contribute to Kristina's expensive medical treatment, which was not covered by insurance because she had been driving illegally.

The accident had another tragic impact on David's life, according to Robert Wagner, because 'just before that I was sure he was going to leave Hjördis for a lovely lady of about thirty-five and was hoping he would. This woman was so in love with him and sat at his feet and listened to his stories, and laughed, and had a joyous time with him. She was *wonderful* for him, and I think he was ready to make the move and would have gone with her when Kristina had the accident and now he could not do it. It would have changed his life.' Jamie's wife Fernanda agreed: 'I knew the woman and he should have gone and lived with her at the end of his life. I can't tell you who she is: she's happily married now.' The woman was English, Jamie told me, 'and I would have been very happy had he left Hjördis for her. By the 1970s he was extremely unhappy with Hjördis. He *hated* her.' One night Niv and Evan Galbraith returned to the chalet to find her slumped, drunk, in the bathtub. 'She was groaning and practically comatose and he was afraid she was going to drown,' said Galbraith, 'and I had to help him get her out and put her to bed, which was embarrassing for him. God knows he tried to have a decent relationship with her but she was very selfish and unhappy with her lot.'

Niv returned to Egypt to finish filming *Death on the Nile* but flew back regularly to Lausanne to see Kristina in hospital and in December he flew her to the London Clinic and wrote to Phil Evans that although she was still very confused and her memory 'very peculiar indeed . . . she is getting rather chippy and rude now which they manfully say is a good sign! (To Matron of starched black . . . "I don't want to watch you taking a shit – why do you watch me?")' In February she returned home to Château d'Oex although Niv wrote to Evans that 'it obviously will be a long time before her little grey cells have sorted themselves out into their proper positions'. He added, 'You are the classic example of guts and I have often talked about you to her. In her own way she is pretty courageous too.'

David Jr was now producing films as a freelance – his first was *The Eagle Has Landed* – and Roger Moore told him to 'stop being such a ponce and give your father and me a job'. From then on Niv and Moore both called him 'Poncey' and he gave them parts in his second film, *Escape to Athena*, a comedy action thriller about a Nazi prison camp in German-occupied Greece in 1944. Moore played the camp's Austrian commandant and Niv a professor of archaeology who is keen to investigate some art treasures in a local monastery. Shooting began on the island of Rhodes at the end of February and the harrowing effect of Kristina's illness is etched in every line of Niv's face, which is suddenly dreadfully gaunt and old.

During Kristina's crisis David could not bring himself to work on the novel at all, despite already having written about 30,000 words of it, though he seriously considered a suggestion by the British publishers Mitchell Beazley that he should write the text for an illustrated coffee-table book about Hollywood while they provided researchers to do all the hard work. He was still determined to escape Putnam's, and went twice to New York to meet executives of the publishers Doubleday with Jamie to discuss how he could escape his next-book option with Putnam's and what he might write for Doubleday instead. 'We all got absolutely shit-faced and had the most extraordinary lunch,' said Jamie. Doubleday's Publisher, Sam Vaughan, told me: 'We all liked him and felt that we ought to publish him even if he didn't make us a lot of money.'

Fernanda Jr and Eugenie were now six and four, and Niv was 'the best grandfather you could ever ask for', their mother told me. 'He would arrive with about ten presents for each of them and he'd get on the floor and play with them, totally involved.' Jamie was astonished to see how popular his father still was in New York. 'People would get out of their cars to shake his hand and doormen would come out to talk to him,' he told me. 'You couldn't just walk with him in this city. I told my eldest daughter to go with Grandad and buy some English papers and when she came back she said, "I'm never going to walk with Grandad again, Daddy. It takes too long. Everyone kept coming up and pinching my cheek and saying, 'What a cute granddaughter.' " It was the same in London: cab drivers would lower their windows and give him a thumbs-up. It was amazing.'

Back at Lo Scoglietto in June the Nivens gave a fabulous lunch for fifty people in honour of twenty-one-year-old Princess Caroline of Monaco the day before she married a thirty-eight-year-old playboy, Philippe Junot, much to the distress of her parents. Caroline was sulky because she felt she was being upstaged by Niv's Hollywood friends, who included Ava Gardner, Cary Grant, Gregory Peck and Frank Sinatra, but it was a beautiful day and 'they gave a wonderful garden party', recalled Leslie Bricusse. 'The views were lovely, the sea went all the way round this two-acre garden, it was *beautifully* planted with wonderful old olive trees with carnations and roses growing out of them, and at the end was the swimming pool and the gazebo and the changing rooms underneath it. There were all these stars, and servants in white jackets, and I was wandering down to the far end of the garden where there was a bronze head of Hjördis and I heard her say to Cary Grant: "So you see, darling, I don't suppose I shall ever have what I really want." I thought: "Fuck you, mate!" '

That evening the Nivens attended a ball for 600 guests at the palace in Monaco and then the next day the wedding in the palace courtyard, and afterwards Niv wrote a warm, sympathetic letter to Grace and Rainier, knowing how upset they were about the wedding. But his relationship with Rainier was not always perfect and there was one occasion when a row in a Chinese restaurant in Monaco nearly ended the friendship. 'They both got rather pissed,' said Roger Moore, 'and Rainier said there was so much crime and unrest in the world that we really needed another war, and Niv said, "How dare you? During the war you sat here in your 'reserved occupation' while the rest of us were putting our lives on the line," and he got up and staggered off into the night. When he woke in the morning he thought, "What the *fuck* did I do? I've insulted the prince in his own principality. How am I ever going to get out of this?" But a despatch rider arrived with a letter from Rainier which said, "Niv, we've been friends far too long to let a stupid little argument upset our relationship." '

In September Kristina was well enough to return to school and Niv flew to London to spend two months filming a six-hour, three-episode TV film that was also released as a much shorter cinema movie, *A Man Called Intrepid*, about Sir William Stephenson, the Canadian who had headed the joint Anglo-American intelligence agency British Security Coordination (BSC) in New York during the Second World War and had been given the code name Intrepid. Niv played Stephenson, who had run a small team of incredibly brave amateur spies in Nazi-occupied Europe and whose greatest coup had been the capture of a vital German Enigma cipher machine. It was a serious role for a change, one on which he worked thirteen hours a day and found so exhausting that he started drinking spirits again and reached every night for a 'big brown umbrella-stand of scotch' to help him sleep. Each Friday he dashed to catch the last plane for Geneva to spend the weekend with Kristina and he was soon to fly to Canada to finish shooting the series there. The strain showed and in the film he looked very old, exhausted, nervous and unhappy. He was sixty-eight and the debonair jester of yesteryear had all at once become a fragile, worried old man with a frightened look in his eyes. 'Suddenly I find I've reached a certain age and you begin to think about the end,' he told Ian Woodward of *Woman's Weekly*. 'What the dickens happens next? Does *anything* happen next?'

He was still surprisingly nervous in front of a camera considering he had made more than eighty films, and was plagued by tense, sweaty hands and lips that stuck to his gums through fear.

A Man Called Intrepid was by no means one of Niv's worst films although the critics thought it was dull and it angered several of Stephenson's old colleagues who felt that it was a sensationalised, romanticised abuse of the truth. When the TV series was transmitted in Britain the wartime head of SOE, the Special Operations Executive, Colonel Maurice Buckmaster, called it 'a travesty of fictionalised espionage activity' and complaints were made to the Independent Broadcasting Authority.

In January 1979 Niv was delighted to hear that Walter Minton had left Putnam's and been replaced by Peter Israel, but he was still determined to move to Doubleday if ever he managed to finish another book. By now he had gone off the idea of the big Hollywood coffee-table book because it would mean too much hard work and was thinking instead of writing a book about backache, he told Greenfield, 'as you and I, and practically everybody else in the world, suffers from it'.

He was also having continual cramps in his right calf and consulted a twenty-nine-year-old English chartered physiotherapist, David Bolton, who was practising in Gstaad and had treated Kristina after her accident. 'He was beginning to suffer the first signs of motor neurone disease though we didn't know that at the time,' Bolton told me at his surgery in London. 'He did half an hour of strict exercises every day and kept himself very fit, and he'd often walk from Château d'Oex to Gstaad, a good forty minutes, and he strode out. We became good friends. As a physiotherapist I embrace very much the body *and* the soul, and you almost become your patient's confessor, and he told me that Hjördis made him very unhappy and depressed, and he never came to understand why she was like that.'

Hjördis consulted Bolton too.

> She said she didn't want to sleep with her husband, and locked him out of the bedroom, and dressed so as not to turn him on. She was very boring, and if you caught her without her make-up she was actually quite ugly. She had alcoholic problems, didn't eat and had a thing about getting old, and you couldn't get her into a meaningful conversation of any sort, so David was a very insecure, sad, melancholy man and his self-confidence wasn't very high. He was forever questioning whether people really did like him. I think he was a damaged child and whatever happened in his childhood he never overcame his lack of self-worth. His eyes always glazed over when he talked about Primmie – that pain was still very raw – and he couldn't understand Hjördis's behaviour, and he didn't deserve it. He was a damned good husband, and he loved and cared for her, cherished her, but she would blame him that she was getting old and for giving him the best years of her life, and if you hate yourself you can despise someone else for loving you. There was enough work there to keep seven psychotherapists busy for all their careers. Without him she would have been a lot worse. With a lesser man she'd have topped herself or drunk herself to death a lot sooner.

I asked Bolton whether Niv's motor neurone disease, which was soon to become increasingly apparent, could have been caused by his deep unhappiness. 'We don't know,' he said, 'but maybe sadness can make our own immunity systems turn against us. Maybe somehow we can give a disease to ourselves through our own depression.' Or as Sam Vaughan put it: 'Maybe the shock of Kristina's accident brought on the disease. After a certain point in a hard-running life you become vulnerable to everything. I think you become eligible for death.'

Niv was also worrying as usual that January about money. Despite all his efforts to avoid tax by living in Switzerland – even his two houses were for tax reasons 'owned' by a company registered in Liechtenstein, Dajani Establishments – he had just had more demands for back taxes both there and in France, and his Zurich lawyers, Staehelin Hafter and Partners, had just sent him a bill for Swiss fr. 200,000 which he queried in a letter to the senior partner, Bill Staehelin, a personal friend, pointing out that 'this year I will be paying in the neighbourhood of $170,000 for the administration and safeguarding of my capital. But I have a nasty feeling that my capital does not generate this sum in interest!' The problem was that he had handed over to Staehelin even the simplest day-to-day household matters and bills, though 'I could easily do it myself if I wasn't so lazy or Hjördis could do it if she had any brain!' as he told his

New York lawyer Lee Steiner. Jess Morgan laughed when I told him about this letter. 'David always watched the fees he paid people even though he could well afford them at that point,' he said. 'He watched our fees closely and he used to complain to me about Lee Steiner's fees!' And he was worrying increasingly about what would happen after his death.

By now *The Moon's a Balloon* and *Bring on the Empty Horses* had sold more than 9 million copies between them and Israel was very keen for Niv to write another book for Putnam's, but despite the change of regime there David was determined to break free and told Greenfield to tell Israel that he considered himself released from their option clause because Mitchell Beazley had offered them the Hollywood coffee-table book for $500,000 and they had turned it down. Greenfield said he would never get away with such a transparent ploy since Niv had never even started work on the Hollywood book, so Niv wrote to Putnam's himself – 'the foul Putnams' as he was still calling them unfairly – to say he was leaving whether they liked it or not, and on the same day he wrote to Vaughan at Doubleday to suggest that he should compile *The Great Book of Lies* for them, an anthology starting with Adam and ending with modern politicians. He was still trying to write 200 words of the novel every day 'but all that happens is that I seem to re-write the same two hundred every other day!' Given the unfair way he was treating the blameless new management at Putnam's, it seems poetic justice that when his butler at Lo Scoglietto was offered more money by one of the neighbours he resorted to equally devious tactics to escape his contract with David: he bored a hole in the bottom of Hjördis's teacup, she was drenched with hot tea and he was sacked.

Despite Niv's fears that his acting career was over he was still being offered the occasional movie and flew to London in April to make *A Nightingale Sang in Berkeley Square*, in which he played the mastermind of a gang of bank robbers. In London he gave as always several newspaper interviews. 'I get very depressed when I think of all my friends dying off,' he told Dan Ehrlich of the *Daily Express*. 'I guess my group has been called up.' He even made a joke about the sudden loss of his healthy good looks, telling Margaret Hinxman of the *Daily Mail* that when he had walked recently into a London delicatessen a woman had asked if he was David Niven and when he admitted it had remarked, 'Well, you're not looking too good, are you?'

It was Kristina's eighteenth birthday on 4 June 1979 and her parents gave her a pair of diamond earrings and a birthday party at Lo Scoglietto to which they invited the Rainiers and their son Prince Albert. Jamie was also there with his two Fernandas and Eugenie, and during their holiday Niv took them out sailing, fishing, swimming and snorkelling every day in his new 22ft boat. The girls were now eight and six, and 'one was the bosun and one the first mate, and they'd have to salute him', said their mother. 'We didn't see him often but when we did he was so excited and really involved and gave a hundred per cent of his time.' Fernanda Jr told me that they used to call Niv Grandfather-With-The-Moustache because their other grandpa was clean-shaven: 'He was a great grandfather, great fun, but I don't think Hjördis liked us particularly. She wasn't a grandmother figure at all.'

Greenfield finally won the Battle of Putnam's when he wrote to Israel to suggest that whatever the legal situation might be, 'I take the view that divorce is rather like rape. One has to lie back with a good grace and, if not enjoy it, at least accept it.' Israel replied with calm dignity to say that although Niv was treating him extremely unfairly 'so be it, then. "Buggered", however, would seem to me a more accurate word than "raped".' In fact he and Putnam's were lucky to have lost David as an author because Doubleday were to make a huge loss by taking him on.

On 27 August 1979 Niv was shattered when he was watching the TV news and heard that his old wartime comrade Lord Mountbatten, who was seventy-nine, had been murdered by an IRA bomb while sailing near his Irish holiday home at County Sligo. 'It was one of only two times that I saw Daddy cry,' said Fiona. 'The other was after Kristina's accident. He was close to Mountbatten and Prince Philip and all the Royal Family, though I heard that my mother once slapped the Queen by mistake at a ball at Buckingham Palace when she was wearing a flowing gown, got up to dance, swung round and knocked into the Queen. My father enjoyed telling that story: he said they were never invited back!' Niv wrote a letter of condolence to Prince Philip, who was obviously a personal friend since he replied with a friendly but typically acid note from Balmoral that read: 'Dear David, It was very kind of you to write at this time. One can only hope that this senseless act may help to galvanise politicians and churchmen into some useful activity. Yours ever, Philip.' There were of course many politicians and churchmen who wondered what it would take to galvanise Prince Philip into some useful activity himself.

A few days later Niv returned to London for five weeks to make *Rough Cut*, an amusing caper in which he played a suave but dodgy Scotland Yard detective, but although the film earned him some good reviews he was annoyed that much of his performance was cut and he was given only third billing after Burt Reynolds and Lesley-Anne Down. He sued the producer, David Merrick, for $1,700,000 for breach of contract plus $91,667 in salary that he claimed he was still owed, plus interests and costs, but was to settle out of court eighteen months later for $125,000.

After shooting *Rough Cut* he flew to India – Delhi and then Goa – to make his last major movie, *The Sea Wolves*, with several ancient chums, among them sixty-six-year-old Trevor Howard, sixty-three-year-old Gregory Peck, fifty-seven-year-old Patrick Macnee and fifty-two-year-old Roger Moore. At first he turned the part down but when Peck insisted that he should be in the picture the producer, Euan Lloyd, raised his offer to $500,000 (£780,000 today) plus $1500-a-week (£2300) expenses and Niv could not resist the easy money. It was yet another war film, this time based on the factual story of a group of elderly Allied ex-soldiers who had hijacked an old rust bucket in Calcutta in 1943 to sail to neutral Portuguese Goa and blow up several German ships. 'It was fun to make,' Moore told me. 'We were all mates, all English except for Greg Peck, and there was only one girl, Barbara Kellerman, and about fifteen miles of straight beach with a colony of hippies, a pharmacy where they sold heroin, and a German nudist camp with highly unattractive guys who would walk down the beach with their dicks between their knees.'

Shooting in temperatures of up to 140° was exhausting and Niv became increasingly worried about his motor neurone symptoms – he had trouble lifting his heel – though he did not yet know what was causing them. In the film he looked tragically old and ill, and was reminded yet again that his generation was passing away when his old love Merle Oberon died of a stroke in Malibu on 23 November 1979, aged sixty-eight. And 'David hated Goa,' said Euan Lloyd. 'He persuaded me to let him return to Europe for Christmas and I let him go on the understanding that he did not ski because the insurance company insisted on it. On Christmas Day I got a telex from him wishing us all a very merry Christmas, and there was a PS: "The hang-gliding is great." '

In India Niv had been struggling with the novel, writing slowly in pencil in school exercise books, but now he wrote in despair to Vaughan: 'I badly need help with this mess that I'm getting myself into! . . . All of it, in my opinion, is totally worthless!' He returned to Goa after Christmas and to strengthen his worrying leg muscles he walked for hours along the beach with Macnee every afternoon. 'We walked eight miles a day for two months,' said Macnee,

> and once when we came to the German nudist part we had Barbara Kellerman with us and all took our clothes off and walked through the nudist village, and the width of his member was something to behold. Then we'd come back for "tea" which was neat whisky in a teapot and soda in a milk jug because no alcohol was allowed, but he always drank – we'd start at about six o'clock – though I never saw him drunk. He talked about the money he had made from *Four Star Playhouse* – he called it The Fortune, all of which was in a tremendous amount of gold – and because I'd already done *The Avengers* he asked me why *I* didn't write a book, and I said, 'Because nothing exciting has happened in my life,' and he said, 'Neither has it in mine. I just made it all up.'

Niv and Macnee discovered that they had a special bond because Macnee's thirty-one-year-old daughter had also nearly died and had to have four operations for a brain tumour, and Niv was deeply sympathetic. 'He was always very kind and fantastically concerned for other people,' I was told by John Standing, who had a small part in *The Sea Wolves*. 'I was forty-six, having an affair with a beautiful American model and in a forlorn state, and he was so nice to me. He took me out to lunch and dinner, shared his car, and back in London the following year he took me to lunch in Chelsea and we got terribly pissed. He was a great bloke.'

During those long daily walks along the beach 'he wasn't at all frail,' said Macnee. 'Everyone gets sick in India, and he said that they had looked into his stomach and found a big black container of liquid which they had dispersed. Motor neurone disease doesn't just come out of nowhere, and I'm convinced it was something he picked up in Goa. Bloody India!' Certainly Niv looks extremely unwell in the movie, very thin and drawn with mournful, staring eyes, and during the last week of filming, in February, he told the movie's publicity director Brian Doyle that he was 'terrified' because he would be seventy in a few days' time. '*Seventy*!' he said. 'And frankly I'm scared. I don't want to be old. I've always felt so young. And I want to *stay* young.'

In February he escaped at last from India. 'That really is a foul place!!!' he wrote to Phil Evans from Château d'Oex. 'India was dreadful and I went from cement to the trots with the greatest regularity and while I was clutching hands around my intestines, other humans stretched out theirs begging me for money.' He went skiing the same day but was appalled to find himself so breathless that he had to lie down and rest twice. He was also starting to worry about Fiona, who was now fifteen and beginning to flirt with teenage freedom. 'I was a good girl and never did anything naughty or took drugs,' she said. 'Kristina and I both smoked and Daddy didn't like it at all because Mummy smoked like a fiend, but he didn't try to stop us. He let me have the occasional glass of wine and although I wasn't allowed to read *The Moon's a Balloon* till I was older he was very open about sex and said, "If you have to have sex please be careful, and if you need me just let me know." You could pretty much talk to him about anything, but I did once make him cross when I stayed out all night after being stuck in Gstaad in a snow storm. Daddy never slept until we got home, he just lay awake waiting for us to come back, and when I came home at eight o'clock, following the snow ploughs, that finger went up and that's all I needed.'

When the Buckleys and Galbraiths were not in Switzerland life was sometimes boring. Hjördis had now completely stopped going anywhere with him – 'you *never* saw them together,' said Valerie Youmans – and Roddy Mann recalled that David was so desperate for company at Château d'Oex that he would invite the local stationmaster up for drinks. The staff at the chalet were also decidedly weird. 'Daddy hired one guy who used to wear little bobby pins in his orangey hair,' said Fiona. 'He always complained about his sciatic nerve, but when Daddy came down in the morning he would be down on his knees bowing to him. Another guy was a complete crook.' Another couple who were employed that winter season of 1980 'were most strange', Jamie told me. 'Every other month the butler would change his name, nationality, and even his relationship with his wife: sometimes she was his wife, sometimes his mistress, sometimes the unknown person who worked in the kitchen. I'd ask François for a glass of wine and he would tell me that François was no longer there but that he, André, would be pleased to produce some! They were kept on only because it was very hard to find replacements in the middle of the season.'

For four years Jamie had been running a spaghetti sauce company that he had bought in 1976 and finally sold in February 1980 at a profit of twenty-five per cent. 'Daddy was very proud of Jamie for that,' said Fiona, and Roger Moore told me: 'He took *tremendous* joy in both his sons. Jamie made $7·5 million [*£9 million today*] when he sold the sauce company and Niv was so *pleased* about it.'

On 1 March Niv was appalled to be seventy, but marked the birthday with a lunch at the Eagle Club to which he invited Evie and Leslie Bricusse, who told me: 'He also invited ex-King Umberto of Italy. It was a weird group.' Hjördis was not there.

Four days later Niv flew to Rome for an audience that Bill Buckley, a Roman Catholic, had arranged with Pope John Paul II, who had no idea that he was a film star but seemed to have a vague suspicion that he might have been a great personal chum of the previous Pope. In saintly mode Niv sent in April another £1000 each to Joyce and Grizel, whom he noted on his chequebook stub by her childhood nickname, Gump, and from now on she was always Gump on the stubs as though he were beginning to revert to childhood himself. Incredibly generous though he was towards his sisters, he could obviously afford it. 'I used to advise him financially,' Evan Galbraith said, 'and he had $14 million [*£17 million today*], in gold bars in some Swiss bank.' By the end of 1980 he had nearly six million Swiss francs invested in a Supplea Trust portfolio, his houses were increasingly valuable and stuffed with dozens of expensive works of art including a Picasso lithograph, two Miró gravures, three Ernsts, a Kandinsky and the Dali. The nine biggest pictures alone were valued by Sothebys at $916,800 (more than £1 million today) in April 1980, and he was about to sign a huge contract with Doubleday for two books. 'David left most of his investments in our hands,' said Jess Morgan, 'but he was a very good investor himself, a big picture guy, and he did very well in gold. He encouraged us to buy gold for him in the 1970s when it was $35 an ounce, and after the US went off the gold standard it skyrocketed to a high of about $850 an ounce and David then sold very near the top. He had great connections in the financial world as well as his entertainment and social worlds.'

At the end of April, knowing that his movie career was all but over, he sent Sam Vaughan parts of the novel over which he had sweated for four years and for which he had eventually hired an assistant to help with research. 'It wasn't a good novel and he wasn't a good novelist,' Vaughan admitted in 2002. 'It wasn't his metier. He told good anecdotes but it's hard to make a novel out of anecdotes.' Phil Evans, to whom Niv sent a copy of the typescript when it was finished, agreed. 'He wasn't really a novelist,' he said, and Alan Gordon Walker admitted that the book was very bad. Still, Vaughan reckoned that it could be improved by his editors and it would be a coup for Doubleday to have Niv as one of its authors, so he was prepared to pay much more for the book than it was worth. 'You're off to a splendid start,' he fibbed in a letter to David on 14 May. 'Don't worry. Whatever problems we might have in the manuscript are fixable. What is irreplaceable is your own gift for story, your soaring sense of humor, and the very real atmospherics of this novel.' Greenfield flew to New York to negotiate the contract and told Vaughan that Niv was insisting on an advance of $1,000,001 for the two books. 'Why the extra dollar?' asked Vaughan. So that Niv could tell everyone that the deal was for more than a million, said Greenfield. It was an absurdly extravagant sum to pay for a bad novel by an author who was quite obviously not a novelist, even though it was to be split into five payments, and Doubleday were never to earn even a fraction back, but all those noughts galvanised Niv into finishing it by the end of the year.

He was now so worried about Hjördis's drinking that he wrote to Belinda Willis, the wife of an old army comrade in Dorset who had beaten her own addiction, to ask her advice, but Hjördis refused to admit that she had a problem or to go for treatment.

At the end of July Peter Sellers died of a heart attack, aged only fifty-four, and his widow Lynne Frederick asked Niv to deliver the eulogy at the memorial service in London at St Martin-in-the-Fields in September. By now he was looking dreadfully old and strained, and when he spoke from the pulpit he was referring as much to himself as to Sellers. 'This brilliant man suffered genuinely, dreadfully, and increasingly, from the classic actors' ailment – insecurity,' he said. 'It was only when Peter was well on his way to becoming what he had set his heart on – a big international success – that he looked down from halfway up the mountain and discovered that he had a very bad case of vertigo. Then he began to question himself, to worry, and truly he suffered. People outside our profession have no conception of the blind fear an actor has of being a failure in public.'

Kristina, now nineteen, left school that summer and Niv settled her into a year-long fine-arts course at Sotheby's in London and a flat at 23 Bruton Street before flying back to the Côte d'Azur. Even though his film career was all but over, he was still able to sign lucrative contracts for doing very little and earned approximately £60,000 for two days' work making a chocolate commercial for Rowntree Mackintosh, but when he flew to New York to see Sam Vaughan and his Doubleday editors about the novel he was suddenly felled by a violent pain in his leg as he walked down Fifth Avenue. 'I thought someone had hit me in the right calf with a plank,' he wrote to a London osteopath, Dr Guy Beauchamp. 'I could only go about 10 yards, then the pain was so bad I had to stop.' Back in England various tests found nothing obviously wrong but the attack was another early symptom of motor neurone disease, and when he returned to Switzerland he found that although he could ski he could not raise his right heel and could walk only flat-footed.

For Christmas he sent Gump and Joyce the modern equivalent of

£26,000, but once again money was cascading into his coffers when he settled his legal suit against David Merrick for some £70,000, Hamish Hamilton agreed to pay him an advance of £42,500 for the new novel, and Hodder another £82,500 for the British paperback rights, though he was still struggling to find the right title because, he said, *Make It Smaller and Move It to the Left* 'does not fit the book at all'. He was still for some reason obsessed by the fey bit of E. E. Cummings doggerel from which he had taken the title for *The Moon's a Balloon* and now suggested the last line of the same verse as the title for the novel, *Flowers Pick Themselves*. 'HATE YOUR TITLE', cabled Sam Vaughan and he had to think again.

At the end of January he flew to Los Angeles to compère an American Film Institute ceremony in Beverly Hills at which a Life Achievement Award was presented to his old friend Fred Astaire, but already the disease was beginning to affect his voice and at the start of his speech he apologised and said that he knew he sounded like a parrot. He had lost so much weight that his dinner jacket and trousers hung loose from his scrawny frame and he realised that something was seriously wrong with him. The doctors still had no idea what it was though one, a Dr Williams, said it could be nervous depression.

Towards the end of February he delivered the last chapter of the novel to all his publishers and suggested yet another dreadful title, *Go Slowly, Come Back Quickly*, a remark that a little black girl had once made to him as he left the West Indies. 'I cannot pretend that David's novel is a masterpiece,' wrote Sinclair-Stevenson in a memo to Roger Machell, 'it is far too rambling and self-indulgent for that. On the other hand, it rattles along amusingly enough, there is a good picture of the perils of Hollywood – and it will sell,' and he told me: 'It wasn't very good and we were reluctant to publish it but we were going to make money out of it. Of course all the stories that Roger had cut from *The Moon's a Balloon* and *Bring on the Empty Horses* were recycled again!' Sam Vaughan realised that the book needed a great deal of cutting and rewriting, and sent his editor Kate Medina to London to help him do it. 'What the novel lacked was a central glue,' Ms Medina told me. 'There were the trees but we never made it into a forest. He did not have a lot of self-confidence about himself as a writer, and he had an inability to concentrate and wouldn't sit still for it, and there was a certain frenetic quality about him. I remember being at the Connaught Hotel and running around a lot and up and down stairs.'

Even after a great deal of professional advice and some extensive rewriting *Go Slowly, Come Back Quickly* was still a very bad novel: slow, pedestrian and embarrassingly amateurish. Even Niv's closest friends thought it was dreadful. 'He couldn't write fiction,' said Roddy Mann. 'His novels were *awful*. Greenfield and I both told him not to write another but he insisted.' Bizarrely the book was dedicated to his old regiment, Phantom, and it told the wartime story of a sexy young Polish American, Stani, who starts off with 'an erection and it hurt', joins the RAF, goes to Hollywood with a beautiful girl who becomes a film star, dislikes the place, and loses her before they get back together again. There are surging loins, thrusting loins, 'perfectly shaped breasts', 'the glorious globes of Pandora's behind', a girl who has 'seen more stiff pricks than she 'as hot dinners' and a sergeant major who is stung by a wasp on the testicles. It is all a pointless, disjointed mess, part hairy-chested adventure, part bosom-heaving romance, interspersed with bits of irrelevant travelogue and absurd coincidence, and all utterly unbelievable. Had it been written by an unknown author it would never have been published, but because Niv had written it the publishers' hype machines went quickly into action. *Go Slowly, Come Back Quickly* was 'a story brilliantly blending love, the excitements of war, the glamour and the off-screen dramas of Hollywood', burbled Hamish Hamilton's early publicity sheet.

Niv flew to New York in May to consult an orthopaedic surgeon, Dr J. A. Nicholas, who told him that his muscle problem might be caused by a pinched nerve as a result of his back injury during the war and gave him a series of exercises to do to build up the calf muscles. But the exercises – and a course of physiotherapy in England – had little effect. 'We were having dinner with him in a Chelsea restaurant,' John Mortimer told me, 'and Penny, who was not yet thirty, said, "Oh God, I've got these terrible wrinkles on my face," and he said, "Even if I took every pill there is in the world I'll still be dead in five years." ' Even so, his energy and will-power were phenomenal. In July he flew to Atlanta to publicise the novel by addressing a convention of booksellers, and he agreed to return for a full exhausting promotion tour of the States at the end of October after Vaughan promised that 'there will be no "signing sessions in public libraries or lavatories" and you will not be given the Edna O'Brien treatment, including the fact that none of us will try to get you in bed. At least none of the guys.'

It was David Jr who gave him his last starring part in a movie he was producing, *Ménage à Trois*, a charming, light-hearted comedy which was later retitled *Better Late Than Never*. Poignantly Niv played an elderly, has-been cabaret entertainer who is trying to scrape a living in a strip club in the South of France where he is booed and hissed by the tourists. He earned $150,000 for seven weeks' work and insisted that his son should pay him a living allowance even though he was living just up the road at Lo Scoglietto. He enjoyed having Bryan Forbes directing and even sang on screen for the first time in his career, Noël Coward's 'I Went to a Marvellous Party', but he looked dreadfully old and skinny, and his voice was so weak and slurred that the studio asked Forbes to dub it. He refused. 'I couldn't do it to him,' said Forbes. 'It would be too humiliating. One night we had dinner on our own at Nice airport and he asked if my marriage was happy and said he didn't have much joy at home. He was a lovely man, very easy to direct and a gent. He'd come on set every day and shake every member of the French crew's hand and say "good morning" and was treated with great love and affection. He was an enchanting character and would still say if he saw a pretty girl, "Forbesie, that's fanciable".' One extremely fanciable girl for him to ogle was David Jr's latest girlfriend, Jaclyn Smith, one of Charlie's Angels. Young David was now thirty-eight and still a bachelor but renowned for his affairs with several beautiful women.

Niv flew to London in the first week of October for the publication of *Go Slowly, Come Back Quickly*. Editing and printing the book had been fraught with problems right until the last minute because he kept changing his mind and demanding alterations to the text as well as the jacket, and a few weeks before publication Roger Machell wrote exhaustedly to Kate Medina: 'Greetings from your fellow-survivor!' She replied, 'I hope and trust you are bearing up under the onslaught.' Just three weeks before publication David rang Hamish Hamilton to say that he approved of the jacket at last. 'Words fail me!' wrote one executive on an internal memo. 'Phew!' scribbled another.

Two nights before the book was published in Britain he appeared on TV on the *Michael Parkinson Show* looking weak, emaciated and uncomfortable. His bright blue eyes were pale and tired, his voice shaky and slurred, and he stumbled over words and looked extremely uneasy. 'Let's face it, my group's being called up,' he told Parkinson. 'I don't view the future with any great longing.' But he added, 'It's been such fun. I've been so lucky. How many people can say "I'm doing a job I love"?'

'In the green room afterwards everyone was saying, "He's pissed,"' Parkinson told me, 'but there was a nurse who said, "No, I think he's had a stroke." I *knew* he wasn't drunk and that there was something seriously wrong, and he knew himself. He was terribly upset and apologetic afterwards and aware that he was slurring his words. "They'll all say I was pissed," he said, but he wasn't.' Sinclair-Stevenson took Niv back to the Connaught 'and he said, "That was a disaster, awful!" and I said, "No, no, you were wonderful," but the following morning he looked absolutely ghastly and said, "I've had rather a shock. When I got back to my room last night there was a message from my Harley Street specialist's nurse, which had been hand-delivered, who said, 'It was such a pleasure to see you on the television but I was so distressed to see that you're obviously very ill'."' Another viewer wrote urging him to contact her doctor father, and in New York Jamie watched a tape of the interview, guessed that his father was seriously ill and urged him to go to the Mayo Clinic in Minneapolis for a major examination.

Niv realised Jamie was right and flew to Minneapolis, where he spent several days having tests. The results were grim. He phoned Jamie in New York. 'The good news is that I didn't have a stroke,' he said. 'The bad news is that I have a form of motor neurone disease and only eighteen months to live.' He returned to New York and Jamie picked him up at the airport, where he found him in amazingly high spirits. 'He had sat next to Tom Brokaw, the NBC anchorman, on the plane,' Jamie wrote in *You* seven years afterwards, 'and I later learned that he had regaled him with stories all during the trip. It is hard to imagine that a man could receive a death sentence and hours later amuse a fellow passenger with anecdotes. But then, that was David Niven. He always gave more to life than he got back from it, and he expected everyone else to do the same. In the car going into town he said, "You know, I have been very lucky, really. Your mother's death has been the only great tragedy in our family. I am fortunate to have gotten this far; I probably should have died in Normandy, and, hell, that was forty years ago. There is absolutely no sense in trying to fool ourselves about the fact that this thing is going to kill me. The secret is to live as best one can, given the circumstances, and get on with it." ... And with that we went to dinner.'

Equally astonishing, Niv told Brokaw during the flight that he had just been given a death sentence and Brokaw kept the secret instead of publishing his scoop, so it was another year before the story broke. Before leaving New York, Niv phoned Betty Bacall. 'Don't go to the Mayo Clinic!' he said. 'They tell you you're going to die!'

Motor Neurone Disease, MND, which is known in the USA as Lou Gehrig's Disease after the baseball player who contracted it, is a mysterious affliction that attacks the spinal cord and motor neurones in the brain, which send electrical instructions to the muscles. Its cause is still unknown, there is no cure, and it affects victims in different ways and at different speeds. Muscles weaken and waste in the arms or legs, then in the face and throat, making it difficult to speak, chew and swallow. Usually unaffected are the intellect, eyes, smell, taste, hearing, touch and sexual performance, and the disease is not contagious, but it is always fatal within two or three years. In September 2002 scientists at Columbia University in New York reported that the disease seems bizarrely to attack the very fittest and slimmest people, like Niv, especially athletes, maybe because vigorous exercise weakens an athlete's resistance to stress, increases the absorption of environmental toxins and speeds up the transport of toxins to the brain. In 2003 it was reported that dozens of highly fit young Italian professional soccer players had contracted MND and the only thing they all had in common apart from football was that they had all been treated at some time with anti-inflammatory drugs. So had Niv for more than ten years, for pain in his leg and foot, but it is impossible to know whether that had anything to do with his affliction.

Vaughan urged him to cancel his American coast-to-coast promotion tour but he had promised and insisted on doing it, flying in just a few days from New York to Philadelphia, Washington, Cleveland, Detroit, Chicago, Minneapolis, Portland, Seattle, San Francisco, Los Angeles, Dallas and Houston. Within a month the book had entered the top twenty list, 'but we didn't earn even half of our advance,' said Vaughan. 'It was something of a disappointment except that we all liked David so much that we didn't go round with long faces.'

Before returning to Europe he went sailing with Vaughan and Buckley, clenched some ropes, and then had trouble unclenching his fingers. The disease was beginning to take a firm grip. Back in Switzerland Peter Viertel urged him to see a neurologist for a second opinion, and he did, but the diagnosis was the same. 'When he got the news he was incredibly gallant,' said Viertel, and Jess Morgan said, 'I spent a couple of days with him in Switzerland just after he returned from the Mayo Clinic and had got the news that there was no hope, and he was philosophical and joking about it. He said, "When it gets too bad I'll just get in my wheelchair and go over the side of that mountain over there." That was a typical Niven joke. He had a wonderful light philosophy of life. He was one of the most wonderful friends I've ever had.'

At the end of November two more deaths underlined how little time he had left. On 18 November Joyce's heart gave out and she died in London aged eighty-one. She left him a diamond and sapphire brooch that had belonged to their mother and most of the rest of her estate of £152,927 (about £368,000 today) to her late husband's brother and his children. A fortnight later Niv was devastated to hear that Natalie Wood had drowned mysteriously at sea off Santa Catalina Island in the early hours of 29 November, perhaps after falling off their boat after a boozy dinner ashore with R. J. Wagner and her current co-star, Christopher Walken. She was only forty-three. Niv was distraught and persuaded R. J. to join him as soon as possible in Switzerland, where he promised to find a chalet for him and his two small children. 'He'd gone through the same thing with Primmie,' R. J. told me, 'and he was so compassionate and loving to me. When we drove to Switzerland he waited in a snowstorm for four and a half hours for us to come up from Geneva so that he could lead us to this chalet that he'd found and stocked for us. He was a true, true friend, caring for me and on the phone every day.'

With Joyce dead, Niv gave seventy-four-year-old Grizel a bigger Christmas present than ever, £11,000 (*about £26,000 today*) which must have been especially welcome because her studio in Fulham had recently been burgled, her possessions smashed, and her precious tools for carving wood and stone stolen. By now she had exhibited her sculptures all over the world, but she was so shocked by the burglary that she was unable to work for several months. 'Daddy was very fond of her,' said Kristina, who was now doing a languages course in London and was soon to work briefly in a London kindergarten.

Niv signed yet another generous cheque in February, this time for £2000 (*more than £4400 today*) which he sent to Trubshawe in Sussex after hearing that he had hit hard times and was battling to care for his wife, who had Alzheimer's Disease. 'She behaves just like a small child of ten,' wrote Trubshawe, saying he was so exhausted trying to look after her that he had to get away for a ten-day break. 'It is a nightmare.' Despite their estrangement Niv immediately offered him money and after wrestling with his conscience for a week Trubshawe replied, 'My dear old David,' and gratefully accepted the money 'most reluctantly' because he was broke and had to find someone to help look after his wife at weekends to ease the pressure. He ended 'with very much love' and wrote at least once more to say that he had hired an elderly woman to help him. 'Much love dear chum – and immense gratitude,' he wrote. Niv did not burden him with his own problem but said merely that he was suffering from 'a pinched nerve in the neck, fuck it'.

It was soon obvious that *Go Slowly, Come Back Quickly* was never going to take off, neither in Britain nor the USA. Reviews and sales were disappointing, and Vaughan told Greenfield that they all needed to think long and hard about what sort of book David should write next if he was to come even close to earning his huge two-book advance. In Britain Rainbird was offering him £100,000 to write captions for yet another projected coffee-table book of Hollywood photos, but in the end he decided to write another novel, an anti-IRA thriller with several autobiographical touches: its hero has joined the army after twice seeing *The Charge of the Light Brigade* – 'this brilliant piece of army recruiting' – and enduring 'the ghastly rigours of Sandhurst', and is now serving in Northern Ireland, where his best friend is Donkey Doubleday, 'always known as Donkey to his friends owing to the really enormous size of his member while Donkey's soldiers fondly referred to him as Excused Shorts'.

Niv soon tired of this story, abandoned it after forty-five handwritten pages, and after agonising for weeks came up with another subject and started scrawling again in longhand in four green notebooks, this time a story with a horse-racing background about a thirty-year-old divorced author who has an affair with a beautiful eighteen-year-old schoolgirl in Switzerland – like Kristina's mother, Mona Gunnarson, perhaps, from the school just across the road from the chalet – and another with a girl who likes being tied up when making love. He wrote 200 pages before giving the book up as well because he had thought of a much more powerful idea and began to write a dreadfully poignant novel about an author with a house in the South of France, an alcoholic Swedish wife and motor neurone disease. His hero, Sandy, whose name is later changed to Ian, has just returned after an exhausting book promotion tour in the States – 'he felt like a whore doing it but once more it had paid off' – and a check-up at the Mayo Clinic in Minneapolis, and is sitting in the garden of his lovely home on the Côte d'Azur near his little boat, *Ladybird*:

> The lush green kikuyu grass between the tortured shapes of the old olives; the citrus trees, the palms, the stone-pines and the spectacular results of Angelo's labours. How he loved it all! He hugged it to him, but he was ill prepared for his reaction to a small bird flashing like a turquoise dart mast high past 'Ladybird' – he burst into tears. Not a gentle pricking of the eyeballs. Accompanied by loud convulsive sobs and heaving breath, tears coursing down his cheeks and spotting his blue silk dressing gown. When Angelo looked up in alarm Sandy groped his way into the house and back to the guest room.
>
> 'It also attacks your emotions,' they had told him. 'Do you laugh

> unnaturally or cry a lot?' His reply had been a trifle pompous. 'I laugh all the time but I never cry,' but here he was howling uncontrollably at the appearance of the first kingfisher of the spring . . . When his sobs stopped he looked in the bathroom for Kleenex. In the mirror he caught sight of his runny nose, blotchy face, red eyes and woebegone expression and laughed out loud, a little too long perhaps but he felt better. The laughter and the tears between them had lit the first spark of hope since he had left Rochester Minnesota ten days before.

That was how he felt and reacted over the last few months of his life as the disease took hold and squeezed the life out of him. 'I wrote him letters increasingly conscious that they and the writing of the book were important to him,' Vaughan told me. 'This was beyond all business. It was friendship. He enjoyed writing, and as he said in one of his letters, writing was his lease on life at the end. He said, "This is all I have," and that was pretty poignant. He was an actor who had lost his voice and so the voice was flowing through his fingers.'

In the unpublished novel Sandy's Swedish wife, Ulla, still seems to care for him and her drinking is not yet completely out of control, but in real life Hjördis's boozing was worse than ever. 'She had blackouts,' Jamie told me, 'and she fell and broke her leg again. She drank upstairs, on her own, and he told me that they found bottles all over the house all the time. She was drinking easily a bottle of vodka a day, he told me. The fundamental problem with Hjördis was that she didn't seem to *get* it. How could you not think this was an interesting, funny man? How could you not want to read his books? How could you not be proud of his success?' The only possible answer is that Hjördis was jealous of him, or mistrusted his success, or was simply by now so alcoholic that she was too helpless to be rational, but 'I don't think there was ever anything *helpless* about this woman,' said Robert Wagner sharply, and Betty Bacall said, 'She was so terrible to David during the last couple of years of his life. She wasn't there for him ever when he needed her. She was drunk, with men, and could not function finally at all.' Anastasia Mann told me: 'I truly believe that Hjördis was evil. She was horrible to David. Towards the end he could hardly speak and she said to me gloatingly, "Isn't it ironic that a man who relied so much on his voice can't even make himself understood?" She was actually *gloating*.' Ustinov agreed: 'I'm sure she must have hated him. She was capable of hatred.' Doreen Hawkins and April Clavell both said Hjördis thought Niv was having her watched and followed. 'She became very strange,' said Mrs Clavell. 'Her mind was not working rationally,' and Valerie Youmans said, 'She was just an awful woman.' Finally, according to Pat Medina: 'It was a finished marriage by then. Poor Nivy. Poor Nivy.'

He was still determined not to lose his sense of humour. 'We saw him skiing cross-country towards the end,' said Mrs Youmans, 'and he said, "By God, I've finally got quick enough to pass somebody! I went whizzing by, but then I turned around and she was about ninety years old!" And then he dropped his glove and said to my husband, "Would you please pick it up for me? I can't." '

In February Niv's old lover Virginia Bruce died in California of cancer, aged seventy-one, and his friend Lesley Rowlatt, who was now thirty-five and working in advertising in New York, married a *Sunday Times* journalist, Peter Watson. 'People may have thought that she was American because she'd lived all her life there and was very feisty,' Watson told me. 'When we came back to London we went to Harrods to buy a bigger bed but nobody helped us and eventually Lesley, this statuesquely beautiful woman, bellowed across at these three salesmen, "Who do I have to fuck to buy a bed in this place?" From time to time Niven would ring up and she would have lunch with him, and she'd get dressed up to the nines. It didn't bother me because I knew almost from the start that our marriage wasn't right: it should have been just a fling.' Niv introduced Lesley to Kristina in London. 'I met her a couple of times,' said Kristina. 'She was very attractive. Daddy presented her to me and said, "This is a friend of mine." I knew her as Lesley Watson and never knew her maiden name.'

In March 1982 Niv made a final trip to Hollywood, where Roddy Mann was now living, writing a column for the *Los Angeles Times*, and took him on a sentimental journey back to all his old haunts including the Pink House, which was still owned by Phil Kellogg. 'He was filled with nostalgia for what now seemed to him a more joyous time, a period when Hollywood was fun and relatively carefree,' said Mann. Then it was back to the South of France to shoot his last two movies, with Roger Moore and R. J. Wagner, because although he was really too ill to make them he had promised the director, Blake Edwards, that he would. For the first time he told several old friends how ill he really was and received a reply from Laurence Olivier that began 'Darling boy' and ended, 'Thank you again my lovely boy for your angelic letter. I really think we had better meet don't you, and quick? . . . All my love dearest friend in the world. Yr devoted Larry.' In his letter to 'Dearest "Phillippo" ' Evans, Niv wrote: 'Struck down by a real "nasty" – Motor Neuron Disease and deeply resentful! Why US? But you are the leader of the brave ones bless you for the example.'

The two new movies were filmed at the same time: *The Trail of the Pink Panther* and *The Curse of the Pink Panther*, two sequels that were put together with out-takes of Peter Sellers's Inspector Clouseau scenes from previous Panther films. Niv played The Phantom, Sir Charles Lytton, again and although his part was very small Edwards gave him top billing because everyone realised that he would never make another movie. 'After doing the last scene,' said R. J. Wagner, 'tears rolled out of my eyes because he said, "I'm afraid you've just seen the last of an actor who had quite a career." ' But now his voice was so weak and slurred that his lines had to be re-recorded by an American impressionist, Rich Little, who made the mistake of telling the Press that he had dubbed Niv's voice. David was mortified and his distress now was such that another actor on the final Panther film, Herb Tanney, said to him gently, 'David, we're all leaving the party soon. It's not just you.'

Also in both films was thirty-six-year-old Joanna Lumley, who wrote later in her autobiography: 'I think many people fell in love with Niven at first sight, and I was no exception ... he was as charming and funny as could be, although he was filled with drugs and feeling ghastly [*and told me*] "The thing about this damn disease is that it makes me do everything in extremes. I can't smile, I have hysterics, I can't feel glum without howling." He then proceeded to tell a wildly funny story about the clinic in America where he underwent tests and had to travel about the hospital holding glass pots of unmentionable lavatorial substances. We clutched each other and yowled with laughter. He tired easily, and was horribly conscious of losing his ability to enunciate clearly. "GOR – ILL – A," he would practise before the take ... but when he said, "Golilla," and everyone said, "Doesn't matter," it did matter, most dreadfully, to him.' When filming ended in mid-July she wrote him a deeply affectionate six-page letter that began 'My dear Niv, my dear, dear Niv' and said, 'I don't think there is an actor living who inspires so much love and loyalty.'

Niv began in desperation to try every form of treatment that was suggested to him to stave off his muscle decay: physiotherapy, exercises, massive injections, squeezing big balls of putty. In London the Bricusses asked him to watch the Wimbledon tennis final between Jimmy Connors and John McEnroe with them at their flat in Eaton Square and he told them about the disease. 'It was the first time I saw him cry,' said Evie Bricusse. 'I remember him saying, "It's very serious. I can ski, darling, I can do anything you want, but I can't fucking walk!" and we held on to each other.'

To Phil Evans he wrote with a marking ink pen because he was losing his grip: 'You have been so incredibly brave with your problem, mine is mini in comparison, but I am copying you and am determined to beat the rap, but it is a fucker when some of the machinery begins to wear out! – I always thought that was reserved for old farts like Winston Churchill but I sense that young farts of 72 are coming into the firing line now and I do so resent it!!' In August newspapers reported for the first time that he was unwell and he was furious when Princess Grace said that he had suffered a mild stroke. Strangers wrote with messages of sympathy and suggested treatments, one lady recommending Super Kelp seaweed tablets and Super Gev-e-tabs, 'both a favourite of Barbara Cartland's'.

He enjoyed one moment of happiness that summer when Fiona, now nearly nineteen, left Le Rosey with an excellent final report – 'Fiona is a pleasure to have around and ALWAYS very helpful and co-operative' – and was offered a place at Geneva University. But his misery must have been deepened unbearably by an adoring love letter that he received early in August from a woman who was possibly the one for whom he was about to leave Hjördis just before Kristina's accident. It was written on the headed notepaper of a company called Hollywood Productions of 20 Canning Place, London W8, and addressed in code to 'Mr McKenzie':

> My Dearest Mr McKenzie,
>
> Such a long time without a word from you. I do so worry about you and hope that everything is fine for you. Many thanks for your lovely letter, which I was thrilled to receive (more please!) and thank you for phoning me here at work . . . no word from you as to whether you would be coming to London or not. I did send you a telegram but I wonder if it ever reached you – perhaps you are away in your Monastry? I just don't know, but one thing I know for sure is that I would certainly like to know that you are alright. You know that I do care very much for you and would always appreciate just a line or two from you. I would die to see you again. A few hours again just the two of us!
>
> I am off to Guernsey tomorrow morning for a couple of days rest, as I have worked terribly hard for the last three months and have nearly had a nervous breakdown as a result of it all.
>
> Will write to you again. Please contact me.

God bless you always,
UG

I have failed to identify the woman or find Hollywood Productions or any of its five directors, but 'UG' was probably short for Ugly – the nickname Niv often gave to women of whom he was especially fond.

Another adoring letter arrived from Joanna Lumley, who said she was 'sick with fear' because he had written to say that despite his weakness he was still snorkelling. 'For God's sake take care,' she said. 'It would be too frightful to read that you had met a watery end partially overwhelmed by rubber equipment. You know what the *Sun* would make of that.' But for all the jollity and joshing his life now was one tragedy after another. On 14 September his darling Princess Grace was killed when her car plunged off the Grande Corniche high above Monte Carlo. Niv was so shocked that he could not go to her funeral because his emotions now were so fragile that he feared he would break down and cause a scene – or, even worse, he might roar with laughter. It did not help that after Grace's funeral Cary Grant came to see him and then, like Grace, told the Press that he had had a stroke. Furiously he denied it, only to be struck another heavy blow when Bob Coote died on 26 November in New York, aged seventy-three. The darkness was closing in.

While Niv was in London for some hospital treatment he hired through an agency a pretty, twenty-eight-year-old, full-time Irish nurse, Katherine Matthewson, who was to look after him throughout his last eight months, became a close friend and tried to brighten his final days. 'She was great and he adored her,' said Fiona, and Jamie told me: 'She was just wonderful and made the end of his life fantastic. At one stage we had nurses for him around the clock but she said she'd take care of him by herself because he became upset with other people.'

At the end of November he went to Château d'Oex for his last winter and wrote to Laurence Olivier: 'I work (no skiing) and sleep and try to write my book – very unsocial I'm afraid because I have a problem swallowing which means I have to eat alone because if anybody speaks to me at the wrong moment they become encrusted with a fine spray of vegetable and saucisse de Vaud! Wine is difficult to keep down too. So I avoid it which makes everyone say how well I look, which is at least encouraging.' He had not lost his sense of humour, and added in a PPS: 'A friend of mine saw *Hamlet* in Johannesburg in Afrikaans – "Omlette, Omlette, ich bin dein Poppa's Spuki"!'

That last Christmas he sent Grizel a final present, yet another huge cheque, this time for £3000 (£6500 today) but he baulked at paying the Swiss fr. 230,000 he was told it would cost him in French export and Swiss import taxes if he shipped his biggest pictures from Lo Scoglietto to Château d'Oex, as he wanted, and he wrote to Sotheby's in London to ask discreetly whether there were any way of smuggling them over the border. With startling indiscretion a Sotheby's official replied on headed notepaper to give him the name and address of a man in London who was 'extremely experienced and reliable in handling jobs of this sort' and would do it for just under £1000. She added with understandable nervousness that 'he wishes to know as little as possible about the property' and 'for obvious reasons I think no correspondence on the subject should pass between you and Sotheby's'. When I mentioned the letter to Jamie Niven in 2002, by which time he was Vice-Chairman of Sotheby's in New York, he said with mock alarm, 'Oh, Jesus! No!'

'When David got really sick Hjördis simply couldn't handle it,' said Evie Bricusse. 'Everybody handles things in different ways but I didn't like her for it. Here was this lovely man in his hour of need and she should have been there for him, but her way was to hit the Fernet Branca. He had no one at the end except the nurse, whom he loved. At the very end, even though he could hardly talk, he used to make me laugh because he'd say this was a good night because she was going to bath him!' Hjördis was in denial, David Bolton told me: 'In that situation people can even be cross and think "How *dare* you die on me? I want a nice, fit man who's normal. How dare you expose me to all this pain and grief?" ' She drank more than ever, which drove Niv to the brink of utter despair and he wrote again to his friend Major-General John Willis, whose wife Belinda had written to him in 1980 about how she had beaten her own addiction, but Willis replied glumly that 'chaps like you and I are going to do nothing to either start or stop things happening ourselves – that can only be the choice or decision of the other person'. Niv could not bear it any longer and decided at last that he had to divorce Hjördis. 'He showed me this letter he was writing to her,' said Fiona, 'saying he wanted to divorce her and take us with him, but it was also a love letter saying how much he loved her and always had and always would. The guy was crazy about her and I said, "You can't tell a woman you love her so much but you want a divorce!" I think he hoped it would stop her drinking but in the end he never gave it to her. After all, where was he going to take us? He was dying. But he refused to believe he was dying and kept holding on to the hope that he would live.'

To cling to life he tried anything. 'I have just switched doctors to a maniac in Paris,' he wrote to General Willis in January, 'who has got me on a horrendous regime which starts at 6 o'clock in the morning sitting for 10 minutes in an ice-cold tub! He squirts me full of all sorts of injections and I am hoping for the best! The leg and hand I can cope with pretty well but the throat is a real hazard.' Gregory Peck suggested that he should try a special sort of ginseng root, to which he replied wittily: '*Caro Fagiolo Vecchio* [Dear Old Bean], Apart from all the great specialists, I have made the rounds of faith healers and quacks, the last being a vineyard worker near Sion with hands like bunches of bananas. He ripped up my records from the Mayo Clinic with a happy laugh and told me that all would be well if I bathed three times a day in olive oil and brandy! Anyway, I'm pressing on, and let's face it, millions of people have worse things than mine.' He drank Guinness, even though he did not like it, because he was told it was good for him, and started kneeling to say his prayers every night, even though he had never been especially religious, and for one specialist he compiled two handwritten pages of heart-rending questions: 'What is the end of the line? Paralysis of legs, arms and tongue? How will I eat if I cant swallow? Will there be great pain?' And finally the question that must have haunted him ever since he had been suddenly overwhelmed by the multiple blows of Hjördis's drinking, infidelity and coldness as well as Kristina's accident. 'Is there any chance,' he asked, 'that stress was the cause of the whole thing? Is the emotional over reaction (tearful feeling) anything to do with the original diagnosis of Dr Williams – Nervous Depression?' Deep in his heart he suspected that he had somehow brought all this on himself, like flowers pick themselves.

He found the new novel increasingly difficult to write, not only because it was hard to grip a pen but also because he lacked inspiration, and he thought it was so bad that he might abandon it and return the unearned part of the advance to his publishers. 'They gave me an *enormous* advance and I can't write a fucking word,' he told Roger Moore, 'but I've had the money for two years now and I've invested it very well, so even if I give it back to them I've made a profit.'

By now writing took him so long that he was dictating his letters, and he wrote to Phil Evans: 'We have lovely weather and gorgeous snow but no skiing for me unfortunately. Never mind. When I get depressed and think "Why me?" I so often think of you and I perk up immediately. You are a wonderful chum and I admire you very much.'

As usual he was worried about money and 'shattered' when Bill Staehelin sent him another huge bill, for Swiss fr. 169,086 for legal services during 1982, even though he was worth at least £20 million and Lo Scoglietto was stuffed with hundreds of thousands of pounds' worth of expensive paintings and dozens of antiques, including six Louis XV fauteuils, a sixteenth-century Venetian cassone, a pair of eighteenth-century rosewood tables, a pair of George III giltwood mirrors, a pair of large eighteenth-century girandoles, several rare commodes and a nineteenth-century Aubusson carpet. He told Jamie that he could no longer afford to employ the nurse until Jamie reminded him that he was incredibly rich and still living on just the interest on his fortune. 'He was even worried that he might not have enough to buy a wheelchair if he needed it!' said Fiona. Despite Hjördis's unending cruelty he worried that after his death she might after a few years not have enough to live on comfortably, and he instructed Staehelin to alter his will to give her a larger share should she somehow survive his children. 'She nagged him all the time about his will,' said Doreen Hawkins.

That last winter in Château d'Oex the Buckleys saw a lot of him even though they could barely decipher what he said. 'He would come round and paint until the turpentine overcame him,' Buckley told me. One of his last paintings started life in February with fluffy pink and white clouds that by the end of March had become grey and black. Yet he still saw humour in all sorts of things. He thought it was hilarious when someone he had not seen for years spotted him in Gstaad, stopped his car, and shouted, 'Niv, how the hell are you?'

'W-well,' he croaked, 'I've g-got this m-motor neu . . .'

'I've got a new motor too!' yelled the friend. 'A Mercedes!'

The trouble with stories like that, said Buckley, was that 'now he had to guard against abandoned laughter because it convulsed him'.

Many of Niv's friends and acquaintances realised that the end was near and urged Downing Street to give him a knighthood before it was too late. 'He deserved one,' said Alexander Walker, 'because of his general popularity and the fact that he represented a popular aspect of the English character, but I just got a formal reply.' One supplicant told me that he wrote to the Prime Minister, Margaret Thatcher, pointing out that Niv had 'had "a good war" and represented the essential values of Britishness in more films than anyone,' and that she replied that as soon as Niv paid all the taxes he had dodged by living abroad since 1946 she would go to see him in hospital and present him personally with a knighthood. When I asked Lady Thatcher in 2003 if this were true her assistant Mark Worthington replied that she 'does not recall having any discussion about an honour for Mr Niven' and that 'a number of non-residents received honours', so the story is 'highly unlikely'. Niv himself had been contemptuous of the British honours system when he had told the *Sunday Mirror* ten years previously that 'titles for film actors really are a lot of balls' because 'actors are vagabonds, despite the fancy trappings', but even so 'he would have liked a knighthood,' said Jamie, 'but he *was* a tax exile and didn't live in England.' Several of Niv's friends agreed, including two who were to be knighted themselves even though they had lived abroad for many years, and he would undoubtedly have been peeved had he known that Rex Harrison would be knighted six years later.

At the end of February Niv and Hjördis flew to London, where he spent ten days in the Wellington Hospital at St John's Wood under the name David Snook, maybe to cock one at the Press, who were now aware that he was seriously ill and following his every move. 'Lesley was very upset when he was there,' said Peter Watson, whose marriage to her was to end a few weeks later. 'Hjördis was quite possessive so Lesley said, "I'm just going to walk around the clinic. I want to be near him. You don't mind, do you?" She borrowed the car and just drove around in a circle. If Niven's friends were urging him to marry somebody else at the end of his life I think it must have been her. She really adored him and she'd have made him happy.' Five years later Lesley Watson married fifty-seven-year-old Viscount Hambleden, and she refused to talk to me about her friendship with Niv.

He made a farewell visit to the Connaught and 'when he was leaving it that last time,' his daughter-in-law Fernanda told me tearfully, 'they had to take him on a stretcher out the back so the Press wouldn't see, and he said, "Oh my God, I haven't paid my bill," and they said, "we're picking up this one." They all loved him.' And then she cried again.

He returned on 7 March to Château d'Oex, where Fiona Thyssen saw him as his life ebbed. 'It was terribly sad,' she said. 'His hands were always so cold and he would sit next to me and say, "Fiona, hold my hand," and I'd sit holding his hand to try to make him warm.' Soon he could no longer eat in public because he could not control his lips or saliva, or swallow properly, and he hated to be seen drooling. Richard Burton came to visit and told his wife, Sally: 'God, he's so wonderful. He's really ill but he's telling jokes about his awful condition.' John Mortimer turned up too. 'When I got to the house,' he wrote in his autobiography, 'Niven came downstairs, gently, almost soundlessly, like a ghost, and when he spoke only the faintest sounds came out of him. "What about a jar?" he greeted me. So we sat and drank white wine and he told me about all the cures he had tried ... We sat together for a long time, until the sun had vanished, and I could hardly hear him when he said: "I think it's having talked far too much during my life that's taken my voice away." ' George Greenfield said in his autobiography that Niv's voice eventually became 'a succession of dalek-like sounds'.

While Niv was in the Wellington Hospital, Hjördis met a doctor there who was to become a close friend of hers and turned up on the Côte d'Azur when they returned to Lo Scoglietto for the summer. Kristina and Fiona both disliked him. 'He was in his early forties and I think there was some Russian or Albanian blood in him,' said Kristina, 'but he spoke German and English fluently, though I didn't like it that he kept bringing bottles of drink for my mother.' Fiona told me: 'I think he was Eastern European. I thought he was dreadful and he may have been having something with Mummy. He was younger than her but she swore by him. He came to the house once with some medical equipment and tried to give Daddy some medication but the nurse said "no". The nurse told me that he was getting a big box of something sent from England for Daddy, and they were all by the pool at one point and Mummy said, "I'm going in with the doctor and we're going to open up the box," and a couple of hours later Daddy came in and the box was still sitting where it had been, which brought into question what they were doing. I didn't want to know. I *hated* him.' Doreen Hawkins once flew from Heathrow to Nice on the same plane as the doctor and as they emerged from the Customs area 'there was Hjördis waiting, and her face lit up when she saw him, and she wouldn't give me a lift to Cap Ferrat, which normally she would have. She said, "This is David's doctor," and I thought, "Well, he isn't actually," because I knew David's doctor. It was awful to see David at the end. He was losing the use of his hands and voice and said, "I keep thinking about Jack all the time. I know what it was like, now." '

Another of Hjördis's admirers was a forty-three-year-old Anglo-Italian painter who lived in Monaco, Andrew Vicari, who became her lover just before Niv died. 'I adored Hjördis,' he told me, 'and I'm proud to have been her lover. She was an extraordinary woman, very beautiful, spectacular, a sort of Viking, a Valkyrie. I went to Lo Scoglietto when David was alive and not yet ill and he regaled us with stories, but they seemed to be an ill-matched, incompatible couple. They were two of the nicest people I've ever met, but she was a *Swede*, and he *knew* that, and she went her own way, and she told me that he used to fuck around all over the place. She had very little sentimentality, whereas Niven was the king of sentiment. I don't know whether he was upset by my fling with her. Maybe. She also told me that he went to a special clinic in Switzerland where they injected him with lambs' testicles, like Charlie Chaplin.'

Niv tried to walk and swim every day with Katherine the nurse and enjoyed a regular evening drive with her around the Cap, but he was weakening fast and by now Hjördis had become blatantly cruel to him. She decided to have the house redecorated even though he was distressed by the strong smell of paint and the noise of the workmen. Soon he could barely walk, write, speak or swallow and 'she would get up from the table,' Ken Annakin told me, 'and say, "There he is. Look at him. He can't tell any of his stories now!" ' Roger Moore told me that a few weeks before Niv died his only exercise was to swim in the pool with a rubber ring: 'He came out and said to her, haltingly and croaking, "I – swam – two – lengths," and she said, "*Aren't* we a clever boy?" I wanted to kill her.' There were even 'stories of her swimming in the pool with younger men – helpers, chauffeurs, staff – and flaunting herself and flirting with them in front of Niv, who by then couldn't swim,' said David Bolton. 'She despised him, I suppose.' Yet despite her own infidelities, said Fiona, she became paranoid about Katherine Matthewson, accused her of having an affair with Niv, and once locked her out on the roof and went out leaving Niv on his own, bedridden. David was indeed very fond of Katherine and one of his last photographs shows him walking hand-in-hand with her at Lo Scoglietto. Even so, said April Clavell, 'he was still infatuated with Hjördis at the end, the way he used to look at her. I think there was genuine love there.'

Many of his friends came to say goodbye: the Bricusses, Willie Feilding, Bryan Forbes, the Manns, Roger Moore, John Mortimer. 'His clothes hung loosely on his wasted frame but the blue eyes still twinkled,' said Mann, and his wife Anastasia added, 'All he could do was to make these gurgling sounds, and when we left he stood at the gate and waved and waved until we were out of sight.' Feilding told me that 'at the end he couldn't have flowers around because the pollen made the MND worse, so I drew him lots of pictures of flowers which he stuck up.' Moore and Forbes flew to the Côte d'Azur together even though Hjördis tried to prevent them. 'He came downstairs in a blazer and silk scarf,' recalled Forbes, 'and to my shame I did what a lot of people do to people in wheelchairs: I started to talk very precisely and loudly to him, and almost his last words to me were when he said haltingly, "I may be dying but I'm not fucking deaf!" We all laughed.' Then, said Moore, 'Bryan spotted the pool through the window and said, "Getting plenty of swimming?" and Niv started to laugh, which turned into tears because there was no difference between laughter and crying.'

Both his sons flew over from America that summer and took him walking around the harbours at Beaulieu and St Jean. One evening a young woman approached them and said to Niv, 'I just want you to know how much joy you have given my family and me over the years. I want you to know that there are so many people who love you.' Several days later Jamie had to return to New York: 'I said goodbye for the last time,' he wrote in *You*. 'He was in the garden, sitting at a table in the sun, looking very small surrounded by the trees and flowers he had planted years before and loved so much ... When I said I would see him again soon, he shook his head sadly and said with great difficulty, "Bye, boy." ' He never saw him again.

On 12 June another old friend, Norma Shearer, died of pneumonia in California aged eighty-one, and Niv said his own goodbyes to friends whom he had not seen for years in letters that took him a couple of painful minutes to write each line. Just before he died he wrote 'a wonderful, pathetic letter' to Deborah Kerr, his 'Hilda', 'that made her cry and she had to go into another room to weep', said Peter Viertel. In it he warned her to beware of working too hard and taking on too much: 'dear old chum,' he wrote, 'don't stretch the elastic too far, because it snaps, and that is what has happened to me.' He wrote to Anthony Quayle that he had discovered what he had always suspected, that he was a coward – 'not true,' said Quayle, 'he had great courage.' He wrote to the boys' old nanny, 'Pinkie' Rogers, and to Phil Evans: 'I fear I am not in your league when it comes to facing up to things.' To help him face up to things a Dr M. M. Bhamgara of Bombay sent him a little story, 'Footprints', by an unknown author, that may have given him some comfort because he kept it until the end:

> One night a man had a dream. He dreamed he was walking along the beach with the Lord. Across the sky flashed scenes from his life. For each scene he noticed two sets of footprints in the sand: one belonging to him and the other to the Lord.
>
> When the last scene of his life flashed before him he looked back at the footprints in the sand. He noticed that many times along the path of his life there was only one set of footprints. He also noticed that it happened at the very lowest and saddest times of his life.
>
> This really bothered him and he questioned the Lord about it. 'Lord, you said that once I decided to follow you, you'd walk with me all the way. But I have noticed that during the most troublesome times in my life there is only one set of footprints. I don't understand why when I needed it most you would leave me.'

> The Lord replied, 'My son, My precious child, I love you and I would never leave you. During your times of trial and suffering, when you see only one set of footprints, it was then that I carried you.'

The tranquillity of Niv's last days on the Côte d'Azur was cruelly shattered when a paparazzo used a telescopic lens to photograph him in the garden at Lo Scoglietto and the harrowing picture, showing him skeletal and gasping for air, was published disgracefully in the English tabloid the *Sun* on 13 July. 'We got that son of a bitch photographer,' said R. J. Wagner. 'He's not taking pictures any more.' David was distraught and decided to fly with Katherine, who was now calling him Pop, to Château d'Oex, where there was less chance of such intrusions. Hjördis chose to stay behind, even though he had only a few more days to live, and he flew by Swissair because he thought he could not afford to charter a plane as usual. 'The nurse was kind but otherwise he was always alone,' said Heidi Donizetti. 'It was awful. He had nobody to cook for him so he sent a man in the jeep from Château d'Oex to the Olden and we prepared special soups with fish and nourishing things that he could take with a straw.' Fernanda Niven told me: 'When he was dying we were upset that he did not have the comfort he should have had.'

Every day David Bolton called in for physiotherapy and Niv tried to swim in Gunther Sachs's indoor pool at Gstaad, but he was failing fast and began to talk to Katherine about death, saying he would like to be reincarnated as a cat, and every night they knelt together and prayed. 'Often it was just him and her in the chalet,' said Bolton,

> and me popping in every day to give her moral support because she was a very young girl and she was there with this man and often overwhelmed by what was going on. The weight of his medical support fell very heavily on her and me, and we were the only people who could understand what he was saying. He was still clinging to every straw and trying to eat some porridgy mixture of rye and mash that he could hardly swallow but that some French quack doctor had said would cure him. By then he knew that he was dying but he never showed that he was afraid to die and was convinced to his last breath that he was going to conquer this. He was desperate and exploited by every cowboy under the sun right up to the very end. It gave him hope but sometimes I had to intervene as it was spoiling the quality of the little life he had left.

Years earlier Niv had told John Hurt that he was terrified of death and would never let himself suffer at the end: 'He said he had a little doctor in Switzerland who would come and put a needle in him if he ever got anything like exactly what he did get, but when it came to it he didn't. He couldn't bear the idea of ending it all.' Eleven years later Hjördis claimed that just before Niv left Lo Scoglietto for the last time he had begged her to commit suicide with him. In an interview with Victor Davis of the *Mail on Sunday* she claimed that Niv had croaked feebly, 'We'll dive into the pool hand-in-hand. Go down three times but only come up twice,' and that from then on she 'was careful to make sure he was never left on his own'. She added genially, 'Of course I knew he had other women. David was very wicked.'

Niv and Katherine were not entirely alone at the chalet. Fiona was there at times during his last two weeks and Hjördis's Swedish nephew, Michael Winstrad, arrived to help lift him. For some reason Hjördis disapproved of this. 'She rang from Cap Ferrat and told Michael his mother was dying and he ought to go back to Sweden,' Fiona told me. 'This upset both Michael and Daddy and was completely untrue. Who knows why she did it?' David Jr and Jamie were in the States, though Jamie was due to come to Switzerland in the first week of August. Kristina was in Geneva, and just before the end Fiona had to go down to her flat there too for a couple of days to get a driving licence.

On Tuesday, 26 July, as a sort of macabre dress rehearsal, Niv's butler Emile Andrey, his cook's husband, died. David too was sinking fast. On the Wednesday night he was deeply distressed to receive a drunken telephone call from Hjördis at Lo Scoglietto. 'She was very cruel about his illness and how he was no longer a man, and she flaunted her lovers in his face,' said David Bolton. 'She refused to come to Switzerland to care for him and he knew he did not have long to go. He had tears in his eyes and her photo on his desk, and he choked as he spoke due to the illness and the emotion. It was a very sad scene indeed.' Niv could not sleep that night and sat up late telling Katherine about Primmie. Bolton saw him again the following morning and 'he looked like a man who had had a minor heart attack. I sent him home, put him on oxygen, and sent for the local doctor.' Hjördis's cruelty had finally left him nothing to live for. Katherine telephoned David and Jamie in the States to ask if she should get him into hospital or put him on a respirator, but they told her to do neither because he had made them promise never to put him on any life support machine. That night once again she sat chatting with him until late and 'he suddenly began talking again about Primmie,' she told Morley, 'and how happy they had been together and how different his life would have been if she had not been killed.' He fell asleep at about 3 a.m. but when she looked in on him at 7 a.m. on the Friday morning, 29 July, he gave her a thumbs-up sign and she went to make some coffee. 'Just as I got to the bottom of the stairs I heard a sort of noise, as though he'd been trying to get out of bed, and when I got back into his room he had the oxygen mask off and gave me a big smile and held my hand and away he went. As quickly as that.' He was seventy-three.

'David chose a beautiful morning to die,' Bolton told me, 'one of those lovely Swiss Alp mornings: blue sky, very quiet, birds singing. Katherine rang me and I went straight over, and there beside his bed was a photo of Hjördis. Half an hour before he died he was still pondering why she was like she was. He was still so devoted to her and he'd never have left her. He thought, "Maybe if I love her a bit more, maybe if I try a bit harder, maybe I'll get the love that I want, and maybe tomorrow it'll be different." I think he was very much like that till his last breath. I think David was an old soul, a deep man tapped into something. I felt very sad. I had never seen the death of someone I loved so close before, and his body was still warm.'

Roger Moore and his daughter Deborah drove up immediately from St Paul de Vence and helped Fiona, Bolton, Alastair Forbes and a local Scots-born Swiss Reformed Church pastor, the Rev. Arnot Morrison, to organise the funeral for the Tuesday. Hjördis did not arrive until thirty-six hours later, on the Saturday afternoon, drunk, driven up from Cap Ferrat by Rainier's chauffeur. 'When she got out of the car,' said Moore, 'her wig was askew and she looked at me and said, slurring, "Are you here for the publicity?" I just left. His was the first death of a friend that really affected me, and I've not been able to watch any of his films since, but I couldn't stay for the funeral because I thought I'd probably end up killing her. Some of us were convinced that had he lived another month they would have been legally separated.' Robert Wagner also missed the funeral even though he was in London on his way to see Niv when he died. 'I didn't go because I was afraid that I'd really have lost it with her,' he said. 'I couldn't have handled it. I left flowers later at his resting place and never saw her again.'

David Jr and Jamie and his family arrived from America on the Saturday night. 'My father had told me that when he died he wanted me to go into his office and take out certain documents and destroy chequebooks,' Jamie told me. 'I had helped him with his will and was extremely familiar with the money that was in his bank accounts and stocks, and what was in safe deposit boxes, and I had all the keys. So I was in his office doing exactly what he had asked me to do – I was actually cutting up his Coutts & Co. cheques because I didn't want anyone to get their hands on them if the house was going to be full of people – and Hjördis came in drunk and said, "Counting the money already, Jamie?" I said, "Get out".'

Hjördis nearly did not bother to go to the funeral at all. 'Rainier told me that she wouldn't have come if he hadn't forced her,' said Alastair Forbes. Bolton, Fiona and Katherine had already chosen the suit in which Niv would be buried. 'It was his favourite colour, dark bottle green,' said Bolton, 'and we took it up to the hospital, and lying in the mortuary next to him was his butler, Monsieur Andrey, who had died three days earlier.'

The obituaries that weekend were long and warm. 'Last of the English Gentlemen,' the *Daily Mail* called him. 'The Perfect Gent,' said the *Daily Star*. 'A man of style,' said the *Sunday Telegraph*. The funeral was at 2.30 p.m. on 2 August in the little Anglican church, St Peter's, in the main street of Château d'Oex, where Kristina and Fiona had been baptised. Prince Rainier came, and Audrey Hepburn, who wept throughout the service, and Capucine, and hundreds of Press photographers, strangers, and almost every villager of Château d'Oex, where the shops were closed for the day in respect. And Kristina was convinced that her real mother was there too, heavily veiled to avoid recognition.

'It was a lovely service, very moving,' said Bolton, but 'Hjördis was a nightmare,' said Jamie. 'She refused to have my brother and myself sit at the same pew as her. Seriously! She was in the front with Rainier and my father's lawyer and her two children, and David, my wife, my girls and I were in another pew.' Willie Feilding was an usher and told me: 'David Jr rang me in a panic and said, "Get over here, the church is filling up with hoi-polloi," so I did and it was. I asked one woman to move and said, "You're in a seat reserved for Richard Attenborough, so please go up into the public gallery," and she said, "I'm not going up there. It's full of winos!" David would have loved that!' The most obvious wino was the widow, who was so drunk that she could barely stand and hung grimly onto Prince Rainier's arm throughout. She was 'pale and shaky', reported Ann Leslie pointedly in the *Daily Mail* the next day, 'smiling with a kind of feverish courage at the congregation.' Another witness told me: 'It was terrible. She had no right to be in a church in that condition.'

The church and coffin were piled with sunflowers and blooms of blue and gold, the colours of Stowe School. The biggest wreath, worthy of a

Mafia godfather's funeral, came from the porters at Heathrow Airport with a card that read: 'To the finest gentleman who ever walked through these halls. He made a porter feel like a king.' They sang Psalm 23, 'The Lord's My Shepherd', and 'To Be a Pilgrim', and listened to readings from St Paul's Epistle to the Corinthians and the Book of Revelation, and the great violinist Yehudi Menuhin and seven students from his music school in Gstaad played the *Andante* from Mendelssohn's 'Octet for Strings in F'. And Niv would have chuckled to know that there were five misprints in the three small pages of the funeral programme. Once again, for the last time, no one had bothered to correct the proofs.

Afterwards the cortège made its way to the little cemetery in the sunny valley just outside the village, surrounded by towering wooded mountains, just off the main road to Bulle, where so many onlookers jostled and hung over the wall that the Rev. Morrison bellowed at them to 'fuck off'. 'I got into trouble over that,' he said, 'but I think Niven would have been proud of me.' They buried him in a double plot, with space for Hjördis to join him one day.

Three months later, in October, there was a memorial service in Beverly Hills where Cary Grant, Gregory Peck and Peter Ustinov were among the mourners, and Fred Astaire, despite being eighty-four, unwell and unsteady, sat between David Jr and Jamie. 'I know that your father would have wanted me to sit here,' he told them. 'The only sad thing is that the roles should really have been reversed.' After the service 'Swifty' Lazar gave a lunch at which Lord Hanson was a guest. 'There were howls of laughter coming from one of the two tables,' Hanson recalled, 'where Cary Grant and all the usual suspects were sitting. They were remembering all his funny stories.'

In London on 27 October a thanksgiving service was held at the church of St Martin-in-the-Fields, where Niv had himself given the address at Peter Sellers's memorial service three years earlier. Trubshawe, now seventy-seven, was an usher and the congregation of 1200 included Prince Michael of Kent, the Duke of Marlborough, Margaret Duchess of Argyll, the Earl and Countess of Snowdon, Sir John Mills, Sir Richard Attenborough, Trevor Howard, David Frost, Joanna Lumley, and seventy-three-year-old Douglas Fairbanks, who had recently been knighted despite not being British. Graham Payn was there too, even though Niv had snubbed him so cruelly after Noël Coward's death, and the church was stuffed with stunningly beautiful flowers, and they sang Psalm 23 again as well as the gloriously rousing 'Onward Christian Soldiers!' and 'Jerusalem' – 'I will not cease from mental fight ... till we have built Jerusalem.'

Once again they heard the Alpha and Omega passage from the Book of Revelation, read this time by a frail, seventy-six-year-old Lord Olivier, and one of the prayers, by St Francis of Assisi, was especially appropriate because it encapsulated what Niv had striven to do for so long in his life, friendships and marriage:

Lord, make us instruments of thy peace.
Where there is hatred, let us sow love;
Where there is injury, pardon;
where there is discord, union;
where there is doubt, faith;
where there is despair, hope;
where there is darkness, light;
where there is sadness, joy;
Grant that we may seek
not so much to be consoled as to console;
not so much to be understood as to understand;
not so much to be loved as to love.

He had followed its precepts right to the very end. John Mortimer, who once described Niv's life brilliantly as 'Wodehouse with tears', gave the address, spoke of 'our joy in knowing a man who gave us so much happiness', and quoted Ernst Lubitsch's remark to Niv that 'nobody should try and play comedy unless they have a circus going on inside. Perhaps that was the secret of David's style. He seemed so elegant and cool, he was so handsome and well dressed, but inside the band was forever striking up, the children were clapping with delight and the clowns were always about to be brought on.' That was just what Niv had striven to do all his life – to make other people happier – and because of it he was deeply loved and widely mourned. In his own way, in the hearts of others, he had built Jerusalem.

Postscript

1983–2003

Niv had always told his sons he would leave them nothing in his will. On their twenty-first birthdays he gave them $21,000 each – '$1000 for each year you've been a pain in the ass' – but after that, he warned them, they would get nothing. 'Nobody left me anything,' he told the *Daily Express* in 1960, and 'one day I realised that the saddest people I knew were my friends with money they'd inherited. They had no drive, no ambition, no reason. All they had was money that some rich daddy had been idiot enough to leave behind. So I decided to spend every penny I earn. I don't want to be the richest man in the graveyard.'

He was of course undoubtedly the richest man in the graveyard at Château d'Oex. Beside him lie his butler and cook, the Andreys, and all around are the poor of the valley: J. P. and Geneviève Exchaquet at his feet, Benjamin and Annesley Chance at his head. Swiss wills are not made public – a year before he died he was still insisting to the French taxman that he was a Swiss resident and Lo Scoglietto was only 'rented for holidays' – but his books had sold more than 10 million copies and had earned him maybe as much as £30 million in modern terms, and he left more than £20 million and maybe as much as £30 million, which would be worth more than twice as much today. In the end he loved his sons too much to cut them out. They had in any case proved that they could make their own way in the world – both were already rich in their own right – and they and the girls each inherited about £3 million at first. The properties and most of the rest of the money were left in a trust to give Hjördis homes and an income until she died, but the trust was controlled by the boys and when Hjördis died in 1997 they and the girls inherited about another £5 million each. Niv also left Grizel £60,000 and Madame Andrey £12,500.

In October the family and friends set up a fund in his name to help research into MND, and a curly granite Scottish cross inscribed with his name and dates was erected on his grave, where the Bricusses had a stunning experience when they went to pay their respects that Christmas of 1983. 'Let's have one last picture of you with Niv,' said Leslie, so Evie stood behind the cross with her arms on it. 'I held up the camera,' he told me, 'and into the frame flew a multi-coloured hot-air balloon going down the valley: not only was it *The Moon's a Balloon*, it was also *Around the World in Eighty Days*. It was a lovely photo. I told Niv Jr about it and he shivered.'

Under Swiss law Niv may lie in his grave only until 2047, fifty years after Hjördis's death, when his body will be dug up and the space used for someone else unless the Nivens' lawyers can find some way to let him rest in peace. If his spirit is eventually so rudely disturbed it should find a home in his old chalet just up the road. 'I feel ghosts here,' said Coco Wyers, who bought the house with her husband after Hjördis's death. 'When we first came to look around the chalet his Oscar was still here, and I have a strong feeling that he is happy we are Dutch and not German! We have changed the house a lot. Hjördis's bedroom was very grubby and messy.' Sue Bongard told me that after Hjördis's death she was shown round the chalet 'and in her bathroom there were eight or ten wigs on styrofoam heads. It was quite spooky.'

After Niv's death Hjördis avoided the chalet at first, lived as a recluse at Lo Scoglietto and drank herself into a stupor every day, which caused numerous rows with Fiona and eventually a permanent rift. But more than a year later Hjördis finally admitted that she needed help and checked into a French clinic for alcoholics – encouraged, I am told, by the doctor friend who 'hung around for a while', said Fiona, and was working in 2003 in London with a medical team called Company Health, though he declined to respond to my numerous requests for an interview. For a while Hjördis seemed miraculously cured, as though somehow she had been liberated by Niv's death. She took up with a gay couple, helped with an AIDS foundation, and was coaxed out for dinners and parties by Andrew Vicari, who continued their affair for a couple of years until they had a row and never saw each other again. Vicari eventually became even richer than Niv after he was appointed the Saudi royal family's and government's official painter, claimed to be the world's highest-paid living artist and was listed in the *Sunday Times* Rich List in 2002 as worth £40 million. 'She was a hell of a nice woman,' insisted Vicari when I met him. 'We all loved her, and people who didn't were just jealous. She loved art and painting and bought several of mine.' His memories of her are irreconcilably different from those of almost everyone else, though I did find three women who became friends of hers after Niv died and who all said she was very pleasant and not drinking at all.

One was forty-six-year-old Jill Hulton, who met Hjördis in 1986, later married the Duke of Hamilton and told me: 'She was charming. Often I'd stay at Lo Scoglietto for the weekend and she'd always send the car to collect me, and when I left Angus [*the Duke*] she lent me her flat in Mayfair. She wasn't drinking at all when I knew her, or if she was it was secretly. She was *nice*. She always spoke about David with great affection and respect, she talked about the first wife, and was very upset about the rift between her and the two sons.' Another titled lady who met and took to Hjördis after Niv's death, Lady Christopher Thynn, said, 'I liked her very much. She was lonely and rather sad and obviously missed David and adored him, but she was charming and very friendly.' Another of Jill Hamilton's friends, Roxie Clayton, told me that Hjördis 'was sweet and spoke fondly about David'.

Eventually, though, she lost her battle with alcoholism and became a heavy drinker again, strange and silent, glaring at people in shops. 'When she went into a village shop she was often drunk and difficult and everybody left,' said Sue Bongard. When the Buckleys and the Bricusses heard how she had treated Niv at the end they would have nothing more to do with her, and she tended to alienate most of her other old friends, even Doreen Hawkins, April Clavell and Betty Bacall, who said, 'I saw her several times in London and about a year before she died she wanted me to stay at Cap Ferrat but she was *horrible* to me for those two days, *so* rude.' She told Vicari, Sue Bongard and others that she was going to marry Prince Rainier and the story was splashed all over the newspapers. Jamie asked Rainier if this were true and the prince replied, 'I don't know where the *hell* that story came from.'

The relationship between Hjördis and the boys became worse than ever. 'Because of the trust we had to have a family meeting in Switzerland every year,' said Jamie, 'and it became so cantankerous and acrimonious that my wife stopped coming with me and said, "I refuse to see that woman. She's just a horrible person."' Hjördis thought that the boys 'were out to get her', said Fiona, but then Hjördis also became paranoid because she thought that Kristina and Fiona were trying to kill her by putting oil around the swimming pool so that she would slip. Eventually she died of natural causes in hospital in Switzerland – a stroke – on Christmas Eve 1997, aged seventy-eight, an insult to all those doctors who insist that a woman should not drink more than two small glasses of wine a day. 'This is not kind,' said Billie More, 'but when Hjördis died I can't think of a single soul who was sorry.' She left ninety per cent of her estate to Kristina, who had always been her favourite, and just ten per cent to Fiona, who had often made it plain she disapproved of her drinking and her treatment of Niv. Hjördis had forbidden the girls to bury her in the grave beside him, which still lies empty, the only double grave at Château d'Oex with just one lonely occupant. 'I want to be free,' she told Kristina, and so she was cremated and her ashes scattered in the Mediterranean at Lo Scoglietto.

David Jr, Jamie, Doubleday and Hamish Hamilton considered whether to publish Niv's unfinished novel about the writer with MND, or have someone else complete it, but decided against after asking Bill Buckley to read it as well. 'He'd written more than 50,000 words,' said Jamie, 'but the manuscript wasn't very good although some of it was rather poignant. It was very honourable and gracious of Nelson Doubleday not to publish it because they had paid my father a huge advance and could have insisted.'

David Jr gave up making movies, enjoyed a string of love affairs with beautiful women and finally married an actress, Barbara Alexander, when he was fifty, in 1993, but they divorced after five years. In 2000 he was married again, aged fifty-seven, to Beatrice Morrison, a rich thirty-nine-year-old divorcée, and still lives in Hollywood, where in 2002 his main occupation was working voluntarily with a road safety charity called See a Child, Save a Child. He has no children of his own – 'I don't have the patience for small children,' he told Vicky Ward of the *Daily Mail* in 1998 – but he does have four step-children.

Jamie became the American boss of the scent and soap makers Floris, ran a company in Houston for five years in the 1990s, and then joined Sotheby's in New York, where he is now a Vice-Chairman. He and Fernanda bought a farm on Long Island and a house in the Dominican Republic but separated in 1995, divorced, and in 2002 he was living alone in New York.

Neither Kristina nor Fiona has married and both are shy, nervous, unsure of themselves, estranged from each other, and have not seen the boys for a long time, yet both could not have been nicer or more helpful to me. It seems a shame but perhaps inevitable that the family has not kept in touch with each other. Kristina, who is now forty-two, took up singing, wrote some poems, had a son, Michael, by the Spanish butler at Lo Scoglietto in 1990, and in 2003 was living with Michael in Lausanne and planning to marry an Italian from Venice, Bernard di Matteo.

Fiona left Geneva University and went to Boston University in 1985, obtained a Bachelor's degree in Professional Studies, a Master's degree in Business Administration, and in1994 went on to study for a Ph.D. on 'the impact of electronic commerce on supply chain management', but was often understandably sidetracked and still working on her thesis in 2003 in Boston where she was lecturing in statistics at the university and was a part-time administrator and student counsellor. 'Dad was very proud of Fiona,' said David Jr. 'He would love her to get a Ph.D.' Now forty, she too has had a son, Ryan, now five, by a black lover who left her when she told him she was pregnant. 'My father would not have disapproved of that so long as Fiona is happy,' said Jamie. 'He was more liberal than conservative and his primary goal was that they would both be happy.'

Grizel created the bronze trophy of a woman, the Bessie, that is awarded annually in Britain to the winner of the £30,000 Orange Prize for women's fiction, and was still alive in 2003, aged ninety-six and living in an old people's home in London, where she was bright, perky, friendly and with a disconcerting resemblance to Niv but too vague to handle her own affairs, so that her lawyer has power of attorney.

Lo Scoglietto, where Hjördis lived on for many years although it was far too big for her on her own, was sold – asking price £15 million – to a New Zealand businessman in 1997, much against her wishes so that she tried to obstruct the estate agents at every turn. Eventually the Niven trustees bought her a smaller house nearby – 'the only house on Cap Ferrat without a view of the ocean,' chuckled David Jr – but she died before she could move. The new owner of Lo Scoglietto, Richard Chandler, has altered the house completely and renamed it La Fleur du Cap, but it is still painted pink, and the pretty little tiled square on the crowded public footpath right outside the front door was renamed the Place David Niven in 1990, though a plaque claims incorrectly that Niv was born in 1909 not 1910. Even after his death he was stalked by misprints and inaccuracies. And across the bay in 2002 Niv's favourite restaurant in Beaulieu, the African Queen, was still displaying an old poster advertising the film with Humphrey Bogart and Katharine Hepburn, the one in which he so nearly starred himself.

In California the Pink House is still pink too and owned by Whoopi

Goldberg, but there are six other houses on what was Niv's property, several of them between the Pink House and Douglas Fairbanks's old mansion next door, which now belongs to Steven Spielberg.

In October 1985 Niv was given the rare accolade of having his face and signature printed on one of a set of postage stamps to mark British Film Year along with Charlie Chaplin, Alfred Hitchcock, Vivien Leigh and Peter Sellers. But how good an actor was he really?

'He was superb,' enthused Patrick Macnee, 'one of the great light comedians. I'd rate him with Cary Grant and Rex Harrison, and he didn't despise acting at all: he had enormous respect for it.'

'He was a wonderful actor,' said Betty Bacall. 'He wasn't a lightweight at all.'

'He was a very fine actor and a total professional,' said Robert Wagner.

'Niv was a damned good actor, a joy to play scenes with, and he listened and gave plenty in return,' said Roger Moore.

John Mills admitted that Niv 'couldn't play Hamlet but he was perfect for light comedy and played it beautifully', and David Jr admitted that 'you wonder why on earth he did some of his movies but even in bad films he was very good.'

'He wasn't a great actor,' said Bryan Forbes, 'but he was a great screen personality, deeply loved, and he never gave a *bad* performance. He never really acted: he was a film star, and there's nothing wrong with that.'

Roddy Mann felt that Niv 'wasn't really an actor at all in the normal sense. That's what he said himself. He knew that he was not a major actor, and in all the hundreds of hours I spent with him he never talked about movies, certainly not his own. I don't think he even liked movies a lot, and he never watched his own because he said he always thought of himself as a young, rather attractive man and yet there was this creepy old character up on the screen. But he was a real pro. He could be as drunk as a skunk the night before but he wouldn't show it and he'd always be right on time.'

Jamie, too, had no illusions about his father's acting. 'I don't think he *loved* acting,' he told me. 'Clark Gable used to tell him, "Just remember it's a nine to five job and you're no different to anyone else: you just go to work. If you ever let it get bigger than what it is it'll ruin you," and there was something of that in my father. He was a consummate professional, would do a good job, and the benefits were enormous, but I never thought he couldn't wait to get at the next movie and do a great job with that. But he was a better actor than he was given credit for. There were some movies in which he was truly brilliant: *Separate Tables*,

Paper Tiger, The Guns of Navarone, Bonjour Tristesse, Dawn Patrol.'

Even so, although Niv made ninety-one movies, 'very few of them made any noticeable contribution to the art of the cinema,' wrote the film critic Barry Norman in *The Film Greats*. 'He was indeed less an actor than a great screen personality; most of the time he simply played himself but that, granted his small but finely honed talent as a light comedian, was enough to save a multitude of mediocre films from total disaster.' And Norman concluded, 'I suspect that generations of movie-goers will continue to watch his films, bad though many of them are, simply because the very presence of Niven makes them feel better.'

What a glorious achievement – to have made millions of people feel better. I suspect that when you first glanced at the jacket of this book it gave you a warm glow and maybe a happy smile. To leave such a legacy is rare, maybe unique, and the man who did it deserves to be remembered and celebrated, even though the moon is not after all a balloon and flowers just don't pick themselves.

Filmography

ALL THE WINNERS (London Film Company, 1932)
Allan Jeayes, Muriel George, Cyril Chamberlain. Produced and directed by Bunty Watts.

WITHOUT REGRET (Paramount, 1935)
Elissa Landi, Paul Cavanagh, Frances Drake, Kent Taylor. Produced by B. P. Fineman; directed by Harold Young.

BARBARY COAST (Goldwyn–UA, 1935)
Miriam Hopkins, Edward G. Robinson, Joel McCrea, Walter Brennan, Brian Donlevy. Produced by Samuel Goldwyn; directed by Howard Hawks.

A FEATHER IN HER HAT (Columbia, 1935)
Pauline Lord, Basil Rathbone, Louis Hayward, Billie Burke. Produced by Everett Riskin; directed by Alfred Santell.

SPLENDOUR (Goldwyn–UA, 1935)
Miriam Hopkins, Joel McCrea, Paul Cavanagh, Helen Westley, Billie Burke. Produced by Samuel Goldwyn; directed by Elliot Nugent.

ROSE MARIE (MGM, 1936)
Jeanette MacDonald, Nelson Eddy, Reginald Owen, James Stewart. Produced by Hunt Stromberg; directed by W. S. Van Dyke.

PALM SPRINGS (Paramount, 1936). USA title, *Palm Springs Affair.*
Frances Langford, Guy Standing, Smith Ballen, Ernest Cossart. Produced by Walter Wanger; directed by Aubrey Scotto.

DODSWORTH (Goldwyn–UA, 1936)
Walter Huston, Ruth Chatterton, Paul Lukas, Mary Astor. Produced by Samuel Goldwyn; directed by William Wyler.

THANK YOU, JEEVES (20th Century-Fox, 1936)
Arthur Treacher, Virginia Fields. Produced by Sol M. Wurtzel; directed by Arthur Greville.

THE CHARGE OF THE LIGHT BRIGADE (Warner Bros, 1936)
Errol Flynn, Olivia de Havilland, Patric Knowles, Nigel Bruce. Produced by Hal B. Wallis; directed by Michael Curtiz.

BELOVED ENEMY (Goldwyn–UA, 1936)
Merle Oberon, Brian Aherne, Karen Morley, Jerome Cowan. Produced by George Haight; directed by H. C. Potter.

WE HAVE OUR MOMENTS (Universal, 1937)
Sally Eilers, James Dunn, Mischa Auer, Thurston Hall. Produced by Edmund Grainger; directed by Alfred L. Werker.

THE PRISONER OF ZENDA (Selznick–UA, 1937)
Ronald Colman, Madeleine Carroll, Douglas Fairbanks Jnr, Mary Astor, C. Aubrey Smith, Raymond Massey. Produced by David O. Selznick; directed by John Cromwell and W. S. Van Dyke.

DINNER AT THE RITZ (New World–20th Century-Fox, 1937)
Annabella, Paul Lukas, Romney Brent, Francis L. Sullivan. Produced by Robert Kane; directed by Harold Schuster.

BLUEBEARD'S EIGHTH WIFE (Paramount, 1938)
Claudette Colbert, Gary Cooper, Edward Everett Horton. Produced and directed by Ernst Lubitsch.

FOUR MEN AND A PRAYER (20th Century-Fox, 1938)
Loretta Young, Richard Greene, George Sanders, C. Aubrey Smith. Produced by Kenneth MacGowan; directed by John Ford.

THREE BLIND MICE (20th Century-Fox, 1938)
Loretta Young, Joel McCrea, Stuart Erwin, Marjorie Weaver. Produced by Raymond Griffiths; directed by William A. Seiter.

THE DAWN PATROL (Warner Bros, 1938)
Errol Flynn, Basil Rathbone, Donald Crisp. Produced by Hal B. Wallis; directed by Edmund Goulding.

WUTHERING HEIGHTS (Goldwyn–UA, 1939)
Merle Oberon, Laurence Olivier, Flora Robson, Donald Crisp, Hugh Williams. Produced by Samuel Goldwyn, directed by William Wyler.

BACHELOR MOTHER (RKO Radio, 1939)
Ginger Rogers, Charles Coburn, Frank Albertson, E. E. Clive. Produced by B. G. De Sylva; directed by Garson Kanin.

THE REAL GLORY (Goldwyn–UA, 1939)
Gary Cooper, Andrea Leeds, Reginald Owen, Broderick Crawford. Produced by Samuel Goldwyn; directed by Henry Hathaway.

ETERNALLY YOURS (Wanger–UA, 1939)
Loretta Young, Hugh Herbert, Billie Burke, C. Aubrey Smith, Broderick Crawford, Zasu Pitts. Produced by Walter Wanger; directed by Tay Garnett.

RAFFLES (Goldwyn–UA, 1939)
Olivia de Havilland, May Whitty, E. E. Clive. Produced by Samuel Goldwyn; directed by Sam Wood and William Wyler.

THE FIRST OF THE FEW (British Aviation Pictures, 1942). USA title *Spitfire*.
Leslie Howard, Rosamund John, Roland Culver. Produced and directed by Leslie Howard.

THE WAY AHEAD (Two Cities, 1944)
Raymond Huntley, William Hartnell, Stanley Holloway, John Laurie, Peter Ustinov, Tessie O'Shea. Produced by John Sutro and Norman Walker; directed by Carol Reed.

A MATTER OF LIFE AND DEATH (J. Arthur Rank, 1945)
Roger Livesey, Raymond Massey, Kim Hunter, Marius Goring, Richard Attenborough. Produced, directed and written by Michael Powell and Emeric Pressburger.

THE PERFECT MARRIAGE (Paramount, 1946)
Loretta Young, Eddie Albert, Virginia Field, Charles Ruggles, Zasu Pitts. Produced by Hal Wallis; directed by Lewis Allen.

MAGNIFICENT DOLL (Universal Pictures, 1946)
Ginger Rogers, Burgess Meredith, Horace McNally. Produced by Jack H. Skirball and Bruce Manning; directed by Frank Borzage.

THE OTHER LOVE (Enterprise–UA, 1947)
Barbara Stanwyck, Richard Conte, Gilbert Roland. Produced by David Lewis; directed by André de Toth.

THE BISHOP'S WIFE (Goldwyn–RKO, 1947)
Cary Grant, Loretta Young, Gladys Cooper, Elsa Lanchester. Produced by Samuel Goldwyn; directed by Henry Koster.

BONNIE PRINCE CHARLIE (London Films, 1948)
Margaret Leighton, Jack Hawkins, Finlay Currie, John Laurie. Produced by Edward Black; directed by Anthony Kimmins.

ENCHANTMENT (Goldwyn–UA, 1948)
Teresa Wright, Evelyn Keyes, Farley Granger. Produced by Samuel Goldwyn; directed by Irving Reis.

A KISS IN THE DARK (Warner Bros, 1949)
Jane Wyman, Victor Moore, Broderick Crawford. Produced by Jack L. Warner; directed by Delmer Davies.

THE ELUSIVE PIMPERNEL (London Films, 1949). USA title, *The Fighting Pimpernel*.
Margaret Leighton, Cyril Cusack, Jack Hawkins. Produced by Alexander Korda and Samuel Goldwyn; directed by Michael Powell and Emeric Pressburger.

A KISS FOR CORLISS (Strand–UA, 1949)
Shirley Temple, Tom Tully, Virginia Welles. Produced by Colin Miller; directed by Richard Wallace.

THE TOAST OF NEW ORLEANS (MGM, 1950)
Kathryn Grayson, Mario Lanza, J. Carrol Naish, Rita Moreno. Produced by Joe Pasternak; directed by Norman Taurog.

HAPPY GO LOVELY (Associated British–RKO, 1950)
Vera-Ellen, Cesar Romero, Bobby Howes. Produced by Marcel Helman; directed by Bruce Humberstone.

SOLDIERS THREE (MGM, 1951)
Stewart Granger, Walter Pidgeon, Robert Newton, Cyril Cusack. Produced by Pandro S. Berman; directed by Tay Garnett.

APPOINTMENT WITH VENUS (British Film Makers, 1951). USA title, *Island Rescue.*
Glynis Johns, Barry Jones, Kenneth More. Produced by Betty E. Box; directed by Ralph Thomas.

THE LADY SAYS NO (Ross–Stillman–UA, 1951)
Joan Caulfield, James Robertson Justice, Lenore Lonergan. Produced by Frank Ross and John Stillman Jr; directed by Frank Ross.

THE MOON IS BLUE (Holmby–UA, 1953)
William Holden, Maggie McNamara, Tom Tully, Dawn Adams. Produced by Otto Preminger and F. Hugh Herbert; directed by Otto Preminger.

THE LOVE LOTTERY (Ealing Studios, 1953)
Peggy Cummins, Anne Vernon, Herbert Lom, Gordon Jackson, Felix Aylmer. Produced by Monja Danischewsky; directed by Charles Crichton.

HAPPY EVER AFTER (Associated British, 1954). USA title, *Tonight's the Night.*
Yvonne de Carlo, Barry Fitzgerald, George Cole. Produced and directed by Mario Zampi.

CARRINGTON, VC (Romulus Films, 1954). USA title, *Court Martial.*
Margaret Leighton, Noelle Middleton, Laurence Naismith, Raymond Francis. Produced by Teddy Baird; directed by Anthony Asquith.

THE KING'S THIEF (MGM, 1955)
Ann Blyth, Edmund Purdom, George Sanders, Roger Moore. Produced by Edwin H. Knopf; directed by Robert Z. Leonard.

THE BIRDS AND THE BEES (Gomalco–Paramount, 1956)
George Gobel, Mitzi Gaynor, Reginald Gardiner. Produced by Paul Jones; directed by Norman Taurog.

AROUND THE WORLD IN EIGHTY DAYS (Michael Todd–UA, 1956)
Cantinflas, Robert Newton, Shirley MacLaine, Charles Boyer, Ronald Colman, Noël Coward, Marlene Dietrich, John Gielgud, Frank Sinatra and

numerous other stars. Produced by Michael Todd; directed by Michael Anderson.

THE SILKEN AFFAIR (Dragon Films, 1956)
Genevieve Page, Ronald Squire, Wilfrid Hyde-White, Richard Wattis. Produced by Douglas Fairbanks and Fred Feldkamp; directed by Roy Kellino.

THE LITTLE HUT (MGM, 1957)
Ava Gardner, Stewart Granger, Walter Chiari, Finlay Currie. Produced by F. Hugh Herbert and Mark Robson; directed by Mark Robson.

OH, MEN! OH, WOMEN! (20th Century-Fox, 1957)
Dan Dailey, Ginger Rogers, Tony Randall. Produced, directed and written by Nunnally Johnson.

MY MAN GODFREY (Universal Pictures, 1957)
June Allyson, Jessie Royce Landis, Robert Keith, Eva Gabor. Produced by Ross Hunter; directed by Henry Koster.

BONJOUR TRISTESSE (Columbia Pictures, 1957)
Deborah Kerr, Jean Seberg, Mylene Demongeot, Juliette Greco, Walter Chiari, Martita Hunt. Produced and directed by Otto Preminger.

SEPARATE TABLES (Clifton–UA, 1958)
Deborah Kerr, Rita Hayworth, Wendy Hiller, Burt Lancaster, Gladys Cooper, Felix Aylmer. Produced by Harold Hecht, James Hill and Burt Lancaster; directed by Delbert Mann.

ASK ANY GIRL (MGM, 1959)
Shirley MacLaine, Gig Young, Rod Taylor. Produced by Joe Pasternak; directed by Charles Walters.

HAPPY ANNIVERSARY (Fields Productions Inc–UA, 1959)
Mitzi Gaynor, Carl Reiner, Loring Smith. Produced by Ralph Fields; directed by David Miller.

PLEASE DON'T EAT THE DAISIES (MGM, 1960)
Doris Day, Janis Paige, Richard Haydn. Produced by Joe Pasternak; directed by Charles Walters.

THE GUNS OF NAVARONE (Open Road Films–Columbia, 1961)
Gregory Peck, Anthony Quinn, Stanley Baker, Anthony Quayle, Richard Harris. Produced by Carl Foreman and Cecil Ford; directed by J. Lee Thompson.

THE BEST OF ENEMIES (De Laurentis–Columbia, 1961). Italian title, *I Due Nemici*.
Alberto Sordi, Michael Wilding, Harry Andrews. Produced by Dino De Laurentiis; directed by Guy Hamilton.

THE ROAD TO HONG KONG (Melnor–UA, 1962)
Bing Crosby, Bob Hope, Joan Collins, Dorothy Lamour, Robert Morley, Frank Sinatra, Dean Martin, Peter Sellers. Produced and directed by Norman Panama.

THE CAPTIVE CITY (Maxima Films, 1962) USA title, *The Conquered City*. Italian title, *La Città Prigioniera*.
Ben Gazzara, Michael Craig, Martin Balsam, Lea Massari, Daniela Rocca. Produced and directed by Joseph Anthony.

THE SHORTEST DAY (Titanus, 1962). Italian title, *Il Giorno Più Corto*.
Marcello Mastrianni, Stewart Granger, Walter Pidgeon, Jean-Paul Belmondo. Directed by Sergio Corbucci.

GUNS OF DARKNESS (Cavalcade–Warners, 1962)
Leslie Caron, James Robertson Justice. Produced by Ben Kadish and Thomas Clyde; directed by Anthony Asquith.

55 DAYS AT PEKING (Bronston–Allied Artists, 1963)
Charlton Heston, Ava Gardner, Robert Helpmann, Flora Robson, Elizabeth Sellars. Produced by Samuel Bronston; directed by Nicholas Ray.

THE PINK PANTHER (Mirisch–UA, 1964)
Peter Sellers, Robert Wagner, Capucine, Claudia Cardinale, Brenda de Banzie, John le Mesurier, Michael Trubshawe. Produced by Martin Jurow; directed by Blake Edwards.

BEDTIME STORY (Lankershim–Pennebaker Universal, 1964)
Marlon Brando, Shirley Jones, Dody Goodman, Aram Stephen. Produced by Stanley Shapiro; directed by Ralph Levy.

WHERE THE SPIES ARE (MGM, 1965)
Françoise Dorleac, Cyril Cusack, John le Mesurier, Nigel Davenport. Produced by Val Guest and Steven Pallos; directed by Val Guest.

LADY L (Concordia–MGM, 1965)
Sophia Loren, Paul Newman, Claud le Dauphin, Phillipe Noiret, Cecil Parker, Peter Ustinov. Produced by Carlo Ponti; directed by Peter Ustinov.

EYE OF THE DEVIL (Filmways–MGM, 1966)
Deborah Kerr, Donald Pleasence, Edward Mulhare, Flora Robson, Emlyn Williams, Sharon Tate, David Hemmings, John le Mesurier. Produced by Martin Ransohoff and John Calley; directed by J. Lee Thompson.

CASINO ROYALE (Famous Artists–Columbia, 1967)
Peter Sellers, Ursula Andress, Orson Welles, Woody Allen, Deborah Kerr, William Holden, John Huston, George Raft. Produced by Charles K. Feldman and Jerry Bresler; directed by John Huston, Ken Hughes, Val Guest, Robert Parrish, Joe McGrath, Richard Talmadge and Anthony Squire.

THE EXTRAORDINARY SEAMAN (MGM, 1968)
Faye Dunaway, Alan Alda, Mickey Rooney. Produced by Edward Lewis and John H. Cushingham; directed by John Frankenheimer.

PRUDENCE AND THE PILL (20th Century Fox, 1968)
Deborah Kerr, Robert Coote, Judy Geeson, Keith Michell, Edith Evans. Produced by Kenneth Harper and Ronald Kahn; directed by Fielder Cook.

THE IMPOSSIBLE YEARS (Marten–MGM, 1968)
Lola Albright, Chad Everett, Ozzie Nelson, Christina Ferrare, Jeff Cooper. Produced by Lawrence Weingarten; directed by Michael Gordon.

BEFORE WINTER COMES (Windward–Columbia, 1969)
Topol, Anna Karina, John Hurt, Anthony Quayle. Produced by Robert Emmett Ginna; directed by J. Lee Thompson.

THE BRAIN (Gaumont International–Paramount, 1969). French title, *Le Cerveau.*
Jean-Paul Belmondo, Bourvil, Eli Wallach. Produced by Alain Poire; directed by Gérard Oury.

THE STATUE (Shaftel, 1970)
Virna Lisi, Robert Vaughn, Ann Bell, John Cleese, Tim Brooke-Taylor, Hugh Burden. Produced by Joseph Shaftel and Anis Nohra; directed by Rod Amateau.

KING, QUEEN, KNAVE (Wolper Pictures, 1972). German title, *Herzbube.*
Gina Lollobrigida, John Moulder Brown, Mario Adorf. Produced by David L. Wolper; directed by Jerzy Skolimowski.

VAMPIRA (World Film Services, 1973)
Teresa Graves, Peter Bayliss, Jennie Linden, Nicky Henson, Bernard Bresslaw, Freddie Jones. Produced by Jack H. Weiner; directed by Clive Donner.

THE CANTERVILLE GHOST (HTV, 1974)
James Whitmore, Lynne Frederick, Flora Robson. Produced by Timothy Burrill; directed by Walter Miller.

PAPER TIGER (Lloyd–MacLean Films, 1975)
Toshiro Mifune, Hardy Kruger, Ando, Ronald Fraser. Produced by Euan Lloyd; directed by Ken Annakin.

NO DEPOSIT, NO RETURN (Walt Disney, 1975)
Barbara Feldon, Don Knotts, Darren McGavin, Vic Tayback. Produced by Ron Miller and Joseph McEveety; directed by Norman Tokar.

MURDER BY DEATH (Columbia, 1976)
Truman Capote, Peter Falk, Alec Guinness, Elsa Lanchester, Peter Sellers, Maggie Smith. Produced by Ray Stark; directed by Robert Moore.

CANDLESHOE (Walt Disney, 1977)
Leo McKern, Jodie Foster, Helen Hayes. Produced by Ron Miller; directed by Norman Tokar.

DEATH ON THE NILE (EMI, 1978)
Peter Ustinov, Bette Davis, Mia Farrow, Maggie Smith. Produced by John Brabourne and Richard Goodwin; directed by John Guillermin.

ESCAPE TO ATHENA (ITC Entertainment, 1979)
Roger Moore, Telly Savalas, Stefanie Powers, Claudia Cardinale, Elliott Gould. Produced by David Niven Jr and Jack Weiner; directed by George Pan Cosmatos.

A NIGHTINGALE SANG IN BERKELEY SQUARE (S. B. Fisz Productions, 1979)
Richard Jordan, Oliver Tobias, Gloria Grahame, Elke Sommer. Produced by S. Benjamin Fisz; directed by Ralph Thomas.

A MAN CALLED INTREPID (Lorimer Productions Ltd, 1979)
Michael York, Barbara Hershey, Peter Gilmore, Nigel Stock, Flora Robson, Gayle Hunnicutt. Produced by Intrepid Productions; directed by Peter Carter.

ROUGH CUT (Paramount, 1980)
Burt Reynolds, Lesley-Anne Down, Timothy West, Patrick Magee, Joss Ackland. Produced by David Merrick; directed by Don Siegel.

THE SEA WOLVES (Uniprom International, 1980)
Gregory Peck, Roger Moore, Trevor Howard, Barbara Kellerman, Patrick Macnee. Produced by Euan Lloyd; directed by Andrew V. McLaglen.

BETTER LATE THAN NEVER (working title, '*Ménage à Trois*) (Golden Harvest, 1981)
Maggie Smith, Art Carney, Lionel Jeffries. Produced by David Niven Jnr and Jack Haley Jnr; directed by Bryan Forbes.

THE TRAIL OF THE PINK PANTHER (MGM–United Artists, 1982)
Peter Sellers, Robert Wagner, Capucine, Joanna Lumley, Herbert Lom, Graham Stark, Burt Kwouk. Produced and directed by Blake Edwards.

CURSE OF THE PINK PANTHER (MGM–United Artists, 1983)
Robert Wagner, Herbert Lom, Joanna Lumley, Capucine, Graham Stark. Produced and directed by Blake Edwards.

Acknowledgements and Bibliography

I must thank all four of David Niven's children – David Junior, Jamie, Kristina and Fiona – for their wonderfully generous support and co-operation in giving me long interviews in Los Angeles, New York, Lausanne and Boston, answering numerous supplementary questions, providing photographs, and letting me see their father's private papers in the archives of the Margaret Herrick Library at the Academy of Motion Picture Arts and Sciences in Los Angeles, as well as his British Ministry of Defence army records and his publishers' records and files for allowing me to quote from his books, letters, manuscripts and other documents. I owe a huge debt to the entire Niven family, from Niv's ninety-six-year-old sister Grizel, who was living in London in 2003, to his daughter-in-law Fernanda and granddaughters Fernanda and Eugenie. Even so, this book is 'authorised' only in the sense that they have spoken to me remarkably openly and given me unrestricted access to Niven's documents. Not one of them asked to read the text for approval before publication.

Niven's closest surviving friends have also been incredibly kind and helpful: Lauren Bacall, Evie and Leslie Bricusse, William F. Buckley Jr, Pat Medina Cotten, Sir Roger Moore, Anastasia and Roddy Mann, Sir John Mills, Sir John Mortimer, Sir Peter Ustinov and Robert Wagner. So have many other actors, producers, directors and writers who worked with him: Ken and Pauline Annakin, Claudia Cardinale, Lesley Caron, Priscilla Dunn, Bryan Forbes, Charlton Heston, John Hurt, Euan Lloyd, Patrick Macnee, Michael Parkinson, Tony Randall, John Standing and Peter Viertel.

I am especially grateful to Sheridan Morley, who wrote Niven's first biography in 1985, *The Other Side of the Moon* (Weidenfeld & Nicolson), was able to interview many witnesses who have since died and has generously given me permission to quote from those interviews. Equally helpful were Guy Evans and Tom McDonald of October Films, who have made a superb television documentary about Niv that is due to be transmitted when this book is published. Other invaluable TV sources were the three *Michael Parkinson Show* programmes on which Niv was interviewed and the BBC's *Living Famously: David Niven* (2003).

I learned a great deal about Niven's childhood, schooldays and early years from Hugh Boynton; John Bridgwood and Karen McGahey of Stowe School's Old Stoics Society; Derek Cannon of St Hugh's School, Carswell Manor, Faringdon; Reg Gadney; General Sir Charles Harington; Niv's sons' nanny Beryl Rogers; his brother-in-law, Andrew Rollo; Colonel Mike Samuelson and Jim Dearden of the Bembridge Sailing Club; Niven's ninety-two-year-old school classmate Dudley Steynor and ninety-year-old school contemporary Frith Banbury. Brigit and Clemency Ames, Governor Hugh Carey and Andy Parlour, the author of *Phantom at War*, illuminated his war years and the twenty-three winters that he spent in Switzerland were described for me by Sue Bongard, David Bolton, Jane Del Amo, Hedi Donizetti, Martine and Ralph Fields, Alastair Forbes, Evan Galbraith, Ken and Kitty Galbraith, Patrick and Sussie Kearley, Gaynor Mazzone, the Rev. Arnot Morrison, Taki Theodoracopulos, Baroness Fiona Thyssen-Bornemisza, Coco and Jan Wyers, and Valerie Youmans. And some of the twenty-two summers that he lived in the South of France were described by April Clavell, the Hon. William Feilding, Virginia Gallico, Lord Hanson, Doreen Hawkins, Billie More, Kathrine Palmer and Andrew Vicari.

Niven's career as a bestselling author was explained by Phil Evans, Kenneth Giniger, Alan Gordon Walker, Peter Israel, Michael Korda, Kate Medina, Walter Minton, Vivienne Schuster, Christopher Sinclair-Stevenson and Sam Vaughan. Others who gave me invaluable interviews include Princess Salimah Aga Khan, Roxie Clayton, Joan Evans, Jill, Duchess of Hamilton, Tom Hutchinson, Jess Morgan, Lady Christopher Thynn, Alexander Walker and Peter Watson.

For help in researching Niv's private papers I am extremely grateful to Barbara Hall of the Margaret Herrick Library in Los Angeles; to Samuel Goldwyn Junior and the Samuel Goldwyn Foundation for permission to quote from Sam Goldwyn's letters; to Hamish Hamilton Ltd for permission to quote from Niv's letters from his British publisher; to Curtis Brown Ltd for permission to quote from his letters from his literary agent; to Joanna Lumley and Sam Vaughan for permission to quote from their letters; and to W.W. Norton to quote e.e. cummings' 'who knows if the moon's a balloon'.

I have also had help from Maurice Baird-Smith DFC; Ann Birch of the Foreign and Commonwealth Office Records and Historical Department; Miss S. Bowry of the Departmental Records department of the Ministry of Defence; Lt-Col O. R. St J. Breakwell MBE and Jimmy Holland of the Turf Club; Miss L. C. Burrows of the Ministry of Defence Army Medal Office; Sally Burton;

Elaine Cleary of *The Times*; Minty Clinch; Kathleen Dickson of the British Film Institute; Benoit Favey; Margaret Flory; Enid Foster of the Garrick Club; the Hon. Nigel Havers; Camilla Hornby; Christopher Horton; Penny Junor; James Leasor; Hannah Lowery of Bristol University library's special collections department; Brian MacArthur; George MacDonald Fraser; Mary-Ann McFarlane-Barrow; Dr Brian Miller; Clive Mitchell; Doug Munro; Dr Mark Nicholls; Nigel Reynolds; Mary Sharp of the Carlton Club; Becky Shaw; Major W. Shaw of the Royal Highland Fusiliers and his assistants W. Gallagher and D. McMaster; Malcolm Shemmonds of the Bank of England; R. Smith of Boodle's Club; Becky Shaw; Jill Spellman of the Conservative Party Archive at the Bodleian Library in Oxford; Mrs J. V. Thorpe of the Gloucestershire Record Office; Dr P. J. Thwaites, Andrew Orgill and Tracey Morgan of the Royal Military Academy, Sandhurst; Richard Webber; and Michael York.

Naturally I read all four of Niven's published books: *Round the Rugged Rocks* (Cresset, 1951); *The Moon's a Balloon* (Hamish Hamilton, 1971); *Bring on the Empty Horses* (Hamish Hamilton, 1975); and *Go Slowly, Come Back Quickly* (Hamish Hamilton, 1981). Three previous books about Niven provided invaluable signposts at the outset: *Niven's Hollywood* by Tom Hutchinson (Macmillan, 1984); *The Last Gentleman: A Tribute to David Niven* by Peter Haining (W. H. Allen, 1984); and *The Films of David Niven* by Gerard Garrett (LSP Books, 1975).

For help with newspaper archives I am grateful to Steve Baker of *The Times* library, Gavin Fuller and Gerald Hill of the *Daily Telegraph* library, and Steve Torrington, the chief librarian of the *Daily Mail*. And thanks to the wonderfully helpful staff of the British Library at St Pancras in London I was able to consult hundreds of relevant books with astonishing speed, most notably the following:

Ken Annakin, *So You Wanna Be a Director?* (Tomahawk Press, 2001)
Noel Annan, *Roxburgh of Stowe* (Longmans, 1965)
Margaret Duchess of Argyll, *Forget Not* (W. H. Allen, 1975)
Mary Astor, *A Life on Film* (W. H. Allen, 1973)
Michael Astor, *Tribal Feeling* (Murray, 1963)
Lauren Bacall, *By Myself* (Jonathan Cape, 1979)
Peter Baker, *Confession of Faith* (Falcon Press, 1946)
Major-General David Belchem, *All in the Day's March* (Collins, 1978)
Gertrude Bell, *Letters* (Ernest Benn, 1927)
A. Scott Berg, *Goldwyn* (Hamish Hamilton, 1989)
Shirley Temple Black, *Child Star* (Headline, 1988)
John Boyd-Carpenter, *Way of Life* (Sidgwick & Jackson, 1980)
Melvyn Bragg, *Rich: The Life of Richard Burton* (Hodder & Stoughton, 1988)
Eric Braun, *Deborah Kerr* (W. H. Allen, 1977)
Kate Buford, *Burt Lancaster* (Aurum Press, 2000)

M. E. Clifton James, *I Was Monty's Double* (Rider, 1954)
Minty Clinch, *Burt Lancaster* (Arthur Barker, 1984)
Joan Collins, *Second Act* (Boxtree, 1996)
Juliet Benita Colman, *Ronald Colman* (W. H. Allen, 1975)
T. Comyn-Platt, *By Mail and Messenger* (Constable, 1925)
Roland Culver, *Not Quite a Gentleman* (William Kimber, 1979)
Nigel Dempster, *Dempster's People* (HarperCollins, 1998)
Paul Donovan, *Roger Moore* (W. H. Allen, 1983)
Faye Dunaway with Betsy Sharkey, *Looking for Gatsby: My Life* (HarperCollins, 1995)
Brigadier John Durnford-Slater, *Commando* (G. Mann, 1953)
Steve Englund, *Princess Grace* (Orbis, 1984)
Douglas Fairbanks Jr, *A Hell of a War* (Robson Books, 1995)
Ian Fenwick, *Enter Trubshaw* (Collins, 1944)
Shirley Anne Field, *A Time For Love* (Bantam Press, 1991)
Suzanne Finstad, *Natasha: The Biography of Natalie Wood* (Century, 2001)
Gary Fishgall, *Against Type: The Biography of Burt Lancaster* (Scribner, 1995)
Michael Freedland, *Fred Astaire* (W. H. Allen, 1976)
———*The Goldwyn Touch* (Harrap, 1986)
Ava Gardner, *Ava* (Bantam Press, 1990)
Martin Gilbert, *Winston S. Churchill* (Heinemann, 1983)
Sarah Giles, *Fred Astaire* (Bloomsbury, 1988)
John Glatt, *The Ruling House of Monaco* (Piatkus, 1998)
Lionel Godfrey, *Cary Grant: The Light Touch* (Robert Hale, 1981)
Stewart Granger, *Sparks Fly Upward* (Granada, 1981)
Benny Green, *Fred Astaire* (Hamlyn, 1979)
George Greenfield, *A Smattering of Monsters* (Little, Brown, 1995)
———*Scribblers for Bread* (Hodder & Stoughton, 1989)
Nigel Hamilton, *The Full Monty* (Allen Lane, 2001)
Warren G. Harris, *Gable and Lombard* (Cassell, 1974)
———*Audrey Hepburn* (Simon & Schuster, 1994)
———*Natalie and R. J.* (Doubleday, 1988)
Rex Harrison, *A Damned Serious Business* (Bantam Press, 1990)
———*Rex* (Macmillan, 1974)
Jack Hawkins, *Anything for a Quiet Life* (Elm Tree, 1973)
Hugh Heckstall-Smith, *Doubtful Schoolmaster* (Peter Davies, 1962)
C. David Heymann, *A Woman Named Jackie* (Heinemann, 1989)
Charles Higham, *Brando* (Sidgwick & Jackson, 1987)
Charles Higham and Roy Moseley, *Cary Grant: The Lonely Heart* (New English Library, 1989)
———*Merle: A Biography of Merle Oberon* (New English Library, 1983)
James Hill, *Rita Hayworth: A Memoir* (Robson Books, 1983)
Lt-Col R. J. T. Hills, *Phantom Was There* (Edward Arnold, 1951)

Allan Hunter, *Faye Dunaway* (W. H. Allen, 1986)
Joe Hyams, *Bogart and Bacall* (Michael Joseph, 1975)
Sir Anthony Jenkinson, *America Came My Way* (Arthur Barker, 1936)
Alva Johnston, *The Great Goldwyn* (Random House, 1937)
Kitty Kelley, *His Way* (Bantam, 1986)
———*Jackie Oh!* (Ballantine, 1979)
Edward Klein, *All Too Human: The Love Story of Jack and Jackie Kennedy* (Pocket Books, 1996)
John Kobal, *Rita Hayworth* (W. H. Allen, 1977)
H. Peter Kriendler with H. Paul Jeffers, *21: Every Day Was New Year's Eve* (Taylor Publishing, 1999)
Gavin Lambert, *Norma Shearer* (Hodder & Stoughton, 1990)
Barbara Leaming, *If This Was Happiness: A Biography of Rita Hayworth* (Weidenfeld & Nicolson, 1989)
Cole Lesley, *The Life of Noël Coward* (Jonathan Cape, 1976)
Joanna Lumley, *Stare Back and Smile* (Viking, 1989)
Alasdair Macdonald, *Stowe House and School* (W. S. Cowell, 1951)
Shirley MacLaine, *My Lucky Stars* (Bantam, 1995)
Patrick Macnee and Marie Cameron, *Blind in One Ear* (Harrap, 1988)
Peter Manso, *Brando* (Weidenfeld & Nicolson, 1994)
Robert Mark, *In the Office of Constable* (Collins, 1978)
Arthur Marx, *Goldwyn* (Bodley Head, 1976)
John Masters, *Bugles and a Tiger* (Michael Joseph, 1956)
Diana Maychick and L. Avon Borgo, *Heart to Heart With Robert Wagner* (Robson Books, 1986)
Graham McCann, *Cary Grant: A Class Apart* (Fourth Estate, 1996)
Jeffrey Meyers, *Bogart: A Life in Hollywood* (André Deutsch, 1997)
John Mills, *Up in the Clouds, Gentlemen Please* (Weidenfeld & Nicolson, 1980)
Kenneth More, *More or Less* (Hodder & Stoughton, 1978)
Joe Morella and Edward Z. Epstein, *Loretta Young* (Delacorte Press, 1986)
Eric Morris, *Churchill's Private Armies: British Special Forces in Europe 1939–1942* (Hutchinson, 1986)
John Mortimer, *Murderers and Other Friends* (Viking, 1994)
Roy Moseley with Philip and Martin Masheter, *Rex Harrison* (New English Library, 1987)
———*Roger Moore* (New English Library, 1985)
Michael Munn, *Burt Lancaster* (Robson, 1995)
———*Gregory Peck* (Robert Hale, 1998)
Ken Murray, *The Golden Days of San Simeon* (MurMar Publishing, 1995)
Cathleen Nesbitt, *A Little Love and Good Company* (Stemmer House, 1977)
Barry Norman, *The Film Greats* (Hodder & Stoughton/BBC, 1985)
Barry Paris, *Audrey Hepburn* (Weidenfeld & Nicolson, 1997)

Andy and Sue Parlour, *Phantom at War* (Cerberus, 2003)
John Pearson, *The Life of Ian Fleming* (Jonathan Cape, 1966)
Roy Plomley with Derek Drescher, *Desert Island Lists* (Hutchinson, 1984)
Tony Randall and Michael Mindlin, *Which Reminds Me* (Delacorte Press, 1989)
Thomas C. Reeves, *A Question of Character: A Life of John F. Kennedy* (Bloomsbury, 1991)
Miles Reid, *Last on the List* (Leo Cooper, 1974)
Jeffrey Robinson, *Rainier and Grace* (Simon & Schuster, 1989)
Gwen Robyns, *Princess Grace* (W. H. Allen, 1976)
Tim Satchell, *Astaire* (Hutchinson, 1987)
Alan Shepperd, *Sandhurst, the Royal Military Academy* (Country Life Books, 1980)
R. Dixon Smith, *Ronald Colman, Gentleman of the Cinema* (McFarland, 1991)
James Spada, *Grace: The Secret Lives of a Princess* (Sidgwick & Jackson, 1987)
A. M. Sperber and Eric Lax, *Bogart* (Weidenfeld & Nicolson, 1997)
Donald Spoto, *Dietrich* (Bantam, 1992)
———*Elizabeth Taylor* (Little, Brown, 1995)
Peter Ustinov, *Dear Me* (Heinemann, 1977)
Peter Viertel, *Dangerous Friends* (Viking, 1991)
Alexander Walker, *Elizabeth* (Weidenfeld & Nicolson, 1990)
———*Fatal Charm* (Weidenfeld & Nicolson, 1992)
———*Peter Sellers* (Weidenfeld & Nicolson, 1981)
———*Vivien: The Life of Vivien Leigh* (Weidenfeld & Nicolson, 1987)
Geoffrey Wansell, *Cary Grant: Haunted Idol* (Collins, 1983)
Nicholas Wapshott, *Rex Harrison* (Chatto & Windus, 1991)
Ronald Warlow, *The 1900 Club and the Conservative and Unionist Party* (1900 Club, 1986)
Philip Warner, *Phantom* (William Kimber, 1982)
Christopher Warwick, *George and Marina* (Weidenfeld & Nicolson, 1988)
Sophia Watson, *Marina: The Story of a Princess* (Weidenfeld & Nicolson, 1994)
Stephen Watts, *Moonlight on a Lake in Bond Street* (Bodley Head, 1961)
Jane Ellen Wayne, *Clark Gable* (Robson Books, 1993)
———*Ava's Men: The Private Life of Ava Gardner* (Robson Books, 1990)
Lana Wood, *Natalie: A Memoir by Her Sister* (Columbus Books, 1984)
Ian Woodward, *Audrey Hepburn* (W. H. Allen, 1984)
Peregrine Worsthorne, *Tricks of Memory* (Weidenfeld & Nicolson, 1993)

Index